The Responsible Journalist

An Introduction to News Reporting and Writing

THE RESPONSIBLE
JOURNALIST

An Introduction to News Reporting and Writing

Jennie Dear and Faron Scott

New York   Oxford
OXFORD UNIVERSITY PRESS

Oxford University Press is a department of the University of Oxford. It
furthers the University's objective of excellence in research, scholarship,
and education by publishing worldwide.

Oxford   New York
Auckland   Cape Town   Dar es Salaam   Hong Kong   Karachi
Kuala Lumpur   Madrid   Melbourne   Mexico City   Nairobi
New Delhi   Shanghai   Taipei   Toronto

With offices in
Argentina   Austria   Brazil   Chile   Czech Republic   France   Greece
Guatemala   Hungary   Italy   Japan   Poland   Portugal   Singapore
South Korea   Switzerland   Thailand   Turkey   Ukraine   Vietnam

For titles covered by Section 112 of the US Higher Education
Opportunity Act, please visit www.oup.com/us/he for the latest
information about pricing and alternate formats.

Published by Oxford University Press
198 Madison Avenue, New York, New York 10016
http://www.oup.com

Library of Congress Cataloging-in-Publication Data
Scott, Faron.
   The responsible journalist : an introduction to news reporting and
writing / Faron Scott and Jennie Dear.
      pages cm
   Includes bibliographical references and index.
   ISBN 978-0-19-973234-0
   1. Journalism--Handbooks, manuals, etc. 2. Journalism--Authorship--
Handbooks, manuals, etc. I. Dear, Jennie. II. Title.
   PN4775.S36 2014
   808.06'607--dc23
                                                        2014008977

Printing number: 9 8 7 6 5 4 3 2 1

Printed in the United States of America
on acid-free paper

BRIEF Table of Contents

TABLE OF **Contents**

Unit 2: Get it in writing

Habits of mind 46

CHAPTER 3   How is news language different? 57

Unit 3: Background for your stories

Habits of mind 128

CHAPTER 6   A journalist's skeptical research 135

CHAPTER 7   Plagiarism and copyright infringement: Stealing other people's stuff 153

Unit 4: Working with sources

Habits of mind 166

CHAPTER 8   Who gets the spotlight? 177

Unit 5: Storytelling in other forms

Habits of mind 260

`CHAPTER 12` **Leading with something different 267**

CHAPTER 13 What about other kinds of news stories? 279

CHAPTER 14 IMHO: Expressing your opinions as a journalist 293

CHAPTER 15 **Conclusion: How storytelling connects to larger forces 311**

Preface

As future journalists, you operate in an environment of great uncertainty, but also great promise: the uncertainty of how changing technology will affect journalism careers, and the promise of what ever-evolving technology offers to you, the storyteller.

A journalism student might well ask, How do I prepare for this uncertain terrain?

We believe a journalist who understands a core set of skills can keep up with whatever's out there—and we believe that's what our book provides.

This is a newswriting textbook that teaches reporting and writing skills from a liberal arts perspective, a markedly different approach from most introductory newswriting texts. This book also teaches that journalism, at its heart, is about being public servants. This means we teach journalism as an approach—one that involves careful thought, ethical decision-making, skepticism, an attention to accuracy and an emphasis on truthfulness—rather than as a vocation with mechanical skills. Embedded in each lesson are brief discussions that give context to the practice. We believe this method is essential to journalism, but even more so because the discipline is changing so rapidly. You will have to bring a journalist's approach to whatever the *new* new media are when you graduate.

Acknowledgments

Thank you, Peter Labella, for seeing our vision for the book. And thank you to the many people at Oxford University Press who have helped us since—in particular, Mark Haynes, Grace Ross, Caitlin Kaufman and Danielle Christensen. We are most appreciative.

Thanks to our two independent editors, Elizabeth Arlen and Caroline Arlen, who helped us whip the book into shape as it neared its final phase.

Thanks to Tom Bartels for his brainstorming sessions with us about everything from design to the best grind for espresso. Thanks also for the image work he contributed to both the book and the website.

Thanks to the many reviewers who gave us such thoughtful comments and insights, and thanks for the time you took with our manuscript at each stage of the way.

Thanks to the journalists like Peter Maass, Cathy Resmer, John Walcott and Bryant Liggett, and to Dr. Leslie Blood, who answered our questions and helped us make this book more accurate. And thanks to Tanya Scott for her precision as she helped with tables, lists and charts.

We also want to thank our students. We started this project for you, and for your fellow truth tellers. You've helped to shape our thinking and the book through your feedback on the beta editions.

Mostly, thanks to both Eric Thompson and Tom for being sounding boards, cheerleaders and patient partners.

> ## ARTWORK
>
> The original illustrations are by Miki Harder, a Durango artist, who worked with us to translate some of the book's most important points into drawings. Thanks, Miki, for your artistic intelligence and for being so quick to understand our ideas and turn them into images that still make us smile.

Reviewers

Jessica Armstrong, Auburn University
Annie-Laurie Blair, Miami University of Ohio
Jeff Boone, Angelo State University
Scott Brown, California State University, Northridge
Scott Burgins, Indiana University
Justin Catanoso, Wake Forest University
Lona D. Cobb, Winston-Salem State University
Mike Dillon, Duquesne University
Michael Doyle, George Washington University
Madeleine Esch, Salve Regina University
Jennifer E. Follis, University of Illinois
Peter Friederici, Northern Arizona University
Andrew Galarneau, SUNY at Buffalo

Ted Geltner, Valdosta State University
Tamara L Gillis, Elizabethtown College
Peter W. Goodman, Hofstra University
Jennifer D. Greer, University of Alabama
Nancy Hanus, Michigan State University
Sue Hertz, University of New Hampshire
Barry Hollander, University of Georgia
Edward Horowitz, Cleveland State University
John E. Huxford, Illinois State University
Alisa T. Jackson, Kennesaw State University
Deidra Jackson, University of Mississippi
Dale M. Jenkins, Virginia Polytechnic Institute & State University
McKay Jenkins, University of Delaware
John Jenks, Dominican University
Valerie Kasper, Saint Leo University
Sharon J. Kobritz, Husson University
Cheryl L Kushner, Kent State University
Ryan Lange, Alvernia University
Roger Lipker, Colorado State University
Herbert Lowe, Marquette University
Ralph Merkel, University of Louisville
Lisa C. Miller, University of New Hampshire
Pat Miller, Valdosta State University
Gregg B. Neikirk, Westfield State University
Sara Netzley, Bradley University
Margaret J Patterson, Duquesne University
Claire Regan, Wagner College
Buck Ryan, University of Kentucky
Yvonne R. Schultz, Mount Vernon Nazarene University
Carl Sessions Stepp, University of Maryland
Benjamin Shors, Washington State University
James Simon, Fairfield University
Scott A. Strain, Laney College
Lydia Timmins, University of Delaware
Joseph Weber, University of Nebraska-Lincoln

The Responsible Journalist

An Introduction to News Reporting and Writing

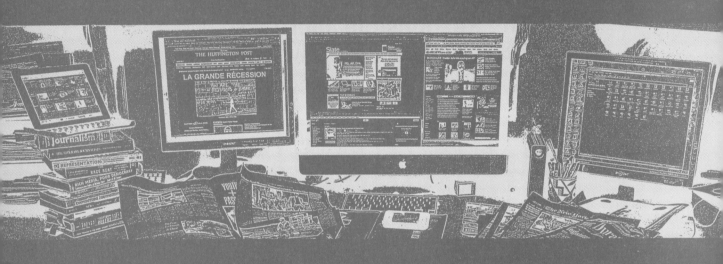

WHAT DISTINGUISHES A GOOD JOURNALIST?

"**THE NEWS MEDIA** help us define our communities as well as help us create a common language and common knowledge rooted in reality. . . . The news media serve as a watchdog, push people beyond complacency, and offer a voice to the forgotten. . . . It is difficult, in looking back, even to separate the concept of journalism from the concept of creating community and later democracy. Journalism is so fundamental to that purpose that, as we will see, societies that want to suppress freedom must first suppress the press." (Kovach & Rosenstiel, 2007, p. 12)

Habits of Mind

A good journalist shows initiative, persistence and curiosity.

Ask managing editors, producers and others who scout for journalistic talent what they look for when they're hiring. They will probably tell you what they've told us: that they want people who practice ethically and present a professional demeanor. They want people who can write well and who also understand cross-media storytelling. They want people who know the importance of background researching and cultivating sources. And then they will typically pause, as one editor did as while he was trying to characterize that one essential quality that good journalists have. They need to have a fire in the belly, he said.

A person with fire in the belly is someone who is passionate and engaged, someone who has initiative, persistence and curiosity (Fig. 1-1). These characteristics are not unique to journalism: A professional in public relations, advertising—any career— might exhibit them. Sometimes you're drawn to a field because you already have a passion for it; sometimes the passion develops as you venture into it and understand its impact and importance.

The stories of three student reporters following illustrate some ways that a fire in the belly manifests itself for journalists.

INITIATIVE

One student landed an internship at his community's main news outlet. On his first shift, he shadowed a professional reporter to that evening's city council meeting.

FIGURE 1-1

About 15 minutes before the meeting started, the professional reporter got a text that he was needed to cover another story. The student was left to report on his own.

He could have simply sat down and checked his phone for texts and emails while waiting for the meeting to begin. Instead, he used the time to introduce himself to city council members. He chatted briefly with each, and asked them to identify the people in the room who had a stake in the meeting's agenda.

In taking this action, the student set himself up to serve the public in at least two ways:

- He met key government and community members, which made it easier for him to interview them after the meeting.
- By building rapport with his sources, he laid the foundation for good reporting then and in the future.

He took **initiative**.

PERSISTENCE

Another student reporter was assigned to cover a 7 p.m. press conference, when the famously press-shy mayor was supposed to announce a multimillion-dollar city road project that was going to make a major traffic artery almost unusable for a year. The student had done her research on the mayor's public position so far and the pros and cons of the project. She'd prepared a list of questions to ask, focusing on why the city wanted taxpayers to ante up for a new project in such lean times.

The December press conference was at the city building, a mile or so away from where the student lived. She didn't have a car—she normally rode her bike, walked, or took the bus—and, by early evening, snow and sleet were icing the roads.

She bundled up, went to the bus stop and waited in the cold. But the bus didn't come. She considered, just for a minute, calling the whole thing off.

But she didn't. Instead, she walked and slid to the house of a neighbor who owned a truck, only to find he wasn't home. She could have surrendered here; instead, she walked and made it to the city building just after the press conference was supposed to start.

No one was there: no mayor, no staffers, no other reporters. Cold and tired, she decided to wait and spent the time looking over the questions she'd prepped. After about 20 minutes, the mayor walked in. The student reporter stood and introduced herself. The mayor was clearly impressed, and gave her a one-on-one interview and the scoop. What's more, the student established herself as a dedicated reporter, which helped her gain access for the remainder of the mayor's term.

That's **persistence**.

CURIOSITY

Another student reporter was assigned to follow up on a press release from the university public relations office. The release said that the state had approved a 5 percent raise in tuition. It seemed to the student reporter that tuition was rising every year

(Fig. 1-2). His background research informed him that, 10 years earlier, his state had funded higher education generously. Now it only paid for about 30 percent of a typical college's budget, and more cuts were on the horizon.

He was curious: Why was this happening—again? Were tuition increases just a fact of life, something students could expect like the rising cost of food? Because of his research, he knew that recent tuition increases were larger and more frequent. He set out to understand the money flow from the moment a student paid tuition to when it went into the state's coffers. He learned the following about education funding in his state:

- Over the last several years, the state had been paying for a smaller and smaller percentage of higher education. And tuition had been rising to fill the gap.

- The state legislature and the governor could have made different choices—they could have continued to pay a larger share of higher educational costs. Instead, they had funded other priorities.

FIGURE 1-2

- Voters had also chosen other priorities. They had voted to limit the amount of tax revenue the state could keep, requiring the state to return any surplus to taxpayers.
- But the university still had to pay its bills. Students had to pick up the difference, and that's why tuition kept rising.

Curiosity drove the reporter to move beyond the face value of the story—the state approved another tuition increase—and understand the mechanics of state budgeting.

He could now connect the dots so that students wouldn't just bemoan constant increases, but could actually see *why* these increases were happening (Fig. 1-3). At the very least, people would better understand changes that directly affected their lives. At best, people would know enough to make more informed decisions from reading his story—something they wouldn't have been able to do if he'd just reported that the budget had been approved.

These students, like professional reporters, share a journalist's habits of mind— a core set of ideals that guides each decision journalists make when they evaluate information, choose sources or tell a story well. Initiative, persistence and curiosity are three of these—an understanding of what makes an interesting story is another. At the beginning of each unit in this book, we will discuss additional habits of mind. The chapters that follow in each unit will focus on the "how to" of practicing good news reporting and writing.

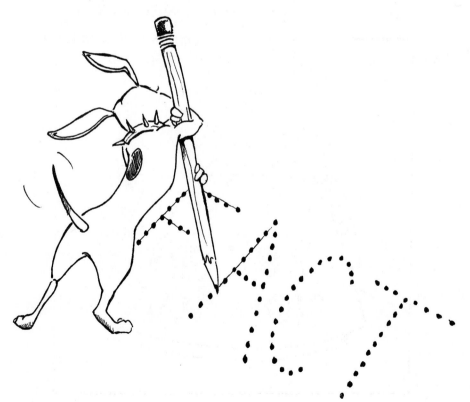

FIGURE 1-3

The journalist we want you to become is a practical idealist, someone who holds the ideals of journalism and its traditions in mind while practicing professional journalistic skills. Practical idealists understand that journalism can be fascinating and fun, and that it can provide people with stories that entertain as they inform. They also understand the impact they and their work have on the people they cover and the audience they serve. So they do their job conscientiously to maximize good and minimize harm. They see themselves as public servants.

Conclusion

As you move forward into the world of news reporting and writing, we want you to take the following ideas with you:

- A good journalist serves people and has a passion for seeking truth and justice.
- A good journalist ferrets out useful information and provides context so that truth is accessible to people, and so that it's possible for them to take action.
- A good journalist crafts a compelling story, thinking ethically and critically every step of the way.

This is the heart of journalism and is where we begin the chapters in Unit 1, with an explanation of why being a public servant is so important to good journalism, why journalists are vital in a democracy, and how to practice ethical journalism.

As you make your way through the chapters in this unit, think about how initiative, persistence and curiosity help journalists fulfill their public duty.

CHAPTER 1

THE PUBLIC'S CHAMPION

Defining News Media in an Era of New Media

You'll often hear people lump all the news media together—as if Google News, which depends mainly on news created elsewhere, and CNN News, whose staff researches and reports its own news, are the same—or as if the *PBS NewsHour*, with its large staff, and a local television station, with a tiny one, are the same. They aren't.

The actual medium affects how journalists tell stories and often what stories they tell, as well as how audiences experience the news (Fig. 1-4). For instance, news on Twitter focuses on technology trends much more than most other news outlets do. And news stories told online are more likely to include multiple graphs and charts, transcripts or recordings of full speeches and interviews than, say, a news magazine or newspaper, which have more limited space.

If you become a journalist, there's a good chance you'll be working in more than one medium. But you also might be working strictly online and for an organization like Yahoo News or Slate News, or maybe for a nonprofit news outlet, or even a group of news organizations.

FIGURE 1-4 The ways people access the news can affect their experience.

"Symbolia," the illustrated journalism magazine for computer tablets, uses a comic-book or graphic-novel-style approach for most of its stories, including its first issue's environmental feature on California's Salton Sea, a story on food and microbiomes and a feature on life in northern Iraq.

Try this: Search for "Bet Against the American Dream," and watch the showtune video created to explain how at least one hedge fund contributed to the financial crisis (Lopez, Holtz & Arrow, 2010). And, if you have time, listen to "The Giant Pool of Money," the award-winning radio story aired in 2008 that helped explain the subprime mortgage crisis in conversational language (Blumberg & Davidson, 2008).

These stories, songs, videos and podcasts were created by different news groups, often in collaboration: ProPublica, an online news organization; National Public Radio (NPR); *This American Life*, a popular weekly radio program that only rarely dabbles in news; and *Planet Money*, a news program that teams up reporters from NPR and

This American Life to report finances for a general audience. Here's what *Planet Money* says about its approach:

> Imagine you could call up a friend and say, "Meet me at the bar and tell me what's going on with the economy." Now imagine that's actually a fun evening. That's what we're going for at *Planet Money.* ("About Planet Money," 2013)

The kind of innovation that made possible *Planet Money*—and its collaboration with ProPublica—is happening all across the country. New journalism ventures like Vox, First Look Media and the latest version of FiveThirtyEight are experimenting with ways to provide readers with more explanation and context with their news stories. And *The New York Times,* once known as "The Gray Lady" for its stodgy tradition of printing so many words and so few photos, now hosts one of the best news sites online. (At www.nyt.com, click on "Video" to see features and news videos. Or you can simply do a site search for "Multimedia" to see examples of graphics, photos and videos all in one place.)

But at the same time that star journalists like Ezra Klein, Katie Couric and Nate Silver are receiving a heady amount of attention, many of the best news organizations in the country are struggling as they try to figure out how to make a profit online (Box 1-1). The changes to journalism are real and far reaching. Large numbers of journalists have been laid off, and we're only beginning to feel the impacts on investigative reporting, or even complete news coverage of the government or large corporations. At the same time, there's good news: People are spending more time with news than they ever have in the past, according to the Pew Research Center's Project for Excellence in Journalism (2006–2013). There's a spirit of collaboration, innovation and imagination that makes this an especially exciting time to become a journalist.

A closer look at news media shows us that amidst the upheaval and innovation and the differences among individual news organizations, the news media do share common traits in their practice of journalism. Great journalism is interesting and compelling. It emphasizes well-researched, meticulously reported facts attributed to credible sources. It follows a particular approach that journalists can use across media platforms, an approach that's been created and modified through a mixture of the traditions and ideals of people in the profession.

> A profound reset is under way. In more than a decade of covering the news end of the media business, I cannot think of a time of greater optimism or potential. Nontraditional operators like Mr. Bezos can afford to adopt a long-term strategy, something he has done rather effectively at Amazon.
>
> *DAVID CARR,* THE NEW YORK TIMES *MEDIA ANALYST*

If People Govern Themselves, They Need a Free Press

Those traditions and ideals of good journalism include a set of cultural expectations, some of which go back at least as far as the founding of the U.S. government.

BOX 1-1

BEZOS BUYS WAPO

A surprising event in 2013 underscores some assumptions about news ownership in the United States, and how those assumptions are changing: Jeff Bezos, the founder and CEO of Amazon.com, bought *The Washington Post* from the Grahams, the family that had owned the newspaper since 1933.

What was so surprising? News organizations like the *Post* are often privately owned, by people or families or corporations, and they make their money through subscriptions and by selling advertising. This is different from models you'll see in other countries, such as ones in which the government helps finance news organizations—the way a government charter set up the BBC and established most of its funding in Great Britain, for example.

The concern with that kind of model, though, is that journalists may have a harder time investigating or criticizing the government if it is also their source of funding. In contrast, defenders of a private system see it as giving news the freedom to perform its watchdog function and provide news that might disrupt the status quo. That seemed to work reasonably well for 200 years in the United States—until the early 2000s (Fig. 1-5).

But by the time Bezos bought *The Washington Post*, the Grahams had lost money for seven years with one of the nation's most influential newspapers, and they couldn't figure out how to fix that. *The Post*'s struggles were similar to those of many news organizations across the country, affecting newspapers, broadcast and cable news—and their online outlets.

When news started becoming widely available on the Internet, traditional news organizations scrambled to make a profit. Most have had limited to no success in selling subscriptions online: People expect information to be free on the Internet, although this may be changing. While there's plenty of online advertising, a large chunk of that money goes to Internet giants like Facebook, Google and Amazon.com.

But polls show that people are reading or listening to more news than ever. So, as long as people are still getting their news, what's the big deal? Many analysts worry that as news organizations have cut back, international reporting and investigative reporting have dropped rapidly. They are concerned that all news organizations are employing fewer journalists, which means fewer people keeping an eye on the public business, on righting wrongs, on making sure the weak have some rights to stand up to the powerful.

And that brings us back to why it was so surprising that Bezos would buy the Post. Why would one of America's most successful technology entrepreneurs invest in an industry that's supposedly dead?

But there are also hopes that new models will emerge. More and more, citizen journalists are honing their skills and traditional newsrooms are learning how to better

> . . . if we are serious about participatory democracy, we must be serious about journalism and its relation to democracy. . . . In fact, in a more sane world, journalism would be among the most prestigious fields in the academy.
>
> *ROBERT MCCHESNEY,*
> *COMMUNICATIONS SCHOLAR*

A BIT OF HISTORICAL REVIEW

When the U.S. government was formed, the prevailing mindset was that most people could not be trusted to govern themselves—they were thought to be too emotional or uneducated, or too easily swayed by persuasive speakers, to have a strong voice in their government.

FIGURE 1-5 Jeff Bezos, the CEO and co-founder of Amazon.com, wasn't the first wealthy individual to buy *The Washington Post*. This photo shows the auction at which Eugene Meyer bought the paper. Meyer was the father of Katherine Graham, whose heirs sold the paper to Bezos in 2013. Part of the unique nature of news in the United States is that it has always included the business element alongside the ideals of freedom and justice for citizens.

integrate their reporting in a way that provides quality journalism. Some news organizations have banded together to fill the gaps in investigative reporting. And some news industry experts hope that Bezos—and other investors, especially from the technology sector—will invest the money and technology know-how to save news organizations and make them better.

The industry has had a jolt to its system, and there are real consequences for journalists and people studying to become journalists. But, as the model of how we gather and communicate news changes, it's also an especially exciting time to be part of that world.

The job of governing belonged to people who had money, education and social status. For people who held this view, it was unthinkable that an ordinary person could be a part of the political process, much less someone who governed.

The founders of the U.S. government thought differently (Fig. 1-6 and Box 1-2). They based their ideas on those of English thinkers such as John Milton (1608–1674) and John Locke (1632–1704) and French philosophers such as

FIGURE 1-6 While the U.S. model was more inclusive than those of most other contemporary governments, large segments of the population could not participate in self-governance until a long time later.

Charles Louis de Secondat Montesquieu (1689–1755) and Voltaire (1694–1778) and others. They believed

- People are capable of reason.

- Education is key to making good decisions, and the press has a duty to help educate.

- The government should allow citizens to engage in robust, open debates about competing ideas, so they can arrive at the best decisions regarding self-governance. (At the country's founding, though, only white, male property owners could actually vote.)

- All ideas, no matter how abhorrent, must be allowed, again so that citizens can arrive at the best decisions.

These assumptions led to the belief that citizens who have enough accurate, thorough information will make wise decisions regarding their own self-governance—such as which candidate to elect, which policies to support, and which positions to believe.

Under this philosophy, the press plays an especially important role: It contributes to self-governance by helping to inform the people. The way the U.S. press originally viewed its role has been called the **Libertarian Theory** of the press, which is also based on the ideas of philosophers like Milton, Locke, John Stuart Mill and Thomas Jefferson (Siebert, 1963). This theory sees the press as a monitor of the government, keeping an eye on those in power and seeking the truth. For people who had been under the rule of the kings and queens of England, who themselves had power struggles with the Pope and the Catholic Church, it was especially important that there be some way to resist power and its ability to corrupt. They had seen too well the havoc that unchecked authority could unleash—and they envisioned the press as one of those **checks and balances**.

THE FIRST AMENDMENT

The First Amendment to the United States Constitution, found in the Bill of Rights, illustrates the founders' commitment to freedom of expression (Fig. 1-7). The amendment is about more than freedom of the press, of course—it's also about things like people being able to choose their religion or hold a protest rally. But regarding the press, the First Amendment says that Congress can't make laws that determine what the press can or cannot publish. Prepublication censorship is called **prior restraint**.

First Amendment rights aren't absolute. The courts must balance the freedom of the press against other interests, such as national security, especially in times of war.

For example, just because a journalist knows troop locations doesn't mean he can report them—troop safety could be compromised. The press also doesn't have the freedom to publish obscene material. However, there are rigorous tests that must be successfully met on the part of those who would limit or punish the press, and, historically, there's a presumption of openness and freedom.

The First Amendment means that the news media in the United States are really quite free from government interference in what they report. That's why the ethical principles are so important: Just because journalists *can* report something doesn't mean they *should.*

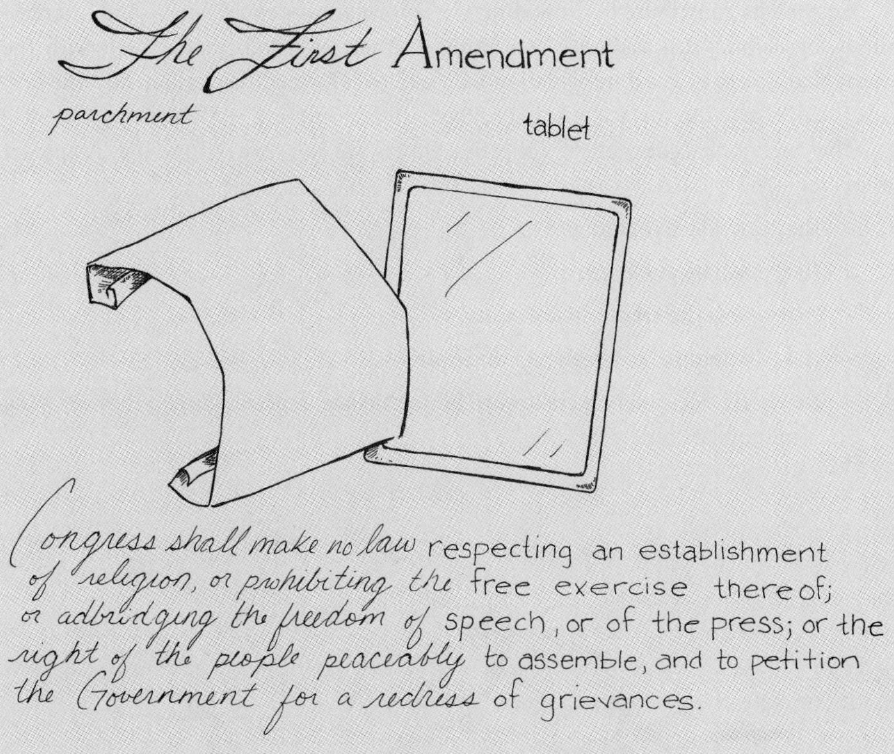

The First Amendment

parchment   tablet

Congress shall make no law respecting an establishment of religion, or prohibiting the free exercise thereof; or abridging the freedom of speech, or of the press; or the right of the people peaceably to assemble, and to petition the Government for a redress of grievances.

FIGURE 1-7

THE PRESS AS WATCHDOG

One metaphor that journalists use for this aspect of their job is the **watchdog function** (Fig. 1-8).

Just as a guard dog is on constant alert, a journalist stays keenly focused on matters of public interest and keeps an eye on the powerful, particularly those who are in a decision-making role—government institutions and officials and corporations and their officers—as well as other prominent people who have power or influence over the lives of individuals, such as a celebrity who is attempting to influence environmental policies or is fundraising for a political candidate.

The assumption is that our government and society itself can't function well without input from people. And people's interactions with their government are much more complicated and frequent than the act of voting. Citizens influence government decisions through online commentary and letters to the editor, attendance at public meetings and workshops, street protests, obedience or disobedience of existing laws, direct complaints or compliments to public servants like teachers and police officers, organization of nongovernmental groups, communications with their elected officials and even word of mouth (Fig. 1-9).

Journalists contribute by providing the information people need—and, increasingly, by helping this audience communicate their own information—all with the hope that access to good information will lead to informed discussion, and the best ideas will rise to the surface, leading to the best decisions and actions.

That means that journalists' collective efforts are the cornerstone that keeps democracy strong:

- They provide access to ideas.
- They evaluate evidence.
- They assess the credibility of sources.
- They distinguish between fact and opinion.
- They push decision makers toward honest debate, especially when they're trying to manipulate public opinion.

FIGURE 1-8 Watchdog.

FIGURE 1-9 Countries with representative governments expect citizens to have access to news and information because citizens participate in government not only through their votes but in multiple—and complicated—other ways. For instance, to show their support for Edward Snowden, demonstrators in Berlin, Germany, wore Guy Fawkes masks and stood in front of the Brandenburg Gate. Snowden, a former CIA employee who also did contract work for the National Security Agency (NSA), revealed details of U.S. surveillance when he leaked hundreds of thousands of secret U.S., British and Israeli documents (Spata, 2013).

Exercises for Chapter 1

EXERCISE 1-1: Visit the student news website of a college or university other than yours. Select a story to analyze. Make a list of the facts in the story and then discuss your answers to the following questions: Will this story help the audience make informed decisions? If so, how? If not, why not?

EXERCISE 1-2: Visit the website of a professional news organization. Select a story to analyze. Make a list of the facts in the story and then discuss your answers to the following questions: Will this story help the audience make informed decisions? If so, how? If not, why not?

EXERCISE 1-3: Search for "Frontline.org." When you reach the *Frontline* website, select one of the stories to watch or one of the multimedia packages to analyze. Take notes as you study the coverage: How do the journalists fulfill their watchdog responsibility? Discuss.

EXERCISE 1-4: Visit the online news site of a college or university different from yours. Select a story to analyze. Take notes as you study the coverage: How do the journalists fulfill their watchdog responsibility? Discuss.

EXERCISE 1-5: Search online for the term "Polk awards." When you reach the Polk award website, select one of the award winners to analyze. Take notes as you study the coverage: How do the journalists fulfill their watchdog responsibility? Discuss.

CHAPTER 2

HOW DO ETHICS AND CRITICAL THINKING APPLY TO EVERYDAY REPORTING?

Imagine a sports team—say, football. Think of the people involved, from players to coaches to team physicians and trainers, to the front office and the league. They are all trying to make their team better, their athletes faster, stronger, and safer. They're doing this to win the Super Bowl, sure, but a big chunk of their work is just about excelling at the game of football. It's about creating a new offensive play that maximizes a quarterback's strengths, and the sense of accomplishment when it's executed perfectly. It's about a team working together, apart from the goal of any individual—and expecting that ethic from each player. It's about creating and enforcing standards that minimize harm to players and maximize fairness on the field.

These are examples of **internal goods**—the moral force driving a person to seek excellence for its own sake (MacIntyre, 1985, pp. 251–253; also cited in Lambeth, 1992, pp. 73–74). Internal goods originate inside a practice. They are still rewards, and people who pursue them usually experience pleasure, as they would for more traditional rewards. The more that people involved strive for these internal goods, the better they and the practice as a whole become.

That's not always true for **external goods**. Fame, fortune and Super Bowl rings are examples of external goods—benefits that people reap as a result of excellence. These are the rewards from outside, or external to the practice. Some external goods are usually necessary. Most people need to make a salary in exchange for their work, for instance. External goods can help to motivate people to do even better work. But too much emphasis on external goods can lead to bad practice. An athlete who is chasing endorsements or glory might dope to win, losing sight of the team and the welfare of the sport (Fig. 2-1).

External and internal goods affect the practice of journalism, too. Excellent journalism includes making decisions ethically; ensuring accuracy; gathering meaningful, useful information; and telling compelling stories. Journalists who pursue these goals successfully earn the internal good of achieving excellence. The better journalists become at these goals, the more the profession and the public benefit. In this chapter, we'll focus on specific goals in the form of ethical principles.

This emphasis on ethics might seem unusual to lay people and critics, who argue that the media are businesses, and therefore only trying to get higher ratings, increase the number of page views or sell papers. However, that's an oversimplification of how

FIGURE 2-1 Lance Armstrong's focus on the external goods of winning at the expense of ethical competition torpedoed his career. Armstrong, the seven-time winner of the Tour de France, eventually confessed in 2013 to using banned drugs to compete. He was stripped of his Tour de France medals and banned from competition.

the industry works. People inside journalism know that for news organizations to achieve external goods for any length of time, they have to pay attention to fulfilling internal goods—to achieving excellence (Box 2-1). Ted Turner, the billionaire founder of CNN

> is lionized by many journalists who worked for him at CNN because he often made decisions that cost money but built the CNN brand. He created the first world news network. He aired documentaries on weighty subjects at a time when CBS, NBC, and ABC had largely abandoned them. (Auletta, 2005, p. 11)

Turner understood that focusing on good journalism could also help the network make money in the long term.

As journalism critics Bill Kovach and Tom Rosenstiel say

> A commitment to citizens is more than professional egoism. It is the implied covenant with the public, which tells the audience that the movie reviews are straight, that the restaurant reviews are not influenced by who buys an ad, that the coverage is not self-interested or slanted for friends. The notion that those who report the news are not obstructed from digging up and telling the truth— even at the expense of the owners' other financial interests—is a prerequisite of telling the news not only accurately but also persuasively. It is the basis for why citizens believe a news organization. It is the source of the organization's credibility. It is, in short, the franchise asset of the news company and those who work in it. (2007, pp. 52–53)

External goods such as a Peabody Award or Pulitzer Prize, or fame and fortune might also accrue as results of good journalism. It's okay—in fact, assumed—that a good

---

BOX 2-1

FACEBOOK CO-FOUNDER SAYS MAGAZINE'S PROFITS LINKED TO QUALITY

When Facebook cofounder Chris Hughes bought and redesigned *The New Republic*, he said he believed the venerable magazine could make a profit because people will always need quality journalism:

> *The New Republic was launched nearly a century ago in a spirit of high idealism. . . . With this issue, we relaunch* The New Republic. *Our goals may be somewhat different from those of the magazine's founding fathers, but we share their unabashed idealism. We believe that our new hyper-information age is thrilling, but not entirely satisfying. We believe that there must remain space for journalism that takes time to produce and demands a longer attention span— writing that is at once nourishing and entertaining. (2013)*

FIGURE 2-2

journalist might *also* be driven by them. But the focus on internal goods defines the good professional journalist.

In this chapter, we introduce a system of ethical decision-making we find accessible and complete: Edmund Lambeth's Eclectic System of Journalism Ethics. We like this system because its framework organizes the key ideas in responsible reporting into five principles—justice, stewardship, freedom, humaneness and truth telling (Lambeth, 1992; Fig. 2-2).

Justice

The principle of justice asks journalists to make sure that citizens are treated the same by those in power. No one should get special treatment, and no one should be arbitrarily discriminated against. This doesn't mean that if a boss gives one person a promotion, everyone else should get one, too—it simply means that there should be a sound reason why that one person got promoted when others didn't. It means that if a television star gets arrested for driving under the influence, he should be treated the same as a non-celebrity in the same circumstance. Someone without power or money should get the same treatment as someone who has both.

When people wonder if there is one set of laws for white-collar criminals and another set of laws for everybody else, when they complain that tax policies unfairly benefit the wealthy, or that the federal government has been taken over by lobbyists, or that public schools in one neighborhood are falling apart and schools in another are not, justice requires the journalist to attend to these stories. A good journalist keeps an eye on the government and its officials, such as the police and the legal system; corporations, such as airlines or agribusinesses or investment banks; and others with power, such as employers. When people aren't being treated fairly, the journalist shines a spotlight on their circumstances to help rectify an unjust situation, serving as the public's champion.

STAKEHOLDERS

When you are making sure that a news story is fair, it helps to identify who the stakeholders are in that story and what their investment is. Stakeholders—the people who might be affected by an issue or event—typically include a story's subject, sources and audience (Fig. 2-3). It's crucial that journalists, not stakeholders, decide what information does or does not get published. But if journalists know who the stakeholders are, they can do a better job of selecting sources, getting closer to the truth and deciding whether publication might be more harmful than helpful. Articulating who the stakeholders are and what stakes are at issue can help clarify any ethical matters you need to consider. Here are some questions to keep in mind:

- Who stands to benefit in the situation being reported?
- Who stands to lose?
- Who needs to know about the situation?
- What is it that they need to know?

FIGURE 2-3 Stakeholders.

FAIRNESS IN STORIES

After you identify possible stakeholders, justice underscores the importance of being fair to them. Stories should be complete, honest and straightforward. They should include all relevant facts, but nothing frivolous, deceptive or misleading. They should not misrepresent facts or leave out important information. Yet fairness doesn't mean you always have to include equal amounts of information for each side. Such misguided attempts to be fair by allotting the same amount of time or space to all stakeholders can even lead to less accurate reporting.

For instance, decades of scholarly analysis and research now point to the news media's misrepresentation of climate change—the extent of the problem, its cause and the extent of expert agreement about the issue. One cause of this has been an attempt by journalists—reporters, editors or producers—to provide balanced coverage.

In 2008, Bud Ward, the editor of the Yale Forum on Climate Change and the Media, wrote about a series of workshops that brought together leading climate scientists and environmental journalists. Ward summarized a growing consensus among journalists about how to approach coverage of climate change:

> Former Washington Post and New York Times science reporter Boyce Rensberger, for instance, affirmed . . . that accuracy trumps balance. While there may once have been a legitimate 50/50 split of viewpoints on some climate science questions, Rensberger argued, the preponderance of scientific evidence had since accumulated to a point where responsible reporters should give the scientific consensus on anthropogenic climate change much greater weight than dissenting claims challenging the mainstream scientific conclusions. The journalistic tenet of accuracy now demands that the established science be given total or near total prevalence in coverage of certain aspects of climate change science. (2008, p. 2)

When journalists strive for balance, they sometimes set up **false debates** such as the one about climate change. By creating and maintaining a false debate, solutions to the situation have been delayed by years. Especially because the United States is such a big player in the climate change issue, the misleading coverage may have contributed to greater injustice by helping to spread misinformation.

FAIRNESS AND DIVERSITY ACROSS COVERAGE

You need to check for fairness within stories, but you should also keep an eye on how fair you are across coverage. Journalists need to be ethical in the choices they make about where to direct their attention, guarding against leaving relevant issues under-covered. For instance, university students who have children need information that students without children wouldn't; students who are also parents are more likely to want information about day care cost and availability, or

> Excellence is what happens when the principles upon which journalists stand are applied to everyone, every community, every class and kind with the same passion.
>
> *KEITH WOODS, NPR'S VICE PRESIDENT FOR DIVERSITY*

what's going on in regional elementary schools. You don't have to cover these issues every day, especially if the number of stakeholders is relatively few, but you can make sure they are on your radar.

At the national level, news outlets have been criticized for providing missing white girls or women a generous amount of coverage but not other girls and women who have gone missing. This means that the plight of some victims is visible and prioritized, while crimes against other victims are invisible. Or perhaps the problem is belated coverage, for instance, of the low pay and lack of safety for Sherpa guides on Mount Everest, where earlier, more sustained news coverage might have helped prevent accidents such as the deaths of 18 Sherpas in the spring of 2014, or at least ensured better compensation for the locals who have died in Everest accidents over the years.

Journalists once had much more access to a wide range of information than the average person. That meant that the role of selecting stories that best served the community was more concentrated in their hands. Now, that's been tempered by people's ability to seek out facts on their own. Those who have Internet access can look at government reports or other primary sources themselves. But this doesn't mean ordinary citizens get all of the information they need from primary sources. They don't. This is true for many reasons: Journalists have training, time and access to key sources that most people don't. That means that journalists remain in a unique position to make the world more just.

Stewardship

If we call someone a good steward of the land, we're suggesting that that person takes care of it somehow. Similarly, when we think about journalists as stewards of their profession, we're saying they are responsible for guarding, even nurturing it. This means that journalists need to think about how their actions can affect the profession as a whole.

One student news organization's financial crisis helps illustrate the principle of stewardship: At midterm, editors discovered an accounting error, and they realized that the newspaper didn't have enough money to publish all of its scheduled weekly print issues. They considered three options:

- They could publish weekly until they ran out of money.
- They could publish less frequently, allowing the newspaper to make it to the end of the term.
- They could publish all of their news online and discontinue their paper edition.

The third option was especially appealing, because the newspaper staff had been planning to switch to an online-only edition in the coming months. However, readers and advertisers had made clear that they preferred some print presence in addition to an online version of the newspaper. How could editors best fulfill their role as stewards of their organization and of journalism?

The editors thought they might turn the predicament into an opportunity: What about publishing news online weekly, and also printing a news magazine every two weeks? The magazine might provide a new and exciting mix of features, photo essays, and literary journalism, or maybe even fiction and poetry.

Then they began to ask about what they, as editors, owed to the newspaper's legacy. The other people who worked at the newspaper surely had expectations about what a newspaper should be, and what kind of work they had signed up for. And what was the editors' responsibility to future newspaper staff members—or even past staff? They talked about what their readers expected and deserved, and about the newspaper itself as an institution. The online newspaper would fulfill its watchdog function of reporting on student government and administration, but did it still have an obligation to do so in its print version? After all, the news organization's funding and its status as a campus organization were based on some assumptions about what a newspaper was or should be. But didn't editors also owe something to themselves as good journalists and to the practice of journalism—like a spirit of innovation and a willingness to experiment? These are the kinds of questions a steward would ask before making a decision with potentially far-reaching impacts on the organization.

The editors in this case decided to finish the term with an online-only edition, which satisfied two key objectives—providing the news while keeping the organization fiscally sound. They took care to explain their decision to stakeholders. They also decided that the biweekly news magazine was a great idea, and debuted it the following term to much success. The combination of the online version and the news magazine offered both breaking and in-depth stories to multiple audiences across media, and it allowed staff members to broaden their range of skills.

As a journalist, the principle of stewardship says, you become part of and responsible to something larger than yourself, your stories, and even your organization. You are responsible to the whole of the practice, its credibility and its future. Journalists who are stewards of the practice set out to do meaningful work that will reflect well on the profession.

You'll see journalists looking out for the profession in many ways: Foundations created by private companies or individuals, such as The Poynter Institute or the John S. and James L. Knight Foundation, educate and assist journalists. Other organizations set out to protect one particular aspect of journalism, such as the Reporters Committee for Freedom of the Press, or Reporters without Borders. And there are organizations that award prizes to encourage excellent journalism, such as the Pulitzer Prize Committee (Box 2-2). It's good to know these organizations exist because you can turn to them for help, and you also may eventually want to participate in them. But stewardship starts with the actions and decisions of individual journalists, who must keep in mind that they contribute to the profession as a whole.

TRANSPARENCY

One specific way that journalists are good stewards is through **transparency**, or being clear about why—and sometimes how—they do what they do. This is a way of treating your audience members with respect, by providing them with the background

BOX 2-2

PRIZE-WINNING JOURNALISM

The following is a list of some of the premier prizewinners in journalism. As you look at these examples, you'll see that the principles of good journalism are evident:

- In 2014, a George Polk Award went to journalists at PBS' *Frontline* for their documentary examining the National Football League's attempts to hide evidence of the links between head injuries and brain disease.
- A 2014 Pulitzer Prize was awarded to *The Washington Post* and *The Guardian US* for their coverage of the National Security Agency's secret spying on citizens. The coverage helped people better understand how the information, first released by Edward Snowden, fit into the big picture of national security.
- A 2012 Peabody Award went to NPR for its coverage of the uprisings in Syria. The coverage provided listeners with in-depth information that helped them understand a volatile situation with global implications.

- A 2012 Pulitzer Prize went to *The Philadelphia Inquirer's* multimedia series on school violence at all levels of the city's schools. The series helped lead to reforms to improve safety for children and teachers.
- A 2010 George Polk Award went to CBS' *60 Minutes* for its news story, "The Price of Oil," which reported that large changes in the price of oil were caused by market speculation rather than changes in consumer demand or the amount of oil available.

These are just some examples of journalists shining their spotlight on injustice—whether it was people asked to bear unfair burdens, like the school children and teachers dealing with school violence, or people reaping questionable benefits, like the oil speculators. For every prizewinner, there are several runners-up—and we encourage you to visit websites such as Pulitzer.org and Peabodyawards.com to see more of the noteworthy examples of journalism.

---

information to better understand how news organizations work. For instance, some news organizations hire an ombudsman to explain news decisions and act as an advocate for the public within the company. During NPR's coverage of the 2012 elections, listeners from both the right and the left criticized the organization for bias. Managing editor David Sweeney invited Lori Grisham, an assistant to NPR's ombudsman, to listen in on a news meeting to gain a better understanding of the tone and kind of conversation editors and reporters had about political reporting—and Grisham shared her experiences in a story for the audience:

> I found a robust conversation, as Sweeney promised.
>
> It was Thursday and Gov. Romney's acceptance speech at the Republican National Convention was the top story of the day. One editor reported that correspondent Ari Shapiro would file a segment for that evening's *All Things Considered*. Another said that Mara Liasson, who had filed an eight-minute story that morning, was preparing another one for Friday's *Morning Edition*. And someone else suggested an update on Ron Paul.
>
> The conversation continued and was low key and factual—a divvying up of responsibilities and ideas. No one knew that I was on the line, but I didn't hear any endorsements, criticisms or diatribes. (Grisham, 2012, para. 14–16)

In the rest of her story, Grisham provided more background about NPR's election coverage methods. Her reporting may not have persuaded listeners who were convinced of the organization's bias, but its transparency showed a basic respect for its audience.

If a news organization makes a thoughtful but controversial decision, it's often a good idea to explain the rationale behind that decision. Such an explanation is usually separate from the news story—a link may take readers to an editorial or a sidebar, for instance. People still may disagree with you, even vehemently, but they've received an explanation of why you made your decision.

That's an explanation people deserve in other circumstances, too. If a journalist who reports on a story has some connection to players in the story—perhaps he has worked for a brother of one of the sources in the past, or his book has been reviewed by an author he is profiling—then the journalist needs to tell the public about that connection. This explanation often takes the form of a parenthetical comment.

You might also see a similar kind of comment in the form of a side note or an italicized paragraph at the beginning of a story if a news team spends a lot of time on an investigation. These short explanations are a way for a news team to let an audience know that the news story is based on much more background research than is readily apparent—that reporters have set up a database or interviewed 50 people whose quotes may never appear in the stories. A paragraph like this can also help the practice, so people realize that many journalists care very much about their communities and are willing to do a tremendous amount of work to make them better.

Journalists are stewards who should consider the history and the future of the organization as they make decisions about what to cover and how to cover it. They must build on what previous staffers have created, keeping in mind what they'll leave for future staffers, particularly credibility and reputation. The principle of stewardship asks each journalist to be a caretaker of the profession and to demonstrate a commitment to it.

Freedom and Autonomy

In the spring of 2013, Nicolas Maduro narrowly won the Venezuelan presidential election. Maduro, who was Hugo Chavez's handpicked successor, had been acting president since Chavez's death the month before. Violent protests erupted as people called for a recount of votes, and journalists were among those targeted by both political parties. Supporters of the opposition candidate attacked a building where two television news stations had their offices. Elsewhere in Venezuela, government officials arrested three journalists who were covering protests and charged them with "destabilization."

Contrast this to what we in the United States would expect after a contested election here. In 2000, when the presidential election was so close that a clear winner didn't immediately emerge, people expected the news media to investigate the process and the aftermath, keeping people informed as to what they found. Also, people felt assured that the government wouldn't arrest journalists, nor allow a major political party to attack them. While the performance of both the press and the United States government during this time have been criticized, look at the underlying assumption: The press would remain free to report critically on the government.

As stewards of their profession, journalists in the United States have often fought to protect this press freedom—the freedom to act as watchdogs of the government and those in power, and to seek the truth. Although that press freedom is balanced with other societal needs, such as national security, journalists enjoy a great deal of latitude in what they can report without prior restraint by the government.

But government can try to interfere in journalists' freedom in other ways, such as in attempts to get information from reporters or keep information from them. Journalists resist such intrusions and commit to guarding the First Amendment against those who would try to limit its protections. That's one way to think about the principle of freedom. The principle also refers to autonomy, which means that reporters keep a professional distance from their sources, and even their audience, so that none of them can have undue influence on a story.

FREEDOM FROM MANIPULATION

People who work in public relations or advertising sometimes create events that are designed to garner media coverage. Sometimes these are what historian and cultural critic Daniel Boorstin called "pseudo-events," or those that don't really have much newsworthiness, but sometimes they are worth covering (1992). Your job as an autonomous journalist is to determine which type the event is.

For example, in the summer of 2011, the Denver Broncos organization sent the "Broncos Country Caravan" around the state. Fans got to meet football players and take pictures with cheerleaders. The pro football team rolling through town was an event that many people wanted to know about—in one town, 5,000 people showed up to see the caravan. If a Broncos public relations person contacted your news outlet, you might decide to put an announcement in the briefs section, where a news outlet often lists upcoming events. But it might also be something that people would enjoy a story about. So even though this was an event clearly designed for Broncos' publicity, you'd still probably cover it with a lighthearted story that the community would enjoy. The distinction here is that you would be covering the event for the community's sake, not the Broncos'. A good journalist knows to ask that question.

In the current climate of spin and celebrity, there's an especially strong need for journalistic autonomy. It can be tempting to agree to what politicians or celebrities ask in exchange for access to them. But journalists need to resist caving in to that pressure. By maintaining autonomy, journalists send a message to the public that they are reporting responsibly and without bias for or against certain cases.

CONFLICT OF INTEREST

Suppose the Political Science Club is bringing a popular speaker to campus, and you're assigned the story. The club president is a friend of yours. You interview her for the story and include a few of the facts she gave you about how much the speaker will cost and how much money the club has raised. Probably anyone writing a story about the fundraiser would do the same. But if people know or learn that you two are friends, they might wonder if your friendship led to the sympathetic coverage. Even if it didn't, your readers might wonder. There may not have been a direct conflict of interest—you'd maintain that the friendship played no role in your coverage—but because there was even the possible appearance of a conflict of interest, your story's credibility is in question.

Typically, conflict of interest is a concern when there's a friendship or a business, family or romantic relationship involved. Similarly, if you report on campus politics, you probably shouldn't be a member of the student Democratic or Republican organization—or the student government. If you are involved with the campus environmental center, you should be wary about accepting assignments for environmental stories. Inform your supervisor of any conflicts like this. The supervisor will make the call: Just because you know somebody doesn't mean there's a conflict. But if there is, the story might be reassigned to another reporter.

A conflict of interest—real or perceived—can also arise when reporters accept free meals, gifts or passes to events (Fig. 2-4).

Publicists sometimes send free passes to news outlets as a way of encouraging coverage. Reviewing movies or restaurants or previewing concerts may provide a real service to your readers. You want them to have enough information to decide whether to go to a restaurant or attend an event. Or, maybe sports fans want a firsthand account of how their team performed. Especially when a media outlet is too short on cash to buy the reporter a ticket, one could argue that accepting free entry is in the audience's interest. The counterargument is that, to maintain independence, the news organization or journalists should pay their way. How critical could a journalist be of the coach or the home team that paid her way in or gave her a free bus ride? How honest can her movie or restaurant review be? Even where the journalist and source have a good and respectful relationship, something can go awry. What if a coach or player is caught with illegal drugs? What if a journalist notices unsafe food practices in a restaurant kitchen? Autonomous journalists avoid conflicts of interest or even the *appearance* of them.

The reason for professional distance is so that you maintain credibility. When readers doubt a reporter's independence, they might lose faith in journalism. If the audience doesn't trust the news, people won't engage with it as they make important decisions. Then journalists are not doing their job.

Humaneness

The principle of humaneness says that reporters should not be simply unfeeling chroniclers of events. Journalists aren't required to relinquish their humanity as they strive for autonomy. The principle of humaneness tempers the traditional injunction

FIGURE 2-4 Journalists should not buy anything for sources nor accept anything from them, not even a burrito.

against becoming involved in the story with permission to help out in a dangerous situation or to show compassion to the subject of a story. Sometimes the balance between being a reporter who is impartial and also humane is difficult to strike.

Consider this passage from Peter Maass, who was a correspondent for *The Washington Post* during the war in Bosnia, describing a visit to a concentration camp there in the early 1990s:

> We were led to a dormitory room filled with about forty bunk beds. It wasn't such a bad place, but of course it was created for our benefit. Until a few days earlier, the prisoners had been sleeping on the hard ground in an adjacent shed. A guard shadowed me all the time, so trying to talk to the prisoners was more fruitless than ever. I slipped my notebook and a pack of cigarettes to Vlatka and told her that I was going outside and hopefully the guard would follow me. As I headed for the exit, I passed the television crew. The reporter was interviewing a feverish inmate lying on a bunk bed. The television light was shining right on the poor

guy, and several guards were hovering about the bed. The inmate was shaking, his blankets moving up and down under the furious heavings of his chest. "Are you being treated well?" the reporter asked. The prisoner's look of terror tightened a few notches more, and he glanced at one of the guards, not knowing how to respond. Obviously he could not speak honestly, but the guard might get mad if he was too fulsome in his praise. The truth would kill, and even the wrong lie would kill.

"*Dobro, dobro*," he gasped. Good, good.

I left the room, feeling sad for the prisoner and angry at the TV crew, which seemed to have crossed a boundary by getting involved in this game. It was sort of Russian roulette. Five empty chambers in the gun, one filled with a bullet. The reporter was handing the gun to the prisoner when he turned the camera on. *Speak*, the reporter asked. *Pull the trigger*. The prisoner was safe while we were around but what happens when we leave and the guards no longer need to put on a show? I suppose that my anger at the television guys was compounded by the fact that I had been doing much the same thing, although at least I didn't need to ask my victims to speak up because the sound level was too low. What were journalists supposed to do? Not go to the camps? Not try to talk to the prisoners? (1997, pp. 48–49)

The journalists naturally wanted to report on the camps, and to interview someone directly involved, like the prisoner. But sometimes it's especially important to think about how we might affect the subject of a story or a source we use. As with the television crew in this example, our sense of mission can lead to a lack of sensitivity, which might result in harm to others. The principle of humaneness tries to prevent this.

Maass concludes that, in this case, it's better to back off. He writes, "The answer might be this: Talk to the ones who are willing to talk, but for God's sake, when a prisoner is shaking in his bed, turn the camera off" (p. 49).

Being humane doesn't mean letting a source trample on your independence. You wouldn't withhold a tough question because it might embarrass a source. And you also have to ask sensitive questions sometimes. When reporting a news story that touches on someone who died, you might have to contact members of the dead person's family. Sometimes you'll have to ask a politician to confirm or deny an allegation of wrongdoing. Humaneness doesn't outweigh the other principles, but it says that you can and should consider it.

In one of the most famous news photographs from the Vietnam War, a naked 9-year-old girl is crying or screaming and running down the road, away from her village and toward the camera (Fig. 2-5). Her clothes have been burned in a napalm raid, and she is obviously in terrible pain. After taking the photograph, journalist Nick Ut gave the girl, Kim Phuc, water to drink and also poured some on her hot skin. Then he loaded her into his car and took her and several of her family members to the nearest hospital.

> Only when Kim Phuc was on the operating table did Nick Ut leave the hospital and head towards Saigon, to bring his film to the AP.
>
> When a newsman later de-briefed Nick Ut for a by-line story of what he had experienced on Route-1, Nick did not mention that he helped Kim Phuc. (Faas & Fulton, p. 2)

FIGURE 2-5 Nick Ut, a photographer for the Associated Press during the Vietnam War, showed the American public the face of war—and was also humane to the subject of his photo. He snapped photos of Vietnamese children fleeing the effects of an accidental napalm drop by the South Vietnamese on its own people. Then he took 9-year-old Kim Phuc (center) to the hospital and made sure she received medical attention.

Ut did not leave his humanity behind, despite the fact that he was in a war zone. He remained professional, keeping himself out of the news story as much as possible, but he was willing to delay turning in his film to make sure that Phuc was safe. Ut went on to win the Pulitzer Prize for his photo, and Phuc grew up to become a United Nations goodwill ambassador working for world peace.

Truth Telling

Ultimately, journalists have to get it right, and that's what the principle of truth telling addresses. Even though the idea of a single, fixed "Truth" is problematic, good journalism is based on demonstrably accurate information. This concept is so important that we'll keep returning to it throughout the book. But to give you a sense of what factual accuracy means for a journalist,

> Telling the truth has always been the simplest and most complicated function of journalism.
>
> *KELLY MCBRIDE & TOM ROSENSTIEL, MEDIA ETHICISTS*

here's an overview that illustrates how an ethical journalist thinks about the quality of information in a story. Let's talk about truth telling at two levels—factual accuracy and contextual truths.

FACTUAL ACCURACY

Factual accuracy requires that information within a story be confirmed. You should double-check the spelling of names and the accuracy of someone's title. You should confirm information with multiple sources, especially if your source has questionable, little or no authority to speak on the topic; if your source has an axe to grind or an agenda to promote; or if the story is controversial.

You should also keep your ears attuned to comments that sound like fact but may not be. They should be verified. Not every person's opinion is equally valid on every subject. Your job is to discern what's supported by sound evidence and what's unsubstantiated. There's a distinction between opinion and well-documented information that you and your audience can trust.

That means that even when you're quoting someone or using actual sound bites, you should confirm that what they say is also correct. Quotes should accurately reflect what someone said, and their substance must also be true. Especially when there is a truth claim—that is, a statement that could be verified, as opposed to a personal opinion—you want to make sure that the information is accurate. And, when that claim is controversial or charged, you need to confirm that it's substantively true. Just because a person says something doesn't make it true or worthy of inclusion in a news story.

Additionally, you should make sure that the way you quote someone accurately reflects what that person said. Typically, a reporter doesn't have the space and readers don't have the time for news to include everything said in many interviews. So it's acceptable and even helpful that you don't include entire quotes. But if you included only a misleading part of a quote, you would misrepresent what the source said. That would be inaccurate, so it would be unethical under the principle of truth telling.

CONTEXTUAL TRUTHS

In addition to factual accuracy, the principle of truth telling asks us to research and report contextual truths. An ethical journalist seeks out and provides relevant material to help people understand the story in the larger scheme of things—to go beyond surface examination.

Contextual truths may not be immediately apparent and may be difficult to ferret out. And not every story is going to warrant extended reporting. People often need information fast more than they need it in-depth, or before they need it in-depth. However, this aspect of truth telling asks the journalist to pause and consider any larger ramifications of a particular event. Then, the journalist must make sure that the context provided portrays the event accurately.

In the following example, what appeared to be a routine, but tragic, accident story turned into a larger discussion of dangerous intersections and how to increase public safety at this particular intersection.

Durango, Colorado, has two major highways running through town. At one of the town's intersections is the entrance to a big-box retailer. Despite the traffic lights, turning into and out of this retail center can be a knuckle-biting experience because traffic is often heavy and the speed limit is 50 mph.

One morning, the driver of a Subaru station wagon turned left into the retail center in the way of an oncoming Dodge Ram pickup truck. The accident killed her and her husband, who was in the passenger's seat. The driver of the truck was able to walk away. The accident was breaking news, and could have been reported as a basic accident story.

But if you're reporting this story, considering your audience, and trying to provide the fullest report you can, you might think about questions like the following: Have there been other serious accidents at this intersection? How dangerous is this intersection compared to others in the city? What can be done to minimize danger at this intersection?

The reporting staff at the local newspaper, the *Durango Herald*, did answer these questions in the first story and in two follow-ups (see Benjamin, 2011a, 2011b; "Walmart," 2011). They reported the following information:

- This was one of the 10 most dangerous intersections in the city, the site of 45 accidents in 10 years, 3 of them fatal.

- There had been fatal accidents elsewhere in the city. The *Herald* reported the number and dates of these.

- Authorities said that the speed of oncoming traffic made accidents at that intersection more "severe."

- Within a week, the state's department of transportation announced it would change the traffic light at the intersection; workers would install dedicated left-hand turn signals so that drivers wouldn't have to negotiate oncoming traffic.

- The department spokesperson confirmed that the signal change was in direct response to the accident.

Imagine how useful this information was to residents. They might have had a general sense of the problems at that intersection, and some feeling that someone ought to do something about it soon. But the coverage here put this accident in the context of other accidents and intersections in town, so a resident could conclude that yes, this was a problem intersection, that there was a fairly easy fix, and that the appropriate agency took immediate steps to implement it. Thanks to journalists concerned with providing context, people had access to enough information to assess the job their government was doing to ensure their safety.

A Caveat

When you seek contextual information, pay attention to the meaning that you generate through juxtaposition of information, when two or more pieces of information are close together and the audience can read them as directly related to one another. You need to make sure that such a connection is also factually accurate.

Consider another accident example: A man drove his truck off a 200-foot cliff into a ravine. Authorities found him dead at the scene. Suppose the accident report listed the following facts:

- The driver was not wearing a seatbelt.
- Authorities thought he might have had a heart attack.
- The roads were in good condition.
- It could have been foggy due to an area storm.
- Empty and broken beer bottles were at the scene.
- No one knew what led to the accident.
- No one knew whether alcohol was a factor.

As you can see, several causes of the accident are possible, and the actual one hadn't been determined. If you wanted to create a story that told the fullest account, does that mean you should publish all of this information, including the fact that beer bottles were at the scene? It's true that the state patrol said the bottles were there. But does juxtaposing beer bottles with the accident information lead the audience to think that perhaps the man had been drinking?

Even if you say that no one knows yet whether alcohol was involved or what led to the accident, if you include the bottles, you're still putting the idea out there. However, you can't confirm that the bottles and the accident are related. In this case, the additional fact, while included in the accident report, might best be omitted from the story.

The answers to all of the questions you ask probably won't be included in every story. Also, realistically, even with the seemingly endless space in online news, you won't have the time or the room to provide all of the context, all of the time. You'll undoubtedly have to leave some information out. But you still need to think critically about each of your stories, discerning for your audience what information will illuminate the current situation.

In the following case study, we'll apply all of the principles to determine the best answer to a particular ethical dilemma. You'll see that we'll have to weigh principles against each other to reach a good decision, backed by reason.

An Ethics Case Study: The Facts of the Case

This case started with a murder. Lori "Star" Sutherland, the mother of a 5-year-old son, worked at a boutique on the main street in Durango, Colorado. At the time, her former boyfriend, Richard Keith Edwards, was under a restraining order for threatening her and for vandalizing her home.

One day, at about 11 a.m., Edwards entered the boutique where Sutherland worked. In a matter of minutes, he had shot and killed her.

After her death, Sutherland was mourned throughout the community. People were shocked that a brutal act had been carried out in the middle of the day in such a public place. They were also especially concerned about her 5-year-old son. After the murder, the boy remained in town, living with his grandparents. Edwards, who immediately confessed to the crime, was taken into custody. Initial news reports covered the shooting and Edwards' arrest.

The following month, Sutherland's autopsy report was released. The newspaper published a story about its contents, including these facts:

- Sutherland had been shot six times.

- Three of the shots were capable of killing her.

- A single shot to her head killed her instantly.

- She had methamphetamine in her system.

- She had a blood-alcohol level of 0.11.

The newspaper (Box 2-3) also included the following information: "In an affidavit, Edwards accused Sutherland of using methamphetamine and neglecting her son by staying out all night" (Benjamin, 2005, para. 12).

After publishing this story, the newspaper received a number of letters to the editor denouncing the autopsy story. They said that what was in the victim's blood was irrelevant and should not have been reported. They also said that the paper should not have included Edwards' statement about Sutherland.

Do these critics have a point? And what would you have done, if you had been the journalist?

The five principles offer a framework to help you decide. You'll want to consider the affected parties and the responsibility, if any, you have to each of them. In this exercise, you can start by identifying the stakeholders and then considering the principles.

WHO ARE THE STAKEHOLDERS?

The son and his grandparents might very well be affected by the way Sutherland's death is reported. Edwards might also have a stake. What about Sutherland—can a dead person still be a stakeholder?

You might also think of community members who were not directly involved. People who witnessed the murder or heard about it might feel they have a right to an explanation of the shooting. After all, don't they have something at stake concerning crimes committed in their midst?

The letters to the editor indicate that at least some people had concerns about the way the story was reported. Also, because the coroner is a public official, community members have a stake in knowing how well she is doing her job.

Can you think of other stakeholders?

BOX 2-3

THE AUTOPSY STORY

Coroner reports shooting victim used alcohol, meth
Durango Herald, May 24, 2005

By Shane Benjamin
Herald Staff Writer

The Durango woman who was shot and killed last month in a Main Avenue store died while under the influence of methamphetamine and alcohol, according to a coroner's autopsy report released Monday.

Lori "Star" Sutherland, 41, was shot six times: once to the head, once in the left wrist and four times to her upper body. The shot to her head was instantly fatal, La Plata County Coroner Dr. Carol Huser said.

Two other shots, one to a lung and another to the lower back, would have been fatal or fatally infectious. But three other shots would not likely have caused her death.

Richard Keith Edwards, 49, has been charged with first-degree murder in connection with the shooting.

In a police affidavit, Edwards said he fired seven shots at Sutherland. The .45-caliber handgun held six bullets in a clip and one in the chamber. According to the affidavit, Edwards said he meant to save the last shot for himself, but he accidentally fired all seven at Sutherland. Where the seventh shot landed is unclear.

The coroner's report details each of the bullet wounds and includes a toxicology report completed in Midland, Texas.

What's next
A preliminary hearing, where prosecutors must prove a crime and the involvement of Richard Keith Edwards, was scheduled for 9:30 a.m. today in District Court.

However, at the request of the Public Defender's Office, the hearing has been rescheduled for a later date.

The toxicology report showed that, at the time of her death, Sutherland had a blood-alcohol level of 0.11—above the legal driving limit in Colorado.

Sutherland was also under the influence of methamphetamine, Huser reported.

But Huser said she couldn't determine exactly when Sutherland took the drug and alcohol, although it would have been within hours of her death.

In an affidavit, Edwards accused Sutherland of using methamphetamine and neglecting her son by staying out all night.

Sutherland was pronounced dead at 12:15 p.m. April 14. The coroner's report of her death is a public record under state law.

Truth Telling:
What Do You Know Is True?

FACTUAL ACCURACY

Is the Autopsy Report Factually Accurate?

Is it factually accurate to say that an autopsy was conducted and a report released? Yes. But does truth telling in terms of factual accuracy require you to report this?

At the very least, your story can inform readers that an autopsy was performed and a report released, which shows that the coroner is obeying the law.

Now the questions become thornier.

Do You Include the Blood Test Results?

Should your story include the test results that show Sutherland was legally drunk and had meth in her system when she was killed? The information is factually true, according to the report. One way to answer the question is to say that, because it's true, it goes in. A journalist shouldn't be in the habit of withholding information.

The counterargument is that an autopsy story should only report the cause of death. The coroner reported that the shot to Sutherland's head killed her instantly. She would be dead regardless of what was in her system.

Do You Include the Murderer's Accusation?

Is there a good reason to include Edwards' statement? It came from a sworn affidavit, so you can reasonably assert that he did in fact make the comment. But is the substance of the comment true? In other words, while it may be true that Edwards *said* Sutherland was unfit, the truth-telling principle asks you to verify that information so you're not repeating an unsubstantiated opinion.

This is not an easy statement to verify. It's unlikely that you could access records of whether complaints of neglect had been filed, or whether the child had ever been removed from the home. This type of information is typically confidential. You should be able to check whether Sutherland has been arrested for drug- or alcohol-related incidents because arrest records are typically open under state laws. You might also try to interview people close to her to find out more. But until you know for sure whether the statement is substantively true, you could say that the requirements of factual accuracy have not been met. So, you can't ethically include it.

CONTEXTUAL TRUTH

Considering the contextual truth of the story might help you clarify your thinking about whether to include the blood test results. For example, at the time this story broke, meth production, distribution and abuse were a serious social problem in many areas around the nation. Data showed a connection among meth use, increases in property crime and increases in child-neglect cases—meth users who are parents are often either too high or too crashed to properly care for their children. Additional data show a pretty firm connection between drug and alcohol use and homicide.

Here you might ask, What is this story about? Some might argue that what was an autopsy-report story has become something more, given the results. Maybe the meth and alcohol *are* related to Sutherland's death. You could follow up with interviews with local law enforcement authorities, social workers and others familiar with meth use. By making these connections in the story, you would provide context that might help people understand how this could have happened.

It's tricky, though. Deciding the drug and alcohol information is relevant is making an explicit connection between the victim's choice to partake and her subsequent murder. It's an example of how, by juxtaposing these facts, you make them appear to be related. You could be seen as suggesting that if Sutherland hadn't been involved with drugs and drunk in the morning, then she might not have been killed.

Humaneness—To Whom?

A good number of the letters to the editor argued that the newspaper had been inhumane to Sutherland and her young son. The letter writers complained that publishing the results of blood tests unfairly tainted her memory and would make life more difficult for her son.

A counterargument might be that suppressing information is the greater harm, and it would affect more people. There are times when information that is painful for victims or their families to hear still needs to be published in order for reporters to be responsible and fair to the public. And a news organization has to be careful about establishing a precedent that it would need to apply in future cases—you have to be fair to each person for whom publication of certain details might prove embarrassing.

Part of the dilemma is that you don't know for sure what the immediate or eventual outcome of publishing the information will be, and you don't know that it would be negative in any case. For instance, publishing the mother's drug and alcohol test results could result in community outreach to the boy, providing a support network larger than that he otherwise would have known. On a broader scale, perhaps including the results would draw people's attention to substance abuse in the community and help address the problem.

A tempting solution might be to ask the family what their preference would be—and that seems like a thoughtful course of action. If the family gave its approval, you would be released from the dilemma. But what if they said no? Either way, the principle of freedom and autonomy warns against giving editorial power to sources—or, in this case, family members. You shouldn't give special treatment to the Sutherland family, letting feelings get in the way of journalistic freedom.

Freedom: Keeping the Decision Independent

The freedom and humaneness principles frequently seem like the two sides of a coin. As you guard journalistic independence, you risk treating people harshly or appearing to be insensitive. Journalists are people, too, so it's natural to share concerns for a victim's family. However, if you become too wrapped up in protecting people's feelings, you risk losing autonomy. The principle of freedom asks you to create that professional distance from the boy, the family and the victim.

How much do you allow humaneness to influence your report? Autonomy asks you to make sure that you don't treat people differently just because you feel sorry for them or because you want to shelter them from bad news or because they are close to you.

Justice: What's Fairest to All the Stakeholders?

Justice requires you to make sure that procedures and policies are applied equally to all citizens, and this relates directly to making sure that the coroner did a complete and careful autopsy. By reporting on the autopsy results, you afford the audience the chance to see that the coroner did her job, came to an official cause of death, conducted the standard tests and reported the results publicly.

The principle of justice also asks you to treat sources and the subject of the story fairly as you go about telling the story. You can hear echoes of the concerns raised under humaneness. Is it fair to include the blood work and thereby imply that drugs and alcohol were related to Sutherland's death? Is it fair to include facts that make Sutherland look bad? (And for that matter, is it fair to exclude facts so that she *doesn't* look bad?)

If you think about the *story* as opposed to the *people* directly involved, some different issues come up. Because fairness also asks you to render the story in such a way that you're not misleading the audience, it's not just Sutherland or her family that you'll be concerned with. The story should be the fairest representation of the event, and that returns us to a question that we've encountered from the beginning of this analysis: What's the story? Is it that the coroner released a report, established the cause of death and did her job? If so, then the story is much narrower than if it's a story about domestic violence.

Stewardship: Stepping Back to Think about Journalism's Credibility

Whether they're learning about a murder in a small town or a war across the world, people rely on journalists to provide information. But they also expect you to be members of the community, and to behave responsibly to others in the community. You can serve the profession and bolster its credibility by making a thoughtful decision that is either self-explanatory or that you explain, perhaps in an editorial. You should avoid the appearance of sensationalizing the story, or of being insensitive. Yet, you must also abide by professional standards of accuracy and freedom, so you can't just withhold inconvenient information. Having worked through the principles individually, let's now consider them collectively as you decide what the most ethical course of action would be.

Making the Decision

Let's start with the decision about reporting the cause of death. The story would include the coroner's determination that the gunshot to the head was immediately fatal, that two other wounds would have been fatal and that the other three bullets were not fatal. This information is factually accurate, and it is in context. It confirms gunshots as the cause of death, which police and previous news stories had indicated and is therefore not inhumane. You are free to report information that is public record, which in fact your watchdog role compels you to do. This decision seems clear: You should report the cause of death.

The decision of whether to include the Edwards comment on Sutherland's drug use and fitness as a mother is also straightforward. Based on accuracy alone, it's hard to ethically justify making it a part of the story—you just don't know if what Edwards said is true. As far as you know, it is an unsubstantiated opinion from a source who could possibly be trying to justify his actions.

Thoughtful people might disagree about these two decisions. But not all conclusions by good people are equally sound. It's important to understand that the ethical principles we're discussing don't dissolve into relativism—this is not a case of "one person's decision is just as good as anyone else's." The ultimate choice should be the one with the best evidence.

But what about the meth and alcohol in Sutherland's system? Our analysis doesn't lead to such a clear-cut answer about whether to include this information. First, there's the conflict between humaneness and the other principles. Furthermore, the drugs weren't the direct reason for Sutherland's death.

They were, however, part of the report about that death. If people already know these details and see that you don't include them, they might wonder what else you weren't telling them concerning this story and others. That could damage your credibility for now and in the long term, which would serve no one's best interest. Furthermore, causing that damage to your credibility would be poor stewardship.

Sometimes the principles will lead to a definite answer, and sometimes they'll conflict. In that case, you have to weight them—see what the strongest argument for the most ethical decision seems to be. Are you, as a journalist, most concerned with the memory of a murder victim and protecting her family? Or does your duty to the public take precedence? If so, there's a strong case to be made that, taken together, truth telling, freedom, justice and stewardship outweigh the concerns that humaneness highlighted.

If you opt for openness, you might not be able to prevent pain to the family. But you might be able to minimize community anger by explaining how you came to your decision. For example, sometimes when news outlets choose to make sensitive information public, an editor or anchor will explain the decision in an editorial comment accompanying a story. Journalists try to make the decision-making process as transparent to the public as possible. The audience still might not agree, but people can see how the journalists are trying to be good stewards.

How the *Durango Herald* Explained Its Decision

The *Herald* did address its readers' concerns two years later, after similar complaints by the families and friends of victims in two other situations. In one case, two motorcyclists speeding down a four-lane highway through town died when they crashed into a pickup truck that pulled out from a side street. Both men were ejected from their motorcycles. The *Herald* reported the results of their autopsies, which showed that both men had cocaine in their systems. In another case, three teens, ages 13, 16 and 18, died late one night when a truck crashed into the parked car in which they were sitting. The newspaper later reported that, according to the autopsies, all three had been drinking alcohol, and all three were too young to drink legally.

The editorial, called "Hurtful Facts," acknowledged the harsh criticisms leveled at the paper, which "centered on the feelings of the families, respect for the dead and a desire not to blame the victims" ("Hurtful," 2007, para. 8). It also said that while people shouldn't blame the victims for their own deaths, the community could learn from those deaths. And while everyone sometimes makes poor decisions, the editorial said

> It is almost always the case that a series of poor judgments formed a causal chain that led to disaster. Sometimes relatively minor factors that would not in themselves cause such a bad outcome also can contribute. We can learn from those, too.
>
> That a woman would show up to work in the morning legally drunk suggests a troubled individual. That she also had meth in her blood says more. Is there a more effective way to get tangled up with dangerously unstable people?
>
> Her killer alone is to blame for her death. But the toxicology report adds context—and an implicit warning—to the story.
>
> The case of the two bikers is simpler. Cocaine is illegal; reporting on its use requires no further justification. Beyond that, its presence in the dead men's systems—especially taken together with "crotch rocket" motorcycles and excess speed—suggests a propensity for risk-taking that is itself a cautionary tale.
>
> The deaths of the three students is the most difficult case, but also the most compelling. A series of things appear to have played into that tragedy. Chief among them were a truck driven 16 consecutive hours, a sheriff's deputy's car parked facing north in the southbound lane (which the State Patrol said was a contributing factor) and the truck driver's not braking immediately.
>
> What, if any, role the students' drinking might have played is unclear, as is exactly what they were doing off the side of the road at midnight. But whatever was going on was sufficient to attract the attention of the deputy, and it is hardly a stretch to wonder if underage consumption was not one factor in how the events of that night unfolded.
>
> That does not mean the students' drinking was the cause of the crash. But it is part of the story. Withholding it would not have made such a sad story any less so. (para. 12–18)

The editors apparently understood the anger in the community and sought to address it. In the editorial, they try not to blame the victims, but they do use the deaths as **cautionary tales**—warnings to the reader about drinking and drugs and death. Readers may not agree with the editors' final decisions or their rationale, but they are reassured that the decisions were thoughtful. The editorial is an act of stewardship in this way and a good supplement to the decision to publish.

However, reasonable people could conclude that the lack of a direct link between the substances in Sutherland's system and her death provides a strong argument against including the information in the story. Then, another option is to leave it out of this story and get to the larger contextual truth some other way. Perhaps you follow up by investigating the issues brought about by this situation, culminating in a later story or package, if one turns out to be warranted. That course of action would address the larger questions of truth telling, justice and stewardship, albeit in a delayed time frame, without forcing you to be inhumane at the same time. If you can establish what your priorities are, then you can try to figure out the decision that will reflect them best.

Which way do the principles lead you? Ethical decision-making requires a journalist to come to a best decision, the one with the soundest reasons and the strongest support. When we use this example in class, we see students often find their personal opinion differs from their reasoned decision. Personally, they want to be kind to the family and honor the memory of the victim, but they decide that, as journalists, they have a larger duty to the truth. They decide they cannot withhold the blood-test results, but they can withhold the Edwards comment. They do want to include an editorial comment with the story.

We're persuaded by their position on the grounds of truth telling, justice and stewardship. We also conclude that the watchdog function of the press compels journalists to report that a public official did her job and to provide the gist of her report. Finally, we agree that the connection among drugs, alcohol, crime and parental neglect warrants further investigation.

We've introduced you to this framework so that you can see the benefit of applying a system of ethical decision-making to all of your stories, seeking out and including information that will fulfill your role as public servant. Of course, myriad factors contribute to how a story gets told, and we will discuss these in some depth in the remainder of the book. Still, regardless of the kind of story, we want you to pause and consider the moral implications of how you report it.

Exercises for Chapter 2

EXERCISE 2-1: Select an in-depth news story. Make a list that answers the following questions: Who are the stakeholders? What do they have at stake?

EXERCISE 2-2: A source for the story you're working on suggests that you meet at the local coffee shop for a snack. You meet the source there and order yourself a beverage. The source orders after you, and then hands the cashier a debit card, telling the cashier to put it all on his bill, thereby paying for your order. What do you do? Why? What issues of freedom and autonomy do you see?

EXERCISE 2-3: You are covering a burglary in one of the dorms. You get an interview with the resident assistant in charge of the dorm. He makes the following statements:

"I told her not to leave her room unlocked."

"The campus police showed up right after I called to report it—it took them, like, just a few minutes."

You also talk to a resident down the hall, who says the following:

"You've got to lock your room—just common sense. Dumb girl. She deserved what she got."

Write a 300- to 500-word discussion that describes which, if any, of this information you would include in the story. Is it accurate? Is it humane?

EXERCISE 2-4: Suppose the Edwards statement was substantively true, and you could confirm it. Using the principles, decide what the best decision would be about whether to publish it. Make a list of issues that the principles lead you to consider.

EXERCISE 2-5: Kevin Carter's disturbing photo of a starving child being watched by a vulture won a Pulitzer Prize in 1994. You can see a small image at pulitzer.org/awards/1994 or search a term like "Kevin Carter vulture photo." As we did for the example in the chapter, go through each principle and identify the issues involved in taking this photo. What about the issues in publishing it?

EXERCISE 2-6: Email a professional journalist to find out about an ethical dilemma she or he has faced in reporting a story. Explain briefly that you're a journalism student and that you'd like to learn about an ethical issue in the professional world. Prepare three or four questions to pose to the journalist so that you get an understanding of the situation. Make clear to the journalist that you'll be using this information in class. Summarize the journalist's response and discuss which principles are involved.

EXERCISE 2-7: Select an evening newscast to watch. Listen carefully for any elements that serve as cautionary tales—that is, implied warnings about how to behave. Write down a description of these elements, if any, and the cautions they present.

GET IT IN
WRITING

Habits of Mind

From the very beginning of their reporting, journalists think about whether and why a story merits attention. They think about how to frame the story so that it's fair and accurate, useful and interesting. And they ask, what makes this story newsworthy?

Think about the last time you grabbed your phone or camera to take some pictures. What did you take pictures of? Why? How did you decide what to include in a picture? What did you do with those pictures? Before reading further, take a few minutes to answer these questions.

When you take pictures, you make decisions about what's worthwhile for a photograph and what's not. The rest of life keeps going on around you, and you can never really capture it entirely. No matter how many photos you shoot, they only reflect what is happening in that moment—a snapshot of time and place.

Now, let's say you decide to post some of your pictures. You'll probably review what you have and edit accordingly, dumping fuzzy or irrelevant pictures. You also might add some captions to accompany the images.

At every step of the way—deciding to take pictures, choosing their content, selecting which pictures to post and writing comments—you create a particular version of the event. It's not the only one possible—you could make different decisions and create another version. As you make choices about what to photograph, you are also deciding what does *not* get recorded. The people who see your posted photos will understand the event in a way that's influenced by the decisions you've made.

Framing

Sociologist Gaye Tuchman (1978) talks about **framing** as the way that journalists create a world for their audience based on a very similar process of selection. She says that what people see, on the nightly news, for example, is limited to what's within the boundaries of the television screen (Fig. 3-1). They see *a* version of reality, created by journalists. The television news constructs reality for the audience, but the reality it constructs isn't complete. It's the same idea as in the preceding camera example: When you decide which pictures to take and to post, you create a particular version of events for your friends to see. The concept of framing can apply to media other than television and cameras. The home page of any news site would be a frame, as would a magazine or newspaper page, the design elements within them, or the ambient sound in a radio package.

The way journalists frame a story is important because, first, what's in the frame is legitimized as important, relevant and most worthy of people's attention. On the flip side, what journalists leave out of the frame is delegitimized and invisible. Second, the way we represent the news that *is* in the frame can influence the way our audience perceives their world. **Agenda setting** is a term referring to the idea that journalists

FIGURE 3-1 The way a journalist frames a story signals what's important.

don't tell people what to think, but they do influence what people think about by choosing what to present (Fig. 3-2).

For example, after the Sandy Hook Elementary shootings, the debate over gun control re-emerged with even more urgency than in the past. The way journalists framed the debate helped to legitimize the terms of argument (Fig. 3-3): Was it about confiscating all guns, or was the emphasis on background checks? Or was it armed teachers in schools? Were people most concerned because so many of the victims were small children? By including some arguments in the frame but not others, the news media suggested that those were the arguments worth paying attention to.

WHAT'S THIS MEAN FOR A WORKING JOURNALIST?

When journalists make framing decisions, we need to think critically and make sure that our decisions are ethically justified, maximizing justice and truth telling. We need to think about the implications of how we frame a story. We don't want to impose the frame too early in the process, or refuse to shift the frame as more information emerges. That

FIGURE 3-2 By snapping this photo at the six-month anniversary of the Sandy Hook Elementary shootings, the photojournalist helped keep the shootings and their link to gun violence on the agenda. What are some ways the photo and the cutline helped to frame the event? The cutline read as follows: "NEWTOWN, CT - JUNE 14: Lindsay Knauf takes a picture of a bus bearing some of the over 6,000 names of people killed by gun violence since the massacre in Newtown at a remembrance event on the six-month anniversary of the massacre at Sandy Hook Elementary School on June 14, 2013, in Newtown, Connecticut. A 26-second moment of silence was observed to honor the 20 children and six adults who were killed at the school on Dec. 14. The event also included the reading of the names of over 6,000 people who have been killed by gun violence. The reading of names is expected to take 12 hours." (Platt, 2013)

FIGURE 3-3A Should guns be confiscated?

FIGURE 3-3B Should background checks be stricter?

FIGURE 3-3C Should teachers carry guns?

would shut down what the story is because we've decided too early what to exclude. Some stories, or parts of them, will always be excluded. The constraints of time and space still exist, both for audiences who will eventually stop clicking on yet another link, and for journalists, who will eventually have to move on to other stories. There will always be criticisms of the journalist's power to decide what gets covered and the privileging of some ideas and censoring of others that result from those decisions. Knowing we are vulnerable to such objections helps drive journalists to strive for fair and accurate framing. But selection is essential to a coherent understanding of reality. It's part of the job.

News Values

One of the ways that journalists begin to construct a frame is by deciding whether to cover a story at all—that is, by determining what news value it has. Experienced journalists often disagree about the **newsworthiness** of a story. But they usually agree about what elements indicate that a story is worth investigating. The terms for these **news values** vary, but they generally include **timeliness**, **impact**, **proximity**, **conflict**, **prominence** and **novelty**.

Timeliness is essential to the very definition of news—what distinguishes it from history or science or any other kind of information: A story should be new, present a new development or link to a current event. If a person is missing, and at the next news cycle the person is still missing and there are no other developments, you might question whether another story is warranted. When the Malaysia Airlines Flight 370 mysteriously disappeared in 2014, some news organizations couldn't resist frequent updates even when there was no new information. But the public gained little from those stories. In the effort to be timely, you can also rush too quickly to file your report and end up with an inaccurate story. Being fast is important, but being accurate trumps being fast.

Impact is one of the strongest news values of this group. Here, we look at who the stakeholders are and calculate the real or probable impact an event will have on them. For instance, campaign coverage is important because the outcome could change people's lives. Good journalists cover the candidates' positions rather than focusing on who is ahead in the polls. Media critics fault such **horse-race coverage**, as it's called, as providing superficial instead of substantive information (Fig. 3-4).

It's possible that once a candidate is labeled a front-runner, that person will get more coverage than someone behind in the polls. It's possible, too, that the attention paid to the front runner will also solidify that perception and unfairly marginalize less popular candidates with important messages to share.

Sometimes a story will concern potential impacts, such as the predicted ramifications of a new law. Covering stories about potential impacts is tricky because consequences are so difficult to predict. Still, reporters should address these because that's how they can help people understand how decisions that others make might directly affect them. For example, when Colorado, Washington and Oregon were voting whether to legalize the recreational use of marijuana, people in those states undoubtedly had questions about what would happen if the initiatives passed. When would

FIGURE 3-4 Horse-race coverage can be exciting, but not very useful.

adults be able to smoke pot anywhere they wanted without fear of arrest? How would that work, given that it was still illegal at the federal level? What would happen if someone was driving while stoned? How would taxes be collected, and where would they go? The election hadn't been held yet, so there was no direct impact, but people still wanted to know about the potential impact.

Proximity refers to the idea that the closer the event is to the audience, the more newsworthy it is. We think of this in two ways: **geographical proximity** and **psychological proximity.**

Geographical proximity means that a story is newsworthy because it's happening in your neck of the woods. A heat wave settling over your city is more important to cover than one that's half a country away. A local audience would want to know how long the high temperatures are forecast to last, what measures they should take to wait out the weather, or any city advisories, for example. Information about a local problem like this could help people make plans (Should I postpone an outdoor project? Should I make sure to check on my neighbor?), and possibly save lives.

Similarly, a state's proposed law allowing gay marriage wouldn't be as newsworthy in terms of geographical proximity outside of that state. However, the new law could very well be newsworthy in terms of psychological proximity. Many people have strong views about same-sex couples being allowed to legally marry, so even if the new law wouldn't affect them directly, they would be very interested in following the story.

Conflict is typically defined as some sort of battle between competing forces or ideas, such as human against human, human against government or human against nature. Reporting on conflicts can be important, provided that the conflict is over real and meaningful action and not just gamesmanship between two people who disagree with one another to advance a personal agenda.

During the tense "fiscal cliff" negotiations of 2013, Speaker of the House John Boehner reportedly told Senate Majority Leader Harry Reid to "go f--- himself" when the two men crossed paths in the White House. The curse made the national media, but was it newsworthy, or a tidbit of gossip? It's probably justifiable to write that, within earshot of reporters, the speaker was disrespectful to his Senate colleague—you could argue that the comment illustrates a facet of Boehner's personality that citizens might need to know. On the other hand, you could also argue that some Democrats were turning an irrelevant incident into a big deal to weaken or criticize a political opponent. Or, you could say that Boehner was just posturing as a tough guy after a brutal election and that reporting the comment plays into his personal agenda and heightens the importance of the conflict to a disproportionate degree. You might also decide that while all three arguments have merit, illustrating Boehner's personality is important enough to take the risk. This is an example of where to think critically about whether and in what sense a conflict deserves coverage.

Prominence refers to the idea that prominent people are newsworthy. The definition usually includes political and business leaders, celebrities, athletes and other well-known people (Fig. 3-5). Because prominent people are often in positions to

FIGURE 3-5 When then-senator Barack Obama first ran for president in 2008, he was already newsworthy because of his prominence as a senator, as a candidate for president, and as the first African-American candidate for president who had a serious chance of winning. Damon Winter, who won a Pulitzer for his photographic coverage of the campaign, said his challenge was finding moments of sincerity among all the carefully staged campaigns: "There are real moments even though the event may have been organized. The challenge is to find those real moments within the context of the staged events" (Fenwick, 2009, para. 8).

make decisions that concern the rest of us, what they do is frequently newsworthy. But not always. If one of your state legislators is coming to town to speak, it's a good idea to report the event so that constituents know what their elected representative has to say. But while gossip and reports of the comings and goings of celebrities might be amusing to some of your audience, your job is to discern whether the actual story is newsworthy and not a waste of valuable time or space.

Novelty is typically defined as a unique or unusual story: It's not news if a dog bites a person, the saying goes, because that happens with some regularity, but if a person bites a dog, that's news because it's unusual. Sometimes novel stories are useful and can alert readers to dangers they may not know about but should, such as a mountain lion attack on a local trail, a case of bubonic plague in a neighborhood that is also rife with vermin, or a house fire that kills a family of seven because the smoke detector didn't have batteries in it. But often, stories get told just because they're weird, which looks like the case with the following Associated Press story.

A man driving a truck hit an oncoming car, killing a woman and one of her young daughters. The crash had a novel consequence: The man had the severed head of his wife in his truck, and it "was tossed into the roadway by the impact" (Alderman, 2006, p. 11A). Police later found the wife's body in the garage of their home, and the man acknowledged involvement in her death. As the police spokeswoman said, "A woman and her child killed in a crash, and a severed head from an earlier homicide: it's nothing short of tragic and bizarre" (p. 11A). It's the bizarre twist, its novelty, that characterizes this story. But how useful is this bizarre information to your audience, and at what cost to your profession and the people involved? Especially because the man is in custody, there doesn't seem to be any danger to the community. Wouldn't publishing or airing the graphic details of this story cause further pain to the wife's relatives and friends, while providing little of worth to the audience? And when you unthinkingly republish information only because it is outlandish, you can diminish people's respect for your news organization, and for news in general. Novelty can be a reason to tell a story, but it usually shouldn't be the sole justification.

For example, when Aron Ralston was trapped in a Utah slot canyon and cut off part of his own arm to escape, the story was novel, but that's not all that made it newsworthy. It also had psychological proximity and conflict (human against nature) that resonated with a national audience. People felt a link to a fellow human who had been in a terrible situation, and many asked themselves, "If I were stuck in a similar situation somehow, would I be able to cut off my arm to save my life?" The story probably inspired horror in many readers, but it also probably inspired empathy just as often.

These six news values inform a journalist's decision about framing. When you examine a police blotter or a meeting agenda, when you hear about a speech or protest, you consider how people might be affected and how deeply. You observe whether something unusual about an event is noteworthy or whether the presence of prominent people deserves mention. And, you can provide helpful insight if you can distill for the audience what core conflicts exist, if any. You probably won't ever hear journalists saying, "I'm going to cover this fire on Main Street because of proximity, novelty and impact," but journalists do absorb these news values, and articulating and understanding them can help you develop a nose for news.

Deeper Cultural Concerns

News historian Mitchell Stephens says that news serves as a connection that allows a society to create a group identity (2007, p. 51). As such, it usually acts as a stabilizing, conservative force, reinforcing society's values and some version of the status quo, although it may also aid calls for reform. Stephens compares the news to our senses; he says that news can act as a "social sense" that allows people to know they're in touch with important events, even those they can't observe for themselves:

> The humanoids in whom our genes developed must have survived in part because they were curious about the "unobserved," with its potential threats and potential rewards. Our compulsive interest in events in the next village may have been born of that instrumental curiosity, but it has grown into a generalized need to remain aware. And it is that need, whatever its origin, that is . . . behind our newspaper reading, and behind our newscast viewing.
>
> We may savor the insights, the stimulation that the choicest news items bring, but we are driven to ingest this mix of current information each day by a hunger for awareness. That is the source of our obsession. (p. 12)

This hunger for awareness also results in a value that often informs the six news values described earlier: **human interest** or emotional interest. People are drawn to stories of ordinary human beings who experience tragedies, or who encounter adventures or miraculously good fortunes—the story of a young woman diagnosed with terminal cancer who touches the lives of community members in her last months of life; the story of a child who donates his allowance to the homeless shelter; or the story of a high-school athlete who is crippled on the field and eventually becomes a small-business owner.

But how do you decide whether to spend your time as a journalist covering such human-interest stories? Furthermore, sometimes it's easy to slide from covering a story because of its human interest into covering it for its sensational value. People usually think of **sensational news** as information that includes graphic details about sex, violence or crime that satisfy an audience's curiosity—a curiosity that's usually viewed as unhealthy and superficial. Critics accuse journalists of sensationalizing the news by emphasizing such details in their coverage.

People's interest in such information goes back as far as we have any evidence of news. Stephens (2007) gives an example of the wide interest in a historical case in which a countess and her lover apparently poisoned a man because he tried to prevent the countess from divorcing her husband. Stephens theorizes that news about a crime like this

> serves important purposes within a society. In raising a hue and cry it can, when necessary, assist in the apprehension of the criminal. In publicizing the punishment that is meted out, it can help deter other potential criminals. And in making the public aware of both crime and punishment, it can help clarify and reinforce the lines of acceptable behavior within a society. Political bonds are also strengthened when a particularly despicable act unites a people in a great chorus of moral outrage. (p. 97)

News about sensational crimes can make people aware of their own personal danger, but, as Stephens points out, that doesn't explain interest in faraway crimes, or those that are unusual and unlikely to threaten readers personally. News about graphic murders or sex may be of vital interest because they're so closely connected to life and death. But they also reinforce common bonds in a society. Stephens concludes that it's human nature to be interested in sensational news stories:

> They can be found in the Roman *acta*; they were spread with enthusiasm by preliterate societies. It is difficult, therefore, to resist the conclusion—however unpleasant and unfashionable—that the bulk of the blame for the amount of sensationalism that continues to appear in the news rests not with media corporations, no matter how greedy, but with our natures. (p. 103)

If this interest in the graphic details of a murder or the sex lives of important political figures is just human nature, what's a journalist to do? Likewise, how does a journalist respond to people's interest in superficial news—human interest or celebrity news stories about subjects such as whether a celebrity couple has broken up this week, a new tattoo that soccer star David Beckham is sporting, the fact that a famous billionaire left $12 million to her dog when she died or what the First Lady wore to a dinner party? Should a reporter feed the hunger for this type of news?

For centuries, plenty of news outlets have. For instance, in England in the 17th century, news pamphlets often described lurid murders or the torture of criminals. In the 18th century, daily newspapers began to change and develop in England—and a little more slowly, in the United States. At a pricey six pennies per issue, these newspapers were purchased mainly by big businessmen and the news inside was tailored accordingly, to include political happenings, shipping news, stock information and other information that affected this audience. In the 19th century, in the United States and England, a number of newspapers dropped their prices for purchase by people who had less money and less education, and who were less likely to be interested in business affairs. The focus of these newspapers—called the "penny press" because they usually only charged a penny per newspaper—changed to more sensational news of crimes and sex, and stories with local color for these blue-collar workers who wanted to know about their corner of the world and be entertained.

Good professional journalists take into account human interest in the news: that people may be widely interested in the biographical stories of famous people, for instance—how a singer became famous, or how a sports figure who received a large salary at a young age became embroiled in illegal drugs. Stories like one about a martial arts instructor who brandished a samurai sword to frighten off a would-be mugger in 2013 may not shed light on world problems, but they might expand our vision of the world just a little—and make audiences smile. And people can be very moved by symbolic events like President Obama sitting down at his desk for the first time.

Good journalists also try to be respectful of their audience. As journalism critics Bill Kovach and Tom Rosenstiel point out, it's wrong to think that everyone wants shallow or sensational information all the time:

> A journalism that focuses on the expert elite—the special interests—may be in part responsible for public disillusionment. Such a press does not reflect the

world as most people live and experience it. Political coverage that focuses on tactical considerations for the political junkie and leaves the merely interested and the uninterested behind is failing in the responsibilities of journalism. A journalism in which every story is aimed at the largest possible audience—all O.J. all the time—actually leaves most of the audience behind.

... Television aimed at women eighteen to thirty-four, or Generation X, or soccer moms, or football fans is likely to alienate larger numbers of the very group at which it is aimed. People are simply more complex than the categories and stereotypes we create for them. (2007, pp. 26–27)

This means that journalists need to rise to the challenge of providing good, helpful information at the same time that they tell their stories well and take into account our common humanity and interests in each other's lives. Kovach and Rosenstiel quote Jack Fuller, president of the Tribune Publishing Company:

"Here is the tension," Fuller told us at a forum of the Committee of Concerned Journalists. "A newspaper that fails to reflect its community deeply will not succeed. But a newspaper that does not challenge its community's values and preconceptions will lose respect for failing to provide the honesty and leadership that newspapers are expected to offer." To be at once the enabler and the goad of community action is a great challenge, but it is one journalism has always claimed as its own. It is a challenge that can be met by accepting the obligation to provide the members of the community not only with the knowledge and insights they need but with the forum within which to engage in building a community. (pp. 180–181)

As you begin to practice journalism, regardless of the medium, you should understand the importance of the frame you construct. It's not a linear process or a decision that should be made once and for all. You or your team will make decisions throughout the news process: what to cover, how to cover it, and how to render it, both in content and design. Each decision that you make depends on what you think is important for your audience to know. We'd like you to keep these concepts in mind as we talk about news content and structure:

- A good journalist understands the importance of a story's frame.
- A good journalist knows how to evaluate the newsworthiness of a story consistent with the journalist's duty to the public.
- A good journalist can articulate the ethical reasoning behind storytelling decisions.

In this unit, we introduce you to characteristics of newswriting, the basic news story, and the multiple media you might use to tell your story. As you move through the chapters, look at how the choices you make—your language, story structure, medium— frame a news story. Notice how the decisions you make about what is newsworthy, or what appears early in a story, affect the version of reality that your audience will get.

CHAPTER 3

HOW IS NEWS LANGUAGE DIFFERENT?

Flash floods rushed through parts of Colorado in 2013, cutting off roads, inundating homes and stranding residents (Fig. 3-6). This was an emergency, and the news audience needed facts about what had happened. A journalist's explicit judgments simply weren't relevant: When you're first learning that a hurricane is hitting the East Coast, are you really interested in a journalist's opinion about the Federal Emergency Management Agency? Or, would you want to know a reporter's opinion about drunken driving when you're trying to find out who was killed in a fatal accident? Of course not.

Journalists craft most news stories to emphasize the information itself, rather than the writer or speaker. They use this style for two main reasons: to be as accurate, fair and humane as possible, and to meet audience expectations that they deliver information efficiently. There are times when journalists refer to themselves or their experiences to help humanize stories or to remind readers that there's a real person behind the reporting. This happens most frequently in blogs, features or news analysis pieces, which are often clearly labeled. But a journalist *starts* by knowing how to provide a straightforward focus on the facts.

57

FIGURE 3-6 During the floods in Colorado, people needed facts right away—such as the information that U.S. Highway 36 between Lyons and Pinewood Springs was washed out and drivers would have to use other routes to get to their destinations.

Newswriting Emphasizes Reports

INFORMATION YOU CAN VERIFY

S. I. Hayakawa was a famous linguist—among many other accomplishments (including being a U.S. senator). In his classic essay, "Reports, Inferences, Judgments," he describes what makes newswriting unique from other kinds of writing. Hayakawa says that **reports** are, most importantly, verifiable statements. The following statements are examples of reports:

- Gasoline costs $5 a gallon.
- It's sunny outside.
- Margaret Thatcher, the former British prime minister, died in 2013.
- Michael Phelps has won 18 Olympic gold medals.
- The city council voted 6–3 in favor of the new ordinance.
- The Sun Bank was robbed at 9 a.m. Saturday.
- A South Korean ferry sank in April 2014, killing more than 260 people on board.

In each case, the statement is about verifiable information (Fig. 3-7). You can go to several service stations and find out how much gasoline costs, or you can look outside

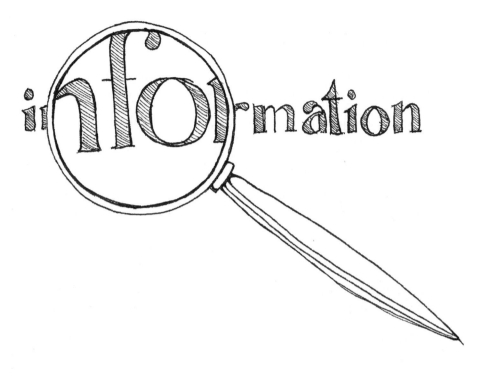

FIGURE 3-7

and see whether the sun is shining. You could talk to people who attended the city council meeting, or check official documents to find out about a particular vote. To find out for yourself about a local bank robbery, you could check police logs or talk to witnesses. While you personally probably can't verify how many people were killed in a foreign ferry accident or the physical state of a former world leader, the information is still verifiable: "the nature of the report is such that, given the proper resources, it can be verified—or, if inaccurate, it can be invalidated" (Hayakawa, 2006, p. 257). People depend on this kind of information every day: If gasoline prices are going up, they may postpone a trip or decide to take public transportation or carpool; if a local weather forecast predicts unseasonably warm weather, they will probably choose to dress and act differently than they would if it predicted a blizzard. National or international news reports can give people information about relatives or friends who live elsewhere, or they can affect people's worldviews and cultural understandings or their travel plans, or they can change their opinions and actions regarding their own government.

Reports are a crucial element of news, and we expect them to be truthful, as Hayakawa points out:

> To a surprising degree, we trust each other's reports. We ask directions of total strangers when we are traveling. We follow directions on road signs without being suspicious of the people who put the signs up. We read books of information about science, mathematics, automotive engineering, travel, geography, the history of costume, and other such factual matters, and we usually assume that the author is doing her best to tell us as truly as she can what she knows. And we

are safe in so assuming most of the time. With the interest given today to the discussion of biased reporting and propaganda, and the general mistrust of many of the communications we receive, we are likely to forget that we still have an enormous amount of reliable information available and that deliberate misinformation, except in warfare, still is more the exception than the rule. (p. 257)

Despite questions about political biases, the influence of corporate ownership of the media and the foundation of truth itself, people still rely on reports produced by the news media to find out about the world around them.

INFERENCES MAY BE BASED ON INSUFFICIENT INFORMATION

Hayakawa (2006) distinguishes between a report and an **inference**, which he defines as "a statement about the unknown based on the known" (p. 258). Here's his example:

> On an elementary level, the difference between a report and an inference is demonstrated in the following statement: "He's afraid of women." This statement does not report; it draws an inference from some set of observable data: "He blushes and stammers whenever a woman speaks to him. He never speaks to women at parties." (p. 258)

Inferences may be mistaken (Fig. 3-8) or may be based on insufficient information—what if the man never speaks to anyone at parties, and is blushing because he's embarrassed by his own stammering?—but, as Hayakawa notes, scientific knowledge is based on such inferences. For example, in an early study, the patients of doctors who didn't

FIGURE 3-8 Making an inference.

wash their hands were much more likely to contract germ-carried illnesses; so, scientists inferred, doctors were transferring germs from patient to patient by not washing their hands. We couldn't live without knowledge based on inferences, and these are, in many cases, scientific—but they're also different from reports.

Think of the earlier example of a reported bank robbery. What if someone made the following statement after the robbery?

> "The Sun Bank has insufficient security."

The statement might or might not be true, but if it's based only on the knowledge that the bank was robbed, it's an inference without enough information to support it. A good journalist wouldn't write it—or even include it as a quote from someone unless that person had evidence or expertise to back it up.

JUDGMENTS SOMETIMES SHUT DOWN THOUGHT

The third category of information Hayakawa (2006) describes is **judgments**, "expressions of the speaker's approval or disapproval of the occurrences, persons, or objects he is describing" (p. 258):

> To say, "It is a wonderful car" is not a report; to say, "It has been driven 50,000 miles without requiring repairs" is a report. "Jack lied to us" is a judgment, while "Jack said he didn't have the car keys, but later, when he pulled a handkerchief out of his pocket, the keys fell out" is a report. Similarly, when a newspaper says, "The senator has been stubborn, uncooperative, and defiant," or "The senator courageously stood by his principles," the paper is judging and evaluating rather than reporting. (p. 258)

Hayakawa says that judgments tend to shut down thought because they are conclusions. There's little for an audience to say after such a conclusion except that they agree or disagree with the judgment. And judgments say more about the speaker or writer's state of mind than about external circumstances. He gives as an example the statement, "She's the sweetest little girl in all the world!" The speaker and listeners might get the false impression that something has been said about the little girl, but the sentence really says much more about the speaker's attitude toward her.

Newswriting is meant to provide information that allows for different interpretations, for differing conclusions and for thoughtful debates. Newswriting strives to emphasize facts and information over judgments, and therefore it uses reports more than inferences, and both of these more than judgments.

Look at the two different story versions following of an imaginary bank robbery:

Judgmental version: *You wouldn't expect a bank robbery right here on Main Street, but sadly, the well-respected and rather staid Sun Bank hit a dark moment in its history yesterday when two men violently robbed it of an incredible amount of cash.*

News style: *Two men held up a clerk at gunpoint at the Sun Bank Monday, taking $200,000 with them.*

The first example makes assumptions about what readers would expect. It also tells readers that they are sad and that the Sun Bank is well-respected and rather staid. While it's true that a gun robbery is violent, the first version's use of the word "violently" raises more questions than it answers. In the second version, we find out more information and get to make judgments for ourselves about what constitutes an "incredible amount" of money.

Following are two different versions of news leads to another story. The first is our rewrite, in which we've inserted more judgmental language. The second is the lead from the original *Los Angeles Times* story:

Judgmental version: Bell is a town where you wouldn't think people could afford to pay their city officials much money, because, unfortunately, residents are poor. But city officials have been paying themselves shockingly high wages, especially the city manager, who pulls in an awe-inspiring salary.

News style: Bell, one of the poorest cities in Los Angeles County, pays its top officials some of the highest salaries in the nation, including nearly $800,000 annually for its city manager, according to documents reviewed by The Times (Gottlieb & Vives, 2010, para. 1).

Note that the second example uses less exaggerated language than "shockingly high" and "awe-inspiring." It also does a much better job of delivering information while allowing readers to determine whether they would be shocked by the salaries or whether $800,000 a year for the city manager of a small town inspires awe.

As you can see from the preceding examples, the same general information may be communicated in reports, inferences and judgments; it's *how* this is communicated—that is, the language—that often distinguishes each kind of statement. Reporters strive to use language that relies most heavily on reports, on verifiable information, in their writing. For instance, if you attend a soccer game, you may notice there's a large crowd. You could say just that: *A huge crowd turned out for the Skyhawks' last home soccer game of the season.* But notice that the word "huge" is a judgment. Perhaps I'm a big soccer fan, and I think that the crowd is meager, especially in light of the team's national achievements. Instead, you could write the following: *More than 500 people attended the Skyhawks' last home soccer game of the season.* In the second example, the statement makes a report that could be verified. Because of this, it allows readers or listeners to make their own judgments—*Wow, a sold-out crowd!* or, *Oh, not that many people attended*, or, *At least* some *people showed up*—while the first statement that a "huge crowd" showed up, doesn't. When people say you should "show, don't tell," this is an example of what they mean: "Huge crowd" tells, but doesn't show; "500 people" shows.

You've probably noticed in the previous examples that modifiers are often a place where such unnecessary judgments appear, and that's a good place to watch out for them. Let's try another example:

A young, pretty woman, Yuriko Yamaguchi, is not the type you'd expect to find working as a mechanic in a grungy gas station.

The first problem with this statement is that news stories are much more likely to describe a woman's appearance and dress than a man's, and the reporter may want to reconsider whether this information is relevant to the story at all. But let's say this is a

FIGURE 3-9

story that takes an in-depth look at Yamaguchi's lifestyle as an example of larger social changes, and the physical descriptions of her and the gas station help to develop character and setting in telling an important story. A good reporter would immediately notice that "young" and "pretty" tell more about the writer's attitude toward the story's subject than about the woman herself. Instead, a news reporter might provide a more specific description:

Yamaguchi, who is 22, wears her black hair in a long braid down her back. She is dressed in a pair of coveralls.

And what about the "grungy" gas station? It would be more helpful to provide specifics:

The ceilings and walls are gray, and the concrete floors are stained with grease.

Finally, note the judgment in the phrase "not the type you'd expect to find." Once again, the reporter is making an explicit judgment, and one that tells more about the writer than about the subject of the story (Fig. 3-9). Maybe a reader has very different expectations about auto mechanics, and what is the "type," anyway? When they report about women or men, old people or young people, low-income or wealthy people, journalists should refrain from stating readers' expectations in phrases such as the following: *is not what you'd expect, isn't the typical little old lady, is surprisingly agile for his age, doesn't drive the kind of car you'd think a millionaire would drive.*

In the example about Yamaguchi, the writer doesn't need to sacrifice relevant detail or information to avoid using judgmental language; in fact, journalists often provide more information and more details through reporting than when they infer or make judgments. In reporting on a trial, a journalist might notice that the person charged with murder doesn't seem remorseful. One way of saying that is the following: *The defendant showed no signs of remorse.* But such a statement includes an inference that the defendant's facial expression is not one of regret, and a judgment that the defendant is failing to show repentance for a crime. Something closer to a report would be the following: *As he listened to the jury's verdict, the defendant fidgeted with a pencil, frowning at times. At one point, he turned and smiled at his attorney. He did not speak to his family or the press as he was escorted out of the courtroom after the trial* (Fig. 3-10). The news audience can decide for themselves whether the defendant should be remorseful or not, and whether his gestures indicate a lack of remorse.

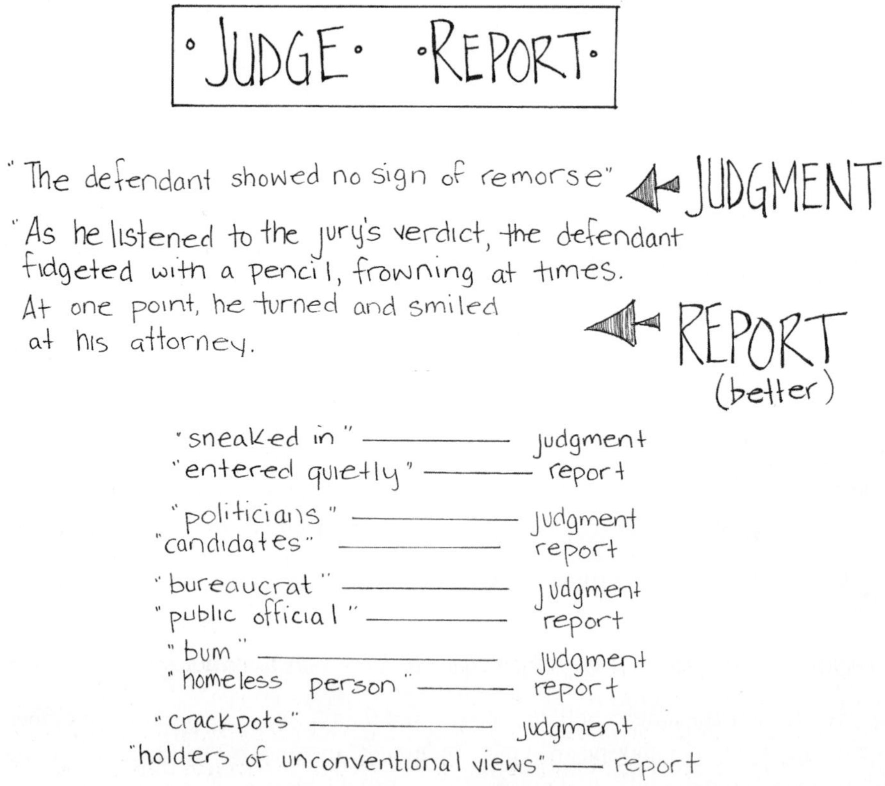

FIGURE 3-10

While any language includes *some* judgment, many words are more explicitly judgmental than others, Hayakawa says:

> Of course, many words simultaneously report and judge. For the kind of strict reporting discussed here, these should be avoided. Instead of "sneaked in," one might say "entered quietly"; instead of "politicians," "candidates"; instead of "bureaucrat," "public official"; instead of "bum," "homeless person"; instead of "crackpots," "holders of unconventional views." A newspaper reporter may not write, "A crowd of suckers came to listen to Senator Smith last evening in that rickety firetrap and ex-dive that disfigures the south side of town," but rather, "Between 75 and 100 people heard an address last evening by Senator Smith at the Evergreen Gardens near the southern city limits." (Hayakawa, 2006, p. 259)

While news reporters *do* call soldiers "insurgents," "warriors," "terrorists," "martyrs," "militants," or "guerillas," they need to carefully ask themselves what justifies those more judgmental names. And in whose opinion? In the United States, people would probably say that the term "insurgent" currently refers to a person who fights against U.S. troops. In another country, people might call someone who fights U.S. troops a "freedom fighter," or simply, "a soldier." What would you call that person in your story? While "soldier" and "fighter" carry their own history and judgments, they are the words we'd recommend because they're less judgmental—and therefore fairer and more accurate.

Newswriting Usually Avoids First-Person References

Another way that newswriting plays down the reporter's role and voice is by avoiding the use of first person. One of the tools in any well-trained journalist's toolbox is the ability to focus on the *information* in a news story, rather than on the writer. Writing like this can take some getting used to, because so much writing and commentary focuses on opinion, and because English classes that teach essay writing spend a lot of time and effort over the years in training you to *have* a voice, to express your opinion and take a stance.

In a way, writing a news story is like taking a step back from this type of writing: You want other people to develop their opinions, and to do so, you're trying to deliver the best information you can. Journalists play an important role in gathering information and determining the public agenda, and their words already have tremendous influence and power. That's one of the reasons that they usually try to step out of their stories.

The most obvious way that reporters remove themselves from news stories is through removing any first-person references: Outside the quotations from sources in most news stories, there is no "I," "we," "me" or "us." You don't see "I think" or "to me" (Fig. 3-11). And although journalists are local and national citizens, they usually try to take the approach of an outside observer. This means that even in stories about the

FIGURE 3-11

United States or the American military, reporters usually don't refer to "our nation" or "our troops." Use of the first person in such cases makes it much more difficult to take a critical, skeptical attitude in reporting on U.S. war efforts or soldiers' misbehavior, or the United States's international political maneuvers. Even on a word level, such involvement by the reporter in a story does a disservice to news audiences, who need to know as much about "our nation"—warts and all—as possible in order to be good citizens and act accordingly.

Although news stories usually avoid using a reporter's first-person opinions, they still report explicit opinions and judgments. However, these are the judgments of sources whose credentials or relevance are given in the story. Your audience should know why these particular opinions are worth hearing. For instance, most news audiences outside your immediate family and friends probably would not care about your opinion about how the United States might improve its economy—but the same audience might care very much about what Federal Reserve Board Chair Janet Yellen thought. This interest in Yellen's opinion might hold true no matter what the audience's political position, because she would be expected to have some power to influence the economic steps the nation took. Stories that include the opinions of unknown citizens about the war might also be of interest to large numbers of people, if those stories are about the reactions of subjects who are identified as soldiers who have served time in Afghanistan or people who are related to soldiers, for instance. This is why it's important to provide a quick explanation of the relevance of your sources to the story through a tag line such as, "who has completed two tours of duty in Afghanistan," or, "who has recently published a book about the U.S. military in Afghanistan."

Because journalists strive to keep explicit references to themselves and their own opinions out of their stories, they rely much more heavily on quotes and paraphrases than other kinds of stories. In an email to friends, you might quote what a professor or another friend has said, but most of the text would be your own reflections or descriptions. In a term paper, you would usually be expected to research information, then summarize and interpret that information and finally use the information as the basis for a hypothesis. You might well quote at length from published work, but most of the paper would be made up of your own summarizing, interpretation and thought process. That's because the point of the paper is usually to reveal your research and thought—the paper exists to reveal something about you.

A news story turns this formula on its head: You, the journalist, are there to reveal the story. When you cover a news story, the emphasis is not on what you've learned personally, as it would be for a class; it's not on your reactions to events, as it might be in messages to your friends or family. The emphasis in newswriting is on facts and events and the interpretations and reactions of those who are involved or affected most directly, or those who have expertise in the area.

Newswriting Is Concise and Direct

FEWER MODIFIERS

As we've seen, one significant difference between reports and other kinds of statements is that reports usually have fewer modifiers—that is, adjectives or adverbs, the words that modify nouns, verbs and other adjectives or adverbs (Fig. 3-12). Modifiers like "huge" or "old" or "very pretty" imply judgments or inferences in a way that observable details like "500 people" or "95 years old" do not.

Newswriting still depends on modifiers—it's very difficult to communicate well without them. It's just that journalists don't use them as often as, say, academics or novelists or essayists. One of the key reasons for this is that news emphasizes verifiable information.

SIMPLE SENTENCE STRUCTURES

Journalists are sparing in their use of modifiers because news audiences expect information to be delivered quickly and efficiently. While good writers still use interesting language in the news, that language is plain and clean of modifiers, flourishes, and

FIGURE 3-12 Brandi Chastain is clearly ecstatic in this famous photo. But instead of describing her as "very happy," a journalist would use more specific language to describe the scene, such as saying that she "pulled off her shirt and raised her fists in victory."

excess. This focus on information also means that, in general, journalists use fewer complex sentences and dependent clauses than other writers, especially at the beginning of a sentence.

Journalists usually introduce the most recent important information as early as possible in a sentence. Look at the following example:

Weaker: *At its monthly meeting this Wednesday, the council approved a new recreation center.*

Better: *The council approved a new recreation center Wednesday.*

Remember the news values we've described: timeliness, impact, proximity, conflict, prominence and novelty. In the first example, the story begins with the dependent clause that focuses on *when*. This information is not the most important information in the story. The news is that the council voted in favor of the new center, and the second example arrives at this information more quickly than the first.

ACTIVE VOICE

But why not start the sentence with the new recreation center?

Weaker: *A new recreation center was approved by the council Wednesday.*

This sentence places the new recreation center at the very beginning of the sentence, but it does so at a cost: The passive construction is not as clear, and it's less interesting and less direct than the active voice. A sentence in the passive voice is one that uses a form of the verb "to be"—am, is, are, was, were—and the past participle of the main verb. In the passive construction, *She was given a present,* the verb "to be" is *was,* and the past participle of the verb "to give" is *given.* This moves the actor to a less prominent part of the sentence—or out of a sentence completely. Passive constructions also de-emphasize the individuals responsible for actions, and in some cases, allow reporters to omit them entirely. In the preceding example, for instance, "by the council" could easily be left out of the sentence. As it stands, the council's role in approving the new center is played down, compared to its place in the better version. Similarly, in the following sentence, readers have no way of knowing who is responsible: *Mistakes were made.* Overuse of the passive voice leaves out important, relevant facts, and fails to hold actors accountable for their actions.

The passive voice can also inadvertently place the blame on the victim of a crime. Keith Woods, now vice president for diversity in news and operations at National Public Radio, discusses the following example of news reporting that dealt with the 1998 fatal beating of college student Matthew Shepard:

> "Police said robbery was the main motive for the attack but that Shepard apparently was chosen in part because he was gay."
>
> The writer uses a verb (was chosen) in the passive voice and attributes the cause of the action—the beating—to the victim, not the perpetrators. The fact is that Shepard was gay every other day of the week and was not murdered. What changed? The motives and actions of his assailants. (2002, pp. 110–111)

Reporters avoid the passive voice for the most part but do use it on occasion, especially when they need to emphasize the victims or objects of an action: *Five children were injured in a car accident* would usually be better than *A car accident injured five children,* even though the second version uses more active language and would also be acceptable. The important news here is that *five children* were injured and therefore this information should appear early in the sentence. In this case, news values make the passive voice acceptable. Also, note that using the active voice here doesn't hold any actors accountable, because *a car accident* isn't an individual or an organization. Of course, if there were someone accountable for the accident, you would adjust your language accordingly.

For similar reasons, journalists avoid starting sentences with "There was" or "There is" whenever possible. In the following sentence, notice that the newspaper's responsibility for a mistake is played down: *There was a misspelling in the newspaper's obituary.* The phrases "there was" and "there is" serve as grammatical placeholders, and are therefore unnecessarily wordy. Whenever you can, it's best to restructure your sentence to avoid using the phrase:

Weaker: *There is no good reason why this sentence can't be rewritten to avoid using "there is."*

Better: *A good reporter could rewrite this sentence to omit the phrase, "there is."*

Newswriting Uses Short Paragraphs

Because of its emphasis on getting to the facts, newswriting uses short paragraphs— a typical news paragraph is only one or two sentences long (Fig. 3-13).

FIGURE 3-13

Look at the following *Al Jazeera* lead about the abduction of Nigerian school girls:

> Heavily armed men have kidnapped more than 100 girls from a secondary school in northeast Nigeria's Borno state and torched the surrounding town, a day after a deadly bombing in the African state's capital (2014).

While the sentence is a long one, it's the only sentence in the first paragraph of the news story.

It's easiest to start by writing news stories with paragraphs limited to one sentence, except for multisentence quotes. When you finish a draft, try going back through your news story and shortening each paragraph to one or two sentences. This should help you learn to adjust to a significant difference in newswriting.

Newswriting Tries to Use Language Fairly

So far, we've focused on the characteristics of newswriting that provide sufficient information efficiently, allowing audiences as much freedom in interpreting that information as possible. Using more neutral terminology also helps journalists to be fair and humane to their sources and subjects.

In the 1970s and 1980s, American society turned a new attention to the power of words because of the conjunction of several forces, including the civil rights movement, the women's rights movement, and linguistic theories that emphasized the power of language. Many different groups—including private and public organizations, educators, and individuals—pressured people to change the terminology they used when there was a possibility that words might reinforce societal discrimination. If language creates meaning, then it stands to reason that a demeaning word can help to perpetuate inequities or misunderstandings.

It's easy to see some of the good results of this movement: Epithets are no longer acceptable because of their history of being used to dehumanize a group of people. Calling someone who can't speak "dumb" is also unacceptable now, because the same word also came to refer to people who were stupid or uneducated.

It's often hard for some people to understand why the use of other words has been criticized or questioned: What does it matter whether you use "girl" or "woman" to describe a 20-year-old female? Or whether you use "policeman" or "police officer"? The hope—backed by a school of academic inquiry—is that if people change their language, their thoughts and actions will also change, and this can lead to reform in social inequality. For instance, if people aren't allowed to say "girl" when they're referring to a grown woman, they're more likely to think of that woman as an equal.

Not all the effects of this movement were positive: Some people were reluctant to speak about touchy subjects for fear they'd say something wrong, and there were surely excesses, or misuses of the social pressures. By the 1990s, a strong backlash against the movement took effect, and "politically correct speech"—a term to avoid because it has been used to demean some important social changes—itself became a term of derision.

Language still reflects deeply embedded societal prejudices and attitudes, and sometimes it's hard to know how to write or speak without perpetuating these. For example, earlier in the 20th century, linguistic customs meant that a second reference to a woman *had* to tell readers whether she was married or single: either she would be *Miss* Brown or *Mrs.* Brown. There was no linguistic equivalent for men, who were always *Mr.* regardless of marital status. *Ms.* was introduced as a way to avoid this unequal specificity, but the fundamental inequality remains.

Journalists can be just as inaccurate by using euphemisms rather than precise terminology. As Woods points out, journalists—and other people—often use words to cover up what they really mean:

> *Blue collar*, an economic term, doubles as a synonym for *white*. *Inner* city is a geographic term, but it is often asked to convey race (black or brown) and class (probably poor). How often have such words as *suburban, urban,* or *mainstream* been used to connote race? How often is *fundamentalist* employed as a clever cover for religious "wacko"? (2002, p. 110)

As a journalist, your job is to write and speak as accurately, fairly and humanely as possible, keeping in mind that telling the news gives you extra power to shape language and attitudes because what you write or say reaches so many people. In fact, the news media are often part of the problem, using stereotypes as shortcuts to communicate more easily. Good journalists must be vigilant in their use of language.

Sometimes, this is easy: Using terms like "firefighter" instead of "fireman," or "police officer" instead of "policeman," avoids reinforcing stereotypes that suggest these people should or would all be male. The same language shift led some people to ask to be called "actors," rather than "actresses," because "actresses" is a diminutive form of the word. Language that treats women as somehow lesser, or doesn't recognize them at all, is inaccurate. Language that treats one group as more human and dignified than another is also unfair. And language that perpetuates hatred—such as disparaging terms for ethnic minorities or for gays or lesbians—is not only unfair and even inhumane, but interferes with the story.

Some people feel they're walking on eggshells when they try to discuss controversial subjects. But it's important to remember that the tricky footing isn't usually caused by trendy oversensitivity; the prejudices are often built into the language itself. For instance, many terms for ethnic minorities reinforce subtle cultural prejudices: *Hispanic* or *Latino* emphasizes the European origins of Central and South Americans while ignoring their indigenous heritage; *Chicano* is objectionable to some people because it was associated with a particular political movement that did not include all Hispanics; and *Mexican-American* implies that some people are less American than, say, Euro-Americans—whose immigrant backgrounds are rarely referred to in everyday usage.

As you're learning the ropes, it's sometimes hard to know the best term to use: Is "Native American" or "American Indian" better? In cases where there is little or no guidance, we suggest asking your subjects how they would like to be called.

Newswriting Is Consistent: An Introduction to AP Style

What does the symbol ;) mean if you include it in a message? You could say it depends on context: It could mean that you're flirting, or joking, or that you mistyped a smiley face. Or you could read the two punctuation marks literally, as a semi-colon and a close parenthesis. The meaning isn't clear.

The *Associated Press Stylebook* is a journalist's way of ensuring clarity, consistency and accuracy across stories and coverage. It's a reference, available online or as a book, that includes usage, spelling and punctuation. If you want to be professional and credible, your work should adhere to a standard, and the stylebook is that standard. Most news outlets use it, regardless of medium.

For example, suppose you are writing a story or a cutline that describes some students standing in line waiting for concert tickets. You'd need to know the proper way to use numbers in this case. Here are some options:

- The 10 students waited two hours in line for concert tickets Monday.

- Ten students waited two hours in line for concert tickets Monday.

- The ten students waited 2 hours in line for concert tickets Monday.

The stylebook will tell you exactly what to do (under the heading, "numerals"). For cardinal numbers, the *Stylebook* says, spell out numbers below 10 and use figures for 10 and above, so the first entry is correct. However, you'll also see that when you start a sentence with a number, you spell it out, unless it's a year. That means that in this example, the second option is also correct. The third option is incorrect because it has the rule backward. "Monday" is capitalized because it's a proper name, and it's spelled out because days always are, unless they're in a graphic (see heading "days of the week").

Under "numerals," you'll see a reference to "ages." That means that if you're looking for the AP style rule on ages, you should seek that entry. Which is correct?

- The boy, 5, called 911.

- The 5-year-old boy called 911.

- The five year old boy called 911.

The "ages" entry tells us that ages for people or animals are always figures. Therefore, the first and second options are correct. The entry also gives some punctuation instruction: When you use the age with "year" and "old" either as a noun or to modify a noun, you connect the three words with hyphens, as the second option does.

Let's look at an example of how the *Stylebook* ensures accuracy. Suppose you are quoting someone who has just received an award for a movie he directed and he says he's humbled by the praise from Quentin Tarantino, a well-known film director. Which of the following is correct?

- "The complement humbles me," Seth Goodman, the filmmaker, said.

- "The compliment humbles me," Seth Goodman, the filmmaker, said.

You would look under the complement/compliment heading to find out which word accurately denotes praise, which is the second option, "compliment." "Complement," you'll find, is defined as a noun or a verb that means completing something, such as, "A full complement of beverages accompanied the meal." If the entry doesn't exist in the *Stylebook*, then the *Stylebook* directs you to—see the heading under "dictionaries"—look in *Webster's New World College Dictionary*.

Many news outlets have a localized version of the stylebook to handle specifics for their region. For example, the name of our institution is Fort Lewis College. People also refer to it as Fort Lewis, the Fort, FLC or the college. The *AP Stylebook*'s entry under "colleges" doesn't give a definitive way to handle this very local example, nor do related entries such as "organizations and institutions." Therefore, the college media needed to create and implement a rule: Spell it out on first reference and abbreviate it as "FLC" in subsequent references. The *AP Stylebook* or stylebooks like it help to ensure consistency for the profession.

Conclusion

Beginning in the next chapter and then throughout the book, you'll see stories where reporters use language in ways that vary. These can be beautiful, descriptive, clever and even heartbreaking. What links all newswriting together and sets it apart from other writing styles is that it depends on reports more than inferences, and more on both of these than on judgments; reporters emphasize verifiable statements about the world, granting readers as much room as possible to draw their own conclusions; and journalists use language that reflects the needs and interests of their audiences. But it's not only audience needs and desires that drive news style. As you've seen, the same information presented in news style can be fairer to subjects and more accurate than it would be if written in other styles.

Exercises for Chapter 3

EXERCISE 3-1: Based on what you have read in this chapter, rewrite each of the following paragraphs in news style:

a. Mandy Corleone, who is 82 years old, doesn't act like a typical old lady. She's sprightly and, even though she weighs only 95 pounds, surprisingly strong. When I was interviewing her, I noticed she was carrying heavy buckets full of water out to her horses. Being a gentleman, I tried to help her, but no way was she going to let me interfere in the process of keeping her six horses happy and well-fed.

b. The not-always-forthcoming executives from several huge oil conglomerates finally lashed out at BP for sloppily making stupid mistakes in its work with the well that caused the tragic spill in the Gulf of Mexico.

   The leaders of Exxon Mobil, Chevron, Shell and ConocoPhillips self-righteously told Congress Tuesday that they would never have made the ridiculous mistakes that BP made in its handling of the drilling and the aftermath of the accident. In my opinion, those leaders can't be trusted: they need to protect themselves from the political backlash, plus Congress has the power to ban all drilling in the Gulf, which is what really needs to happen.

c. Apple has received an incredible number of orders in a single day for its most recent, cool technology: 600,000 iPhone orders.

   The company was pretty shortsighted, however, especially considering it's supposed to be at the cutting edge of technology. Neither Apple nor AT&T could deal with the amazing response yesterday, so they couldn't process the anxious customers for most of the day.

EXERCISE 3-2: In the following paragraphs, change the wording to make it more accurate and to avoid stereotyping. In each case, discuss why the original is less accurate or contributes to unfair stereotypes:

a. A woman was robbed of $450 on Main Avenue yesterday, according to a police report. Police are looking for an African-American wearing a blue T-shirt in connection with the crime.

b. Mrs. Bill Clinton was U.S. Secretary of State.

c. Children who are deaf, dumb and blind are eligible for federal or state education aid, according to the report.

d. The man and his wife were both charged in a Ponzi scheme.

e. Policemen and firemen organized the annual fireworks.

f. The man, who was Caucasian, had robbed seven banks in a month.

EXERCISE 3-3: For one of the words listed in the following, think of all the denotative meanings, and then all the connotative meanings you can. (Remember that *denotative* refers to the explicit meanings of a word—think "large plant with spreading branches" for tree, or "four-legged canine" for dog. *Connotative*, on the other hand, refers to secondary, cultural meanings that become attached to words—"symbol connected with environmentalists," for tree, or "trusty companion" for dog.) Then, look the word up in a dictionary (online, you can go to dictionary.reference.com). Compare that meaning with the ones you had already written down.

Patriot
Tweet
Freedom
Nature
Red
Fast

EXERCISE 3-4: Look up one of the words from the preceding list at urbandictionary.com. What are some of the meanings there?

EXERCISE 3-5: Write three or four paragraphs describing an event or part of an event you observe: It can be something that would appear in the news, like a speech or a parade, or it can be simple goings-on on campus—a lecture or discussion, people playing disc or walking to classes, or construction on a building. Describe the event in the first person ("I saw . . . ," "I said . . . "). Then, "translate" your paragraphs into third person.

CHAPTER 4

HOW DO YOU TELL A BASIC NEWS STORY?

The Inverted Pyramid: An Introduction

Imagine that you have missed a class with an important lecture. You knew ahead of time you would be absent, and you asked another student to take notes for you. She wrote the following:

The teacher walked in. He wore the usual white shirt, red tie and chinos. He seemed to be in a good mood (you know how rude he is if he hasn't had his second cup of coffee!), and he started off class kind of sarcastically, asking us, "How about those Broncos?!" when he knew they'd just lost by 41–7. He first went over what he called some "housekeeping matters": He said we would be getting our tests back soon, that he hoped we had taken the time to go see the movie sponsored by the political science department, and he made a joke about the weather. Then he began discussing what's going to be on the test next week. He said to be sure to study Hayakawa on reports, inferences and judgments . . .

Your unstated expectation is that "lecture notes" includes what's important for you to know for tests and assignments and your own edification, and nothing else. People who watch or read the news also have a set of expectations about how journalists will

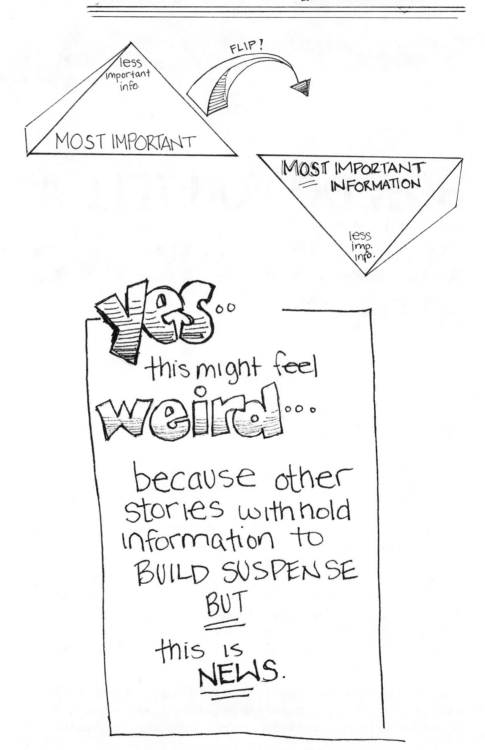

FIGURE 4-1

tell their stories. The most common is the **inverted pyramid**, a story that starts with the most important information for an audience and delivers the rest in descending order of importance (Fig. 4-1).

But what's "most important"? For journalists, it's what's most newsworthy to their target audience. That relevancy is determined from news values like the six elements we've examined: timeliness, impact, proximity, conflict, prominence and novelty.

Breaking news about an event that has just happened may show up first on Twitter or in a video clip on YouTube or in some other raw, clipped form. But the first full news story about it is almost always told in some version of an inverted pyramid. This kind of story is also useful to journalists because news audiences have learned how to interpret it quickly.

BEGIN WITH WHAT'S MOST IMPORTANT AND SAVE THE REST FOR LATER

Again, the most important elements of a story—the fact that a new president has been elected and his margin of victory, for instance—top an inverted pyramid (Fig. 4-2). Other details—the president's political history or information about his biography—are delivered later in the story because they are not as timely and are often part of the public record already. Readers sometimes skip the bottom section of the pyramid, although they risk taking in the "sound bite" without valuable context. While these

FIGURE 4-2 The lead gets to the point of the story right away.

details are less exciting than what comes at the top, they are still the foundation and add depth.

You can see that the very act of organizing your news stories telegraphs information to readers. Journalists are usually signaling to their audience that information at the beginning of a story is important—and that facts near the end don't have as much impact or relevance to their lives. Let's say you're telling your friend about an accident you witnessed on your way to class. You might begin such a story like this:

You: *"I was on my way to Spanish class yesterday morning, and I saw this huge crowd over at Elm and Third. A car smashed into a truck, and you wouldn't believe how bad the car looked . . ."*

But as a journalist telling the same story, you wouldn't include these kinds of details at the beginning. Instead, you'd say something more like the following:

Journalist: *"A car hit a truck on the corner of Elm Street and Third Avenue Wednesday."*

What's most newsworthy is the new information that could have a large impact on audience's lives: A serious accident has just happened.

A NEWS STORY EXAMPLE

Let's look at an example from a *Miami Herald* story about a student's free speech rights on Facebook:

> A student who set up a Facebook page to complain about her teacher—and was later suspended—had every right to do so under the First Amendment, a federal magistrate has ruled.
>
> The ruling not only allows Katherine "Katie" Evans' suit against the principal to move forward, it could set a precedent in cases involving speech and social networking on the Internet, experts say.
>
> The courts are in the early stages of exploring the limits of free speech within social networking, said Howard Simon, the executive director of the Florida ACLU, which filed the suit on Evans' behalf.
>
> "It's one of the main things that we wanted to establish in this case, that the First Amendment has a life in the social networking technology as it applies to the Internet and other forms of communication," Simon said.
>
> In 2007, Evans, then a senior at Pembroke Pines Charter High School, created a Facebook page where she vented about "the worst teacher I've ever met."
>
> But instead of other students expressing their dislike of the teacher, most defended the teacher and attacked Evans.
>
> A couple days later, Evans took the page down.
>
> But after Principal Peter Bayer found out about it, he bumped Evans from her Advanced Placement classes, putting her in classes with less prestige, and suspended her for three days. (Sampson, 2010, para. 1–8)

Take another look. When does the student's actual complaint get introduced into the story? And when do you learn the name of the student? The court ruling in the lead is more important for the audience to know than what the student actually wrote. The court ruling is the new information—the timeliest—and it has the broadest impact. The details about how the student was punished for her complaint are at the end of the excerpt. The fact that Evans was punished for criticizing a teacher is important and interesting because freedom of speech is essential to a working democracy. But the exact ways in which she was punished—being kicked out of certain classes and suspended for three days—have far less potential impact.

AVOID SUSPENSE WHEN YOU'RE DELIVERING NEWS

You already tell different kinds of narratives: stories about what you did last summer, tales about concerts you've gone to or jobs you've had, jokes and anecdotes, book reports and essays, emails, tweets and other posts—these are just a few examples. The frame for each is different because your audience is, and so is the information and how you communicate it to achieve the best effect.

Journalism is another way of telling stories. Its main purpose is to deliver the information to the audience efficiently. This is probably going to feel weird at first, and that's because the end comes first in most inverted pyramid news stories. That's contrary to the typical rules of entertainment. For example, fairy tales, folk stories and historical fiction have a structure that builds suspense by withholding the most recent and important information until near the end of the narrative: "The storyteller, having given a promise of astonishment, narrates in chronological order, leaving the surprise—what Aristotle calls 'Reversal of the Situation'—for last" (Mindich, 1993, p. 1).

But straight news structure has very different narrative rules. It doesn't use chronological order, but starts with the information that will have the most impact on the audience, based on news values and your news judgment.

This doesn't mean there aren't exceptions to this structure. There are. Profiles are one example. Literary journalism is another (Boxes 4-1 and 4-2).

In the 1960s and 1970s, literary journalists experimented with a new kind of newswriting that emphasized a different kind of storytelling. In their stories, these writers—Joan Didion, Hunter Thompson, Tom Wolfe, Norman Mailer and others—drew attention to themselves, used more literary techniques such as elaborate descriptions and metaphors, and didn't begin those stories with the most newsworthy information. You'll still see the effects of literary journalism in many stories on blogs, news magazines and feature pages, where characteristics such as first-person references, more attention to descriptive details and experimental narrative structures are more likely to pop up than they were before the literary journalists. With their experiments, these writers raised questions about the limitations of the inverted pyramid style, questions that have lingered for some journalism scholars and practitioners about how big a role the writer's voice should play in a news story.

Even within journalism, then, there are many different kinds of narrative, and in Chapter 13, we'll show you ways you can explore other techniques. But first we'd like to focus on what remains an essential way to tell a news story.

BOX 4-1

LITERARY JOURNALISM IS THE *UN* INVERTED PYRAMID

The definition of literary journalism wobbles from era to era, and from writer to writer. Anthologists sometimes reach back to include 18th-century writers like Daniel Defoe and James Boswell, or later writers like Martha Gellhorn, Walt Whitman and George Orwell.

But most agree that in the 1960s and 1970s, a new wave of journalists was conscious of experimenting with something different. This group included people such as Hunter Thompson, Joan Didion, Norman Mailer, Gay Talese and Tom Wolfe. These writers blurred what had become traditional boundaries between fiction and journalism: They included dialogue in their stories about news events. They turned articles into narrative stories. They took delight in using the first person—so much so that the writers sometimes became as central to their pieces as the people and places they wrote about. They immersed themselves in the culture and lives of their subjects for days, weeks or even months in order to better understand those subjects. They observed carefully, and then used the descriptive details they had amassed to convey a sense of character and place in their stories.

Over time, many of their practices have been absorbed into long-form journalism that has appeared in even the more traditional news outlets. Journalists are combining these techniques and multimedia more and more to tell important news stories in innovative ways, and we see the traces of this movement in many of the well-written blogs and other creative pieces of journalism online or in current magazines.

YOUR AUDIENCE HELPS DETERMINE A STORY'S FORM

A news audience is drawn to the news for information. Writers may use humor or suspense or even colorful descriptions, and audiences may enjoy these literary devices, but the fact remains that the primary purpose of newswriting is to provide information. No matter what the medium—the Internet, radio, television or print—this approach holds true.

As news has moved to the Internet, where the initial presentation of stories is limited by the size of a computer screen, the inverted pyramid seems a natural fit: If readers want to delve more deeply into a story, they click on a link to read more and learn the details that led up to the newsworthy event. On the first page of a website, however, readers need to see what makes a story worth reading—the fact that the famous author Gabriel García Márquez has died, as opposed to information about whether novelists are as influential as they once were. For stories about breaking news, that's usually what's most important—the crucial information in a story or update.

BOX 4-2

HERE'S WHAT LITERARY JOURNALISM LOOKS LIKE

FIGURE 4-3 Joan Didion.

FIGURE 4-4 Hunter Thompson.

When Joan Didion (Fig. 4-3) writes about difficult subjects—violence, civil war, death—she avoids sentimental language, relying instead on her sharp details to evoke feelings in her readers. The following is an excerpt from *Salvador*, a book about El Salvador during its violent civil war in the 1980s:

> The place brings everything into question. One afternoon when I had run out of the Halazone tablets I dropped every night in a pitcher of tap water (a demented gringa gesture, I knew even then, in a country where everyone not born there was at least mildly ill, including the nurse at the American embassy), I walked across the street from the Camino Real to the Metrocenter, which is referred to locally as "Central America's Largest Shopping Mall." I found no Halazone at the Metrocenter but became absorbed in making notes about the mall itself, about the Muzak playing "I Left My Heart in San Francisco" and "American Pie" (". . . singing this will be the day that I die. . . .") although the record store featured a cassette called Classics of Paraguay, about the pâté de foie gras for sale in the supermarket, about the guard who did the weapons check on everyone who entered the supermarket, about the young matrons in tight Sergio Valente jeans, trailing maids and babies behind them and buying towels, big beach towels printed with maps of Manhattan that featured Bloomingdale's; about the number of things for sale that seemed to suggest a fashion for "smart drinking," to evoke modish cocktail hours. (1984, pp. 80, 81)

Hunter Thompson's descriptions of the events he covered were so extreme that another journalist came up with a new term for what Thompson was doing: *gonzo journalism* (Fig. 4-4). His over-the-top accounts convey a strong sense of place and character, as you can see in the following excerpt from Thompson's essay, "The Kentucky Derby is Decadent and Depraved" (originally published in 1963, then republished in *The Great Shark Hunt: Strange Tales from a Strange Time*):

> I got off the plane around midnight and no one spoke as I crossed the dark runway to the terminal. The air was thick and hot, like wandering into a steam bath. Inside, people hugged each other and shook hands . . . big grins and a whoop here and there: "By God! You old bastard! Good to see you, boy! Damn good . . . and I mean it!"
>
> In the air-conditioned lounge I met a man from Houston who said his name was something

FIGURE 4-5 Sonia Nazario.

FIGURE 4-6 Jon Krakauer.

or other—"but just call me Jimbo"—and he was
here to get it on. "I'm ready for anything, by
God! Anything at all. Yeah, what are you drinkin?"
I ordered a Margarita with ice, but he wouldn't
hear of it: "Naw, naw . . . what the hell kind of
drink is that for Kentucky Derby time? What's
wrong with you, boy?" He grinned and winked at
the bartender. "Goddam, we gotta educate this
boy. Get him some good whiskey . . ."

I shrugged. "Okay, a double Old Fitz on ice."
Jimbo nodded his approval. (1979, pp. 24–25)

Sonia Nazario's series about a Honduran boy's journey to
the United States to find his mother was awarded the Pulitzer
Prize, and she later turned the series into a best-selling book,
Enrique's Journey (Fig. 4-5). In the following excerpt, she uses
her interviews with Enrique as well as her own experience
retracing Enrique's journey to describe part of that journey:

By early afternoon, it is 105 degrees. Enrique's
palms burn when he holds on to the hopper. He
risks riding no-hands. Finally, he strips off his shirt
and sits on it. The locomotive blows warm diesel
smoke. People burn trash by the rails, sending up
more heat and a searing stench. Many migrants

have had their caps stolen, so they wrap their
heads in T-shirts. They gaze enviously at villagers
cooling themselves in streams and washing off after
a day of fieldwork and at others who doze in
hammocks slung in shady spots near adobe and
cinder-block homes. The train cars sway from
side to side, up and down, like bobbing ice
cubes. (2006, p. 82)

Jon Krakauer (Fig. 4-6) became famous for his book
about the tragic 1996 Everest blizzard that killed eight
climbers in two days. In the excerpt from *Into Thin Air*
following, Krakauer describes seeing Everest from the
plane as he flew from Bangkok to Kathmandu on his way
to start that climb:

The ink-black wedge of the summit pyramid stood
out in stark relief, towering over the surrounding
ridges. Thrust high into the jet stream, the
mountain ripped a visible gash in the 120-knot
hurricane, sending forth a plume of ice crystals
that trailed to the east like a long silk scarf. As I
gazed across the sky at this contrail, it occurred
to me that the top of Everest was precisely the
same height as the pressurized jet bearing me
through the heavens. That I proposed to climb to
the cruising altitude of an Airbus 300 jetliner
struck me, at that moment, as preposterous, or
worse. My palms felt clammy. (1997, p. 36)

Inverted Pyramid Leads

A news **lead**, which is sometimes spelled *lede*, is the first paragraph of a story. A good lead is the gist of a news story. It's usually made up of one sentence (now and then, two). It's not too long, not too detailed, but not overly simplified either. Consider CNN.com's lead following in one of the first stories about the Haiti earthquake in early 2010 (Box 4-3):

> A major earthquake struck southern Haiti on Tuesday, knocking down buildings and power lines and inflicting what its ambassador to the United States called a catastrophe for the Western Hemisphere's poorest nation. (Simon et al., 2010, para. 1)

This lead is an example of the way to start a story using the inverted pyramid structure. Thousands of stories were eventually written about the earthquake, estimating how many people were hurt, telling individual accounts of miraculous rescues or heartbreaking losses and describing the devastation, the causes of the earthquake, relief efforts and later vandalism in the streets. But the initial stories started with something similar to the preceding CNN lead: A major earthquake hit Haiti on Jan. 12.

While experienced journalists start stories in different ways, when there's an important breaking story, they use a basic news lead that does the following:

- Answers the basic questions: *who, what, when* and *where.* If the most important information centers on *how* or *why*, these may also be answered in the lead (a roof fell in because of a heavy snow load, or Twitter shut down because people were responding to Michael Jackson's death). Otherwise, how or why something happened is often more complex information that will be answered in the rest of the story.

- Is brief and to the point. The rule of thumb for written news stories is that a lead is somewhere around 20 to 35 words. The rest of a news story will add background and detail.

- Gets to the most important information right away—the information that will have the most impact and be most helpful to its audience.

- Uses a simple, direct sentence structure.

- Captures an audience's attention so they keep watching, listening or reading.

WHO, WHAT, WHEN, WHERE— AND SOMETIMES HOW AND WHY

Most news leads try to answer four of the six basic questions: *who, what, when* and *where.* Notice that although it's in shortened form, the beginning of a news story includes basic information similar to that in other stories: setting, introduction of

BOX 4-3

WRITING A BROADCAST LEAD

Just as online and print texts do, audio and video news starts with the most salient information first. This is one of the most important basics you need to know as a beginning journalist.

But you'll also notice some differences in the beginnings of news stories in different media. In news written for video and audio media, there's often a **"throwaway line"**—an alert to listeners and viewers who may be busy doing something else. For example, note the first, incomplete sentence that begins the CNN news story for television following:

> *Breaking news this morning. The Haiti country has been hit by a devastating earthquake; up to 3 million people are affected. In just seconds from now we're going to take you straight to the capital city and let you know what's going on as daylight now hits the country. (CNN Newsroom, 2010)*

The opening of this television story, in contrast to the CNN.com lead for an online story, gives the listener a chance to tune in before delving into the news. You'll notice the same characteristic in the ABC News lead following:

> *Now to Syria and what could be a breakthrough tonight in the effort to dismantle their chemical weapons. There is word from that team of weapons inspectors that so far Syria has kept its promise—the plants where those weapons were made now destroyed. (Marquardt, 2013)*

These throwaway lines would seem awkward if you were reading them on a website or in print. They're incomplete and a little vague. But in other media, they serve as helpful, efficient ways to catch a listener's ear.

You might have noticed something else about both leads: They use present tense. The CNN television news story announces that Haiti "*has been* hit"; in a written story, you'd be more likely to read that Haiti "*was hit.*" The ABC News lead says "There *is* word" from the weapons inspectors that Syria will uphold its part of the deal.

That emphasis on what's happened most recently underlines the immediacy of the medium. The same is true for the following radio news lead:

> *Howard University, here in Washington, D.C., has hit a rough patch. As one of the country's most prominent, historically Black schools, Howard is also one of the top undergraduate sources for African-American doctors, scientists, and engineers. But faculty there recently voted no confidence in leaders of the school's board of trustees. (Lo Wang, 2013)*

While the actual vote is in the past—"faculty there recently voted no confidence"—the first two sentences emphasize the present.

This is not always true for broadcast news stories: You'll see and hear stories written in the past tense. But you'll notice that overall, broadcast stories emphasize their up-to-the-minute currency.

Broadcast stories also tend to use a more conversational tone. A broadcast news lead is more likely to address its audience directly, as the first example

characters, and introduction of a sort of plot tension. The setting and character introduction answer *where* and *who*. The *what* might be a conflict or timely event (Fig. 4-7).

If the answers to *how* and *why* are the most newsworthy part of the story, those get answered in the lead, too. Otherwise, these answers are more complex and are therefore relegated to later in the story. Sometimes, the answers to how and why aren't known yet, and will be reported in later stories, called **follow-up stories**, or sometimes **folos**.

does: "In just seconds from now we're going to take you straight to the capital city and let you know. . . ." Broadcast stories are spoken, and spoken language is usually less formal than written language. The "rough patch" in the lead about Howard University might show up in a story written for online or print—but its casual tone would be less common in those media. The "here in Washington, D.C.," in the same story is a less formal way to remind listeners where the university is.

Write a broadcast lead

The best way to understand some of the differences between an online news lead and one written for radio or television is to try writing one. Choose a lead from a print or online news source, and rewrite it for radio or television. Follow these steps:

1. Try adding a throwaway line. Reporters use many different kinds of introductory sentences to broadcast stories, but the following are three types that occur commonly:
   a. Reporters write throwaway lines as transitions from other news stories, as the news lead about Syrian weapons inspections does. You can signal that your story deals with a similar subject to the previous one ("In related news. . . .), or you can signal that you're moving from one general topic to another: "On the political front. . . ."
   b. A throwaway line may help shift the tone— "Now, we turn to the lighter side of Thanksgiving. . . ." This is important if your story is funny or lighthearted, or if it's tragic or especially serious.
   c. If the news is an important breaking story, you might use some form of the "Breaking news this morning" from the first example. At Nelson Mandela's funeral, for example, CBS News led with, "It was a remarkable moment in history today. . . ."

2. A broadcast story often uses present tense. Change the lead to the present tense where appropriate. These leads should still be grammatically correct, however—that is, you still wouldn't say, "Car hits bus." You'd say, "A car has hit a bus."

3. Change the tone of the lead to make it a little more conversational. As you can see in the previous examples, this isn't usually a radical change. Is there a place where you might address your audience in the second person— "you"—as the example about the Syrian weapons inspections does? Is there a place where you might use a more colloquial expression?

4. Broadcast sentences tend to be even shorter than those for other media. Notice in the Haiti news lead that the first sentence is very short, and the second sentence reads as if it were two short sentences.

5. One of the best methods for making your lead easy to understand is to read it aloud to yourself: Are there places where you find yourself stumbling, or where the wording is difficult to get through? Are there places where a sentence takes too much time to fully comprehend?

Following is the first paragraph of a story for *The Washington Post*:

The National Security Agency and the FBI are tapping directly into the central servers of nine leading U.S. Internet companies, extracting audio and video chats, photographs, e-mails, documents, and connection logs that enable analysts to track foreign targets, according to a top-secret document obtained by The Washington Post. (Gellman & Poitras, 2013)

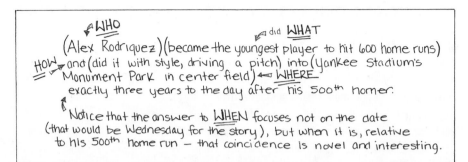

FIGURE 4-7 (Blum, 2010, para. 1).

This is a traditional, inverted-pyramid-style lead. It answers the question *who* (the NSA and the FBI) did *what* (tapped into the servers of U.S. Internet companies). Because the tapping has been an ongoing process, the answer to *when* doesn't appear until later (in 2008, when the government "began six years of rapidly growing data collection").

Note that even within the lead, information follows the inverted pyramid style: The sentence starts with the most important information and delivers the rest in descending order of importance. For instance, in this story *who* did *what* is the most newsworthy. This is information about a government body spying on its own people. The FBI and NSA are prominent and have apparently failed in their responsibility to the people they serve; this is information the public needs to know. In contrast, the answer to *why* is not the most important information in this lead—so this comes later in the sentence.

This checklist of questions can help you make sure you're not missing something important ("oops—almost forgot to include the date") as you begin your story. You can see that it's not set in stone: Sometimes, the *how* may be the most important information, for instance, or the *where* may be clear from other information on the website. Even in the example here, the reporter has to use careful news judgment to decide what goes in a lead.

BREVITY

Try this: Go to cnn.com. Click on the headline for a recent news story. Count the number of words in the lead, and then the number of sentences. Do the same for four other stories on this site. How many words were in each lead? How many sentences?

Most of the time, the answer is somewhere between 25 and 35 words, and only one sentence. (When we tried this in 2014 the average number of words in 10 story leads was 30.)

You'll definitely find longer leads—*The New York Times* and *The Wall Street Journal* are known for their expansive first paragraphs, for example. But in general, most journalists strive to write brief first paragraphs that include the most important facts and not much else. As you learn to write news stories, it's helpful to count the number of sentences and even the number of words in a lead. As a beginning journalist, try keeping your leads to one sentence. This is an easy item to double-check and edit accordingly. If the number of words in your lead is over 35—or even 25—you probably need to revise. As we've noted, you'll definitely see leads made up of more than one sentence. But once you start counting the number of sentences in leads, you'll find that most of the time, it's limited to one or two.

LEADS INCLUDE THE MOST IMPORTANT DETAILS

Try creating a lead based on a set of facts from a fun story that had deeper implications about the commodification of nearly everything in U.S. culture:

- Adam Burtle was a student at the University of Washington.
- He was a part-time automotive technician, and he lived in Woodinville, Wash.
- Burtle was 20 years old.
- He posted an item for sale on eBay Inc.
- The item was his soul.
- On Feb. 1, 2001, bidding began at 5 cents. (For some of the many news stories about Adam Burtle attempting to sell his soul on eBay Inc., see USAToday.com, ABCnews.com or the Chicagotribune.com.)

Remember that the lead is the most important, recent information—the surprise or resolution of the story. You don't want to clutter the lead with details that lessen its impact, so you probably wouldn't include the student's name, his part-time job, or even his age, unless that was unusual. You probably wouldn't include the exact time the bidding started, or Burtle's day job. Instead, you'd start with the newest information, and your lead would probably be something like the following: *A University of Washington student put his soul on sale on eBay Inc. Wednesday—and the opening bid was 5 cents.*

The lead is also a good place to answer the question of why the reader should care about this story—this is often referred to as the *so what*? In our preceding example, there are multiple answers: because Burtle seemed to be mixing up something spiritual and ephemeral with commerce, and because eBay was symbolic of the growth of the Internet, therefore Burtle's attempt was symbolic of the growth and audacity of the Internet community itself.

DELAY PRECISE IDENTIFICATION

Because the lead is where a journalist tells a reader why a story is important and worth reading or listening to, you don't want to fill it with clutter. That means that even though you're answering *who, what, when* and *where*—and maybe *how* and *why*— there's a good chance you won't be specific in the answers to all those questions in your first paragraph. The lead doesn't usually include exact times. It doesn't usually give exact addresses, and it may not give the full name of an organization, if that name is long.

This is all information that's usually crucial to include in a news story—but not in the lead. For instance, you might say in your lead that an event happened near

San Francisco. Later in your story, you'd fully identify the place as "Pacifica, California, a suburb outside San Francisco." By delaying the full identification of the place, you could write a smoother, clearer lead that helped readers immediately figure out what was important and how relevant it was to their lives. Let's look at a couple of extreme examples. In the first, we include all the identifying details:

Weaker: *Manuel R. Samosa of San Francisco, California, and Georgie M. Black of New Orleans, Louisiana, were apparently trying to play football on the Durango & Silverton Narrow Gauge Railroad Train when they fell off the train on their way to Silverton, Colorado, at 10:54 a.m. Tuesday, according to a statement from Assistant Public Relations and Communications Officer Ruby Millane.*

In a rewrite of the same lead, we've removed most of the identifying details so readers can quickly get an idea of what's happened:

Better: *Two visiting tourists were apparently trying to play football when they fell off the train to Silverton Tuesday morning, but are in stable condition at Mercy Hospital, said a train company official.*

Notice that in the second example, there's room to provide the more important information about how badly hurt the two people are. In both cases, the leads tell something about *who, what, when, where* and *how,* but the second lead is more general. The journalist fills in the details of the tourists' names, the official's name and title and the train company's exact name—but in a more useful and elegant way, later in the story.

News leads also don't include names, unless the people named are especially well-known or important: You would name President Obama, but not usually Jean-Pierre Bleger, the owner of a small local bakery. Here's an example from the *Christian Science Monitor:*

The man accused of twin terrorist attacks in Oslo will remain behind bars for the next eight weeks as police continue their investigation, a judge announced this afternoon after a closed court hearing. (Radosevich, 2011, para. 1)

The presumption here is that readers knew about the attacks. But when this story was posted, many people were still unfamiliar with the name of the accused terrorist, so he wasn't identified until the next paragraph:

Anders Behring Breivik made his first appearance in an Oslo court today following his arrest on Friday for the huge bombing of government buildings as well as the shooting rampage at a Norwegian Labor Party youth summer camp that killed 76. Authorities today revised the death toll from the original estimate of 93 killed. (Radosevich, 2011)

Note that this second paragraph provides the more specific information such as the name of the summer camp, the number of people killed and some of the details about Breivik's progress through the court system.

In a story about a car accident or a fire, the names of the people involved usually wouldn't be in the lead:

Two local men were seriously injured when their car collided with a motorcycle on Main Avenue Tuesday night.

A Durango family used an upstairs deck to escape a fire that burned their house to the ground early Sunday morning.

But, as we saw previously, if there's a reason to expect that many of your readers will recognize these same people, the leads would include their names:

Gov. Jonas Samson and his son, Marvin Samson, were seriously injured when their car collided with a motorcycle on Main Avenue Tuesday night.

Mayor Mary Stevenson and her two children used an upstairs deck to escape a fire that burned their house to the ground early Sunday morning.

You can see from the previous examples that the decision about whether to identify any people in your lead depends on news values: Are these prominent or newsworthy people, outside the event that has just launched them into the news? If so, you'll probably want to include their names in the lead. If it's someone who holds an important office but whose name readers might not recognize, you can often compromise by identifying that person by position in the lead, and providing his name in a later paragraph:

The governor and his son were seriously injured when their car collided with a motorcycle on Main Avenue Tuesday night.

Waiting to give someone's full name can be helpful when a person has a long name or title, or when you have a lot of other information to deliver in the lead:

The U.S. needs to acknowledge that Turkey massacred Armenian people during and just after W.W. I, the Armenian ambassador told students at Durango's high school graduation Saturday.

For a story such as this, a journalist would typically identify the Armenian ambassador by name in the second paragraph.

Delaying the identification of the people in your story until after the lead allows you to get to the most important information first—unless their names *are* the most important information. This practice of saving details for later or omitting them altogether signals to readers which information is most likely to have some effect on their lives or some relevance. It's also efficient—it helps people get to what's important quickly.

THE LANGUAGE OF INVERTED PYRAMID LEADS

Efficiency and telling readers what's most important are also two of the reasons that journalists tend to keep their language simple and direct. In general, the basic structure of the first sentence in a news story is simple and straightforward: It's subject—verb—object. The subject is a noun, a person, place or thing. The verb is an action. The object is another noun that the action happens to.

You can think of this as being one of two possible kinds of sentences: Who did what? OR: What hit whom? For instance, look at one of the sample leads in this chapter:

*A major **earthquake** (what) **struck** (hit) **southern Haiti** (whom).*

Most of the other words in a sentence—those besides the subject, verb and object—are modifiers of one kind or another. In the example, *a, major* and *southern* are modifiers. For leads, you usually want to minimize the number of modifiers, but you can see that journalists still need to use some adjectives and adverbs to clarify the facts.

GOOD LEADS ARE LIKE POETRY

The best journalism is an art. It has a set of traditions, rules and conventions that shape its form—and the form challenges journalists to create more powerful language than they might have without its constrictions. Like poets, journalists have to think about each word and how it relates to the next; they have to consider how it functions in a sentence, asking each word to do more work, in order to pack more meaning into a small space. Poets say that this challenge can be thrilling. It's harder work, but the poem they end up with is more interesting and creative because of the conventions. In a news story's lead, the same sort of challenge presents itself.

Let's look at two contrasting examples of leads reporting the same event: When Barack Obama was first elected president in 2008, the media across the country emphasized the news that he would be the first African-American president. An Associated Press lead got straight to the point:

> Barack Obama swept to victory as the nation's first black president Tuesday night in an electoral college landslide that overcame racial barriers as old as America itself. (Espo, 2008, para. 1)

This lead is fine, and well reported: It includes the most important information, uses a simple sentence structure, omits unnecessary details and answers *who, what* and *when* (and the *where*—"Washington"—was answered in a **dateline**, the place where the journalist did his reporting). But a *Los Angeles Times* reporter managed to relate similar information in a more poetic way:

> Barack Obama, the son of a father from Kenya and a white mother from Kansas, was elected the nation's 44th president Tuesday, breaking the ultimate racial barrier to become the first African American to claim the country's highest office. (Barabak, 2008, para. 1)

This lead also includes the most important information, omits unnecessary details and answers *who, what* and *when*. But in this case the writer includes a more nuanced description of Obama's heritage, and therefore alludes to the complexity of race and U.S. cultural heritage itself by juxtaposing Kenya and Kansas. The writer emphasizes this contrast through the **alliteration** of those two very different places (Fig. 4-8).

He includes other alliteration, too—"**b**reaking the ultimate racial **b**arrier to **b**ecome" and "**A**frican **A**merican to **c**laim the **c**ountry's . . ." His wordsmithing enhances his lead without losing focus on its purpose: to deliver the news clearly and succinctly.

° ALLITERATION °

IS several words close together that start with the same letter or sound.

HERALD
BIPED BITES BOXER
Breaks bicuspid then bolts...

FIGURE 4-8

Beyond the Lead

The storytelling in a simple news story about a murder can seem natural, as if the reporter did little to shape the narrative or arrange the bits of information gathered. But as soon as you start pulling information together for your own news story, you may sometimes feel more like pulling out your hair. As reporters move from writing the lead of a breaking news story to organizing the rest of their information, they have to think about that organization in several different ways. Just as they do for leads, journalists continue to prioritize information according to basic newsworthiness.

Let's start by taking a look at how journalists prioritize information in a basic news story. Imagine that you're assigned to do a story for a Chicago news outlet about a neighborhood attack. You've already talked to your sources and gathered the following information (this information is based on a real news story that ran in Chicago BreakingNews):

- At about 1:45 a.m., 16-year-old Alexander Mercado of the 5500 block of Higgins Avenue was sitting in a parked car in the 4100 block of North Albany Avenue, said Police News Affairs Officer Robert Perez. That's in Chicago's Albany Park neighborhood.

- Mercado was with two other people whom police have not identified: an 18-year-old man and a 21-year-old woman.

- At about that time (1:45), someone walked up and started a conversation, Perez said.

- Soon after that, a suspect opened fire into the car, police said.

- The 18-year-old man was wounded. Mercado was also shot.

- The 21-year-old woman switched places with one of the gunshot victims and drove to the 4000 block of North Whipple Street, where she called police.
- The woman said the gunman fled the scene in a dark-colored vehicle. No one was in custody for the shooting.
- Mercado was taken to Illinois Masonic, where he was pronounced dead. The 18-year-old man was listed as stable at the hospital, Perez said. (Williams-Harris, 2010)

Think about the information: What is timeliest and has the most impact? That is your lead. Remember to keep it simple here:

A 16-year-old was killed and a man wounded this morning while sitting in a parked car in Chicago's Albany Park neighborhood. (Williams-Harris, 2010)

Notice that neither of the victims is named in the first paragraph. That's because the news is that two people were attacked, and where they were attacked—while sitting in a parked car. But what comes next?

THE SECOND PARAGRAPH

What are your most pressing questions after reading the first paragraph? Typically, the second paragraph (and often the third and fourth) fills in information that couldn't be treated in the first paragraph. This can mean relevant details like the time or location of an event, or the name of a specific, but not famous, person. You still don't want to overload the reader here—it's no fun to read stories that are written like lists, with no narrative. If you've got a lot of details, you might try combining a couple of them into one sentence, or you might provide the most important details here and save others for the fourth or fifth paragraph. For our example, readers might want to know: Who is the 16-year-old—is it someone I know? Did he die right away? In the second paragraph, you'd expect to get at least the name of the person who was murdered, and you do:

Alexander Mercado, 16, of the 5500 block of Higgins Avenue, was pronounced dead at 2:23 a.m. at Advocate Illinois Masonic Medical Center, according to the Cook County medical examiner's office.

This second paragraph fully identifies the murder victim, giving his name and address. Often, news organizations will omit an exact street address to avoid alerting burglars that a residence might be empty or particularly vulnerable.

This paragraph also provides the official details about Mercado's death—on whose authority we have it that he died, and what time that fact was determined. It's a short paragraph, but readers learn quite a bit: We know that Mercado was taken to a hospital, and that proper procedure seems to have been followed—that the county medical examiner's office was involved. That's important because it's a medical examiner's public duty to analyze suspicious deaths. People need to know that Mercado wasn't left languishing on the streets for hours somewhere and that the violence used against him wasn't ignored by the law.

From the first two paragraphs of this news story, the audience learns what's most newsworthy and enough details to understand something of what's going on. But readers might be wondering at this point, what more do police know about how or why Mercado was killed?

THE THIRD PARAGRAPH

After you provide some brief background, you need to move the story forward, to keep the plot moving. One way to do this is to give more explanation, context and details by providing a chronological description of the main event—in our example, the crime. Remember, the news story itself is not told in chronological order until it reaches the description of the crime. For most stories, you need to be sure that you've provided enough basic background information first, before you return to the beginning of the crime and follow events in the order in which they happened. Here's how this reporter wrote the third paragraph:

> Mercado, an 18-year-old man and a 21-year-old woman were sitting in a parked car in the 4100 block of North Albany Avenue, said Police News Affairs Officer Robert Perez. About 1:45 a.m., someone walked up and started a conversation, Perez said. (Williams-Harris, 2010)

By telling readers what police know about the actual crime, the reporter helps to answer how Mercado was killed. Readers might want to know this because it tells them something about their own personal safety and about the community in which they live.

LATER PARAGRAPHS

After beginning with the most important information, providing some basic background information and introducing the voice of one of your sources if possible, stories follow one of several patterns. The reporter may continue to develop the central issue, interspersing context such as background and history with responses from those involved. Stories may introduce other important issues, or they may immediately introduce other speakers, especially if those speakers offer other, valid, content. Or they may continue a chronological description of the main event.

Let's look at the way the reporter organized the Chicago Breaking News story, with the first three paragraphs included again as a reminder:

> A 16-year-old was killed and a man wounded this morning while sitting in a parked car in Chicago's Albany Park neighborhood.
>
> Alexander Mercado, 16, of the 5500 block of Higgins Avenue, was pronounced dead at 2:23 a.m. at Advocate Illinois Masonic Medical Center, according to the Cook County medical examiner's office.
>
> Mercado, an 18-year-old man and a 21-year-old woman were sitting in a parked car in the 4100 block of North Albany Avenue, said Police News Affairs

> Officer Robert Perez. About 1:45 a.m., someone walked up and started a conversation, Perez said.
>
> Soon after the suspect opened fire into the car, police said. The woman switched places with one of the gunshot victims and drove to the 4000 block of North Whipple Street, where she called police.
>
> Mercado was taken to Illinois Masonic, where he was pronounced dead. The 18-year-old man was listed as stable at the hospital, Perez said.
>
> The woman said the gunman fled the scene in a dark-colored vehicle. No one was in custody for the shooting. (Williams-Harris, 2010)

After the first three paragraphs, the reporter continued the chronological description of the crime. At this point, the reader also wants to know why someone opened fire, but it's obvious that the reporter doesn't have that information. So the audience learns what the reporter does know about the crime: that soon after someone walked up and started a conversation, the suspect opened fire into the car, and that the woman drove the two victims to a place where she could call for help. There's a slight deviation from chronological order when the reporter stops to tell us what happened to Mercado and the wounded man, and then we return to the crime and learn that the gunman fled the scene. Finally, we learn the police response or lack thereof: In this case, no one was in custody for the crime when the story was first published.

Notice that the story ends with some sense of what readers can expect next: We infer that police perhaps have a suspect, but no one has been arrested. That probably means that police will try to determine who's guilty and follow up with an arrest. But the story doesn't have a real conclusion. The reporter doesn't try to wrap up the narrative with a flourish or a generalization, because what comes at the end of an inverted pyramid story is what's least newsworthy. That means that whatever the pattern, news stories don't usually have a conclusion; they just stop. They don't end with important information. For instance, a story about an important trial wouldn't end like this:

Weaker ending: *The defendant was found guilty on 10 counts of felony, and has been sentenced to 20 years of prison.*

That information would come earlier in the story. News stories also don't end with surprises:

Weaker ending: *Doctors thought Jolene Harrison would never walk again. But 15 months after her surgery, she shocked both the surgeons and her family when she took her first steps yesterday.*

Such endings can work well for fiction, but in a news story, they may mean your readers never find out what's really going on. That's because audiences may choose not to click on the next link, or they may change the channel or stop reading before the end, where it's too late to say whether a new law was passed, or that someone taken to the hospital after an accident ended up dying. You may be able to write a final paragraph that has a finished feel by reporting what readers can expect to happen next

("Brown's next court date is June 12"), or by returning to an idea from early in the story. But it's also okay to stop with the last bit of information.

News stories, unlike other kinds of narratives, can come to an abrupt end.

Exercises for Chapter 4

EXERCISE 4-1: For each of the following fact sets, change the order of the sentences so that you start with the most important, newsworthy information and deliver the rest in descending order of importance. Write an inverted pyramid print lead for the story. Be able to explain why you prioritized the information you did, and why you chose to include—or exclude—particular details.

Fact set A:

- A train ran into a pedestrian at 2 a.m. Wednesday.

- The train was owned by Amtrak. It was carrying 100 passengers.

- The pedestrian died immediately.

- The train was pulling out of the station in Denver, Colorado, when the pedestrian walked across the tracks and in front of the train.

- Police said the pedestrian apparently thought he could make it across the tracks because the train was going slowly as it pulled out of the station.

- An Amtrak spokesman said the engineer immediately applied the brakes, but the train simply did not have the capability of stopping in the short amount of time between when it became evident the pedestrian would try to cross and the engineer's response.

- Police are awaiting blood alcohol tests on the pedestrian, whom they have declined to identify until family members are notified.

- The train was delayed by six hours. Police said they had no plans to make an arrest or detain the Amtrak engineer.

- Amtrak said it would pay the engineer and his co-pilot for a week's leave of absence and provide funding for any counseling if they wished.

Fact set B:

- A house caught on fire.

- It was a two-story house.

- Six people were inside at the time of the fire.

- They were two brothers, aged 6 and 8; their 12-year-old sister; an 11-year-old cousin; a 9-year-old neighbor boy; and a 13-year-old boy.

- The teen escaped by jumping from a second-story window, onto a porch roof and then to the ground. He escaped without injuries.

- Everyone else died.

- No adults were home.

- The house did have two smoke detectors, but they had no batteries.

- The fire was called in at 1:42 a.m. Thursday. Firefighters arrived on the scene about six minutes later.

Fact set C:

- There was a car accident yesterday at about 5 p.m. that injured one person.

- It was at Camino del Rio and Seventh Street.

- There was one car, a 2006 Honda Civic, heading south on Camino del Rio, turning left onto Seventh Street.

- It was driven by 20-year-old resident Tim Breace.

- The other car, a Ford Bronco, was driving north, and it hit the car turning left.

- One person was injured, a pregnant woman, 32, named Jane Pulley.

- They sent her to Mercy Medical Center for observation.

- There is no further word on her condition.

- She was the one in the blue Bronco.

- Northbound traffic was redirected through downtown for about an hour. It was rush hour.

- Southbound traffic was slow, but it was not detoured.

Fact set D:

- On West Second Avenue between 25th and 26th streets on the north end of town, there was a water problem.

- The City of Durango Public Works Department determined that the old pipes and probably the water main had been leaking for some time, and as they were made of clay, had probably at least partially corroded. The department dug up the street and replaced the works. In the process, workers realized the leak would have led to a sinkhole soon if no action had been taken. They fixed it in time.

- Since then, the weather has been snowy and icy, so the residents of the street have been living with axle-breaking ruts where the city just filled in the construction holes with a dirt mixture.

- The city had to wait until spring to repave.

- The weather currently has been sunny and dry, and the city thinks it can get the street filled and repaved before the next storm.

- From March 2 to March 6, West Second Avenue between 25th and 26th streets will be closed to all traffic so the city can do this repaving.

- Residents will have to park on side streets during this time, but at least after six months, the job will be finished.

EXERCISE 4-2: For each of the previous fact sets, write an inverted pyramid story. Be able to explain why you prioritized the information you did, and why you chose to include—or exclude—particular details.

EXERCISE 4-3: For each of the previous fact sets, write a broadcast lead. How does it differ from a print lead?

EXERCISE 4-4: Go to Google News (http://news.google.com/), where you'll see headlines and a sentence or two from the top stories in the news for today. Choose two stories; for each of these, click on the link and read the rest of the story. Is this particular news story told in inverted pyramid style? What makes it so—or what prevents it from being an inverted pyramid?

CHAPTER 5

THE STORY
CHANGES
WITH THE MEDIUM

In 2013, *The New York Times* won a Pulitzer Prize for a multimedia story about an avalanche that buried a group of skiers, killing three people (Branch, 2012). It did so in a way that seamlessly integrated several different kinds of storytelling: On its website, the story began with a dramatic photo of snow, followed by an article with vivid descriptions of the group's experiences. Next to the text, people could click on video clips of interviews with survivors or family members, humanizing their experiences by letting them speak in their own words. One clip shows skiers swooping through fresh powder, focusing on the rush of backcountry skiing and why people might pursue this often-risky sport.

Viewers could also take a computer-animated fly-through of the snowy mountains where the group had been skiing; another computer animation depicted the storm that hit late the night the group ventured out. Readers could click to hear audio of one of the skiers, Elyse Saugstad, calling 911, or a recording of the agonizing call a dispatcher made to the ski patrol. And historic black-and-white photos showed the wreckage after a 1910 avalanche that killed 96 people near the same spot.

What's especially interesting about this story is that technology has allowed the news media to tell it in ways that they couldn't before. A print-only story that included the quotes from all the video clips and audio would fall apart—it would feel like a string of quotes without the structure to hold it together, or like a big mass of gray text. A half-hour broadcast news show simply wouldn't have enough time for so many interviews. Even if you had an hour-long show, you would have to sacrifice too many other stories and too much background explanation to give voice to this many people. The *story itself* is different because of the media through which it is told.

This is an example of how online multimedia can allow for depth and breadth beyond what linear storytelling allows. This lets more people have access to information, and allows a diversity of voices access to the world stage.

Here's another example: As part of its coverage of the 2011 Arab Spring, *The New York Times* posted 23 videos, averaging about 40 seconds each and featuring a comment by a member of "A New Arab Generation" (Farrell et al., 2011). The journalists let people speak to the camera in their own words, in their own language, so the audience could hear and see the diversity of ideas firsthand. One man tearfully described how the Libyan revolution was not for him, but for his children and grandchildren. A Moroccan man discussed how foreign and impossible the idea of democracy seemed. A woman from Gaza said it was time for young people to become the leaders. The sources came from several Middle East countries, and all but two of them were in their 20s. Their job titles ranged from teacher to entrepreneur to social worker, and some were students.

If people wondered, who are these revolutionaries changing the world?, the global audience could now see and hear some of them. Here, too, the means by which a story was told affected what that story could be.

In this chapter, we'll be looking at some of the differences in news told in various media (Box 5-1). As new technology is introduced, people keep coming up with innovative ways to apply it to communicating the news. Reporters have tried bundling tweets together into one story full of sharp bursts of energy. They've made up games and cartoons to help their audiences understand complicated news stories. Reporters have told more interesting stories about budgets by creating interactive graphics that help readers understand the numbers. And they'll keep making changes in the ways they tell news stories, using new technologies or new applications of old technologies—so who knows exactly what your news stories will look like in, say, four years? You'll need to be able to think about the strengths, weaknesses and possibilities of whatever media you have available. And we're pretty sure that no matter what, those stories will have some kind of video, audio and/or text.

The most important narrative characteristics of news are those that are shared by stories in any medium. These are the traits that distinguish news stories from other kinds of stories—like a greater dependence on sources, attention to source reliability and diversity, focus on accuracy, attention to ethical principles and a story structure that puts the most important information at the beginning. But there are also important differences in the ways in which stories get told in different media.

BOX 5-1

A COMPARISON OF STORYTELLING ACROSS MEDIA

Radio Transcript Example
National Public Radio, All Things Considered

Waves pound Maryland coast as hurricane nears
By Larry Abramson and Audie Cornish
October 29, 2012, 3:00 p.m.

ROBERT SIEGEL, HOST:
From NPR News, this is ALL THINGS
    CONSIDERED. I'm Robert Siegel.
AUDIE CORNISH, HOST:
And I'm Audie Cornish.

Begins with general intro or throwaway line . . .

Powerful winds, heavy rain, flooding and widespread power outages, and Hurricane Sandy has not yet made landfall, although it is expected to this evening. The category one hurricane is moving faster than predicted, packing 90-mile-an-hour winds, and it's barreling directly towards southern New Jersey and Delaware.

. . . then repeats with more specific info

SIEGEL: For millions of people throughout the Eastern Seaboard, the ferocity of Sandy is already undeniable, and we're going to hear about its impact from our reporters out on the coast. Public transportation systems have been shut down, rail service suspended and thousands of flights cancelled. Many bridges and tunnels are closed. The New York Stock Exchange and other markets are closed today and again tomorrow.

Doesn't overwhelm listeners with too many numbers

. . .

SIEGEL: New Jersey's governor, Chris Christie, expressed frustration with people who are not complying with mandatory evacuation orders.

Introduces speaker before sound byte to avoid confusion

GOV. CHRIS CHRISTIE: I'm very concerned about the people who refused to adhere to my mandatory evacuation order and said they were going to ride it out. They are—let me make this as definitive as I can: They are now in harm's way, and I don't know whether we can get them out or not.

Includes sound byte of governor speaking

. . .

LARRY ABRAMSON, BYLINE: Well, Audie, we're up on the fifth floor of a hotel room, and I can see a very angry bay. I think it's the Isle of Wight Bay that is just roaring onto this barrier island. As you know, this is a thin strip of sand a couple of miles off of the coast, and the wind and the water has been getting more and more intense.

Uses ambient sound of wind and waves that you can hear in the audio version

Describes the setting because audience can't see it

Print Example

The New York Times

October 30, 2012 Tuesday
Late Edition—Final
Storm picks up speed and disrupts millions of lives

BYLINE: By JAMES BARRON

Uses past tense

Hurricane Sandy battered the mid-Atlantic region on Monday, its powerful gusts and storm surges causing once-in-a-generation flooding in coastal communities, knocking down trees and power lines and leaving more than five million people—including a large swath of Manhattan—in the rain-soaked dark. At least seven deaths in the New York region were tied to the storm.

Often uses longer sentences

The mammoth and merciless storm made landfall near Atlantic City around 8 p.m., with maximum sustained winds of about 80 miles per hour, the National Hurricane Center said. That was shortly after the center had reclassified the storm as a post-tropical cyclone, a scientific renaming that had no bearing on the powerful winds, driving rains and life-threatening storm surge expected to accompany its push onto land.

Provides more depth and details (compare with the CNN.online storm reclassification reference)

The storm had unexpectedly picked up speed as it roared over the Atlantic Ocean on a slate-gray day and went on to paralyze life for millions of people in more than a half-dozen states, with extensive evacuations that turned shorefront neighborhoods into ghost towns. Even the superintendent of the Statue of Liberty left to ride out the storm at his mother's house in New Jersey; he said the statue itself was "high and dry," but his house in the shadow of the torch was not.

The wind-driven rain lashed sea walls and protective barriers in places like Atlantic City, where the Boardwalk was damaged as water forced its way inland. Foam was spitting, and the sand gave in to the waves along the beach at Sandy Hook, N.J., at the entrance to New York Harbor. Water was thigh-high on the streets in Sea Bright, N.J., a three-mile sand-sliver of a town where the ocean joined the Shrewsbury River.

Provides descriptions of sound and visuals

Online Example

Sandy wreaks havoc across Northeast; at least 11 dead
By Matt Smith, CNN
Updated 1:32 AM EDT, Tue October 30, 2012

Provides frequent updates

Uses deck or brief summary at beginning of story

Story Highlights

One New York hospital evacuates 200 patients; another turns to backup power
At least 11 U.S. deaths have been blamed on Sandy
"Extraordinary" amount of water in Lower Manhattan, Bloomberg says
Jersey Shore police: "The whole north side of my town is totally under water

Often provides ways for audience to participate

Have you been affected by Hurricane Sandy? If so, share your images and footage with CNN iReport, but please stay safe.

(CNN)—Though no longer a hurricane, "post-tropical" superstorm Sandy packed a hurricane-sized punch as it slammed into the Jersey Shore on Monday, killing at least 11 people from West Virginia to North Carolina and Connecticut.

Sandy whipped torrents of water over the streets of Atlantic City, stretching for blocks inland and ripping up part of the vacation spot's fabled boardwalk. The storm surge set records in Lower Manhattan, where flooded substations caused a widespread power outage. It swamped beachfronts on both sides of Long Island Sound and delivered hurricane-force winds from Virginia to Cape Cod as it came ashore.

. . .

Superstorm Sandy's Wrath

"I've been down here for about 16 years, and it's shocking what I'm looking at now. It's unbelievable," said Montgomery Dahm, owner of the Tun Tavern in Atlantic City, which stayed open as Sandy neared the Jersey Shore. "I mean, there's cars that are just completely underwater in some of the places I would never believe that there would be water."

. . .

Breaks story into chunks with subheadings. This subhead also serves as a link to updates and photos.

Sandy makes landfall

Thumbnail photos that appeared with this story linked to videos with raw footage of the storm.

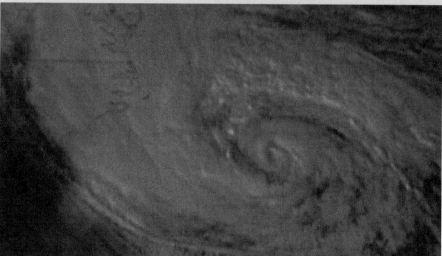

Video Script Example

This column lists the visuals

Begins with general intro or throwaway line

New York streets scenes today:
nyc_update: last shot
APTN 103332 Pan from rough waves
crashing against Harbour
103336 Waterfront restaurant boarded
up and roof blowing in wind
Massive flooding, buildings without
power
VICTORIA SANDY NY 121412
APTN 103359–103426
flooded tunnels—VICTORIA SANDY
NY 120749, 120800, 120857
Subway shots—VICTORIA SANDY
NY 121444

10:33:27 US Superstorm 7
APTN 103344 SOUND BITE: (English)
Nana Visitor, New York City Resident:

blacked out Manhattan last night
ny_lights_outs
VICTORIA SANDY NY 121339

BLOOMBERG

This is what an interview subject said ("SOT" stands for "sound on tape")

NEW YORK WAS A CITY IN SHOCK TODAY—
EVEN DESERTED IN PLACES—AFTER
A NIGHT OF FEAR, FIRE AND FLOOD.

A RECORD STORM SURGE OF 13 FEET
POURED INTO PARTS OF LOWER
MANHATTAN, BROOKLYN AND QUEENS
AS "SANDY" HIT. THE RUSH OF WATER
CLOSED MAJOR COMMUTER TUNNELS
LINKING MANHATTAN WITH OTHER
BOROUGHS, CONTRIBUTING TO
THE WORST DAMAGE TO THE
SUBWAY SYSTEM IN ITS 108 YEARS. . .

"(SOT): last night we could look down this
street here and we saw the river coming
toward us, and it actually looked like
something out of a movie. It was unbelievable."
EQUALLY UNBELIEVABLE -- WINDS OF AT
LEAST 80 MILES AN HOUR BLEW OUT THE
BRIGHT LIGHTS THAT USUALLY DOMINATE
THE MANHATTAN SKYLINE.
SOME ONE MILLION HOMES AND
BUSINESSES IN AND AROUND THE CITY
LOST POWER.
TODAY, MAYOR MICHAEL BLOOMBERG
APPEALED FOR UNDERSTANDING AMID
WARNINGS THAT IT COULD TAKE DAYS
TO RESTORE ALL TRANSIT SERVICE
AND POWER. . .
11:05:52 we have begun the work of clearing
and reopening bridges and roadways, both
of which will take some time and the best
way New Yorkers can help us get this done
quickly is to stay off the roads. The work of
getting our mass transit grid and our power
grid restored however is going to take more
time and a lot of patience. 110617

This is what the reporter said

Refers to video

Doesn't overwhelm viewers with too many numbers

Fire in Queens	BUT NO AMOUNT OF PATIENCE WOULD MAKE
VICTORIA SANDY NY 122020, 121950	GOOD SOME LOSSES. IN QUEENS, FIRE DESTROYED AT LEAST 100 HOMES AND FORCED FIREFIGHTERS TO TRUDGE THROUGH WAIST DEEP WATER TO RESCUE THE TRAPPED.
Staten Island Tanker VICTORIA SANDY NY 121034 + PKG	ELSEWHERE, CRASHING WAVES HURLED A TANKER SHIP ASHORE ON STATEN ISLAND. . .
cars floating—DISC	FLOODING ALSO SWEPT UP CARS FROM CITY STREETS AND CARRIED THEM AWAY. . .
STILL of contruction site STILL of building with side missing GROUND ZERO FLOODING + BUILDING COLLAPSE	AND WATER RUSHED INTO THE CONSTRUCTION SITE WHERE THE WORLD TRADE CENTER ONCE STOOD, AS HIGH WINDS TORE AWAY THE FACADE OF BUILDINGS.
Construction crane coming loose yesterday, dangling today YOUTUBE VIDEOS	THE WIND ALSO BLEW A CONSTRUCTION CRANE FROM ITS PERCH NEAR A LUXURY HIGH-RISE IN MIDTOWN MANHATTAN. . . WHERE IT DANGLED TODAY. THOUSANDS OF PEOPLE WERE FORCED TO LEAVE THE SURROUNDING BUILDINGS.
Hospital evacs—VICTORIA SANDY NY 121437	AND 200 PATIENTS HAD TO BE CARRIED FROM NEW YORK UNIVERSITY'S TISCH HOSPITAL OVERNIGHT AFTER ITS BACKUP GENERATOR FAILED.
APTN 103058 PEOPLE WALKING BK WATERFRONT PARK	THIS MORNING, MANY PEOPLE WERE STILL TRYING TO TAKE IT ALL IN. . .
APTN 10:33:27 US Superstorm 7 103433 SOUNDBITE: (English) Melissa Terrick, New York City Resident:	"(SOT): It wasn't it was never really raining that hard, the wind wasn't blowing that, that hard last night either. So, its just to see how much, how much just happened with even not a lot of rain, not a lot of rain, is crazy."
LaGuardia/Newark Liberty/Kennedy Airports	THE STORM KEPT ALL THREE NEW YORK AREA AIRPORTS CLOSED TODAY.
NYSE, REUTERS 2606CC	AND THINGS WERE QUIET ON WALL STREET, AS THE WEATHER SHUT DOWN THE NEW YORK STOCK EXCHANGE FOR A SECOND STRAIGHT DAY—SOMETHING THAT LAST HAPPENED IN

News Stories in Print

The shorthand name for news media, *the press,* is a reminder that news created on printing presses—newspapers and news magazines—has been with us the longest. But reading the *news* on paper now sometimes seems paradoxical because the information is old by the time a press can produce individual newspapers or magazines and distribute them. Reading the news in print is a tradition or habit for some people, and even a little nostalgic or romantic for others. But creating news in print provides many readers with benefits that have nothing to do with tradition or romance.

In print, you can scan information in a way that's difficult to do in other media. In seconds you can skim through pages of headlines, photos and stories. In contrast, video and audio news programs are more linear in the sense that one story follows another, so you don't have simultaneous access to stories as you do with print. Similarly, while you can use a search engine to look for particular news stories online or scan headlines or photos on a website, the format can't present as much information to the human eye all at once the way print can.

Print also allows people to reread information, which gives them more control in that sense. If you don't catch a name on a radio or television show, you have to wait until the interviewer or announcer repeats it—and hope that she or he does. If you don't catch it on a podcast, you still have to pause and then try to track down the name again. This is true for numbers and facts, but also for complicated information. If a point is dense, readers can reread a particular paragraph however many times it takes to understand it. And readers can read at their own pace, or stop reading one article at any point and move on to another (Box 5-2).

Sophisticated or nuanced information is easier to communicate in print stories because of this characteristic. And newspaper stories tend to treat more complex ideas than broadcast stories—or sometimes even online stories—because the articles can be so much longer. Broadcast stories don't have time to equal the space available in newspapers, and individual stories created for news websites tend to be relatively short, although a website may have just as much information in separate stories. That means readers often turn to newspapers for depth about issues that may not be

---

BOX 5-2

TIPS FOR PRINT WRITING

- Use the past tense, except for headlines.
- Provide more depth and information when appropriate.
- Refer to related photos—but no need to explain these, because they should include their own, separate captions.
- Provide descriptions of sound and visuals when appropriate.
- Provide details about numbers and figures in stories where these are relevant.

available elsewhere. They also read differently in print than they do online. When people listen to news stories or watch them, the assumption is that there will be distractions. That appears to be true for information online, too—you always know that a different news headline or a fun video or perhaps a Facebook update from a good friend is only a click away.

Furthermore, newspapers and magazines provide a combination of depth *and* mobility unlike other media. It's still tricky to know where you'll have Internet access if you're in another country or an out-of-the-way place. And at the beach, for instance, you can ruin a newspaper (cost: about 75 cents) or an iPad (cost: about $400 to $900). A cellphone might link you to more up-to-date information, but reading one long story, much less multiple long stories, on a tiny screen is difficult.

Finally, back to the romance and nostalgia: Print stories are still actual things, as opposed to bits, that people can save, and they do. They keep obituaries and wedding announcements. They buy newspapers when an important event like 9/11 happens, and they save those. And they still look to newspapers to preserve daily history. While online stories can disappear into the ether, libraries and newspaper archives still do a better job of saving old newspapers in some form. These are what historians still turn to in order to find out what happened in the past—at least for now.

Radio News Stories: An Overview

A radio reporter on the scene can make a story memorable in a way that print cannot. The radio reporter communicates the actual experience—its sound—providing texture and context. When a hurricane is approaching, a radio story may record the sound of the wind, rain or waves, allowing listeners to feel on some level that they too are on the scene. During the Chicago teacher strikes in 2012, NPR journalist Becky Vevea reported from the picket lines outside an elementary school (2012). As Vevea interviewed teachers, listeners could hear car horns and excited voices in the background. In this case, listeners experienced the texture of the scene better than readers did.

And media with audio help to convey the tone of how someone says something. Is there a note of humor or sarcasm in what that senator just said? Does she pause thoughtfully, or state something forcefully and immediately? The media that deliver sound can provide a level of nuance in quotes that print can't. In a radio story about a computer hacking camp, reporter Steve Henn interviewed a camper who was looking for bugs in the games on his parents' iPad (2012). Although the reporter *told* listeners that the camper, Charlie, was 6 years old, hearing Charlie's childish voice made a deeper impression—and helped to powerfully convey the unusual skills and interests of some of the youngsters at the camp.

Radio is a relatively inexpensive way to reach masses of people, including those who can't afford a computer. When Haiti's 2010 earthquake disrupted telecommunications and electricity there, radio was the medium through which people were able to communicate most information—whether lost loved ones were still alive, and where and how to get emergency help.

Radio is also a medium that allows its audience to multitask. You can drive or exercise or cook and eat your dinner while listening to the news. Of course, this is also a disadvantage for radio reporters: Because they don't have to be, your listeners are not focused on information in the same way the people reading the news are. This has practical implications for choosing to communicate particular pieces of information by sound, and for how you do so.

Because the audience is often doing something else—or several other things—while they're listening to news, reporters have to think about how much listeners can absorb, realizing that they can't go back and reread information they miss.

Language for radio and also for television is even plainer and more direct than it is for print. On a sentence level, this means that most sentences should be a maximum of about 10 to 15 words long. The stories themselves vary in length. You'll hear that news stories for radio are about 10 to 15 seconds long. But that all depends. News stories for the BBC are usually 2 to 3 minutes. Typical news stories for NPR are 3 to 4 minutes. Check with your news organization first.

Omit details that you would usually include in a written story, such as the middle initials for people's names (there are exceptions, such as George W. Bush, where you need the initial to distinguish him from his father); people's ages, unless these are especially relevant or newsworthy; and exact addresses.

The form of those sentences also needs to be as clear and simple as possible. Avoid overusing dependent clauses at the beginning of sentences, and avoid long or complex dependent clauses altogether.

Weaker: *While the senators disagreed about many of the issues under discussion, they passed a bill by the end of the session.*

Better: *Republicans and Democrats have passed a bill based on a compromise on controversial items.*

To keep language easy to absorb, radio and video stories avoid using many numbers. Of course, when numbers are the story, you need to provide them for listeners and viewers. But while a written story on the city budget might include 10 or more numbers, a visual story might limit itself to one or two. Usually, you'll want to round off numbers. If the city's budget is $51,233,202, you would say "about $50 million."

As you've seen for broadcast leads, radio and video writing also differs from other newswriting in that broadcast stories usually emphasize the present tense to underscore immediacy.

Written: *Rivers and creeks rose to dangerous levels in Southwest Colorado after this weekend's rainstorms.*

Broadcast: *Rivers and creeks are at dangerous levels in Southwest Colorado after recent rains.*

Written: *A homeless man was shot fatally as he lay sleeping on Main Avenue in Durango last night.*

Broadcast: *Police are searching for the murderer of a homeless man who was shot to death on Main Avenue last night.*

Using the present tense for broadcast news often means using the "-ing" form of a verb rather than the simple present tense. Note how the following example sounds like a headline, rather than the first line of a story.

Weaker: *Police search for the murderer.*

While broadcast journalism does use the past tense at times, most of the information is rendered into either present tense or present perfect tense: A plane *has crashed* into the building. In contrast, written stories describe events in the past tense: A plane *crashed* into the building, or *flames billowed.*

For radio, the sounds of words and how they are pronounced becomes more important. At the AP Style website, members can check standard pronunciations. For instance, after the Boston Marathon attack, the site posted the correct pronunciation of one of the suspects, Dzhokar Tsarnaev. After other news events, it posted the pronunciation for Utoya Island, the island where a Norwegian man killed 69 people at a political summer camp, and the place, Abbottabad, where Osama bin Laden was shot. You can also look up how to pronounce the names of people like Beyoncé Knowles, the pop singer, or Reince Priebus, a prominent Republican leader.

Because the emphasis is on what you hear, the best radio stories will include the actual voices of people and characteristic background sounds called **ambient sound**— as they did in the previous sample stories about the Chicago teacher strike and hacking camp. Listeners can't see what you're talking about, so stories should explain audio unless it's already clear what background noises are.

WRITING A RADIO NEWS STORY

You've seen in Chapter 4 some tips for writing broadcast leads:

- Audio or video stories often begin with a throwaway line to get your audience's attention.
- Audio or video stories often—though not always—use present tense.

But how does the rest of a radio story differ from a story written for print or online (Box 5-3)?

After the lead, your news story will proceed in the same order as a story for print: You'll be filling in details as you go, providing specifics about the *who, what, when, where* and, often, *how* and *why*. However, a radio story is much less likely to use quotes than a written story. The reporter still paraphrases and sums up much of what interview subjects say. But instead of quotes, you're more likely to include **sound bites**— short excerpts from recorded interviews, or the equivalent of quotes—from interview subjects.

BOX 5-3

TIPS FOR RADIO/AUDIO WRITING

- Begin with a general intro or throwaway line to draw the audience's attention to the topic, then repeat with more specific info.
- Use short leads.
- Use plain, direct language that's easy for listeners to absorb.
- Use fewer details than for print—usually, that means omitting facts like middle initials in names and people's ages.
- Use simple sentence structures and avoid complex or long dependent clauses.
- Avoid using too many numbers.
- Use present tense to emphasize immediacy.
- Check pronunciation of names and words.
- Include ambient sound where appropriate.

Introduce Sound Bites Clearly

For radio, the story needs to clearly introduce each new speaker. For example, NPR's *All Things Considered* began an important news story in 2013 this way:

> The former president of South Africa, Nelson Mandela, has died. The man who led the country's transition from apartheid to democracy was 95 years old. Here's how the current President Jacob Zuma made the announcement today.
>   PRESIDENT JACOB ZUMA: Fellow South Africans, our beloved Nelson Rolihlahla Mandela, the founding president of our democratic nation has departed. (Beaubien, 2013)

Note the "here's how"—the reporter directly tells listeners who is about to speak. Let's look at the two major kinds of radio stories.

A Story with Voice-Over

For this kind of story, an on-air reporter or announcer reads the introduction and then plays a recording with most of the news story. Your introduction works like a lead: It may have a throwaway line and it gives the most important information from the story. It also needs to introduce the reporter. As you read the following example from *Marketplace*, notice the short sentences and the conversational tone of the writing:

> There was a big win for local governments and environmentalists in Pennsylvania this week. The state supreme court tossed out a big part of what's known as Act 13. It's a state law in Pennsylvania that would let gas companies drill anywhere without having to worry about local zoning laws. Think: fracking. Marketplace's Adrienne Hill reports: (Hill, 2013, para. 1)

As you can see, the reporter's introduction doesn't need to be anything fancy—listeners just need to know who's about to speak.

Now, try writing one. Start with a print or text online story. Be sure to choose one that includes a quote by paragraph two or three in the story.

- Add a line that introduces the subject—your throwaway line.

- Introduce the reporter. Try using the same format as the *Marketplace* example previously—the name of the news agency followed by the reporter's name.

- Revise the first paragraph for shorter sentences and a more conversational tone.

As the story continues, so do the informal tone and generally shorter sentences. Notice that for the following sound bite—when Jordan Yeager, an attorney for opponents to the law, speaks—the reporter explains who is speaking *after* the fact. That works here because the sound bite is so short, and because his voice is so different from hers:

> **Hill:** Act 13 made some folks' blood boil. It stripped local governments of the ability to say where energy companies could put fracking wells and where they couldn't.
>
> **Yeager:** "So it completely eliminated local control and consideration of local concerns."
>
> **Hill:** Jordan Yeager is an attorney at Curtin & Heefner. He represented some of the groups that opposed the law. (2013)

Now, let's get back to your own rewrite. For the next couple of paragraphs, try the following:

- Continue to use shorter sentences and a more conversational tone. This can often be as simple as breaking one sentence into two—the previous sentence could be broken down this way: "Use shorter sentences. And use a more conversational tone." Also, remember the tips for writing for radio: Don't overwhelm your audience with numbers or specifics that make it hard to absorb information.

- Next, introduce the "sound bite" (the quote in paragraph two or three in the original). You can do this by naming the speaker and his expertise or relevance, as the *Marketplace* story does with Yeager after the fact.

- Add a transition back into the rest of the story—do you need to refer to the speaker again?

A Story with Sound Bites

This kind of story doesn't use a separate introduction; it simply incorporates about two or three sound bites from interviews into the story, although longer stories often include more. Think of these as being like quotes in a written story. Just as you would for print news stories, you select sound bites because they're especially well said, because they give some sense of who the speaker is and how she or he speaks or because they sum up important information well.

Choose another print or online text story, again being sure to select one that includes a quote by the second or third paragraph.

- Start with the lead: Add a line that introduces the subject. Revise the tone to make it more conversational and shorten sentences.
- Introduce the speaker in your first "sound bite" (the quote in printed form).
- Add a transition and revise the tone of the paragraphs between this and your next sound bite.
- Introduce the speaker, even if it's the same speaker as earlier. You can say something as simple as: "Again, John Yeager," or you can write a more elegant introduction by paraphrasing something he says, or even his main point: "John Yeager says it doesn't have to be that way."

Communicating by sound alone can take some getting used to. Now what happens when you add visuals?

Adding the Visual Element

Television and video viewers don't have to imagine the sights for themselves—the images are right in front of them. This is the key difference from radio or print stories, and that dependence on images is both the strength and weakness of visual media. When a magnitude 9.0 earthquake shook Japan in the spring of 2011, text descriptions simply couldn't do justice to the story. But on television or in video clips, you could watch the tsunami wave build at sea and move toward the shore (Fig. 5-1).

FIGURE 5-1 This photo shows the impact of a tsunami wave in Miyako, Japan, in a way that print simply could not.

Helicopter footage showed the water and debris approaching and then flooding fields and towns. There were breathtaking shots of vehicles, boats and buildings—some of them on fire—surging like a river across the landscape. Viewers in the United States were connected to what their fellow humans were experiencing half a planet away. Television can communicate the faces and voices of people speaking out about their causes or injustices. It can show people making helpful changes to their own lives or their communities. It can show people in need and inspire viewers to action.

However, if you're watching television, you may have limited patience for watching a person talk at you for anything like the time that you'd be willing to spend reading a news story. The power of the medium is its video footage. But journalists with video cameras might not have access to an important court case or committee hearing. Or the footage of a particular meeting may be so dull or poorly lit that it can't be broadcast. In these cases, the television news story about the issue is often cut short. In contrast, it's easier to get footage of car accidents or crime scenes, and these tend to be visually interesting. So it's sometimes tempting for television news to air or post stories that have good visuals, as opposed to those that are most important.

While newspapers often include photographs, the medium forces readers to look at stories and photos separately. In contrast, television audiences must absorb both what is said and what they see at the same time. Remember that you're telling your stories in two ways, even if the visuals are simply video of the anchor reading a script. This is one of the reasons to keep the writing very basic. Like radio stories, those with visuals use shorter sentences, few dependent clauses, and few numbers. Remember that most television stories are much shorter than written stories. Typically, you may have 15 to 30 seconds for a story. While different newsreaders may take differing amounts of time, you have about four seconds per line, or eight lines to tell a 30-second story.

While readers of the written word are accustomed to stories that never mention accompanying photographs, visual stories almost always need explicit references to graphics or video footage as soon as they appear. If angry people are carrying signs, you need something in your lead that says where they are and what they're protesting before you launch into "Congress is debating a law banning late-term abortions." If the story starts with a shot of the anchor reading the script and then moves to the protest, you're okay. As soon as the video clip appears in the story, though, you need to refer to it. Garth Kant, a former CNN producer who has written a textbook on writing television news, gives this example:

> I saw a story begin with the anchor's script describing a bomb scare at London's Heathrow Airport. The problem was the video showed a van. It stopped the anchor in his tracks. (Apparently he didn't have time to preread his scripts, but that's another story.) Eventually the script made it clear that authorities suspected there was a bomb in the van, which was parked at the airport. The total disconnect between what the viewers were seeing and what they were hearing could have been avoided by mentioning the van in the first paragraph, or by showing footage of the airport first, or by starting the script on camera and mentioning the van at the beginning of the second paragraph. (2006, p. 55)

Remember that your viewers will usually have an image as an anchor reads. If that image doesn't relate to what the anchor is saying, or is left unexplained, the story will make no sense to viewers. Of course, you don't want to go to the other extreme and repeat information that viewers can see for themselves onscreen; your explanation needs to provide additional explanation and context. Reporters using video can often drop the descriptions that are necessary for radio and print reporters.

Broadcast and Web stories often emphasize immediacy by showing the scene or playing audio. They also emphasize the present tense. They are meant to give you up-to-the-minute reports about what the state of affairs is right now, as opposed to last night or even a few hours ago. Another aspect in stories like these is the frequent updates. The updates might be completely new stories, major updates of important stories, or minor updates, sometimes in the form of more detailed or more accurate information.

WRITING A TELEVISION OR VIDEO NEWS STORY

When you write for video, you write to the visuals (Box 5-4). From the very beginning of your reporting, you think about what's going to be on screen because that determines what you need to include in the script. For example, in Box 5-1, you can see the connection between the script and the visuals: The script describes road closures and the video makes clear why the closures had to happen—because there's so much water.

Mastering the interplay among visuals, sound and script takes time to learn to do well, as does learning what makes a good picture or effective sound. The following exercise introduces you to the feel of matching words to pictures, and the symbiotic relationship between them.

BOX 5-4

TIPS FOR TELEVISION/VIDEO WRITING

- Use short leads.
- Use plain, direct language that's easy for listeners to absorb.
- Use fewer details than for print—usually, that means omitting facts like middle initials in names and people's ages.
- Use simple sentence structures and avoid complex or long dependent clauses.
- Avoid using too many numbers.
- Use present tense.
- Explain in your story what's going on in related video.
- Don't repeat information that viewers can see for themselves.
- Provide frequent updates.

Let's walk through a story about a unique composter at Fort Lewis College. Here are the facts:

- The Rocket Composter turns an estimated 20 to 30 percent of the school dining hall's food waste into nutrient-rich soil for the campus vegetable garden and flower beds. In its first academic year, it turned an estimated 24.5 tons of food waste into compost.

- Unlike most composters, this one can break down meat and dairy in addition to vegetables. The composting process consists of four phases. This composter is also unique because it only takes 10 days to two weeks to break down food, as opposed to the more standard four to six weeks.

- Before the composter, only 1 to 2 percent of the food waste was composted. The rest went to the landfill.

- One study estimated that students generated an average of a quarter-pound of waste per student per meal, for a total of 102,977 pounds per academic year.

- The composter is 13 feet long and about 3 feet in diameter. It cost $60,000 and was paid for by the school.

- Students initiated the drive to get the composter.

- The food service contractor pitches in by letting the composter attach to its waste system. Employees also help by separating food and putting it through a pulper, which prepares the food for the composter by grinding up the food and removing much of its moisture.

- Students from the campus Environmental Center maintain and feed the composter. (A. Brooks, personal communication, January 6, 2014)

Let's say that we're preparing this story at the end of the composter's first year of operation. Based on the previous information, determine the story's angle, keeping in mind the news values and ethical principles. Is it that the composter has just completed its first year of operation? That it turned more than 24 tons of waste into compost? That students spearheaded the effort, which was then supported by both the school and the company that provides food service? That students average a quarter-pound of waste per person per meal—and here's the solution?

At the same time, think about the visuals for the story as a whole. For instance, you'll want to show the composter somewhere in the story, so people know what one looks like—but the composter doesn't move much. How do you add motion to the story, maximizing the benefits of video? Panning and zooming in and out are not good options, nor is a handheld shaky-cam approach. So, what visual action will draw viewers into the story? Do your answers shift the frame of the story at all? The way you order the elements?

Also, think about your interviews. Is there a credible source who could talk about why the viewer should care about the composter? Is there someone who could show how much food 24.5 tons is? Where would you interview that source? An office may be quiet, which is good to keep natural sound from becoming intrusive, but an office isn't too dynamic visually.

This story lends itself to what's called a **package**, which is a type of story that includes several elements, such as the following:

- A **stand-up**, which is where you are on camera, speaking to the viewer. Stand-ups are useful for transitions and for closing the piece.

- A **voice-over (VO)** where you or someone else talks while video plays. The audio complements the video, but doesn't describe exactly what the viewer sees happening on screen—that would be too redundant.

- A sound bite from your interview with a source. You select sound bites that move the story forward—by adding emotion, a well-turned phrase and new information, for example. Another term for sound bite is **sound on tape** (SOT).

Once you have a general plan, you or your team will go out to shoot the video, including the interviews. Ask your sources lots of questions, so you'll have plenty of material to select from for sound bites. If your interview subjects ramble when they answer you, or don't really answer the question, it's okay to ask again to see if you can get a more succinct response.

You will shoot extra footage, including some **B-roll**, which is related footage shot in the field that you can select from later to illustrate a point in your script or use for transitions if you need to. B-roll can range from a wide shot of your campus to a close-up of a person's hand turning a lever on the composter. Quality images can make the story, so it's worth taking the extra effort to visualize what you need.

It's also important to shoot **establishing shots**, which are those that give an overview of each location. You see these in television and movies all the time. For example, picture a movie that starts like this: The opening scene is an urban downtown. The camera zooms in on a high-rise building and then looks through one window in the building, where we see a group of people around a conference table having a conversation. We know that we will next go into that room and hear what's going on. And when we are inside the room, we understand that it's the room inside the window of the building in the city that we first saw. That's what an establishing shot does; it gives a sense of place. In news stories, you can use establishing shots to orient your viewer, as bookends for the story—intros and outros—and also as transitions.

Also, look for opportunities to shoot video with compelling **natural sound (Nat Sound** or **NatSOT)**, which is video with ambient sound that's good enough to use without narration. You've also seen these before: a shot of a playground full of children, with their laughter and squealing voices; a shot of a garden, with bees buzzing and birds tweeting; cars passing by on a road, with sounds of their engines and whoosh. You can use video like this for effective intros, outros and transitions. Just a few seconds of video with natural sound invites the viewer into the story.

You won't use all of the footage you have. The goal is to not have to make a second trip for more video.

When you've gathered all of your material, you'll create a script to serve as your blueprint for pulling your package together. You're juggling visuals, sound, script and narrative—so where do you go from here? Writing your script is not likely to be linear: You probably won't start with a throwaway line and write straight through to your conclusion.

A good place to start is by identifying your strongest visuals and the information that will accompany them. Another early decision is which sound bites and any natural sound sequences you'll use because you'll write intros, outros and transitions around them. Once you've taken these steps, you'll see what information is still missing from the story, which you can supply in your own voice-overs and stand-ups. Your story can close in a few different ways. For example, you can summarize the main point, let viewers know what's on the horizon and end using video with natural sound.

If you're creating a 90-second package, you can see that this is a lot of information to squeeze in. Let your visuals pull as much weight as they can, and keep the words to the minimum you need to convey the important information. After each draft, read the script aloud, and if your tongue trips up, that's probably a good place to edit and shorten.

The best visual journalists remember what makes their medium powerful: image and immediacy (Figs. 5-2 and 5-3).

The script always takes into account accompanying visuals, providing enough explanation when it's needed but never boring viewers with repetition of information they can see for themselves. Stories are updated frequently and emphasize their immediacy through using the present tense. Stories tend to be shorter and use relatively simple language that can be absorbed by listeners who don't have the chance to reread complex sentences or double-check lists of numbers for themselves.

FIGURE 5-2 Ice covers equipment after firefighters extinguished a Chicago warehouse fire, a scene conveyed visually in a way that print could not do.

FIGURE 5-3 A photographer was able to communicate some sense of the deep feelings that many onlookers—and one nun in particular—felt upon seeing the white smoke that signals a new pope has been selected.

Online News Stories: An Overview

Online news includes all the media, of course: text, audio and visual. So an online news story *could* be created for any of them. But what we mean here by "online news story"—and elsewhere in the book, except where noted—is a news story in text form written for an online news site, though one that may well appear with audio, video, photos, graphics and links.

You'll notice that online news stories differ from website to website: They may be lengthy stories with a sophisticated tone, like those on the InsideClimate News or *The New York Times* websites, for instance, or they may be brief and more conversational, like those on the Huffington Post or Salon.com websites.

In addition, because the Internet allows readers more control in terms of how they gather news, stories and websites are created with that in mind. Instead of passively receiving information preselected for them by editors or even individual reporters, Internet readers expect to play a more active role.

Unlike broadcast or print journalism, a website typically provides more and different kinds of information about an issue. For one thing, there's almost an infinite amount of space for including information that journalists would often have to omit from a story. Many links are to raw information: A reporter doesn't have to create a transcript of a speech, because the speaker provides one. And the video of a speech doesn't involve writing a voice-over or editing a story, as a television speech story does. So, while a website journalist would usually select only the most relevant and well-put quotes for her story, she might include a link to video footage of the entire interview with a source. Journalists need to be on the lookout for times when this kind of additional raw information can enrich an online story.

Web journalists typically add links to related stories or graphics on their own sites or others. In a story for print or television, the reporter couldn't provide such depth. Readers then get to choose how much, if any, of this information they want to access.

Just as they can with print stories, readers move through written online stories at their own pace, slowing down, backing up and rereading denser material. While reporters still strive for plain, direct language, sentence structures may be more complex and longer online—closer to the writing style in print than in broadcast.

In online news, you'll notice an additional focus on immediacy. Journalists bring audiences to the scene as events unfold, in real time or close to it. In the 24/7 news cycle, news is updated hourly—or more frequently—for hot news and every few hours for other major stories. It's this immediacy that sets online news media apart, and has affected stories on every level, including their organization and even the language they use.

WRITING AN ONLINE NEWS STORY

If you're writing or rewriting a story for your news organization's website, you need to keep some key points in mind (Box 5-5).

Online News Stories Use Brief Summaries or Decks

Online stories are more likely to use **decks**, or secondary, longer headlines that provide more explanation. Because online readers may need to click one more time on a news website to see a full story, this additional explanation helps them decide whether they want to read more. Such summaries or explanations are typically one or two sentences long. They usually focus on providing straightforward information, rather than trying to be catchy. Here are three examples.

In general, BuzzFeed uses longer headlines with more explanation than most other news organizations—but it still provides a second, deck headline with more details.

BOX 5-5

TIPS FOR ONLINE WRITING

- Break stories into small chunks.
- Consider including links to additional raw material, such as interviews or video footage.
- Look for related stories or graphics and provide links when appropriate.
- Make sure you consider carefully the sources of material you link to.
- Provide frequent updates—and make sure these are accurate and meaningful.

For instance, BuzzFeed introduced a story with the following headline: "13 News Organizations sent a letter to Syrian rebels asking them to stop kidnapping journalists" (Nashrulla, 2013). Think about your first questions after reading the headline. You might ask: Are the 13 news organizations well-known and well-respected, or are they tiny and extremist? You might wonder what was so different about what the Syrian rebels were doing that would prompt news outlets to take this extraordinary measure. BuzzFeed provided the answers to just these questions in its deck headline:

> The New York Times, Washington Post, BBC and others asked the Syrian rebels to free an estimated 30 journalists being held in the country. (Nashrulla, 2013)

Salon.com provides a one- or two-line expansion under each of its headlines. For instance, after the headline, "Pope Francis slams super salaries for the rich while the poor survive on 'crumbs,'" Salon included the following:

> Growing inequality requires "timely rethinking of our models of economic development and . . . a change in lifestyle." (McDonough, 2013)

In this case, the story is about a speech, so the quote in the explanatory deck seems especially appropriate. The sentence doesn't really summarize the story, but it provides more details about what the pope said.

Online News Stories Link to Other Information

While you're researching a news story, keep in mind what other information might be relevant or useful to readers:

- If your news story deals with a report, it's helpful to link to the actual report website so your readers have a chance to check details for themselves.

- If you're reporting about a story that appeared elsewhere in the news—when the *Washington Post* and the *Guardian* first reported the leaks about U.S. surveillance in the summer of 2013, for instance—you should link to those stories.

- If your news story deals with a speech, it's helpful to link to video or a transcript of the speech.

- If your news story is an ongoing story or if it's especially complex, it's often helpful to link to earlier stories on your news site.

It's easy to provide too many links—by taking readers to, say, the Federal Aviation Administration home website simply because your story mentions the organization, or the White House website if President Obama's name is in your story. Think in terms of what's useful to your audience—and if your story has more than three or four links, take a close look to be sure they are all helpful, relevant and necessary.

You should also be aware of the kind of site your story links to—whether it's another news story from your own organization, say, or the original data your story is about. In general, the sites you link to fall into several categories:

- They may connect to websites with actual reports, data or other information (say, a U.S. Census website, or the Bureau of Labor Statistics website).

- They may connect to stories from other news sites.

- They may connect to other media on the same news site, such as audio or video of raw interviews.

- Or they may connect to other stories from the same news site—either archival or current.

In any of these examples, a reporter needs to be sure that she or he is connecting to a reputable source. Although reporters might go to Wikipedia as a starting point for research, they don't typically connect readers to this site because it's not a primary source, and its information might be outdated. And while you might link readers to a BBC or CNN story that did the original reporting on an issue or for video your news site can't provide, you wouldn't typically link them to the Drudge Report for factual information because it's a website based primarily on opinion, and it doesn't have a good reputation for credibility. And you wouldn't link readers to a Facebook page or tweet that appeared on Twitter unless you were sure of the person or organization behind the information. Journalists are not usually *legally* responsible for the credibility of the sites they link to, but they are *ethically* responsible. Just as is true for your own reporting, you don't want to contribute to the echo chamber of rumors and unauthenticated information.

Keep an eye on the overall patterns in your stories: Are you only linking readers to stories on your own news site? If so, you might want to do a little more research about what else is out there. Or, if you seldom link to stories reported by your own news organization, you probably should do a little more research in the archives so you can provide your readers with a better sense of the local history and context of an issue.

Online News Stories Are More Likely to Use Subheadings

This is true for long print stories, too, but it's helpful to divide your online stories into chunks of a few paragraphs each, with subheadings that let your readers know the focus of each chunk.

For instance, Bloomberg News uses very short subheadings just to give a sense of the focus of each section of a news story. In a story about a drop in foreclosures, a subhead announces that "Foreclosures Plummet," and details the drop in foreclosures in the next three paragraphs. Another subhead, "Florida's Turnaround," leads into a section about the state with the highest foreclosure rate, and "Jacksonville Prices" transitions into the section about one city in Florida where house prices were rising (Bloomberg News, 2013).

The Center for Investigative Reporting's story about a nursing assistant who was never punished after multiple allegations of physical abuse includes subheads with slightly more explanation: "Employees offer conflicting stories," "Delay in contacting police," and "No charges filed" (Gabrielson, 2013). Here, the subheads help to tell the story.

How do you decide where to use subheads? If your story is longer than 10 to 12 paragraphs, you should at least consider using them. Look at the section about pods in Chapter 13 for a discussion about how to group information in creating stories; you might try providing a subhead for each pod. If you're really struggling to decide how many you might need, try providing one subhead for every four to eight paragraphs.

And what should your subheads look like? Ideally, these provide a little more information than the two-word headings Bloomberg provides, but not much. Three to five words is usually plenty ("White House remodel is a statement"). It's okay to use a noun phrase ("Frequent remodels"), although a verb can make your subhead more dynamic ("Every president remodels"). Again, think of your audience: Does your subheading help someone who's skimming?

Conclusion

The medium for which you are writing will influence how you tell any story. But what's most important for journalists to learn about telling news stories are the characteristics shared across platforms: The story starts with the most important information, quotes appear early on in a story to develop sources' "characters" for readers, background details establish setting, and the narrative explains what happened, how and why.

Exercises for Chapter 5

EXERCISE 5-1: Search the student-run news site at three schools other than your own. Do they use multimedia elements? If so, list how. Is anything particularly effective? Are there any ideas you could localize?

EXERCISE 5-2: Begin a log for yourself where you take note of how news sites use the different media and which media work best for what kind of information. Start by going to a news site such as that of *The New York Times,* PBS' *Frontline* or *The Christian Science Monitor*—although any number of news sites will work. Look for a multimedia package and study it thoroughly.

a. List the various media the package incorporates.

b. Briefly describe the content of each element.

c. What, if anything, do you find effective?

d. Can you think of other elements that would add to the package?

If you keep up this log, over time you will get a sense of what each medium offers, and this can help you conceive of your own multimedia package.

EXERCISE 5-3: Using the fact sets in Chapter 4 exercises, write a 20-second radio news story. Be able to explain why you prioritized the information you did, and why you chose to include—or exclude—particular details.

EXERCISE 5-4: Using the fact sets in Chapter 4 exercises, write a 30-second voice-over television news story. Using the two-column format like in the PBS example, write the audio in caps in the right column. In the left column, describe some visuals that would run at the same time. Does adding the visual element change the audio choices you make?

EXERCISE 5-5: Suppose you're part of a team doing a package on common stressors for first-year students.

    a. Search the archives of other colleges or universities that have addressed common stressors for first-year students or something similar.

    b. What related issues would you want to address? Make a list of these issues.

    c. Make a list of questions you'd want to answer in this package.

    d. Brainstorm about how various media could help tell the story.

    e. In writing, pitch your plan as specifically as possible.

EXERCISE 5-6: Suppose you're part of a team doing a package on where students' tuition and fees go, from the moment they pay.

    a. Search the archives of other schools that have addressed where students' tuition and fees go, or a related subject.

    b. What related issues would you want to address? Make a list of these issues.

    c. Make a list of questions you'd want to answer in this package.

    d. Brainstorm about how various media could help tell the story.

    e. In 500 to 750 words, describe your plan as specifically as possible.

BACKGROUND FOR
YOUR
STORIES

Habits of Mind

Journalists are gatekeepers of information: They help point readers and viewers to what is important, and what is accurate and relevant. This role has shifted from the historical one in which journalists decided what information people might or might not see in the first place. As the Internet has exponentially increased ordinary citizens' ability to participate in reporting news, journalists and nonjournalists alike have much more, and quicker, access to information—and misinformation.

When protesters toppled their governments in Tunisia and Egypt in 2011, analysts wondered how big a role the Internet—and, specifically, social media like Twitter and Facebook—had played in the revolutions. People set up rally times and places via Twitter, and they communicated information to each other on Twitter and Facebook. With the help of the Internet, they were able to discuss ideas and to discover that many people agreed with them. But were the social media essential to the 2011 Arab Spring—a movement that initially seemed to be leading to the birth of much more democratic societies? Or were people already on the brink of demanding more democratic governments, and would they have pushed for revolutions regardless of the new technology?

These issues have important implications for journalism, because they also raise questions about whether something radically different is shaping how people communicate the news. The Arab Spring protests are especially significant because, at least in their initial phases, they spoke to the larger purposes of journalism in a democracy: freedom, justice and people seeking a voice in their own government.

Figure 6-1 summarizes several views of the role played by social media in the Arab Spring protests and revolutions, as described by communications scholar Deen Freelon. We see a bit of truth in each of these views. Some people did seem to overstate the role of the Internet in the 2011 revolutions, but the Internet still provided more access to the powerless, a new platform for spreading ideas and a way for untrained journalists to report on unfolding events. And many analysts agree that while the Internet did not *cause* the protests and revolutions in the Middle East, it did *speed up* and *facilitate* these movements (Kirchner, 2011).

Of course, people have always had avenues outside the news to communicate information—using copy machines to print fliers or posters, or sending messages through the mail or using the telegraph. But the Internet has shifted the kind of participation nonjournalists can have. Jeff Jarvis, a media consultant, articulates one of the strengths for which Internet journalism is often praised: "With the Internet, we all have printing presses and broadcast towers. No one has to beg anyone for access anymore" (Farhi, 2006, p. 40).

FIGURE 6-1 Deen Freelon, a communications scholar, classified views about technology's role in the Arab protests into four groups. He said the first group saw the Internet as giving a greater advantage to those who had traditionally had fewer resources and less power. The second group saw the Internet as providing a public sphere to discuss their ideas in a new way, and the third group saw the Internet as allowing untrained journalists to participate in reporting the news. The fourth group saw the Internet as a "revolutionary nicety"—as something that didn't contribute much, since after all there were successful revolutions against tyrannical governments long before the Internet existed (2011).

Ordinary citizens can report issues that the main-stream news media omits, or that corporations or people in power might be less likely to report. Such **citizen journalists**—people who are typically untrained and unpaid volunteer news gatherers—are often on the scene before trained news reporters have time to make it there.

A person whose house is in a hurricane's path is already at the news site, while reporters have to travel there. A protester in Syria may have close-up video of military attacks when international reporters have been excluded from the country. Such firsthand observations have always been a valuable part of the news. What's different now is that those reports are more often transmitted to the public without the filter of a professional news reporter. At best, information gets out more quickly under this scenario, and professional news organizations follow up by confirming facts and providing more in-depth reporting.

Analysts have also noted, however, that the Internet can be used to intentionally spread misinformation. For instance, hackers used the Associated Press Twitter account in 2013 to say—falsely—that President Obama had been injured in two explosions at the White House. And government operatives in Sudan have created fake Facebook protests in order to arrest whole gatherings of protesters.

> The digital age has made journalism's principles more important—not less. These ethical dilemmas are now the province of anyone who wants to produce news—even only momentarily in special circumstances—and of everyone who consumes it. Ethics is no longer just the concern of professionals.
>
> *KELLY MCBRIDE & TOM ROSENSTIEL, MEDIA ETHICISTS*

The Internet can be manipulated and misused by those in power, just as they have done with other media.

So what does this mean for journalists? In the past, media owners and journalists played a stronger role as society's **gatekeepers** of information—the people who decided what information passed through the gates of the news media, which sources were given a voice, what topics garnered attention. But because many more people have greater access to information, powerful media owners don't have the same kind of control they once did. Sources can sometimes reach wide audiences directly, without going through the news media. But—and it's important to remember this—gatekeeping still plays a crucial role (Fig. 6.2). It's just a more nuanced one. And journalists continue to influence what people know about their communities and the world. That means that journalists must constantly make gatekeeping decisions.

When you begin reporting, you'll notice that only a fraction of the information available actually makes it into your story. Furthermore, any particular story is only one of the myriad possible stories that could be told. Journalists decide what information makes it into individual stories. People need to know what's important from a meeting, without all the procedural business and daily minutiae. They need to know about potentially life-threatening conditions, about changes in the government or legal system that affect their lives, about financial news, science and ideas. They must be able to rely on journalists to provide information that is accurate and not based on false or unsubstantiated rumors.

FIGURE 6-2 Journalists must assess sources and information to make sure that what's presented is credible and accurate.

This role of gatekeeping is essential, but with so much at stake, it's easy to see why journalists have been criticized: for not only deciding what seemed truthful, but for sometimes making choices undemocratically and for too often focusing on wealthy or powerful sources while keeping out the poor and the powerless. In the 2012 U.S. presidential election, for instance, a voter might easily have been surprised to see the names of Libertarian Party candidate Gary Johnson, Constitution Party candidate Virgil Goode or Green Party candidate Jill Stein on a ballot. That's because the news media did very little reporting on presidential candidates other than those fielded by the Democrats and Republicans. But both Stein and Johnson had their names on ballots in enough states to gain the electoral votes to win the presidency, at least theoretically. Would nominees from other parties have a better chance at being elected if the news media included a few other candidates? If so, that seems a very powerful gatekeeping role to grant the press.

As people's use of the Internet has become more sophisticated, so has their participation in the news conversation. For instance, not only do journalists help determine what people are talking about, but they also influence the hierarchy of news—which of the issues is most important. But social media have allowed untrained journalists to filter the information, and to play a larger role in deciding what other people read. For instance, social media sites like Reddit allow the audience to say which websites or posts are most interesting. This means that readers can easily turn to a website of audience votes to decide what news stories to read for the day, rather than letting ABC News or NPR decide for them.

In the excitement about these changes in communication technology and its possibilities, journalists shouldn't lose their sense of perspective. New media existed before the Internet, and with each of these a period of freedom has been followed by more rigid control of the new medium. The Internet and its subsets are tools created by people, and people make mistakes. Reporters need to understand the Internet—not necessarily Internet protocols, bits or computer language, but rather the idea of how it works and why. You'll learn about that in the following chapters, and you'll start to learn about how to navigate the Internet as a journalist.

A Bit of Internet History

You can find out the names of world leaders and diplomats with a quick Internet search, and you can learn where most of them are living or traveling today—and maybe where they ate dinner last night. You can do the same for Beyoncé, Albert Pujols or Warren Buffet, to name a few. It's also easy to learn embarrassing information: You can see the nude photos of Prince Harry in Las Vegas, or videos of Charlie Sheen's very public meltdowns in 2011.

This kind of information about places around the world *right now* has never been available before, nor have so many people had such extraordinary access to information.

FIGURE 6-3 Two programmers stand in front of the ENIAC, which was one of the first computers.

It's easy to think of the Internet as a place—like an information superhighway, as it was once called—where facts and videos and pictures are exchanged, games can be played with strangers, possessions can be bought or sold. But the Internet was created by people, and continues to be improved, limited, fixed and misused by people. The fact that the people who invented the Internet's precursor in the early 1960s were a small, tight-knit group of computer scientists with particular goals has repercussions for how people are still connecting online today (Fig. 6-3).

One of the first key groups of computer scientists came together because of a U.S. government project: the U.S. Department of Defense's Advanced Research Projects Agency. ARPA, as it was called, was developed in the context of the 1960s and early 1970s Cold War between the United States and what was then the Soviet Union.

The main focus for ARPANET—the precursor to the Internet—was to provide backups in case of nuclear war: If the United States were bombed, military leaders wanted functioning communications networks in place. That initial goal, and the organization behind it, meant that the system's redundancy and survival were prioritized over such commercial concerns as privacy or the security of individual sites, as well as making them user-friendly for consumers and reasonably priced.

ARPANET's initial connection of a few computers at different locations laid the foundation, but what made the Internet workable across nations was the invention of a **protocol** allowing computers and smaller networks to connect with each other. Odds are, the computers you use to access the Internet all use the Internet protocol developed by Internet pioneers Robert Kahn and Vint Cerf. When Tim Berners-Lee, a British engineer working with other computer scientists at M.I.T., added hypertext language to produce Web pages, a transfer protocol and URLs (uniform resource locators) to that protocol, the World Wide Web was born. (The Internet is the network of interconnected computers and computer networks; the Web, which is part of the Internet, is made up of digital pages that allow us to access it.)

Given its size and impact, the Internet is a surprisingly freewheeling and spontaneous medium. Internet historian Jane Abbate attributes this in part to the Internet's particular background: "the group that designed and built ARPA's networks was dominated by academic scientists, who incorporated their own values of collegiality, decentralization of authority, and open exchange of information into the system" (1999, p. 5). Berners-Lee felt very strongly about making his idea free to the public; he didn't apply for a patent or charge fees for it. And at least in its early stages, the medium has made it easier for large numbers of people of different classes and backgrounds to exchange ideas and information.

That means that as this unit examines how journalists find and evaluate information, the Internet will be central to our discussion. When untrained journalists participate in the conversation of news, journalists help to filter this part of the conversation for their audience. Ideally, journalists never try to control the conversation. Instead, they do everything they can to keep it healthy. They listen carefully to what people are saying, to news tips from strangers or sources, to complaints and criticisms—and then they go check these out before passing them on. Journalists minimize the spread of rumors through fact-checking and good contextual reporting. They help to minimize vitriol on news sites, while still allowing as many voices into the conversation as possible. And they admit only the best, most accurate and verifiable information into a story, while keeping out erroneous or frivolous information.

In this unit, we introduce you to conducting background research with a journalist's skeptical eye. We discuss how to assess the credibility of a website, a blog post, a tweet or other crowd-sourced piece of information, so that you can ensure its accuracy before you use it yourself. We also talk about the ownership of content, online and offline, so that you can avoid plagiarism and copyright infringement.

The chapters in this unit should help you sharpen your ability to discern the people behind websites and blogs—the content creators and owners and their agendas—and to evaluate their credibility.

CHAPTER 6

A JOURNALIST'S SKEPTICAL RESEARCH

Filtering for Accuracy: Two Examples

Journalists play a dual role in gathering facts: They are expected to filter through the massive amounts of information in places like the blogosphere, Internet searches, Twitter feeds or the rumor mill to find what's accurate and actually helpful for a general audience. They're also expected to know how to seek out good information in the first place. Two stories help to illustrate these essential roles.

When news of the Aurora theater shootings was breaking, the *Denver Post* used social media both to gather information and to keep people up to date. The *Post* won a 2013 Pulitzer Prize for the resulting coverage, including its Twitter posts. From the tweets in Box 6-1, you might notice the repeated requests for witnesses such as this one:

> "Were you at the Aurora #theatershooting? We need to talk to you. Please reply, email newsroom@denverpost.com or call 303-954-1300."

BOX 6-1

USING SOCIAL MEDIA TO REPORT BREAKING NEWS

Figure 6-4 shows an excerpt from the *Denver Post*'s tweets during the Aurora theater shootings. The *Post* received a Pulitzer Prize for its reporting, including its Twitter coverage. Note the request for witnesses, as reporters try to gather more information. Also notice that even in the excitement of the moment, the reporters are using the medium to provide specific facts—as opposed to retweeting speculations—about what's going on.

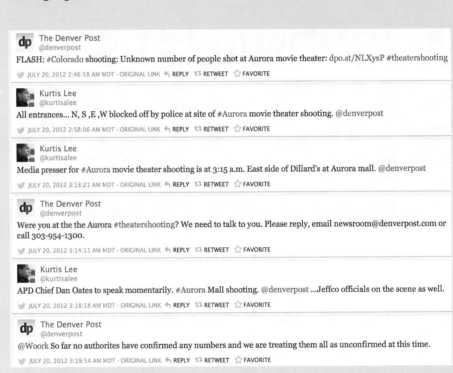

FIGURE 6-4

These call-outs were an efficient way for the *Post* to reach sources who had witnessed the tragedy firsthand, and they resulted in much stronger reporting for the news organization.

More and more frequently, social media users are the first to publicize breaking news. After users report that an event has happened, professional journalists provide verification, and further details, depth and context. At best, the two kinds of newsgathering work together: Citizen journalists contribute timely information, and professional journalists follow up with important—and fact-checked—details.

The *Post* reporters' tweets about the Aurora shootings sometimes reveal a cautious approach to what they were hearing on the street: "So far no authorities have confirmed any numbers and we are treating them all as unconfirmed at this time." More than two hours later, the *Post* finally provided those numbers, attributing the estimates of the number of people wounded and dead to a police officer. This meant that the *Post* didn't repeat wild rumors or unsourced guesses about how many people were affected by the tragedy.

Contrast that caution with something that happened during another tragedy, the Boston Marathon bombings. While police were still trying to find out who might be responsible for the crime, many people got caught up in the frenzy of the hunt. This included CNN, Fox News, the Associated Press and the *New York Post*, all of which incorrectly reported the arrests of people who were not suspects.

A particularly egregious mistake happened when one social media organization attempted to help: A Reddit user started a thread, FindBostonBombers, to try to use **crowdsourcing**—soliciting information from citizen journalists—to find the culprits. Users in that subgroup posted photos of people they said looked suspicious. Several innocent people, including a university student who had been missing for a month, were named as suspects or even as criminals. The Reddit general manager, Erik Martin, eventually apologized for the harm to innocent people. And in an interview with the *Atlantic Wire*, the user who started the thread said the following:

> When someone on Reddit says something is suspicious, it's no different from someone on the street saying it. There's a big difference between journalistic integrity and the opinion of some guy on Reddit. Reddit should never ever ever be used as a source, unless there's actually some proof there. It's no different from a newspaper printing "a guy on the street said, 'My mate told me that this guy is a bomber.'"(Abad-Santos, 2013, para. 14)

Journalists shouldn't repeat—or retweet—information they haven't carefully verified.

You can see that the effects of using unfiltered sources are mixed. On one hand, citizen journalists can often provide varied information more quickly than traditional journalists. On the other hand, they can create an echo chamber for incorrect information, increasing its damaging effects. Mistakes—and their harmful effects—are amplified by the fact that people are able to pass information along so quickly.

Unfiltered sources have always been around, but the social media and the Internet itself have led to a rapid rise in their influence. This rise is a force journalists now have to reckon with. They can learn about breaking news events from the social media, and they can build on the work of citizen journalists to get accurate information to an audience quickly. Professional journalists must verify information from citizen journalists—or in the rare cases when this is not possible, note that they haven't. Good journalists must know where to look, how to look and when to double-check. Learning to find and evaluate information is a skill you can apply in using social media or apps or doing online searches—or anywhere in your reporting (Fig. 6-5).

FIGURE 6-5 A journalist sifts through information to find useful, relevant facts—the way a person might pan for gold.

Time to Start Searching

In your role as a journalist, you're more likely to be frustrated by the overwhelming amount of information than by its limits, at least at first. Let's say you're assigned a story about Facebook privacy at your university. The assignment asks you to **localize** a national issue by reporting on how it involves or affects people in your area. Of course you'll be interviewing local sources, but you'll need background information first. That means you'll include the Internet in your research—but if you're not careful, you may be swamped. When we typed *Facebook privacy* into the search box in the spring of 2014, a Bing search brought up 169,000,000 results. You can narrow the search with more specific terms—you might start with *"Facebook privacy" and university campuses*, which dropped the number of results to 42,800 in our sample search.

You also need to know what's already been published locally about the issue you're covering, and what specific local concerns have surfaced in the past. That's why,

FIGURE 6-6

when you are given an assignment, your first move should be to read or watch the archived stories from your own news organization. Those stories provide information and context (Fig. 6-6). Depending on the topic, you may want to do a keyword search and look at several years of coverage. Perhaps you discover, for instance, that the campus erupted in controversy two years ago when police checked Facebook and then used that knowledge to raid a party where students were using illegal drugs. At this juncture, you could track the story to learn what happened to the students involved in the raid and whether campus authorities changed their policies concerning their own use of Facebook.

No matter where you're searching, you should take notes and you may want to save a couple of key stories. This is one of the ways that reporters develop an understanding about which issues are newsworthy. When you interview sources for a related story and they mention, for instance, that campus police keep a careful eye on Facebook, you'll know that this issue might have particular resonance for your audience because of previous conflicts.

As you read through past news coverage, remember that this job is background research. You never know what errors a journalist made in the initial reporting. And even when the original story gets corrected, other websites may pick up the story without realizing it includes a factual error. That means it's essential to verify all information that you use in your story.

Searching the Internet

SEARCH ENGINE INSIGHTS

Your search for background information about an issue will probably lead you to an Internet search engine such as Bing, Google or Yahoo! You can approach these with a little more sophistication by using the extra filters provided by the search engines. On Google, for instance, you can do the following:

- Click on "Search Tools" and filter results by time, making sure you only get results from, say, the past week, or limiting your search to a custom range of dates.

- Limit your results through Search Tools by typing in your location—or the location of a breaking news event.

- Use characters in the search box to filter results. For instance, using a minus sign before a phrase can help eliminate an unrelated but common usage. If you were searching for information about Halloween but didn't want information about the movie, you could type in: *Halloween −movie*. Or, if you were researching race information about the Boston Marathon for a sports story, you might type something like the following into the search box:

    Boston Marathon −explosion −bombing −suspect

- Use an asterisk as a placeholder in an exact-phrase search. This is helpful if you can't remember a particular word, phrase or name:

    Diary of * Frank

- Look up Google's Advanced Search to find the latest or more search functions (other search engines use similar phrasing and have some of the same functions).

Search engines are handy tools, but flawed. That's because the value of an efficient search engine isn't based on *finding* information but *ranking* it. Clearly, search engines are not objective or neutral. In fact, there are companies whose primary purpose is to help organizations improve their website ranking with Google and other search engines. While it's often a good idea to begin with a search engine or to use such a search for background, a professional reporter uses a more sophisticated method of finding news.

WEBSITES FOR JOURNALISTS

One place reporters can begin is at a site set up specifically for journalists. For instance, the Society of Professional Journalists maintains the Journalist's Toolbox (http://www.journaliststoolbox.org/). Some of the site's links help you find information more efficiently. Under "Mobile Journalism" in the column on the left—when we went to press—you could scroll down to "Recommended Apps for Journalists" for a list of some handy apps ranging from one that helps you listen to live police or other emergency radio to an app that helps you look up public documents and other information by ZIP code.

The site also provides links that deal with journalism as a profession: A "Journalism Jobs" section links to job search databases and resources. There's also a "Design/Visual Journalism" category with links to design contests, instruction and free software for maps and charts. Other categories provide links to information and databases for particular story subjects, based on current newsworthy topics or ongoing coverage areas.

If you were doing a story about the local economy and wanted to provide context in your story by showing how your state or city compared to others, you might start by looking under the Journalist's Toolbox heading "Business Resources." One link, "Consumer Price Index," leads to the federal government's Bureau of Labor Statistics, which provides the most recent regional consumer price index—and maps with regional and national comparisons, definitions of the CPI and how it is calculated, as well as unemployment figures, wage statistics and so on. You could provide your audience with graphics that show visually what's going on regionally. You could find out more specifically which parts of the local economy were suffering or prospering— perhaps tourism has dipped, but local industries are doing well, or maybe the jobless rate is better than in other parts of the country, but local prices are higher compared to salaries. These kinds of context and statistics create a story with real information, in contrast to one that simply quotes local chamber of commerce officials or real estate agents.

Such journalist-oriented sites are helpful because they are filtered with a reporter's needs in mind. Experienced reporters also look to other kinds of sites to provide context for routine stories. For instance, a vast collection of data is available at the U.S. Census website at www.census.gov. (The Mobile Apps Gallery site notes that there's an app for this site, too.) For a story about minimum wages, you might use this site's information to compare the average income in your home county to that in the rest of the state, or the rest of the nation. These figures are painstakingly accumulated across the country, and they give us some of the best numbers available about people in the United States.

Other federal, state and local government sites can also serve as excellent sources of information. The sites don't include all the information the government has, but they often have more than enough for a series of news stories.

WHAT DOES A JOURNALIST USE FROM THE WEB?

Good journalists turn to the Internet for facts and statistics that are likely to be more accurate online than elsewhere—or at least, *as* accurate as they would be elsewhere. Journalists should be fairly comfortable getting information from scientific studies, comprehensive plans, government reports and court documents online, as long as they get the information from primary sources. For instance, if you can look at an actual court case, the information about what was said is more likely to be accurate than someone's memory of the event. The Internet is probably the best place to look for a regional comprehensive plan proposed by the U.S. Forest Service. And there's a good chance that the U.S. Geological Survey's website on river levels over the years is the best place to go for the most comprehensive data on changing river levels. If it's relevant to your story to use an organization's mission statement or rules, you're probably going to get those from the organization's website.

In most cases, you would also talk with human sources, as they can interpret and explain in a way that bare data can't. As a journalist, you need to think about how you can get the best facts, and how to make sure that you're not pulling them out of context.

As you comb the Internet for information, it's important that you continue to take a reporter's critical approach, prioritizing truth telling and accuracy. Journalists do *firsthand* reporting. That means you wouldn't quote from, say, a Google News report on Afghanistan, because that's secondhand information. Under normal conditions, a journalist wouldn't quote a CNN news feed or someone else's blog. This might very well be helpful information, but you don't know how accurate it is until you check it out for yourself. That's why so much of what you gather online will simply be background material for a news story and you'll have to verify everything for yourself before you include it in a story. You'll also want to be sure that websites you do quote from are from credible sources.

Website Credibility

Websites are created by people in real time, and good reporters retain an awareness of who the people are behind any particular site, whether they really are who they say they are, what their motivation is in writing about an issue, whether they can speak with authority on the subject and how accurate and timely their information is (Fig. 6-7).

IDENTITY AND MOTIVATION

One of the first ways you can get a hint about the identity of a site's creator is through the URL. If the address ends in "gov," there's a good chance it's an official government site and therefore may have sufficient authority for you to use as a reference or even to quote, depending on the type of information and the kind of story you're writing. If the URL ends in "org," the site is often a nonprofit organization. If it ends in "edu," the site creator is probably affiliated with a college or university. This may mean the

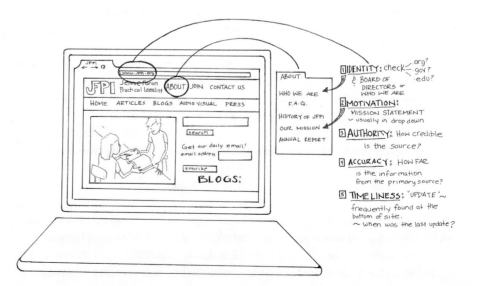

FIGURE 6-7 Checking website credibility.

author is a professor or researcher with expertise in the field—or it may mean the author is a student who created the site for a class project. If the site's name ends in "net" or "com," it's probably a commercial site, created for a private business. Checking the URL is important because it can give you an indication of whose agenda a site is promoting.

But the URL is just the first step in finding out who created a site. You need to be careful of sites pretending to be something they are not. For instance, a website that *looked* like the official World Economic Forum in 2010 linked viewers to video clips of world leaders. One of these featured Queen Elizabeth II addressing the forum with the following:

> My government's overriding priority is to ensure the stability of the crown's land-holdings taken in colonial economic dominance. My landholdings are essential in ranking me as the very richest individual today. The source of our financial treasure was a violent plundering of the southern hemisphere. Going forward, legislation will commence to allocate some of my lands to ensure fairer, more just distribution for those victimized and to improve the livelihoods of the world's poor. (Yes Men, 2010)

While the video actually does portray the queen, her words were dubbed in by a group called the Yes Men, as were those of other world leaders in similar video clips on the site.

If you go to www.whitehouse.net, the Web page that will appear on your screen is not affiliated with the official site of the White House. It's a parody site—now dated, but still active when we went to press—and if you refresh your browser, this is easy to tell. But not all sites make it so easy for readers to determine whether the author is who he or she pretends to be. This is one of the reasons that we urge extreme caution in quoting from websites.

Once you're sure that a site is legitimate, you'll need to find out the agenda or motivation behind the site's owner. At most credible websites for organizations, you can click on a button that says something like "about us," or "mission statement." Here, you'll usually find a quick description of the organization, and often a sense of its official mission or purpose.

One place to look for additional information about an organization is its board of directors. Most websites have a link for "board of directors," or a similar button. For instance, if you go to the website of CBS News, you can click on the "About CBS" button at the bottom of the page, and, at the top of the next page under the "About CBS" tab, click on "Board of Directors." As you read through the capsule biographies, note what other jobs and directorships each member of the board holds. Why do you think a particular person might have been selected? Are there patterns that emphasize particular agendas rather than experience in the relevant field?

AUTHORITY

Once you determine who created a site, whether that person or group is who they pretend to be and what their motivation is in providing information, you still need to think about what authority lies behind that information. A biographical site about Cesar Chavez created by a college student may include correct information, but that student writes with little authority. How would you know whether the student had any background in migrant worker issues, was trained in proper research skills and had the time to apply those skills—or plagiarized from other sources and took short-cuts in doing the work? Although professional historians make mistakes and some have even been known to plagiarize, you have some assurance that they were trained in historical research, that others have overseen some of their previous work and that they have some background knowledge in the field.

What makes scholarly research reliable is that it is conducted for the public good and the public store of information. Researchers are expected to follow rigorous methods for a piece to be accepted by the scholarly community. The most reliable research is subjected to peer review, where several experts independently review a piece to make sure that the method used, the data collected and the conclusions reached meet high standards. Scholarly research that's publicly funded should be especially immune from interference. However, over the course of many years, government funding for public knowledge has decreased, leaving private enterprise to pick up in its place. That's one reason you have to be vigilant even with research that originates at colleges and universities.

As you think about whether a particular source has authority, remember that government sites are often created with the public good in mind, rather than a narrow agenda or self-promotion—although this is not always the case. Nonprofits *sometimes* pursue community goals, but you have to keep in mind that nonprofit status can be used to screen a political or religious agenda. And an organization with an explicitly stated bias can still serve as an authoritative source on some issues. Try this: Go to the Volunteers of America's website. Under "About Us," click on a link to "Our Ministry of Service," and you'll see a few details about the Volunteers of America's religious focus:

> In addition to being one of the nation's largest and most comprehensive human services organizations, Volunteers of America is an interdenominational church—a church with a distinctive ministry of service ... Many of Volunteers of America's religious beliefs and practices can be traced in a direct line to the Methodist reforms and revivalism of the 18th century, and the social gospel movement of the 19th and early 20th centuries. (Volunteers of America, 2013b)

Despite its explicitly stated biases, the Volunteers of America provides some of the best information available about the homeless and people in need:

> At Volunteers of America, we are more than a nonprofit organization. We are a ministry of service that includes nearly 16,000 paid, professional employees dedicated to helping those in need rebuild their lives and reach their full potential. (Volunteers of America, 2013a)

It's a journalist's job to seek out biases such as these and make a reasoned judgment about how accurate information from a source will be on a particular issue. Even after you determine that a source is trustworthy, you still need to include enough background about the organization to let your audience confirm that decision for themselves.

ACCURACY

The likelihood that a site provides accurate information is closely related to its sources. The most important factor to consider is how far the information is from the original, or primary source of information. The further away from the primary source, the higher the probability that errors have been introduced.

In those few cases where you actually use information directly from a website—government statistics, for instance, or perhaps an organization's mission statement, when that's relevant to the news—you'll need to double- or even triple-check that you've copied the information down correctly and credited the source. This is standard procedure for scientists in the field, and it's also standard for journalists. Good journalists incorporate a systematic procedure into their practice. That's how reporters serve their audiences well and preserve their own reputations for accuracy. You can do the first check when you copy down the information. Look again at the original and make sure it matches your notes. When you're completing your story, do a third check: Does the information in your story match your notes? This method seems painstaking at first, and it does involve extra work and thought. But eventually it should become an almost unconscious routine—and it's part of what sets journalism apart as an especially valuable set of skills.

TIMELINESS

Timeliness is often linked to accuracy. For instance, information that was deemed accurate in 1960 or even last year may have been corrected or modified since then. Pay attention to how recent a website's information is. The U.S. Census is updated every 10 years, so you know that although national comparison figures may be one or two years old, they may be the most recent available. However, you might still be able to find specific local information or data from other organizations that's more recent.

When you talk with a human source, you usually have a good sense of how recent her or his information is. Is it based on a recently released report, last night's meeting or an incident that happened a year ago? This is often trickier to determine from a website. Still, reporters have several ways to search for how recent website information is:

- You can start by checking for the date when the site was last updated at the bottom or top of the Web page.
- If there's no date, you can sometimes get an idea of how recent information is by noting the dates in the content. If something that happened in 2014 is mentioned, for instance, you know the site was probably updated at least that recently.
- Look for links to other sites and make sure these are "live."
- You can look for contact information and email a staff member.

> Not only can the past never really be erased; it co-exists, in cyberspace, with the present, and an important type of context is destroyed.
>
> *JONATHAN DEE, NOVELIST AND NONFICTION WRITER*

Keep in mind that it's harder to tell how recent information is online than it is in the offline world. Authors may update parts of a website and not others. Events that happened long ago can appear more recent online. A mistake or an urban myth on the Internet often lives on long past the time such information is easily available offline. Hoaxes or false rumors may get corrected once—or twice or ten times—and still show up in current blog posts, websites or the latest set of forwarded emails.

BLOGS AND AGGREGATOR SITES

Blogs written from a journalist's point of view, just like editorials, focus on opinions rather than independently verifiable information. Although a reporter may write both news stories and a blog, a blog is commonly thought of as more of a diary or commentary.

Blogs can add new angles and information not available elsewhere. If someone reads several good blogs, the format often allows for multiple opinions and voices, and it's often creative and even irreverent (see Chapter 14 for more about the difference in writing such blogs and standard news reporting). Blogs can provide helpful analysis and additional reporting, as in the case of talkingpointsmemo.com, which won the George Polk Award for its news reporting, or "drezner.foreignpolicy.com" named by *Time* magazine as one of the best 25 blogs of 2012 and written by international politics professor Daniel Drezner.

But rumors and unvetted information abound in the blogosphere. For one thing, blogs are typically composed by individuals working alone, which means there's no team double-checking information. As the Pew Research Center's Project for Excellence in Journalism pointed out in one of its *State of the News Media* reports, "Unlike a news organization where a group of minds is behind the selection of stories and the editing process, blogs are truly one-person shows" (2006, para. 3).

Blog journalism is like the subset of editorials, news analysis programs or opinion pages you'll find in other news media. That is, it provides a very valuable service, helpful information and a different angle on the news, but it's not held to the same standards as news stories. And news travels much faster in the world of blogs than it does through regular broadcast news or newspapers, so there's less time to confirm information and double-check for accuracy.

While bloggers often post their own opinions or stories based on anonymous tips, most of the news that shows up on blogs is usually produced elsewhere. That means that readers are getting their information from a secondary source. This is also true for **aggregator sites**, websites that compile information from other news organizations, although sites such as the Huffington Post and Yahoo News also provide news from their own reporters.

What does this mean for a journalist? Most journalists keep up to date on what's happening by checking several news sources, including aggregator sites, which also provide useful analysis and filtering. But keep in mind that on aggregator sites, you'll find blogs and news stories, which are not the same thing. The opinions and analysis in blogs may provide tips for you to follow up on. They are usually valuable in providing background knowledge and understanding and they are a great way to stay up to date on issues, trends or fields; but that's the extent of how you would use them as a journalist. When you start gathering information that goes into your news story, you must do your own firsthand reporting.

Social Media for Journalists

The social media like Facebook, Twitter, LinkedIn or Instagram are a subset of the Internet. They introduce an additional filter that can be especially useful to journalists. For instance, the information about a particular professional may already be available on the Internet, but you can find that information on LinkedIn more quickly. That filtering and grouping of like information makes the social media a good place to get story tips and sources. They are also a powerful and efficient way for journalists to communicate with their audience.

News agencies often use the social media—right now, they're most likely to use Twitter or Facebook—to reach out during a big news event to find people who might have been affected. For instance, after Hurricane Sandy, news agencies turned to the social media to find people who had lost power or had to leave their homes; after the Boston Marathon bombing, news organizations asked for people who had been close to the explosions to contact them.

Journalists also use the social media for enterprise stories. For instance, after a factory fire in Bangladesh killed 1,200 people in 2013, more factory workers are using social media to communicate about poor or unsafe conditions—making it easier for journalists to follow up and report those to the public. Or if you're doing a story about a downturn in the economy, you could reach out on Twitter to ask for people who had lost their jobs or homes or might have other related stories to tell.

As they do for any other information gathering, journalists have to be careful not to be fooled by misinformation through these media (Fig. 6-8).

By the time you're a working journalist—and as you move along in your career—a new set of social media, apps or some other kind of filters will have superseded at least some of those that are most popular now. Realizing that social media are in a state of flux doesn't make your knowledge about them irrelevant, however. If you know the ins and outs of how a good journalist uses a current social medium, you're more likely to be good at applying a journalist's skeptical approach to whatever comes next. A journalist should know how to use each new medium or filter to find information and sources, and also how to step back and look at it critically.

When you use either Facebook or Twitter, you have to ascertain for yourself that a source is the person she or he claims to be. In its early coverage of the 2011 Tucson massacre, CNN went to Facebook for a picture of the suspected killer, Jared Lee Loughner. Unfortunately, the photo CNN aired was *not* of Loughner, but of another young man who was unconnected with the crime.

How can you avoid repeating a mistake like this? For Facebook, you can look at a user's bulletin board if it's public. You'd expect friends to be reacting in some way if

FIGURE 6-8 This photo was widely circulated on the Internet during Hurricane Sandy in 2012, supposedly showing the hurricane arriving in New York City. Snopes.com, a fact-checking website, says that's false: "This one is indeed a real image, but not one of Hurricane Sandy: it's a photograph of an April 2011 thunderstorm in New York City taken through a tinted window" ("Hurricane Sandy Photographs," n.d.).

the person involved is accused of being involved in a major crime; you might also try contacting Facebook friends to confirm that the page you're examining does, in fact, belong to that person.

In general, you'll need to take a journalist's skeptical approach to online identities. How do you do this? The following list uses Twitter as an example of the kind of critical analysis you can apply to the social media to verify someone's identity:

- You can start by checking how long someone has had a Twitter account at http://www.howlonghaveyoubeentweeting.com/. If the account just started up yesterday or last week, you'd be suspicious of that person's information.

- You can check how often a person tweets. A person who sets up a Twitter account as part of a hoax might not have much Twitter activity. If this is the person's first tweet or if he hasn't tweeted for months, that might be a reason to be more skeptical.

- You can also check who and how many people he follows, and who and how many people follow him. If these people or organizations are outlandish or extreme—or if they are especially trustworthy—that can give you some clues to the person's interests and credibility.

- Twitter account users have an option to include a photo. If an account includes a photo of a real human being, it's not proof that that's the person but it provides another clue.

- If the account user makes his or her name public, you can use a search engine—perhaps paired with words like "spam" or "misinformation" to see what comes up.

- Whenever you can, call the person to verify. You can ask for more identifying details and you can ask the person to retell the story or events she has described on Twitter, and then listen for discrepancies. You can ask the person for other witnesses to contact and corroborate what she is saying.

- None of these checks alone guarantees someone's identity, but each helps. (Several of these tips are based on a presentation by Craig Silverman, who writes and teaches for the Poynter Institute, and Mandy Jenkins, former social media editor at the Huffington Post and now interactives director at Digital First Media, at the 2012 Online News Association Conference.) (Silverman & Jenkins, 2011)

Even after you have double-checked someone's identity, you need to think about the pool of sources you're querying. For instance, a Pew Research Center study found the following:

> Pinterest, the online pinboard, has attracted 15% of internet users to its virtual scrapbooking. Whites, young people, the well-educated, those with high income, and women are particularly likely to use the site. (Duggan & Brenner, 2013, para. 2)

You have to take into account that social media sites are not representative of the general population. This means that you need to resist the urge to simply send a request to your own Facebook friends for sources and information—because that too often means recruiting sources just like you.

Journalists have to be careful about how they solicit sources for a story. Just because you're addressing a general audience doesn't mean it's okay to push for a certain kind of answer or to be insensitive to potential sources. Just as you do for particular websites or any other kind of information, you should ask yourself the following questions:

- In what ways is this particular medium or filter less accurate than what I'm accustomed to? More accurate?

- What are its strengths for getting useful information to my audience efficiently?

- What are its weaknesses?

- How much of this device or filter's popularity among journalists is based on something helpful it has to offer in gathering or delivering news, and how much is based on its being the latest trendy technology?

EVALUATING SOCIAL MEDIA VIDEOS

As you saw with the video clip of Queen Elizabeth II, even photographs or videos can easily be faked or modified. In those rare cases when journalists are cut off from first-hand reporting, they have sometimes relied on video clips or photographs from social media. But they still bring a journalist's critical approach to these. Mark Little was one of the co-founders of Storyful, a site that helps users sort through and verify tweets and other online pieces. Little describes how this verification worked for a video clip early on during the 2011 protests in Egypt, when it was often difficult for international journalists to gain entry into the country:

> This video records the ebb and flow of a pitched battle between riot police and protestors on the Qasr al Nile bridge in Cairo. The video was shot by Mohamed Ibrahim el Masry, who was staying at a hotel overlooking the bridge.
>
> Our curators discovered the video on Facebook and quickly contacted Mohamed to confirm he was the original creator of this remarkable footage.
>
> The team used Google earth to check the location of the bridge and Mohamed's vantage point. Using social media channels Flickr and Panaramio, Storyful compared Mohamed's video with other user generated content shot on ground level. (Little, 2011)

After they verified the video, Little said the team asked Mohamed's permission to upload the video and share it with other news organizations. Just as they do for other information, journalists can take steps to help verify and confirm that photos or videos are what they claim to be:

- They can double-check satellite images or street maps to see that the background in an image matches the place where a photographer claims to have been.
- They can call to talk with the person who supposedly recorded a moment, and double-check the uploader's history.
- They can see who retweets a video or information, and how often.
- For videos in a foreign language, journalists can have interpreters confirm that people in the background are saying what someone says they are saying, and that the local accent matches that in a video.

In some cases, crowdsourcing can even help journalists determine that a particular set of information is fraudulent or incorrect. Journalists bring their skills of careful fact checking, source confirmation and independent verification to every medium.

Going Offline

Not all information is online. Sometimes, documents may be legally public but people are concerned that posting them on the Internet makes the information too easily available. For instance, do people really want everyone to have instant access to all the details of public court cases? Some states have chosen not to post marriage or birth records online, in order to provide some protection of people's privacy. A person can still go to the courthouse and request that information—this just takes more time and effort. Often, older documents are not scanned and made available on websites because the time and cost to do so would be prohibitive. Sometimes, a private business or even a government agency would rather people didn't find out about some information. And sometimes, information stays in hard copy form because that's the way it's always been done. As you research offline documents, you should take the same critical attitude in examining the source's identity, motivation, agenda and authority, as well as the timeliness of the data.

One of the important sources to keep in mind is the government. Which government records are available online differs from state to state, and information such as government meeting agendas or voter registration records may not be available online. Information recorded before the advent of the Internet, such as property sales or assessments, may not be online yet. Some state and government agencies keep certain public records, such as driver's license information or vehicle ownership records, off the Internet, although some of this information may still be available in paper form. Births, deaths, marriages and property transfers are all public information, although these records may or may not be available online. Such records can provide ways to check accuracy, to find out basic biographical information about an important but reluctant story subject or to learn information about business dealings of public interest.

Sometimes, a particular government agency's report may not be available online. While Congress provides Congressional Research Service Reports online to congressional offices, private citizens have to request these as paper copies. The full texts of Congressional hearings are available as paper copies, not online. Also, other documents that would allow you to check on an industry's past record—such as environmental compliance reports, for instance, or the personal records of a public person, such as that person's marriage certificate or college degree—may not be on the Internet.

As you acquire the knack of doing background research—whether online or offline—you'll start to develop a feel for why the journalist's approach is so valuable. A good reporter knows how to find information in the first place, but also brings an extra level of skepticism and critical analysis before presenting it as fact.

Exercises for Chapter 6

EXERCISE 6-1: Do a Google search on the term "jaguar." Analyze the types of results you get: Are they sponsored links and ads? Information about your term? Does the type of information change if you click on page 10? On page 20? Try the same search using a different search engine. Do you see any differences in the results? Any trends across search engines?

EXERCISE 6-2: Go to journaliststoolbox.org. Click on one of the categories, and, under that, a couple of links. Describe briefly the kind of information you can find there.

EXERCISE 6-3: Assume that you are assigned to create a news story about nutritional guidelines. For each of the following websites, apply the website evaluation criteria described in the chapter and discuss what kinds of information you should and should not obtain from that website for your story.

a. www.fda.gov

b. www.mcdonalds.com

c. www.OrganicValley.com

EXERCISE 6-4: Go to a website of your choice. Who created the site? Who are the main people responsible at the organization? How much can you find out about them from the site? Is this a credible organization in its field? What is its mission? How do you know? How far is the information from its primary source? When was the site last updated?

CHAPTER 7

PLAGIARISM AND COPYRIGHT INFRINGEMENT

Stealing Other People's Stuff

Plagiarism

As Cathy Resmer was reading through her blogroll one morning, she clicked on another blogger's site and read a paragraph about an upcoming Peking Acrobats show (Resmer, 2006). The paragraph looked very familiar: It had appeared as a calendar spotlight on *Seven Days*, the Vermont news site where Resmer was then a staff writer. "He had ripped off an entire spotlight," Resmer said (personal communication, January 6, 2010). What was more, the other blogger—who worked for *Explore New England*, managed by *The Boston Globe*—had failed to cite or link to *Seven Days*.

The original calendar post was relatively short, about 100 words, but it had involved staff time and labor. "Each of those calendar spotlights is written by our calendar person—and that's a full-time staff position—and then edited and proofread," said Resmer, who is now associate publisher at *Seven Days*. "It's not something we just put up on the Web. It goes through a pretty rigorous process" (2010). Resmer later learned

153

several other mini-reviews had been taken from the *Seven Days* blog and posted on the *Explore New England* blog, again, without any reference to the original.

Resmer tried to contact the blogger. When he didn't respond immediately, she called the blogger's editor. The offending posts were removed, the site itself was deleted and the blogger was let go.

The blogger who lifted the uncredited paragraphs from *Seven Days* was fired for **plagiarizing**: He was using other people's work without giving them proper credit (Fig. 7-1). Such credit—for being first with a story, for doing investigative journalism, for writing thoughtful or well-crafted pieces or for simply doing the work of ordinary, daily reporting—can be crucial in building a person's or a news organization's reputation, and it often translates into economic value. Resmer said that while it might be easy to think about the information on the Web as free, "We are paying someone to create that content, paying an editor to edit, and paying a proofreader to proofread it and paying a Web designer to put it up on the Web" (2010).

FIGURE 7-1 Plagiarizing is using someone else's work without giving proper credit, and that credit has real economic value.

This means the organizations that provide information have to make money in some way—through charging advertisers or subscribers or other news organizations, for instance. In fact, billions of dollars are generated through making such information available to the public.

Journalism leans much more heavily on original reporting than many other kinds of research. Because journalism depends on immediacy and timeliness, if your story's only sources are other websites, books and magazines, then your story is already dated. Other people's information is also not as close to the primary source, who may be able to provide updated information or further explanation.

If there's a tragic car accident that results in the death of a student at your university, you might be tempted to copy quotes from Facebook to use in a news story about the accident. But you don't have permission to use the quotes, and you may not know for sure that you've got the correct Facebook account. It's also hard to be sure that the information is current: What if someone doesn't update her or his information very often?

Or let's say there's a controversial change in zoning in your town, and you turn to a local historian's blog or book on the history of the county. Either one may serve you well for background information and context, but you'll probably get better historical information for your particular issue by setting up a live interview with the historian. If NBC News publishes a story about social welfare in Chicago, don't rely on that news site for your statistics. Call the sources or look up the information yourself.

There are two important exceptions to this rule of thumb: If another news organization broke the story, your story may need to refer to the original news piece, although you would still do your own, original research. The second exception to the rule that good journalists avoid relying on other news organizations as primary sources occurs when a news organization *is* the news. For instance, in a story about Nate Silver's *FiveThirtyEight* blog analyzing election statistics, a reporter might quote from the blog. Or in a story about Amazon CEO and founder Jeffrey Bezos' 2013 purchase of *The Washington Post,* a reporter might well quote from *The Washington Post.*

In a few rare cases, unethical journalists plagiarize consciously: They simply insert directly quoted material into their stories without using quotation marks or crediting the authors. But while such plagiarizing is easy to do, it's also easy to catch. Journalists have large audiences, and someone is likely to recognize material from the original and report it to the original author and the larger community.

Frequently, plagiarism problems are not intentional thefts. They are the result of inexperienced student reporters diligently researching the Internet for background information, and then cutting and pasting information into their notes. Sometimes, student journalists don't keep good track of what is quoted material and what they've already put into their own words. Sometimes, they read a phrase or sentence early on in their research, and by the time they start writing, that phrase feels like their own original writing.

FIGURE 7-2

AVOIDING PLAGIARISM IS A SKILL

The good news is that the ability to avoid plagiarizing is a skill—something you can practice and learn (Fig. 7-2). The solution to forgetting where your information originated is relatively easy, but it requires an extra step in taking notes: Simply mark all such background quotes clearly, with a bold heading that says something like, "Quotes," and include the source and date. As you paste information into your story, consistently ask yourself its source: Where did you get dates? Numbers? Facts? In each case, you should be able to trace the information to your own original reporting or attribute it to a source. While this is a basic step, it's part of what separates good professional reporters from those who simply don't have reporting skills. It's part of your fact checking.

Another mistake can happen if you don't understand the difference between **paraphrasing** and plagiarizing. Again, avoiding such plagiarism is a skill you can learn. Try some practice right now.

Imagine you're doing a story that examines how students at your university use social media. You do some research and find a Pew Research Center study that says the following:

> Social network users are becoming more active in pruning and managing their accounts. Women and younger users tend to unfriend more than others.
>
> About two-thirds of internet users use social networking sites (SNS) and all the major metrics for profile management are up, compared to 2009: 63% of them have deleted people from their "friends" lists, up from 56% in 2009; 44% have deleted comments made by others on their profile; and 37% have removed their names from photos that were tagged to identify them.
>
> Some 67% of women who maintain a profile say they have deleted people from their network, compared with 58% of men. Likewise, young adults are more active unfrienders when compared with older users. (Madden, 2012, para. 1–3)

You check Mary Madden's credentials and then you put in a phone call to her. In case she doesn't get back to you in time, you also schedule several other interviews, including one with a professor at your university who has published research on social media use.

However, you'd still like to communicate the specific information in the study, and you'd like to include research from the Pew Research Center because it's a well-respected national agency. Let's say your story includes this statement, which combines information from the first sentence of the excerpt and the part that starts after the break:

Paraphrase A

Social networkers are getting more active in pruning their accounts, especially women and younger people. Almost 70 percent of women users say they have deleted people from their network, compared to not quite 60 percent of men, scholars say.

Here, you've attributed the information—to scholars—and you've changed the actual words from the original. Furthermore, you've rearranged the order from the original by taking information from two different paragraphs. Good enough?

No—and here's why: First, the credit is to anonymous scholars, not to Madden, the author of the article whose wording your own story so closely parallels—or even the Pew Research Center. The acknowledgment of "scholars" is anonymous. The first task here would be to give credit to Madden.

Secondly, while you've changed words like "becoming" to "getting" and omitted "managing," the wording in the proposed story is much too close to the original. Substituting a few synonyms isn't the same thing as paraphrasing, which means putting an idea into your own, original words. The difference between good paraphrasing and a copy too close to the original can be subtle, so let's look at some of the specific problems here:

- The most blatant, unacknowledged thievery is the use of entire phrases from the original: "more active in pruning" and "women . . . say they have deleted people from their network." It's pretty easy to check for such repetition of entire

BOX 7-1

FIVE WAYS TO AVOID PLAGIARIZING BY MISTAKE

Avoiding plagiarism is a skill, and one you need to start practicing as soon as you begin reporting. Here's a list of steps to take so you don't inadvertently forget to give others credit for their original work:

1. Keep to a minimum any cutting and pasting from Web pages. After all, you're going to need to double-check any information for yourself anyway.
2. Whenever you *do* paste the work of someone else into your own notes or documents, place quotes around each paragraph, just as you would in your story, and note the source.
3. For other people's work in your notes, also add a heading, including who said it and the web address: *Quote from X (www.xxx.org)*.
4. Clearly mark where the borrowed information begins and ends, and be sure to mark it at the beginning of each new page, in case you cut off a heading.
5. As you put together a story, ask yourself the source of each piece of information. This will not only help you avoid plagiarizing, but will also help you to be more accurate.

sentences or phrases. If you need to use someone else's exact words, simply put them inside quotation marks and credit the source.

- Note that Paraphrase A uses "pruning," a relatively unusual word that comes straight from the original. In any paraphrase, you'll have to repeat words like "the," "and," "a" or more common words relevant to the subject matter—in this case, "men," "women" and "social network," for instance. But other, less common words can help you identify phrases or ideas that you need to paraphrase better or quote.

As a journalist, you'll often act as a guide to others in the world of information, linking people to other facts, videos and sites and letting them know what's out there. With practice and careful attention to good note taking, paraphrasing and attribution, you should have no problem avoiding plagiarism (Box 7-1).

Giving credit where it's due is one of the essential skills of a reporter, and you'll continue to improve in the art of good paraphrasing, knowing what to quote and how to credit others gracefully. For now, the most important thing is that you do provide such credit to original writers and producers of information.

Copyright and Fair Use

Even with attribution, if you use too much of someone else's work in your news story, you may be breaking copyright laws, the laws concerned with a person's right not only

FIGURE 7-3 Ideas can't be copyrighted until they are set in a fixed form. Society benefits from creativity, and copyright protection provides incentive for individuals to create and invent. But copyright limits exist so those creations eventually make their way into the public domain.

to get credit for her original creations, but also to make money from them. Journalists are affected in three major ways by copyright and fair use issues:

- They need to be aware of their own rights to the information they create or publish (Fig. 7-3).
- They need to know what's okay to include within the stories they publish with their news organization.
- Some journalists need to know what's okay for them to include in something they publish themselves, such as a blog or website or social media.

The government protects copyright because the public benefits when people pursue scientific and creative ideas. If creators or inventors lose their financial incentive, the fields of science or art may suffer. There's a tension between this desire to motivate scientists and artists, on one hand, and the need to make their ideas and creations available to everyone else to build on and use, on the other. That's why works eventually end up in the **public domain**, where they are available for everyone's use (Box 7-2).

By the way, while the focus here is on copyright laws, patents and trademarks are another set of laws that protect inventions and corporate names. Copyright has to do with written and artistic expressions, but the other two focus more on inventions, logos and designs.

BOX 7-2

WHAT'S PUBLIC?

Works that are not protected by copyright belong to the public domain, which means they are available for anyone to use without permission. Most works created by government employees when they are working in their official capacities are in the public domain (Figs. 7-4 and 7-5). For instance, an entire video created for a national park might be available for use on your news site. And sometimes people in the private sector immediately give permission for anyone to use their creations without people having to apply for further, individual permission. Such works belong to the public domain. And when a copyright expires, authors have no choice: Their works enter the public domain.

Sometimes, people intend to share their work from the very start without special permissions or fees. These artists and creators don't want to wait decades before their works enter the public domain. Creative Commons, for instance, is an organization that provides easy-to-use copyright agreements for users to make their works more accessible. You can use the Creative Commons website to find free or affordable photos, or background music for a commercial video. For this site and others like it, individual agreements may differ, so be sure to double-check so your use of any particular work is legitimate.

FIGURE 7-4 Dorothea Lange's photo of Florence Owens Thompson, a migrant pea picker, is one of the pictures that brought Lange renown. Because she took these photos for the federal government—they were part of a month-long assignment for the Resettlement Administration—the photos are in the public domain. You can look in places like the Library of Congress for photos you can use without paying a fee or seeking out the artist for permission.

FIGURE 7-5 Russell Lee was another photographer paid by the federal government, and many of his pictures are also available through the Library of Congress. This photo shows a group of people registering at the Santa Anita reception center as part of the forced evacuation of many Japanese-Americans to internment camps during World War II.

WHAT CAN BE COPYRIGHTED—
AND FOR HOW LONG?

Remember that the foundation of the U.S. government rests in part on a belief that the free flow of ideas is essential to people being able to govern themselves. That's one of the reasons that an *idea* or a *fact* cannot be copyrighted, but a work can be. So if you want to discuss an idea from a blog or news program in your own blog, copyright shouldn't be an issue. Or if another reporter has an idea that someone should do an investigation of laws protecting copyrights for plant seeds, the idea doesn't belong to that reporter and can't be copyrighted. But if the reporter wrote an investigative story about the same issue, the particular expression of that idea—that is, the story itself—would be protected. That means that plots are difficult to copyright—Shakespeare probably based the story of *Romeo and Juliet* on an earlier poem by a different author, and *West Side Story*, in turn, was based on Shakespeare's play, as was the 1996 movie, *Romeo + Juliet*, to name just three. But a particular scene from *West Side Story* is the creative expression of an idea—and the kind of artwork that is usually copyrighted.

Because an idea can't be copyrighted, journalists wouldn't need to get copyright permission or credit the major facts—that is, the ideas—of a news story, especially one that's been widely reported. For instance, it is a fact that the eastern United States experienced a large hurricane in October 2012, or that Steve Ballmer retired as CEO of Microsoft in August 2013. Neither of these facts can be copyrighted. Of course, as soon as you report more specific details, you need to confirm those for yourself rather than relying on other people's reports.

SOME COPYRIGHTED INFORMATION
IS FAIR GAME: THE FAIR USE DOCTRINE

However, because of the government's concern about protecting free speech, you can use some material without the copyright holder's permission under the **Fair Use Doctrine**. This doctrine was developed because courts decided that without it, copyright laws might stem the flow of ideas and free speech. For instance, the courts have ruled that a private film of the assassination of John F. Kennedy and biographical information about the multimillionaire Howard Hughes are important to the public interest—even over the objections of copyright holders. But even if you believe it's in the public's best interest to publish parts of a copyrighted work without permission, the courts will take into account how such publication might affect copyright holders (Box 7-3).

The courts are most concerned with your purpose for using a work, how much of it you use, what kind of work it is, and whether it affects the author's ability to make money from the work (Box 7-4).

BOX 7-3

HOW DO YOU KNOW WHETHER YOUR USE IS FAIR?

In determining whether your use of copyrighted material is a fair use, the courts have focused on four key issues:

1. The purpose and character of the use
2. The nature of the copyrighted work
3. The amount and substantiality of the portion used in relation to the original work
4. The effect of the use on the potential market for the original work. (Student Press Law Center, 2011)

Purpose of use: In considering the purpose or character of the use of copyrighted material, the courts have been more likely to protect education, scholarship, criticism and comment than commercial use. But when an Internet bulletin board posted the entire text of a copyrighted news article for reader comments from the *Los Angeles Times*, a federal court ruled against the website in *Los Angeles Times v. Free Republic* (2000).

The nature of the copyrighted work relates to whether the main purpose of the original work is artistic and creative, as opposed to informative. Facts, ideas and elements of news can't be copyrighted, although the particular structure or way of telling those facts or news can be, even if information is paraphrased. For instance, if another news organization reports the fact that a meeting took place, the information itself can't be copyrighted. However, the way the journalist wrote the story can be, and the video of the meeting on the local television news website isn't yours to download without permission. The fact that a fire broke out on Main Street, or that the president is giving a speech at your university, or that a Supreme Court justice is resigning, is information that cannot be copyrighted.

Courts also take into consideration whether a work is one that can be used only once, like a sudoku puzzle or a workbook, as opposed to a work that retains its value through repeated use.

The percentage of the work published: It would be nice if the courts had ruled that you could use up to, say, 5 percent of a work without infringing on someone's copyright. But there's no such ruling, and no magic number that says it's okay to publish a certain percentage of a work without the author's permission. Courts *have* considered what proportion of the work was used. That means if you're doing a story on the death of a pop star and you quote a few lines of relevant lyrics, you're probably in safe territory: You haven't included the whole CD, or even the entire song. But if you include the singer's music in the Web version of your story, you'll also need to keep the proportion of any particular song you use to a minimum.

If you include four minutes of a 10-minute video on your website, then the public may lose interest in buying the complete video from the artist. If your newspaper publishes a full-page copy of someone's poster, there's a possibility that people will hang the page from the newspaper on their walls and forgo buying the poster. If you include too much of a short story in a news article or post, the public may not buy the anthology to read the rest.

Effect of the use on the value of the work: Finally, courts have also taken into account whether publishing part of a work without the copyright holder's permission significantly diminishes the copyright holder's ability to make a profit from the work. Remember that the purpose of the copyright laws is to make sure that science and the arts are pursued, that people will make money from either selling their works themselves or selling them to others.

BOX 7-4

WHEN WOULD A JOURNALIST BE IN DANGER OF VIOLATING COPYRIGHTS?

Copyright issues will concern you as a journalist most often when you are referring to or including works by other people in your story. The laws are changing rapidly, so the important thing is to be aware that your rights to include works from others may not always match common practice, or even what seems like common sense. Journalists need to know that embedding videos or music in their websites without permission could be a problem. So could reprinting whole poems, works of art, entire articles or long passages from other texts without permission. Copying big portions might take away from a person's ability to make money from the original. Therefore, you don't ever want to simply download material to your blog or news site. Besides, if you're online, it's usually easy enough to simply provide a link to the copyright holder's website.

While the courts haven't ruled definitively on the issue, linking to other websites with copyrighted material isn't usually an issue. Such links make it clear you're taking someone to another site, a place with a different author. However, if you tried to use a link to claim someone else's work as your own, you might subject yourself to the possibility of a lawsuit—that is, if your site had a link that took a person deep into another website and implied you created material that was actually by another person.

Likewise, linking to a video on YouTube or another site shouldn't be a copyright problem for journalists. However, embedding a video clip created by someone else into your own site might be. Again, the courts have not ruled definitively on whether someone has given you implied permission by including a code in a video that enables it to be shared.

But it's not always clear who actually owns the copyright. Although controls have been tightened after some recent lawsuits, videos still sometimes show up on YouTube that include copyrighted material, such as a musician's songs or clips from other videos. While the creator of the video may have contributed the work to the public domain, the musician or creator of the excerpted video may not have done so. And if someone sends you an email or writes you a letter, the author—not the recipient—retains the copyright. That means you may not have the right to publish a particular email or letter on your site or in your newspaper.

Furthermore, you may not own the rights to your own work. For instance, if you are employed by a news organization, it may own the rights to future publication of your stories, photographs, video or audio recordings. Before trying to republish your work or sell it to someone else, you'll want to check your contract with your news organization. Usually, the copyright for news you've published—and even information, photos or video footage you've gathered while on the job—belongs to the news organization for which you work. Typically, it's relatively easy to renegotiate rights to your work if you'd like to republish it somewhere else. After all, burnishing your own reputation often helps your news organization, too. And editors and producers are often sympathetic or even encouraging to journalists who hope to make a name for themselves or bring in additional income in creative ways. You need to check the policy at your organization, and respect that policy.

Exercises for Chapter 7

EXERCISE 7-1: If you wanted to tell a friend about plagiarism, what would you say? How would you describe it?

EXERCISE 7-2: Why would someone say that plagiarism is stealing?

EXERCISE 7-3: For each of the following scenarios, discuss the issues and considerations that come up regarding plagiarism and copyright. For example, would each raise a warning flag for you? Would you have to get permission from the copyright holder? Does fair use apply? What would you decide?

a. To illustrate a story on literacy, the design staff wants to create the image of a Scrabble board, with tiles arranged so they spell out: "Can Johnny Read?"

b. For an editorial cartoon, the illustrator wants to show Spiderman coming to the rescue of the beleaguered president. The thing is, the illustrator is *really good* and Spidey looks exactly like the original, and the president looks almost lifelike.

c. You're doing a story on this year's graduating class. The class motto is a quote from Albus Dumbledore in one of the Harry Potter books.

EXERCISE 7-4: How long do you think that a songwriter's copyright should last? Why?

WORKING
WITH SOURCES

Habits of Mind

Journalists know that striving too hard to achieve objectivity can actually weaken a story. Instead of trying to be objective, good journalists strive to be complete, fair and accurate. Furthermore, they know that being aware of one's personal biases can help a reporter mitigate their influence.

Your Position, Your Judgment and Your Practice

A group of researchers created a video that features two teams in a room—one team in black shirts, the other in white shirts—each passing a basketball to teammates. They asked their research subjects to observe the video and count the total number of basketball passes. What they didn't mention: In the midst of the game, a gorilla walks through the room.

The researchers, Chabris and Simons and their colleagues, say that they weren't concerned about how many times the teams passed the ball, because that's not really what they were testing. In fact, they wanted to see how observant the viewers were: Did they see the gorilla?

About half of the observers did not. The researchers report a typical conversation following the viewing:

> **Q:** Did you notice anything unusual while you were doing the counting task?
>
> **A:** No.
>
> **Q:** Did you notice anything other than the players?
>
> **A:** Well, there were some elevators, and S's painted on the wall. I don't know what the S's were there for.
>
> **Q:** Did you notice *anyone* other than the players?
>
> **A:** No.
>
> **Q:** Did you notice a gorilla?
>
> **A:** A what?!? (2010, p. 6)

When the researchers showed people the video a second time, telling them not to pay attention to the ball players, everyone saw the gorilla. Some people were so incredulous that they missed it the first time around; they thought surely the researchers must have switched videos (p. 7). The researchers conclude:

> It's true that we vividly experience some aspects of our world, particularly those that are the focus of our attention. But this rich experience inevitably leads to the erroneous belief that we process *all* of the detailed information around us. In essence, we know how vividly we see some aspects of our world, but we are

completely unaware of those aspects of our world that fall outside of that current focus of attention. (p. 7)

As this research shows, people don't see everything, even what's right before their eyes, especially if they are too focused on a specific task.

This phenomenon of "inattentional blindness" has interesting implications for journalists. It's tempting to think that reporting is a matter of simply seeking the self-evident truth and describing it for your audience. The Opaque Gorilla research pokes a hole in this assumption. We're likely to be blind to facets of a story—and not even know we've missed anything. This underscores the importance of thinking critically, not just about the story, but about yourself, your biases and your **position**—or worldview. Such self-awareness might help you recognize your blind spots and therefore mitigate their influence on your work.

Lenses: A Metaphor for Worldview

One way to think about your position is through the metaphor of lenses. When you slip on a pair of sunglasses, the color of the lenses alters your vision. Along the same lines, your biases and interpretations color the way you see the world—and the stories you tell (Fig. 8-1).

FIGURE 8-1

For media scholar Stuart Hall, even talking about a rock involves interpretation. He says that objects come to mean something only as we communicate about them:

> Things "in themselves" rarely if ever have any one, single, fixed and unchanging meaning. Even something as obvious as a stone can be a stone, a boundary marker or a piece of sculpture, depending upon what it means—that is, within a certain context of use. . . . It is by our use of things, and what we say, think and feel about them—how we represent them—that we give them a meaning. (1997, p. 3)

The choices we make in reporting and creating a story involve our interpretation at some level. (And journalists don't control the whole meaning-making process: The way people understand your story will involve interpretation on their part, which we'll discuss later.) Your position, and therefore your bias, comes into play in every story—that's unavoidable. But if you can anticipate where it might affect your judgment, you can control its influence as you set about telling the most responsible story you can.

For example, many people saw the aftermath of the Sandy Hook Elementary School shooting as a chance to renew the effort to pass gun-control legislation. New bills were introduced and people across the country worked to get them enacted during what they saw as a small window in which public sentiment might make the new laws possible. At the same time, many people opposed to greater gun control saw those efforts as a rushed response to a complex problem, and one that might have long-term consequences for individual rights. Even some of the families who had lost someone in the Sandy Hook shooting took stands on opposite sides of the issue.

How might a journalist, knowing she has biases, keep them in check as she reports on the issues? For example, what if the reporter's personal position is that further governmental gun control interferes with individual rights? She believes the Second Amendment protects the right for citizens to bear arms, and that it's dangerous for the government to start down the slippery slope of further regulation. She's anti-gun control. That doesn't mean that the reporter has to go out and find someone in favor of gun control to include in a story just to balance out her stance. But what she would want to do is make sure that her anti-gun control stance, based on her position concerning individual rights, doesn't blind her to issues the community might find useful to consider. And the reporter, by keeping a critical distance from her own views, can ensure that she performs her public duty by providing relevant and useful information.

Objective Reporting

Educating yourself about your biases and knowing where your blind spots might be are part of being a good journalist. If a reporter has to use judgment just to decide whom to interview—that is, before that reporter even starts to write a news story—then what about the idea that journalists are supposed to be **objective**? Given the questions about concepts as elementary as whether or not you're seeing a gorilla, this now seems easier said than done. When people say that one goal of journalism is to be objective, they generally mean that journalists should keep their opinions out of their reports and include just the facts (Fig. 8-2).

This argument assumes that there is an objective reality and that the objective reality can be discovered and described in words that precisely reflect the event. In this tradition, the reporter has been compared to a court reporter who records trial proceedings verbatim. But we've already seen some of the possible problems with this.

BIASED JOURNALISM

The opposite of objective journalism is commonly criticized as being biased journalism. When people say the media are biased, they are suggesting that journalists are including their opinions, politics or agenda in a story that is supposed to be objective. Biased is bad, this school of thought says, because it interferes with the objective truth. One problem with this view of how to be a good journalist is that it assumes that there is one truth out there to find. However, this model is too simplistic.

FIGURE 8-2

Remember that there is an objective reality, but the assumption that the journalist can always find the one truth and report it exactly doesn't take into account the journalist's interpretation.

A BRIEF HISTORY

The idea of objectivity in journalism hasn't always been around. Most scholars put its emergence in the 19th century, against a backdrop of a convergence of influences, such as journalism's moving from craft toward profession; an increasing popular preference for reason, empirical science and factual data; and new technologies at the time (see, e.g., Bennett, 2005; Carey, 1989; and Schudson, 1978).

For instance, the development of the telegraph allowed for quick dissemination of news over long distances, as opposed to strictly local news or long-delayed national news. The telegraph sent messages over wires using electrical impulses, typically in the dots and dashes of the Morse code. A reporter could send the facts of a story over the wire, in code, to the newspaper that was to print it, where a different person would reconstitute the story for publication. It was an expensive technology, however, so the journalist had to be very concise as he sent the facts to the receiving end, and that meant trimming the story down to the bare essentials—just the facts (Carey, 1989, p. 211).

At around the same time, in 1846, the publisher of *The New York Sun* organized with four other New York City papers to speed news of the Mexican War to the city using a combination of mail and the newly emerging telegraph technology—a consortium that eventually expanded and became the Associated Press (Associated Press, 2010). Not all of the member newspapers shared the same politics, though, nor did all of the audiences, so this was another incentive for reporters to strip their language down to the basics, to increase the possibility that their stories would be picked up and carried in more newspapers.

Both the changes in technology and the emergence of the Associated Press are part of the history of journalism's objectivity ideal. Media scholar James Carey (1989) describes how news stories had to shift toward an objective tone that could hold up over distance:

> The wire services demanded a form of language stripped of the local, the regional;
> [sic] and colloquial. They demanded something closer to a "scientific" language,
> a language of strict denotation in which the connotative features of utterance
> were under rigid control. If the same story were to be understood in the same way
> from Maine to California, language had to be flattened out and standardized. . . .
> The origins of objectivity may be sought, therefore, in the necessity of stretching
> language in space over the long lines of Western Union. (pp. 210–211)

This meant that the expectation that the news would be written in an objective tone was not something inherently part of news; instead, it gradually arose from people's reactions to a new technology—the telegraph. When news first started, then, people didn't assume reporters would try to be objective. For instance, the earlier advocacy press often had close ties to politicians or political parties and would unabashedly root for them and against their opponents, like a Rush Limbaugh today. Most big cities had at least two newspapers, and usually each one would be affiliated with a different party. But as information became more widely disseminated and the audience became more diverse, this degree of overt position would no longer suffice for news stories. So journalists sought to remove it from their copy.

CRITIQUES

While purely objective reporting isn't possible, this common goal created conventions that reflect some agreement among professionals about how to go about their practice. The goal was to provide a report that was as complete as possible, fair to all stakeholders and accurate, so that the audience would have enough information to make wise decisions. Yet, even by the middle of the 20th century, journalists were criticized for falling short of their responsibilities to their readers.

Incomplete Reporting

The creators of what came to be known as the **Hutchins Commission** (the informal name given to the Commission on Freedom of the Press) were two wealthy, powerful, private individuals who set out to determine what the press' duty to the public and to democracy was, and how free the press was to fulfill that obligation. Henry Luce, the founder and editor-in-chief of *Time* and other magazines, funded the three-year study. He criticized journalism for being too sensational and lacking substance. Robert Hutchins, the president of the University of Chicago, agreed to organize and, later, lead the committee. It sought to examine the state of the U.S. press and make recommendations about how it should serve democracy better. Although subject to some criticism upon its release in 1947, the report is considered a milestone in journalism history partly because it underscores the importance of the press in a democracy and its obligation to serve the public. The Commission said that the news media's "objectivity" often led to a more superficial kind of journalism:

> [T]he press has developed a curious sort of objectivity—a spurious objectivity which results in half-truths, incompleteness, incomprehensibility. In adhering to objective reporting, the press has tried to present more than one side to a story; but in doing so, the suggestion is, the media have not bothered to evaluate for the reader the trustworthiness of conflicting sources, nor have they supplied the perspective essential to a complete understanding of a given situation. Instead of assuming that two half-truths make a truth, the Commission says in effect, the press should seek "the whole truth." (Peterson, 1963, p. 88)

As early as the 1940s, the news media's attempt at objectivity was being criticized as leading to incomplete journalism. The same critique was evident more than a half-century later in editor Brent Cunningham's article, "Toward a New Ideal: Rethinking Objectivity in a World of Spin" (2003). In it, Cunningham makes the case that the news media's attempts at objectivity have often led to important gaps in news coverage.

He gives as an example President George W. Bush's March 6, 2003, press conference. Bush, who was talking about U.S. plans to invade Iraq, "mentioned al Qaeda or the attacks of September 11 fourteen times in fifty-two minutes" (p. 24). Cunningham points out that none of the reporters present pushed the president on the implicit connection he was making between the September 11 attacks and the invasion of Iraq, despite the fact that "there was no solid evidence of such a connection." Because the reporters were trying to avoid appearing biased by introducing a topic on their own, they didn't challenge the president. The result, Cunningham says, is that important questions were left unasked by much of the mainstream media, and therefore, many people were less informed.

As a further example, Cunningham points out that before the U.S. invasion of Iraq, very few news stories dealt with the subject of complications after the invasion. The president wasn't bringing up the topic, so reporters felt it wouldn't be objective for them to raise it. After Bush introduced the subject on February 26, 2003, "aftermath" articles became very common: "It was as if the subject of the war's aftermath was more or less off the table until the president put it there himself," Cunningham writes (p. 25).

By trying to remain objective in the sense of dutifully playing the stenographer, the press let the source control the agenda and therefore the story (Fig. 8-3). This sort of journalism can turn a journalist from an information seeker to a source's accomplice, which probably won't help the audience understand anything but the source's message point.

FIGURE 8-3 Recording only what your sources say is like being a stenographer in a courtroom. Good reporting is more active, requiring much more critical thinking than that.

Passive Reporting

Cunningham says that these are significant gaps in news coverage that are caused, at least in part, by the news media's conventional understanding of objectivity. Journalists allow "the principle of objectivity to make us passive recipients of the news, rather than analyzers and explainers of it" (2003, p. 26). He says that reporters often allow the principle of objectivity to serve as a rationale for "lazy reporting": "If you're on deadline and all you have is 'both sides of the story,' that's often good enough" (p. 26).

This type of reporting, Cunningham says, too often turns up in the news: A reporter gets two conflicting versions of the truth, and rather than digging to the bottom to find out whose version is correct, she simply reports what the two sides say about the problem and leaves the reader to decide which is right—even if there's not enough information to make a rational decision (Box 8-1 and Fig. 8-4).

BOX 8-1

AVOIDING FALSE BALANCE

If a strictly objective report isn't possible—or even desirable—how does a reporter satisfy the goal of providing an accurate account of an event?

An excerpt from an article by *The New York Times'* Michael Slackman illustrates how to use contextual information to counter a potentially misleading government claim about an event. Slackman gives the audience useful details to help them more accurately evaluate the situation. Slackman's story recounts a 2006 situation in Cairo, where Sudanese migrants had created a squatter camp in a well-to-do neighborhood to pressure the United Nations to help them relocate to another country. After three months, the police ordered the squatters to leave. The squatters refused, and "the police attacked." The story continues:

> So many were left dead, and the international condemnation was so embarrassing, that President Hosni Mubarak has told the attorney general to investigate.

> But the government's official position is that the Sudanese were to blame. Magdy Rady, the government's chief spokesman, said the Sudanese injured their own people by trampling those who collapsed, and he said they also attacked the police, injuring more than 70 officers.

> The Sudanese were unarmed and many were barefoot. The police were wearing riot gear, including helmets with face shields, and wielded truncheons. (2006, p. A3)

The third paragraph shows how unlikely the government's claim was, particularly in saying that the unarmed and barefoot Sudanese injured scores of officers who were dressed in full gear and had serious weapons. The reporter signals to the audience that the evidence conflicts with the officials' statement. That is, by using factual information to provide context, the reporter can indicate that what the government says may not be true. This is different, of course, from trying to advance a personal agenda—Slackman is not sneaking his opinion into the story. Instead, he's broadening the scope of the story beyond the government official to include a fuller description of the event, an account that speaks for itself.

FIGURE 8-4 Here, a Jewish settler who has defied the law to remain in the West Bank resists Israeli security forces who are trying to evacuate her. If a journalist simply tried to report both sides of the situation, you can see that wouldn't be doing justice to the complexity of the issues. Not knowing whether this woman is being treated justly or not would frustrate many readers. Why is she being relocated, and on whose orders? Why is she there in the first place? Who are the people in the background? Is something on fire in the rear of the frame?

The problems with this passive kind of reporting are easier to see in hindsight. As Cunningham points out, African-Americans were clearly being terrorized during the lynchings of the 1890s. If a journalist only reported what white government officials said and what African-Americans said and left it to readers to figure out truth for themselves, then many of them wouldn't—and didn't—figure out the truth.

Even if a completely objective transcript of reality is probably impossible, we don't want to toss out the gist of what journalists are concerned with when they invoke the objectivity ideal: an accurate, fair, contextualized report free from unfair manipulation by the reporter. You can see this attempt manifested if you look at the Society of Professional Journalists' Code of Ethics (www.spj.org), particularly sections that direct journalists to be accurate, to refrain from advocating a certain argument and to refrain from editing out views with which they don't agree.

Conclusion

People used to think about the news media as serving as a mirror of society, reflecting it exactly. But the stories journalists create are the products of many decisions.

This filtering role is so foundational to what journalists do for audiences that they need to make these decisions consciously, and to be aware of their own positions.

The key here is that you do bring in bias, so you must do so in a thoughtful, ethical way. That means trying to include a diversity of sources so that you're more likely to include multiple positions. The goal is to provide relevant, accurate and fair coverage that audience members can use to make decisions about events that have an impact on them.

This unit focuses on sources, including source selection, conducting an interview, quoting and paraphrasing sources in your story and working in depth with them when you cover a beat. As you make your way through the chapters in this unit, look for moments where your biases could influence your decisions, and determine whether and how you could mitigate their influence.

Your sources will have their own biases. Where and when might these show up in the reporting process? Think about how you would handle those occasions and the information you get.

CHAPTER 8

WHO GETS THE
SPOTLIGHT?

*". . . news is not reality, but a sampling of sources' portrayals of reality,
mediated by news organizations"* (Sigal, 1986, pp. 27–28)

Beyond Convention and Convenience in Source Selection

In 1955, Lamar Smith, an African-American farmer, was working to register other African-American voters in Mississippi. Because some whites threatened to shoot any African-Americans who showed up at the polls, Smith urged the people he registered to cast absentee votes, and the number of absentee ballots rose from 600 to about 1,100 in the Democratic primary. Upset at Smith's effectiveness, several white men went to the courthouse square and shot and killed Smith in broad daylight. Here's what Gene Roberts and Hank Klibanoff, who wrote a book about the news media's role in the Civil Rights movement, say happened after the murder:

> Newspaper coverage was of little value in ferreting out what had happened or why. . . . The dominant Jackson newspapers, *The Clarion-Ledger* and *Daily News,* sent a reporter to Brookhaven who filed a report that ran as the main story in the next day's combined Sunday edition. The story—with the four-column headline "Links Shooting of Negro with Vote Irregularities"—shifted the blame for Smith's

death to Smith himself, saying he had been "linked to voting irregularities" in urging Negroes to cast absentee ballots.

The newspapers were able to ascertain quickly that Smith had once been convicted of bootlegging but never managed to report why Smith had urged Negroes to vote by absentee ballot. That and subsequent stories never explained what the law on absentee voting was or whether Smith was within his legal rights. No effort was made to interview anyone other than the district attorney, the sheriff, the chief of police, and the shooter. Friends and associates of Smith were not interviewed, so that even as he went to his grave recognized in the Negro community as a fearless political organizer, he appeared in the white press as a cipher, a schemer, and an aging bootlegger. (2006, pp. 81–82)

As Roberts and Klibanoff point out, the white press failed partly because its reporters interviewed only the official sources. In making their choices about which sources to interview, these reporters may have satisfied many of their readers, but their stories were inaccurate. This example illustrates how important it is to select sources thoughtfully—to interview people from a range of different viewpoints and backgrounds for controversial stories, to talk to people who are most likely to have accurate information and to know something about your sources' potential biases and prejudices (Fig. 8-5).

FIGURE 8-5 Malala Yousafzai is a Pakistani teen whose activism for girls' education drew international attention after she was shot in the head by the Taliban on her way home from school one day. When U.S. journalists shone their spotlight on her and her cause, they were going beyond official sources to report the story. On the other hand, when *everyone* started interviewing Malala, the issue of overexposure arose: What about other people who stand up for the rights of the powerless? What about people in other countries—is Malala the only one?

WHAT'S NEWS DEPENDS ON WHOM YOU INTERVIEW

In his classic work, "Who? Sources Make the News" (1986), Leon Sigal says that much of what is considered news is determined by the sources reporters choose to interview, and that those choices tend to be governed by convention and deadlines, rather than what is most important (Fig. 8-6). Sigal, who taught government at Wesleyan University, was particularly intrigued by the dominance of government officials in the news media. In his essay, Sigal makes the following points:

- Ordinary people appear in the news infrequently, compared to public officials or celebrities.

- News is often reported in terms of personalities, rather than abstract issues.

- The people who show up in the news media are there because they are news sources, and who sources are depends on how reporters gather news.

Sigal also notes that reporters need regular news they can count on, which means that when they make systematic checks for news, they return over and over again to the same types of sources: to government workers, to police officers or to elected officials. In what Sigal defines as the "**convention of authoritative sources**," reporters have come to think of hierarchical status as equal to the quality of a news story—the higher an official's position within an organization, the better a source, according to this theory. Sigal worries that "The convention of authoritativeness has so strong

FIGURE 8-6 Journalists have to remember that where they shine the spotlight of attention brings visibility, and therefore power, to particular sources and the people and causes they represent. And the opposite also holds true.

a hold on journalists that they will take the word of a senior official over that of sub-ordinates who may be in a better position to know what the government is doing from day to day" (p. 20). This attitude also means that a reporter may be less likely to report on a loosely organized association in which hierarchy is hard to determine.

A reporter with enviable access to very powerful sources may not be closer to the truth; instead, he may simply be providing another, perhaps more personalized, version of the official story of events.

In contrast to the reporter with powerful sources, a reporter who interviews sources who are closer to actual events may get a version closer to the truth. This is a good example of why better reporting sometimes avoids the convention of authoritativeness—because those with the highest authority may have more vested interests in hiding the truth.

Sigal makes the further point that reporters' social locations help to determine their sources. Reporters usually work in offices, which are situated in particular cities in particular parts of a country. They move within definite social circles and come from particular cultural backgrounds. All of these factors affect how they hear and report the news. This means that places like New York City and Los Angeles and Chicago get better news coverage than rural areas of the country where large news organizations have no bureaus. Reporters tend to cover issues affecting people who also work in offices, who have accessible telephone numbers and easy access to cars or public transportation—as opposed to migrant workers, or small farmers, for instance.

Sigal concludes that as readers of the media, we need to at least be aware of the arbitrariness of who makes the news. He points out that the sources who make the news help to determine who gets and keeps positions of power, and that if government officials get to define what's most important and what issues reporters cover, then those officials have an inordinate amount of power (pp. 36–37).

DON'T LET SOURCES TURN YOU INTO PROPAGANDISTS

Two other media theorists, Noam Chomsky and Edward Herman (2002), express some of the same concerns about sources. Chomsky and Herman believe that the mass media have become, in effect, an instrument of propaganda for the dominant social and economic groups in the United States and they argue that an important factor in this unhealthy role is the misuse of sources (p. 307). Like Sigal, Chomsky and Herman say that because the media need a steady flow of information, they tend to return to sources who will deliver news and leaks and press conferences at a steady pace. This means that a majority of news sources represent the wealthy and powerful—government agencies and large corporations, who can afford to hold press conferences and produce numerous press releases. This coverage comes at the expense of those who represent people without such resources, such as the working classes, the poor or even grassroots organizations.

While the critiques of sources by Sigal, Herman and Chomsky have different emphases, all point to problems in the ways in which journalists select sources. And all three agree that, at least in this aspect, the conventions of journalism stand in the way of providing fair and accurate news coverage. The obstacles center around convenience, unquestioned assumptions and conventions and issues of power. All three theorists suggest that the news is distorted from the very start because of the ways in which reporters choose sources.

For these critics, the biggest problem is not some crass self-interest in selling more newspapers or gaining corporate advertisers; it is a more nuanced recognition that news traditions and convenience drive source choices. Unfortunately, a problem with such complex roots has no quick and easy solution. For Chomsky, the very social and democratic system needs to change before sources can be more equitably chosen. But reporters can work within the current system and still make fairer, better choices in selecting sources.

Good Practices

We've pointed out some of the deep concerns that theorists like Sigal, Chomsky and Herman have about whom journalists choose to interview. But as a working journalist, you also need to know what other reporters assume about the details of practicing good journalism.

From your very first story, you may need to be thinking of the lessons we've just discussed—you may be asked to report on someone charged with a crime, for instance, and need to know that it's important to talk to someone who can represent that person, in addition to police officials. But when you get your first few story assignments, you also may find yourself simply wondering, Who is someone, *anyone*, I could call as a source?

Let's start with thinking through sources for a basic news story, and then we'll look at a more challenging example: In August 2005, a couple in Durango, Colorado, were sitting on their deck overlooking the river when a mountain lion attacked the woman from behind, leaping onto her shoulders and then bounding off (Rodebaugh, 2005). The woman's injuries were minor—the lion left puncture wounds on her shoulder and face and scratched her ear—but the incident seemed newsworthy for several reasons: Mountain lion attacks in the area were very unusual, and the circumstances in this case were particularly rare because the lion had attacked someone on her deck, and because the attack had been relatively harmless; the lion's audacity seemed to be evidence that wild animals might be growing less timid around humans, a possibility that people in the area needed to know about so they could take appropriate precautions; and the attack called "attention to the close quarters that humans and wildlife share in Southwest Colorado," as a newspaper story observed, and this change in boundaries between wild and human habitat has had far-reaching consequences (Rodebaugh, para. 1).

If you were assigned to write the news story about the incident, you'd probably figure out pretty quickly that you'd need to talk with an official—someone from the sheriff's department or Division of Wildlife. Such a person would be most likely to know the answers to questions about whether wild animals were becoming more aggressive and therefore area residents needed to take more precautions, how often similar incidents had happened in the past and whether the victim of the attack seemed to have done anything especially dangerous or improper—had she been feeding deer or mountain lions, for instance?

Tracking down an official source wouldn't be too difficult, because that's typically how journalists learn about accident and crime stories such as this in the first place: They check a police blotter regularly to find out about stories that may be important to their community. For a story this unusual, you would also do your best to talk with the victim: Had she seen mountain lions in the area before? Did she have any idea she was being stalked? A reporter might then try to find out more about how rare such animal behavior is—again, from the Division of Wildlife or some such agency. The reporter might also check with the hospital or someone who could discuss whether the woman's injuries were worrisome.

Beyond simply reporting the event, a journalist could serve readers by talking to an animal behaviorist about why the lion might have attacked, and the best possible ways for humans to respond in similar situations to keep from being injured or killed.

In this case, the reporter interviewed the Division of Wildlife regional manager, the San Juan Basin Health Department's regional epidemiologist about the likelihood of the lion's having rabies and both the woman who was attacked and her husband, who was a witness (Fig. 8-7).

Notice how we thought about whom to interview for this story: We asked first about why the story was newsworthy and interesting to the community. That led us to a list of relevant questions that we'd expect people to ask. Then we thought about who might have the best, most accurate answers to those questions. You'd usually expect the victim of the attack, for instance, to be able to speak most accurately and with most authority about the details of the incident—although you'd always want to be sure there were no questions about the credibility of that source. In this case, there weren't. But the victims are unlikely to know the statistics about area mountain lions in general, so you'd turn to an official for this big-picture information.

Let's look at a different kind of story: In November 2006, a homeowners association in Pagosa Springs, Colorado, ordered a resident to remove a wreath shaped in a peace symbol (Munro, 2006). The resident refused to stop displaying the wreath, and was threatened with a $25-a-day fine. At the time, tensions were still high about the U.S. invasion of Iraq, and the wreath was interpreted by some people as an anti-war statement. The story was newsworthy because it touched on deep feelings about a national war at a local level, and because it revealed the possibility that an important right—freedom of speech—was threatened. People would probably want to know what motivated the resident who hung the wreath, and why the homeowners association responded the way it did. That means that a journalist reporting on the story would need to talk to the resident who hung the wreath in the first place, and someone from the homeowners association. Ideally, the reporter would talk with several neighbors to try to get a sense of how controversial the wreath was and whether the resident had been antagonistic in the past.

VICTIM   WITNESS   DIVISION OF WILDLIFE   ANIMAL BEHAVIORIST

"...describe what happened."

"How does this type of attack happen? What will happen to the mountain lion?"

"Why would a mountain lion attack someone sitting on her deck, so close to town?"

reporters

FIGURE 8-7 For every story, journalists need to think about who are the best, most credible sources. In the news story about a mountain lion attack, some sources could provide firsthand information about what happened, and others could talk about mountain lion behavior and how to prevent an attack on people and pets—useful, relevant information.

In the initial news story in *The Durango Herald*, the reporter interviewed the resident, Lisa Jensen, who hung the wreath, and the homeowners association president, Bob Kearns. The reporter also looked at the letter from the association, and a public letter posted on a website from the chairman of the subdivision's committee. Part of the issue turned on different interpretations of the meaning of the peace symbol: Jensen said the wreath was not an anti-war statement, while Kearns said the symbol was an "anti-Christ sign" (Munro, para. 10). In a laudable attempt to get to the bottom of this issue, the reporter also quoted from a 1972 reference work on symbols (a human source would have been better because that would have provided a primary and up-to-date source).

The examples of the controversial peace wreath and the mountain lion attack show how professional reporters think about selecting sources on a very practical level. We'd also like to provide you some basic guidelines for source selection that professional journalists are expected to know. For instance, a good journalist would be horrified if you chose to include your friend as a source for a standard news story about the presidential election, or if you quoted another local website about the resignation of the mayor rather than talking with the mayor yourself. And you also need to know that some widely publicized practices—like using anonymous sources or making up composite sources—are used only rarely or frowned on by the most respected journalists. To prepare you for making good professional choices, we have included a list and explanations following of some of the basic practices good journalists follow when selecting sources.

CONFIRM FACTS WITH MORE THAN ONE SOURCE

For any news story you write, you need to rely on multiple sources. Even if your story is just about the speech that a paid speaker made, your job is to provide accurate news, and whenever you interview only one source for a story, there's a stronger possibility that that person's view is inaccurate or is not representative of your community.

How many sources is enough? A rule of thumb when you're working on a contentious issue is to confirm facts with at least three sources. For a less controversial story, it's important to confirm all information with at least two sources. If one source remembers a fact incorrectly or twists it slightly, you're likely to catch this through checking with a second source.

However, the answer is not simply getting two points of view for every story. People sometimes talk about getting "the other side," as if there were only two. Typically, however, there are multiple sides to an issue, and reporters serve their readers poorly by thinking in bilateral terms. For instance, after the president gives his annual State of the Union speech, news networks usually call on a high-ranking member of the opposite party for reaction. This approach ignores differences within each party, as well as points of view outside the group of elected politicians who share the same city of residence, similar jobs, methods of gaining power and general ideas about how government should work. Media scholar W. Lance Bennett writes that interviewing just Democrats and Republicans on any issue simply provides information from the two groups of people who hold government power:

> While this may satisfy some minimal standard of "fairness" by presenting two sides of most issues, it is important not to confuse "two sides" with "both sides," much less "all sides." ... If we divide the political world differently, into categories such as "powerful versus powerless" or "insiders versus outsiders," the two sides admitted into most news debates begin to look like powerful inside minorities given vast media preference over any number of outsiders who might wish to challenge their privileged position. (1996, p. 27)

A good reporter strives to interview multiple sources—and because accuracy is so important in journalism, a reporter should confirm with as many sources as necessary to ensure that accuracy.

ALLOW PEOPLE TO DEFEND THEMSELVES

At the very least, a reporter should talk to a person or representative from each of the stakeholders affected by an event or decision, such as an election, a controversial

Supreme Court decision or a protest on campus. It's especially important to call on a person or representative of a group who is criticized or attacked by another source in a story. But what if that person is unavailable?

Your story needs to be as fair as possible, and to make clear to readers that you did your best to be fair. In some cases, this means including a line such as the following: "Calls were not returned by deadline," or, "Efforts to reach X were unsuccessful before the *Journal* went to press." But reporters should be very careful not to insinuate that someone was avoiding their calls if that was not the case. If you work on a story for two weeks, you know that your congressional representative is in town, you call her office every other day and no one returns your calls, then it's fair to write that "X did not return repeated telephone calls." But if you only have a few hours to gather information and allow a source to respond, you may need to hold the story if you can't reach that source. On rare occasions when time runs out and you are unable to reach a source, it's appropriate to run a story noting that fact, as long as you make it clear that the source was not actively avoiding you.

REPORT DIVERSITY

Beginning reporters tend to choose sources who are convenient and easy to talk to. These sources might share the same economic class, professional and educational bracket, race and ethnicity as the reporter. When people talk about "diversity," they mean many different things: They may mean including members of the ethnic minority most significantly represented in their area, such as Cuban-Americans in Miami, or Asian-Americans in parts of the Pacific Northwest. They may mean including a specific group, like people over 65. What we mean here by "**reporting diversity**" is that accuracy demands that over the course of time in your reporting, you interview a range of sources who approximate the range of views and backgrounds in your community.

You can begin by looking around your community, observing for yourself the different kinds of people who live there. In your news organization's archives, what groups of people show up? Journalists have to develop a healthy curiosity about the world around them, learning to ask questions about who lives in their communities. You can read the obituaries and marriage announcements in your local newspaper; over time, these give you some sense of the individuals and families in the area. You can look up census information about the ages and incomes of people living in your area, and find out something about the **demographic** characteristics of the community. You can ask questions about different socioeconomic groups: Where do the homeless people in your community go—do they sleep in the streets in the summer? Are there shelters and soup kitchens?

No matter where you live, it's important to get a sense of the history of the community—for example, through finding out about the different waves of immigration. Again, you can do this by looking through news archives, and you can also talk with locals and read about local history. For instance, before Durango, Colorado, existed, the Ute Indians used the area as a seasonal hunting ground. The town itself was founded by a railroad company transporting ore from nearby mountain areas. In the late 1800s, most of the immigrants in the area were from Great Britain and Ireland, the next largest group came from Germany, and a small contingent from China (Smith, 1992). Very few African-Americans lived in the area, but the Ku Klux Klan operated a branch and conducted raids on Mexican-Americans and Catholics. Later, miners were followed by ranchers, and eventually people came for the outdoor lifestyle and then wealthy retirees began to resettle in Durango. Understanding those waves of immigration and different lifestyles helped a journalist, for example, who was reporting on a controversy about Durango residents in a wealthy neighborhood who bought sheep to give their border collie something to do. As an informed journalist, she understood some of the tensions among long-time residents and ranchers, developers and wealthy newcomers that might underlie the controversy, and was able to put into perspective claims about newcomers.

Here's another example of what reporting diversity means: At Fort Lewis College, the student population in 2013 was 57 percent white, 22 percent American Indian, 9 percent Hispanic, 1 percent African-American and 2 percent foreign (6 percent identified as "two or more races," and 3 percent did not answer the question on applications) (Fort Lewis College Institutional Research, 2013). Other differences exist, too: Some students are very wealthy, while some aren't quite sure how they're going to pay for their housing, or their next meal. Some are "non-trads," students older than the 17- to 22-year-old age bracket considered the norm. Some were drawn to FLC because they want to ski or hike in the surrounding mountains. Some came to play soccer or cycle with award-winning teams at the top of their divisions. Some came because FLC is less expensive than other colleges. And some take care of children while also working and attending classes. A reporter writing a story about FLC students would try to think about as many of these kinds of differences as possible.

For instance, a reporter assigned to do a story about a tuition increase at the college would interview students whose families had no trouble paying for college, and those for whom finances were a struggle. The reporter might also check with non-trads, or be sure to talk with students who had their own children to take care of. A reporter who was looking for story ideas would be conscious of talking to students from different and overlapping groups—those from different financial circumstances, age groups and so on.

Covering Race and Ethnicity

Let's take a quick look at a source issue that the news media have long been criticized for: coverage of racial and ethnic minorities in the United States. For example, the stories that journalists tell about nonwhites too often fit into stereotypical narratives— they're stories of struggle and crisis, or feature stories about holiday celebrations. Journalists will turn to minority sources for stories they perceive to be *about* race and ethnicity, but not for their other stories.

Reporters often fail to include the voices of nonwhites more routinely partly because their source lists are made up of white experts. This can be true no matter what the reporter's own race or ethnicity. The majority of sources for news stories that don't explicitly cover race are white because this is the group that has historically been powerful in the United States. The news value of prominence tells us that powerful people make the news.

The historical customs that help to decide who is most visible and powerful were around long before you, and will probably affect your reporting in some way no matter what your personal history. And it's not that there's some essential white or African-American or Filipino-American viewpoint—that by interviewing a Filipino-American source, you'll get "the Filipino-American view." But the more diverse your list of contacts, the more likely your stories will reflect who your community really is—and cover issues that have important implications for the people who live there.

So how do you do a better job of reporting about people who aren't white? In 2012, National Public Radio received a $1.5 million grant from the Corporation for Public Broadcasting to deepen its coverage of diversity. With the money, NPR hired or reassigned reporters and editors to form a project team, and one of their first projects was a blog that looked at issues in the national news from the angle of race and ethnicity. That regular, conscious coverage of diverse groups automatically has helped to normalize news stories about them. Story subjects ranged from an analysis of African-Americans' views about gays, to "hicksploitation," or white stereotypes on television, to a study on the wealth gap between whites and people of color. And stories that started with the project team seem to be popping up more and more in NPR's other coverage.

As part of that blog, reporter Gene Demby also wrote a series of three essays that examined neighborhoods where populations were in flux—and the complexity of race and stereotypes in those neighborhoods. For instance, one essay focused on hip-hop in Oakland, Calif., long considered an African-American community, where white people now make up the biggest group in the city.

> What's happening in Oakland is definitely gentrification, but it's not the way we often think of gentrification. It's not white people pushing out black folks; in Oakland, it's black folks leaving of their own volition, black folks being pushed out, black folks staying, and *everyone* else moving in…. The city, like the culture, is shifting from *ours* to *everyone's*. The old-fashioned models have broken down. (Demby, 2013, para. 5)

Another of Demby's essays looked at the way hip-hop music and slang were being used by people who weren't African-American: "Several critics summoned a familiar narrative about appropriation: white people, again, co-opting some piece of culture created by people of color," but something more complex was going on, Demby said:

> Cecelia Cutler, a linguist at New York's Lehman College, says that when kids who aren't black traffic in hip-hop slang or African American Vernacular English— even if they aren't themselves hip-hop fans—they're not trying to mimic blackness, per se. They're calling upon this language to signal (or "index," as linguists like to say) some of the postures that people associate with hip-hop—coolness, toughness, hipness, swagger, *separateness*. The black part is being referenced, but it's not quite the point. In some circles, Cutler said, hip-hop-inflected black speech has become a kind of prestige English. (2013, para. 22)

The reporting and news analysis in these blogs moves beyond simplistic stories about ethnic groups or about race itself to try to further people's understanding of the issues.

Of course, not everyone gets a $1.5 million grant to do a better job of reporting on race. And including diverse sources in a thoughtful way can be a complex endeavor. But simply challenging yourself to examine your sources and story patterns is a good start. And it's essential to good journalism: Stories that don't include diverse sources and subject matter are often inaccurate. Mark Trahant, the author of a book on American Indians in journalism, gave this example: Few Native Alaskans were being represented on television or in print journalism in a state where the native population was 17 percent. Jeanie Greene, the host of a rare television program about American Indian village life, said most of the television in Alaska looked as if it were about some other state—or planet: "'It's like an alien planet—you never see yourself on TV,' Greene said. 'To see yourself on TV is an amazing thing'" (as cited in Trahant, 1995, pp. 33–34).

While we've used ethnic background as an example here, it's just one possible lens.

Within every group are subgroups of people of different genders, different social classes, different levels of education—and they often have different interests and issues that good journalists will try to discover. Remember that seeking diverse sources means seeking out a range of sources who approximate a range of different views and backgrounds in your community.

> . . . white people don't all have the same kinds and qualities of privilege. Some white people have less opportunity and less power because they're working class. Just because someone is white, or even a white man, doesn't mean he's part of the ruling class.
>
> *SHERRY LINKON, CO-FOUNDER OF THE CENTER FOR WORKING-CLASS STUDIES AT YOUNGSTOWN STATE UNIVERSITY*

BE AWARE OF BIAS—OR ITS APPEARANCE—WHEN YOU SELECT SOURCES

Sometimes, the most relevant sources have at least the appearance of a strong bias about a newsworthy issue. You would still interview them. But, it's often important to also interview sources who are *not* directly involved in an issue or event. For instance, 33 workers were trapped for several months in 2010 inside a Chilean mine after part of the mine collapsed. Eventually, tensions arose between the miners and the government officials about the best way to help them survive a long ordeal. In this disagreement, the government officials told friends and family members to keep communications upbeat, because it would be easy for the miners to become dangerously depressed. In some cases, letters were censored when officials thought they were inappropriate. But many of the miners said they needed to know what was really going on, and they needed to be able to trust communications from family and the government.

This meant reporters knew that with this particular issue, both miners and government officials would have either a strong bias on the issue, or the appearance of such a bias. Even if a government official honestly believed censorship was in the best interests of the miners, readers might believe that the officials took that stance to protect their own actions. In this case, journalists knew it was important to include both miners and officials despite their apparent biases. But reporters also turned to outside experts about whether to censor information to isolated people, based on the experiences of astronauts or explorers who also had been cut off from the rest of the world for long periods of time. These sources, who were not directly involved in the issue, were less likely to hold deeply entrenched views.

The opposite can also be true: Journalists are often extra careful to include those sources with a strong agenda or bias in politically charged situations. When Congress debates the federal budget or a controversial bill, for instance, reporters make sure they interview both the Democrats and Republicans involved—knowing that such politicians are biased or will appear biased to their audiences. They make sure that they identify the political parties of politicians they quote, thereby letting readers know about the possibility of a hidden agenda driving such quotes. In the same way, a reporter would usually note in a story about a political issue that a source works for "the Heritage Foundation, a conservative think tank," for example. When sources have taken an explicit political stance or have leanings that might be relevant to a story, professional reporters are careful to point these out.

Journalists do their most helpful reporting, however, when they move beyond quoting representative Democrats and Republicans to pointing their audiences toward the truth. That happens through researching the facts of the case.

DISTANCE YOURSELF FROM SOURCES

When you need to interview a student who may be affected by a news event, you should not interview your friends—or your enemies. You should never interview your relatives. There is an obvious conflict of interest for any of these sources, and a reporter should avoid even the appearance of such a conflict. Even if you think you can do solid, fair reporting by relying on people you know well on a personal basis, your readers won't think so. You may get such sources past your editor, who doesn't know who your friends are. But other people notice, and this practice erodes the credibility of a news organization.

INTERVIEW PRIMARY SOURCES

We pointed out earlier that you should avoid quoting from other news sources because they take you farther away from the primary source. The same idea holds true for interviewing people: If you talk with a senator's spokesperson, the answers you get may well be what the senator wants you to hear. But will they be as thoughtful, or for that matter, as close to the truth about what the senator really thinks as they would have been if you had interviewed the senator? Or let's say you hear from a friend that the student body president might resign. You would need to confirm that information with the president—the primary source—directly.

INTERVIEW EXPERT SOURCES . . .

When they think about different kinds of sources, journalists need to consider their sources' expertise. As you decide which sources to interview for a particular story, a good rule of thumb is to try to interview at least one expert and at least one person who is directly or indirectly affected by events or issues under discussion. Let's look at an example.

In November 2010, the *Boston Globe* published a follow-up story about several high school soccer players who were suspended after they were accused of hazing their teammates. Here are the first three paragraphs of the story:

> Educators and sports officials from around the state are defending the suspension of members of the Needham High School girls' soccer team for allegedly hazing younger teammates, saying the sharp response was necessary despite the furor it caused.
>
> "These events have to be handled firmly and directly," said Tom Scott, executive director of the Massachusetts Association of School Superintendents. "It's not just the students directly involved; it's the whole culture of the school. Everyone is watching how the adults are going to respond, and if the adults don't send a message with some degree of severity, it's as if they're condoning it."
>
> "The only thing I can say is that hazing is a form of bullying," said Glenn Koocher, executive director of the Massachusetts Association of School Committees. "I would say parents are responding almost as they always do, but when things cool down, people generally see that the school has taken an appropriate response." (Abel & Noonan, 2010, para. 1–3)

Look at the "expert sources" in this excerpt: In addition to Scott and Koocher, the story also quoted a Massachusetts Interscholastic Athletic Association spokesman, the Needham Public Schools superintendent and the police chief.

It's easy to imagine that lots of people would have strong opinions about why the school chose to suspend the students. But only a school official, such as the principal or superintendent, could speak with authority about the school's choice. Because your job as a journalist is to seek truth, you need to talk with sources who know what's really going on. In this story, the parents didn't make the decision to suspend the soccer players; they can speak with authority about how their families' lives were affected by that decision or whether they think the school should have acted differently, but they usually wouldn't have direct information about how the decision was made. When possible, it's essential to talk with decision-makers.

An expert source can often provide a sense of the big picture: For a story about why the music program is being discontinued, the dean of a particular college might well be able to provide you with the numbers of music majors compared to business majors. If the dean is unwilling to talk, you may want to interview chairs of music departments at other colleges to ask whether there has been a similar trend elsewhere, or whether economic forces or changes in musical tastes might be factors.

Even when local experts are available, you may want to seek out additional expert sources. In an attempt to provide context and a sense of the big picture, journalists often seek out national or regional experts to provide analysis of an issue or trend. In the Needham school story, notice that the reporters moved beyond local experts. If the community was suggesting that local school officials were somehow unfair or wrong, then their expertise could become less authoritative. By interviewing the executive directors of the state association of school committees and the state association of school superintendents, the reporters at least consulted with people who were less likely to be biased by local connections or rivalries.

State or national experts can give a sense of perspective: If your university's student enrollment is down or tuition rises significantly, it's helpful to know whether colleges across the state or the country are experiencing a similar trend.

Finally, if you fail to check with those in power for a relevant story, you may lose credibility and access. If, based only on student comments, you wrote a story saying the college paid too much for a new building, the vice president of finances might well be reluctant to talk with you for your next story. And you may lose credibility with your editors and audience, who perceive the vice president of finance as the one with the expertise. Checking with experts is often a convention with so much use and custom behind it that it has become necessary in order for a story to earn the respect of readers and other journalists.

. . . BUT ALSO INTERVIEW THE PEOPLE AFFECTED BY AN ISSUE

Reporters can lean too heavily on "experts," however (Fig. 8-8). Remember Sigal's "convention of authoritative sources," which reinforces hierarchy and returns reporters too often to the same sources. Including citizens who are not experts on a particular issue does not mean simply doing person-on-the-street interviews, however. An online poll that asks people whether they support or oppose the president's health care plan doesn't help anyone:

> With this simplistic approach, the media often set up two extremes, usually represented by experts and spokespeople on opposite ends of the spectrum. Then, citizens are asked to take a side on an artificially polarized and oversimplified issue. From there, attention turns back to the experts and spokespeople; debate devolves into a fighting match between two extremes—neither of which represents the positions of most people—and the public finds itself disenfranchised. (Barger & Barney, 2004, p. 198)

However, you can include differing viewpoints in a way that contributes substance and color to your story and encourages people to become involved in issues that affect them. In the Needham school story, for example, reporters also talked with a senior at the high school, a junior, the football coach, a father of one of the soccer players and the godfather of one of the suspended students. The story gave a sense of the sharp differences among the affected groups, and the reasons for their opinions—and that, in turn, gave readers a way to come to a reasoned conclusion about the events so far.

As you seek the stories of those affected by the larger issues you report on, we'd like to provide a caution: Bennett, the media scholar critiques **personalization**, which means

FIGURE 8-8 Occupy Wall Street presented a unique challenge to journalists trying to report accurately. The movement intentionally had no official organizers. That meant that anyone a reporter interviewed couldn't begin to represent the organization as a whole.

turning complex stories that should be about context and the issues themselves, into more superficial stories based on individual personalities. One example Bennett gives is that of a news story about welfare-to-work programs that starts by telling the story of an individual who was happy to be getting a job (2005, p. 52). Bennett points out that "the article did not mention the large-scale social, political, or economic implications of the program cuts until paragraphs eight, nine, and ten" (p. 53). The article dealt with these briefly, then returned to its focus on the individual. The problem here is that the experiences of the individual affected by the issues discussed in the story are told *at the expense of explanations of the issues themselves.* That is, there's nothing wrong with including the stories of individuals who are affected by policy changes; what makes this bad journalism is a version that's one-sided and reductionist because the story's entire focus becomes about that one individual's experiences. It's still important to interview people who are affected by the issues, but you need to remember that those personalities should not overshadow the issues.

As you decide whom to talk to about the decisions made by administrators or changes pointed out by experts, you'll also need to think carefully. Follow these three additional rules in reporting from affected sources:

- Choose someone in a position to comment because of that person's knowledge. If you're trying to get student reaction to a new chemistry building, you probably wouldn't interview an English major—unless you wanted to talk with some students in a chemistry class for non-majors, and then also some chemistry students. Either way, it should be clear to you why you've chosen these particular sources. If you're getting reaction to a controversial campus election, you might talk with a political science student, or someone who has served on the student senate in the past for their presumed expertise. However, you really don't want to quote someone who not only doesn't care, but also doesn't know anything. The source you choose must be knowledgeable about the aspects of the issue on which the person comments; otherwise, that person's opinions are uninformed and may be, at best, useless to your readers. In the worst case, such uninformed opinions may even be damaging because they foster false rumors or spread disinformation about issues. For instance, if you were to interview an uninformed person who said they had heard the chemistry building was unsafe, your story might conceivably lead to unnecessary and costly investigations, or it might prevent some student from taking classes in that building.

- Second, you need to be clear to your readers about why this person's views matter. If you decide to interview students in the chemistry class for non-majors, identify them: "Carlos Jones, an anthropology major who is taking Chemistry for Consumers this semester, said he thought the new chemistry labs were up to date, but he wished the money had been spent on the proposed recreation center instead." Always offer some identifying information on your sources that shows why their views are relevant.

- As you seek out interviews with people affected by the news—and this holds true for your expert sources as well—avoid falling into the trap of deciding ahead of time what information you'll get. The more experience you have, the more you'll be tempted to "go out and get a quote" from someone, with a preconceived notion of what that quote will be. Such an approach is unfair to your sources, because rather than thinking of them as fellow human beings who may have something interesting to say, you are thinking of them as conduits to sound bites or quotes.

AVOID USING ANONYMOUS SOURCES

In 1974, Richard Milhous Nixon resigned from his job as president of the United States. Despite presidential controversies before and since, the event shocked the nation and rocked the world of journalism. The presidential scandal had repercussions for journalism because Bob Woodward and Carl Bernstein, two reporters from *The Washington Post*, were influential in discovering and publishing information that helped lead to the only presidential resignation in U.S. history. Two years earlier, police had discovered burglars in the Democratic national headquarters in the Watergate building in Washington, D.C. In the following weeks and months, Woodward and Bernstein helped to uncover and publicize ties between the burglary and its cover-up and top White House aides. When Woodward and Bernstein later published an account of their investigation, *All the President's Men,* they described the most famous anonymous source in American journalism, "Deep Throat." Because of the apparent power and influence of Woodward and Bernstein in contributing to the fall of an American president, investigative journalism and the use of anonymous sources gained glamour and popularity after the publication of their book. Ben Bradlee, the editor of *The Washington Post* at the time, approved the use of the anonymous source although Bradlee required the reporters to tell him Deep Throat's real name, and to corroborate information from him with at least one other source.

Despite Woodward and Bernstein's success, we do not recommend using anonymous sources. "There's an assumption out there that we [use anonymous sources] all the time and it's not a big deal. But we don't and it is a big deal," says Mike King, an editor at the *Atlanta Journal-Constitution* (as cited in Rosen, 2003, p. 50). If sources are not named within a story, readers can't verify information for themselves, as the same article points out, citing the philosophy of *Syracuse Post-Standard* editor Mike Connor:

> Connor likes the idea of being able to give his readers such conclusive information in a story, such "scientific proof," that the accuracy is beyond doubt. "Ideally newspaper reporting is built on a solid foundation of fact that any reader could go out and gather the same facts," he says. "When you have unnamed sources, that's impossible." (Rosen, p. 49)

When sources remain unnamed, they don't have to stand behind their words. That means they're less likely to be concerned about getting facts straight, or thinking about consequences. Those criticized by an anonymous source have no recourse, no way to "face" their accusers. And when you use anonymous sources, you're also asking your readers to take more on faith than they usually do. Readers have no way to verify the information or be sure that you're not making it up.

But what if there is an issue of great public interest, and the only sources you can find to talk about the issue refuse to allow you to use their names? If you chose to use anonymous sources in a story, you would not be alone. The media continue to quote anonymous sources on a daily basis. Again, we firmly believe that the cost to journalistic credibility, to readers and to those who are criticized, is too great to justify such a use. But the reputable journalists who *do* use anonymous sources point out that they do so very carefully, and that they follow the procedures required by their news organizations. If there is an issue that you feel is essential for your readers to know about, and the only way to provide that information is through using anonymous sources, we recommend that you follow a few key steps:

- Make sure the reason a source asks to be anonymous is acceptable—that is, that you are not allowing someone to avoid accountability for an action or statement for which that person should be held accountable.

- Discuss the issue with your editor or producer before you grant anonymity, and get approval.
- Tell the source they will remain anonymous unless you are served a subpoena, in which case you will obey the law and reveal their name.

Reporters can be held legally responsible to the courts for information they know, and courts often do not exempt reporters from subpoenas, despite those reporters' promises to sources to keep their identities private. For instance, in a U.S. Supreme Court case, *Branzburg v. Hayes* (1972), the court ruled that the First Amendment does not give a journalist the right to refuse to appear before a grand jury, or to refuse to answer their questions about the identity of a source. Reporters who fail to obey a court subpoena may go to jail.

In a well-known case in recent years, Judith Miller of *The New York Times* and Matthew Cooper of *Time* magazine both conducted interviews with anonymous sources who disclosed the identity of CIA agent Valerie Plame. Revealing a CIA agent's identity can be illegal, and in the resulting court case, both journalists were threatened with prison sentences unless they would name their sources. The Miller and Cooper example is especially convoluted, which points to one of the problems with using anonymous sources: The CIA had sent Plame's husband, Joseph Wilson, to Niger in 2002 to find out if Saddam Hussein had tried to buy uranium there (see Hertzberg, 2005, or Liptak & Newman, 2005). Wilson, a former Foreign Service officer, reported that he found nothing to indicate such a possibility. Wilson's information was apparently ignored, and after the war began, he wrote an opinion piece for *The New York Times* about his findings, suggesting that the Bush administration had tried to drum up evidence of weapons of mass destruction where none existed. Soon after, columnist Robert Novak wrote a column revealing Plame's identity as a CIA agent, and then Cooper published a piece in *Time* magazine. Miller never even wrote a story about the subject. At the last minute, Cooper's source released him from their confidentiality agreement. That source was Karl Rove, President George W. Bush's political adviser. Miller served almost three months in prison for withholding information about her conversations with her anonymous source, I. Lewis "Scooter" Libby, the chief of staff for Vice President Dick Cheney. Ultimately, Libby released Miller from her promise of confidentiality and she was released from prison. And Libby himself was convicted of lying under oath in connection with leaking Plame's name to the press. But notice that Miller's sacrifice for professional integrity was tainted because she was protecting a source who was accused of manipulating the news media to take revenge on Wilson. And note that while you may promise your sources anonymity, there's no guarantee that the courts will shield you in keeping that promise.

The same Supreme Court case, *Branzburg v. Hayes* (1972), also recognized a reporter's right, in some situations, to withhold information from courts. The court stated that to force reporters to reveal their sources, the government must show (1) probable cause to believe that the journalist has information relevant to a specific illegal action, (2) that the information cannot be obtained by some other means, and (3) a compelling and overriding interest in the information.

SHIELD LAWS HELP—BUT DON'T DEPEND ON THEM TOO MUCH

Many states have enacted **shield laws** to protect reporters who hope to shield the identity of their sources. However, these shield laws vary radically from state to state and ultimately may not offer much protection for reporters or their sources (Fig. 8-9).

And reporters can also be held legally accountable to the sources themselves: If you promise your sources anonymity, that promise may be legally binding. In the landmark *Cohen v. Cowles Media Co.* (1991) court case, the U.S. Supreme Court ruled that reporters had violated an implied contract when they published the name of an anonymous source. A source told reporters for the *St. Paul Pioneer Press Dispatch* and the *Minneapolis Star and Tribune* he would provide them with information in exchange for a guarantee of anonymity. The reporters agreed and the source gave them what seemed to be incriminating information about one of the candidates for Minnesota lieutenant governor. But the information turned out to be about minor offenses with extenuating explanations. Furthermore, the source was working for another candidate's campaign. When the newspapers' editorial staffs met independently, they decided that if they published the information, they were ethically bound to include the source's identity because of his personal interest in damaging the reputation of another political candidate. The stories ran with the name of the source, Cohen, who was fired the same day that the news stories were published. Cohen sued the newspapers' publishers, Cowles Media, and won for breach of contract. This has set a precedent that an agreement between a journalist and a source can be considered an enforceable contract.

FIGURE 8-9 Shield laws provide limited protection for reporters, but vary from state to state. Check your state's laws at www.dmlp .org or www.rcfp.org.

To sum up: Using anonymous sources can raise questions of credibility and can allow your sources to escape accountability. It can create legal problems with the courts if you are asked by a court to reveal sources, or with sources, if you decide later to reveal those sources' names. While the courts provide some limited protection in the form of shield laws, reporters ultimately can be required by the law to reveal their sources. We do not recommend using anonymous sources, but if you decide to do so, we advise using the checklist just outlined.

DON'T FABRICATE SOURCES OR QUOTES

In 2012, Jonah Lehrer's book about Bob Dylan was published and quickly became a bestseller. But Lehrer's career came crashing down when *Tablet* magazine revealed that Lehrer had apparently made up several Dylan quotes in the book, and had certainly cobbled together others from different contexts. The *Tablet*'s Michael Moynihan, a self-described "Dylan obsessive," contacted Lehrer to ask about the quotes:

> Over the next three weeks, Lehrer stonewalled, misled, and, eventually, outright lied to me. Yesterday, Lehrer finally confessed that he has never met or corresponded with Jeff Rosen, Dylan's manager; he has never seen an unexpurgated version of Dylan's interview for No Direction Home, something he offered up to stymie my search; that a missing quote he claimed could be found in an episode of Dylan's "Theme Time Radio Hour" cannot, in fact, be found there; and that a 1995 radio interview, supposedly available in a printed collection of Dylan interviews called The Fiddler Now Upspoke, also didn't exist. (2012, para. 8)

Lehrer subsequently apologized and was fired by *The New Yorker,* and his deceptions made headlines across the country.

In 1981, Janet Cooke, a reporter for *The Washington Post*, won a Pulitzer Prize for her reporting on the effects of heroin trade in poor neighborhoods in the city. Her story focused on Jimmy, an 8-year-old boy who had become a heroin addict after his mother's boyfriend introduced him to the drug. The story was a well-told investigative feature that drew attention to a worthy cause. Unfortunately, the story was false: Cooke later explained that Jimmy was a composite source, her own creation based on stories she had heard from multiple sources. When she couldn't find a child like Jimmy who would go on the record, she decided to make him up. Subsequently, the newspaper returned the Pulitzer Prize, and Cooke and the *Post* suffered humiliation and disgrace.

Stephen Glass, a reporter for *The New Republic*, not only created stories and sources, but created fictional websites to make those sources seem valid. He was fired from the magazine in 1998—and a movie, *Shattered Glass,* was later made about his journalistic transgressions. Journalists continue to succumb to this temptation: *The New York Times* reporter Jayson Blair and *USA Today* reporter Jack Kelly were fired after their news organizations learned they had made up parts of news stories.

Perhaps a reporter's aim in making up a quote or source is noble, as Cooke's seemed to be. Maybe your source talks for a long time and beats around the bush so much that there's no succinct quote you can use from what they have said. Or maybe you're hoping for more colorful language. Your source may even tell you, "You know what I mean—make it sound good."

But if you act on any of these impulses, you're endangering your own credibility and that of your news organization. Your source will know that you've made up the quote, and sources often talk to other people. Furthermore, what you're writing is no longer journalism. Good fiction often attempts to communicate a deeper truth through made-up events and people, but journalism uses a different method: It reports real events and real people and what they actually said.

Finding Sources

Once you identify the people you need to contact, how do you find them? Sometimes, this is easy: You can usually look up the local government directory online to find out county commissioners' names and phone numbers, for instance. The same is true for most government officials or businesses. But what if you're looking for someone who's not an official?

ASK EACH SOURCE FOR OTHER SOURCES

For most news stories, you'll know how to contact at least a couple of sources. Experienced reporters also know to ask each of these for ideas, names and contact information for other sources. For instance, if you're trying to piece together a story about computer hacking at your school, you can probably figure out how to reach a professor or a computer science major you can interview. Before you finish the interview, you can ask for ideas about other sources. Sometimes, this can lead you to multiple sources, and each of these sources has the potential to lead you to others.

GET OUT ON THE STREET

The old-fashioned way to find information is to get out on the street and talk to people—and this is still a powerful tool (Fig. 8-10). For instance, if you're covering a residential fire, you can knock on neighbors' doors to find witnesses. Sometimes, it's especially helpful to simply show up at places: You might walk to the fire department during a time when firefighters aren't busy, see who's there and interview them. If someone scrawls a racist epithet on a professor's door, you can go over to the professor's office and see who has offices nearby. There's a good chance those people are acquaintances or colleagues who know the professor. If you go to the scene of a newsworthy event or issue, you're likely to find sources you would not have otherwise. And sources are usually more likely to talk with you in person.

DON'T FORGET YOUR OWN CONTACTS

Reporters don't interview their own friends and families as sources for news stories. But they absolutely *do* talk to their own friends and families to find out how to contact

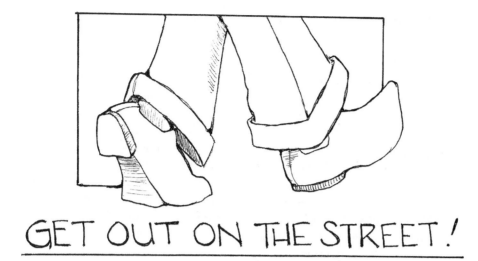

GET OUT ON THE STREET!

FIGURE 8-10 "Shoe leather" is a classic journalism term for getting out of the office to interview people in person and do firsthand research.

other sources. If there's a controversy in the sociology department, think about the friends you have who are sociology majors. Ask other staff members at your news organization if they know people who might be involved. If you know any professors well, ask them for ideas about whom to contact.

USE SOCIAL MEDIA

Professional news organizations also actively solicit information from citizen journalists, a practice called crowdsourcing. As a reporter gathering news, you might ask your readers for tips or help for a continuing story; you might ask for insider sources for an investigative piece; or you might ask for people who have experienced the effects of an issue or trend firsthand.

In April 2007, a Virginia Tech student killed two people in a dormitory and then shot 30 more people at Norris Hall, a campus classroom building. The Virginia Tech newspaper, the *Collegiate Times*, won special attention for its coverage—even though the editor in chief, Amie Steele, had only been on the job three weeks. Here's what she and her staff of fellow student journalists did:

> The Collegiate Times tapped into the vast social networking resources on the Internet to help track down names of the dead. At 10 p.m., Steele assigned two reporters to mine the wildly popular Facebook and MySpace, along with other sites, for posts that could provide clues. They also turned to contacts such as classmates and faculty for information. Many on the paper's staff had friends who knew students in classes at Norris Hall that day. Once they had names, they could check for profiles on any of these sites.
>
> If they found a profile, they searched for messages such as "I miss you already" or "RIP." They then sought confirmation from friends or family members. The students pulled an all-nighter, posting the first names at 4:07 a.m. "To us, it was just crazy to

have CNN quote our list of victims and for huge media outlets to be citing us as their source for information," says Steele. (Ricchiardi, 2007, para. 18–19)

Notice how creative the student journalists were in using the social media: This was when Facebook (and MySpace) were still very new. And the students started with information from personal contacts and used this to make their online searches more efficient.

But journalists need to treat social media with the same skepticism they do other sources. For instance, notice that the *Collegiate Times* journalists also confirmed the information they found at Facebook and MySpace with other sources. It's all too easy to create a hoax message or site—as happened when someone hacked into the Associated Press Twitter account in 2013 and tweeted that the President had been injured, or when the *Salt Lake Tribune* used a MySpace page for information about a man accused of shooting a corrections officer (Spencer, 2007). The page turned out to be a hoax page, and the information was incorrect.

The social media are great places to start looking for additional sources, to get ideas and to get possible contact information. But you will need to confirm everything. Remember that most of the information at a site like Facebook is uploaded by the subject of the profile. That means the person is projecting a particular image of themself, the one that they wants the public to see. And Brant Houston, the James L. Knight Chair in Investigative and Enterprise Journalism at the University of Illinois, warns that you need to respect people's expectations of privacy when you use social media for information you intend to make public:

> "Even though it's totally public, or potentially open to the public, it might be of such sensitivity that you don't want to be the journalist who promulgates it because it has nothing to do with the story." (as cited in Spencer, 2007, para. 31)

This means that information you find on Facebook or LinkedIn or Twitter should be subject to the same tests you apply to information from other sources:

- Is the source who they say they are? Do they really have the credentials they say they do?
- Does the source have the authority to speak on the particular issue you're covering?
- Is the information timely?
- Is the information accurate?

WHEN YOU'RE STUMPED FOR SOURCES, THINK CREATIVELY

Sometimes when you call to ask a source for an interview, the answer will be an unequivocal, "No." In some cases, there's little or nothing you can do about this. But if the story is important enough, you can keep trying, and use your imagination. Journalists at *The Nation*, a leftward-leaning political magazine, noticed some news stories and court cases that suggested a larger-than-usual number of attacks on Iraqi citizens. To find out more information, here's what reporters did:

> *The Nation* interviewed fifty combat veterans, including forty soldiers, eight marines and two sailors, over a period of seven months beginning in July 2006. To find veterans willing to speak on the record about their experiences in Iraq, we sent queries to organizations dedicated to US troops and their families, including Iraq and Afghanistan Veterans of America, the antiwar groups Military Families Speak Out, Veterans for Peace and Iraq Veterans Against the War and the prowar group Vets for Freedom. The leaders of IVAW and Paul Rieckhoff, the founder of IAVA, were especially helpful in putting us in touch with Iraq War veterans. Finally, we found veterans through word of mouth, as many of those we interviewed referred us to their military friends. (Hedges & Al-Arian, 2007, para. 23)

The reporters obviously realized that finding U.S. veterans willing to speak on the record about Iraqi citizen deaths would be difficult. Rather than settling for anonymous reports or no story at all, they thought creatively about how to find sources they could name in their story. In this case, this meant writing queries to organizations. And notice that while most of those organizations were against the war, one—the Vets for Freedom—was for it. And as the reporters interviewed each source, they asked for the names of additional possible sources.

In this example, reporters had to move beyond simply calling an official source to get their story. Because they pushed a little harder to come up with other possible sources, their reporting was more truthful, more interesting and more helpful to their audiences.

Exercises for Chapter 8

EXERCISE 8-1: Select one of the news stories following and identify any issues you see with the choice of sources. Are any of the sources problematic? Are any of the sources especially good ideas? Make a list of pros and cons for each source.

a. For a story about a drop in car sales, a reporter calls the largest car dealer in town, a man who is also the reporter's uncle.

b. For a story about grade inflation, a reporter with limited time talks only with the following sources: the student body president, a student majoring in business, a student majoring in art and a student majoring in science.

c. For a story about a tuition hike, a reporter on deadline and with limited time talks only with the following sources: the college president, the college controller and a member of the college's board of directors.

d. For a story on a new local business, a student does a long and thorough interview with the business' owner. Is that enough?

EXERCISE 8-2: Select a long news story, such as one you might find in a news magazine. What types of sources did the reporter use? Are there voices that should have been included, but weren't? If so, what are they, and why should they be given space? Write a description of what you find.

EXERCISE 8-3: Select one of the story ideas following and use archives and social media to identify, by name or by job title, **four** possible sources. List these and describe why they would be good sources.

a. A controversial political speaker is scheduled to visit your campus, and you learn that a student organization is planning a protest during the speech.

b. Your university has decided to raise its admissions standards. Under the new standards, 5 percent of the current student body would not have been admitted to the school.

c. A wildfire breaks out, threatening nearby wilderness areas. The next few days are supposed to be especially windy.

EXERCISE 8-4: For a news story assigned to you in class, use archives and social media to identify, by name or by job title, **four** possible sources. List these sources and describe why they would be good sources.

EXERCISE 8-5: You are assigned a story on what happens when someone is arrested for driving under the influence of alcohol. You want to localize the story by finding students who have had this experience. However, all of the students you find don't want you to use their name. How do you proceed? How do you make your case to your boss?

CHAPTER 9

HOW DO YOU
CONDUCT
AN INTERVIEW?

On June 22, 2010, *Rolling Stone* magazine published an article about Gen. Stanley McChrystal, the head U.S. commander in Afghanistan. Less than two days after its publication, that article helped to topple one of the most powerful military men in the world. Here's an excerpt from reporter Michael Hastings' profile:

> The general prides himself on being sharper and ballsier than anyone else, but his brashness comes with a price: Although McChrystal has been in charge of the war for only a year, in that short time he has managed to piss off almost everyone with a stake in the conflict. Last fall, during the question-and-answer session following a speech he gave in London, McChrystal dismissed the counterterrorism strategy being advocated by Vice President Joe Biden as "shortsighted," saying it would lead to a state of "Chaos-istan." The remarks earned him a smackdown from the president himself, who summoned the general to a terse private meeting aboard Air Force One. The message to McChrystal seemed clear: *Shut the fuck up, and keep a lower profile.* (2010, para. 16)

But McChrystal's 2010 profile in *Rolling Stone* was anything but low-profile. The quotes that commenters—and, apparently, the president—objected to were those that showed disrespect for civilian commanders. For instance, Hastings said that McChrystal and his staff members joked about Vice President Joseph Biden:

> "Are you asking about Vice President Biden?" McChrystal says with a laugh. "Who's that?"
>
> "Biden?" suggests a top adviser. "Did you say: Bite Me?" (Hastings, 2010, para. 18–19)

Many critics agreed that McChrystal's behavior was inappropriate: He knew he was with a reporter and his public criticism of his commanders was insubordinate. But while the general and his staff members did not question the accuracy of the quotes, some staff members said the reporter had misled them or been unclear about what was off the record. One conversation, for instance, took place in a bar when the men had been drinking heavily. Some of them thought that what they said at the bar was private.

We've retold this story here because it vividly demonstrates how much impact a journalist's work can have on a source: Hastings' article led to the general losing his post and ended his army career of more than 30 years. Because appearing in the news can have all kinds of consequences for sources—including significant changes to their lives—reporters need to be very, very careful to treat those sources with respect. That doesn't mean it's necessarily wrong to write a story that may contribute to the end of someone's career or that may reveal someone's unethical or criminal actions. Making this kind of information public can be an important part of your job. Rather, treating your sources with respect means remembering that sources are fellow human beings, and treating them with empathy and humaneness. It means being sure that you quote them accurately and in context. It means being honest with them.

In some sense, writing articles about other people decreases the control they have over their own stories. After all, the reporter gets to decide what to include and what to omit, which points to emphasize and how they all fit together into a narrative. But, paradoxically, writing stories about other people also gives them more control over their own narratives. That's because accurate journalism can help your sources get their versions of events out to the rest of the world.

When a student from our college died in a tragic accident several years ago, the student newspaper was reluctant to do a story. Editors and reporters didn't want to bother the family, who were obviously dealing with a life event more important than chatting with a college reporter. But it turned out that the family *wanted* to tell people about the young man who had died—what he was like, who he had been and what they loved about him. Talking to journalists allowed them to tell the community more about the person they knew so well.

Humane reporters remain acutely aware of the vulnerability of their sources, but they're also aware of what good interviewing and careful journalism can offer those sources. From your first interaction with a source through the representation of that person in your final news story, a journalist can have significant power over the world's view of the source. That means you owe your source respect in the form of accuracy, courtesy and humaneness—a practice that starts before you even arrive at your first interview.

Research Ahead of Time

Being prepared for an interview is one of the ways reporters treat sources with respect. It also makes for a better interview. If you're interviewing a college dean about the controversial firing of a professor, you need to know if that dean has been in the news lately. You may need to understand the basics of tenure and the college's firing policies. If you don't know about relevant issues, your sources may treat you with contempt or give you canned answers that provide little substance or insight.

Even when you're reporting on issues that aren't controversial, doing basic background research will make the difference between an underreported story and a well-informed one. For a story about a guest speaker on campus, for instance, you might not be able to interview the speaker ahead of time, but you could call the organizer and find out her expectations, the costs of the speaker and who the organizations are that are funding the speaker and why they've chosen to invite this person. You could also do some online research about the speaker and the topic.

Likewise, if you were assigned to cover a city council meeting, you'd usually request an agenda and then call a city councilor or the mayor or city manager to discuss it. You might find that you needed to contact other sources ahead of time if you were on a tight deadline afterward, or you might simply be able to ask more informed questions and take better notes during the meeting.

Your research should help you get a general idea about a story's direction before your first interview. For instance, if the guest speaker's topic is, "What communities can do locally about climate change," you'll have a pretty good sense of what the speech will be about just from finding out the topic ahead of time. But there's a delicate balance here. A well-prepared reporter has an idea of a story's direction, but remains flexible. A speaker might say something unexpected, for example. And from your very first interview, you need to communicate this balanced approach: You should have the background knowledge to see the most likely news angle, and you should have the openness to recognize the implications of a surprising comment or see a better angle.

Plan Your Questions

Doing the background research and planning for a story is a multifaceted process: You'll need to organize your thoughts, to think carefully about the kinds of information you'll need, to think about which sources you need to interview. You shouldn't re-report what's already out there; you should advance the story by bringing in new information and insight.

Most reporters write out a list of questions before going to an interview. In fact, until you've conducted a lot of interviews, you should spend some time doing this and refining your questions. The kind of story you're writing will affect what questions you'll ask. For instance, if you're doing a few paragraphs on a car accident, then you don't need the anecdotes and examples that you might want in a longer, issues-oriented story. You simply need to be sure you know the basic information essential to an accident story, which you'd usually get from the officer in charge:

- Who was involved?
- How much damage did the accident cause?
- Who was hurt and how badly?
- When and where did the accident happen?
- How did the accident happen? (This is usually a description.)
- What possible impact is there for your news audience? If it's a car accident, is there an especially dangerous intersection people need to know about? Was the driver doing something dangerous that people should avoid?
- Who responded to the accident—police? Firefighters? How long did they take to arrive at the scene?

Reporters quickly learn to keep either a mental or written list of such questions for any interview, so they don't get back to the office without some essential facts.

You should also keep in mind how your questions affect what your story will look like. Your story will be too short if you simply ask a list of factual questions: "Where did you go to college? What is your full job title?" These are questions that ask for short-answer responses. If you ask only closed-ended questions like these, you may be prepared with plenty of questions and still return with only enough material to write a few sentences such as the following:

> "Ralph Jenkins, a chemistry professor originally from Wisconsin, has worked at this college for 20 years. He enjoys reading."

To find out more from your interview subjects, it's helpful to ask open-ended questions such as, "Could you give me an example? Or, "Do you remember one time in particular when that happened?" Or, "What would be the impact on students?"

It's also important not to force the story to go in a preconceived direction. One way that reporters do this is by asking **leading questions**—that is, questions that lead to a particular response (Fig. 9-1). Let's say you're doing a story on Mark Zuckerberg, one of the founders of Facebook, and you interview two former Harvard students who sued him, accusing him of stealing their idea. You ask the following:

Weaker: *"Weren't you angry at Zuckerberg?"*

That's a leading question. A question like this tries to pull an interview subject in a particular direction, based on a reporter's own preconceived notions. You can still give your interviewees a chance to air their feelings, however:

Better: *"What did you think when you found out Zuckerberg had started Facebook?"*

This second question is more honest reporting, and it allows for more complex responses. If your interviewee is angry at Zuckerberg, he can still say so. But if he was angry at first and then felt saddened, or isn't angry at all because he doesn't

FIGURE 9-1 The way you ask a question helps determine whether you're leading your sources in a particular direction or allowing them to respond organically.

take the situation personally, or had a fascinating and original response to what he says Zuckerberg did, he has the chance to say so.

Leading questions aren't necessarily negative. Let's say you interview Zuckerberg's favorite professor and ask him the following question:

Weaker: *"You're probably pretty proud of Mark, aren't you?"*

Again, you're heading the interview subject in a particular direction. Questions like these can result in less-truthful responses. The professor might subconsciously feel he's a bad person if he doesn't say he's proud of Zuckerberg, but what if he feels something more interesting—or would simply use a different word to describe those feelings? For example, what if the professor felt something more like the following:

> I'm impressed with what Mark's done in some ways, but I have mixed feelings about what Facebook provides to the world. I worry that the friendships and threads are based on superficial connections, and that these are threatening our culture's deeper community.

To allow for a more nuanced answer like this, you'd have to ask a better question:

Better: *"When you realized what a success Facebook had become, what was your response?"*

While you need ideas ahead of time about what your story is, sometimes sources will say something quite different from what you expect. This is yet another reason why it's so important to really listen to what the subjects of your interviews are saying. In fact, sometimes you'll see that by following up on an unexpected answer or comment, or simply letting a source pursue a different conversational direction, your story will develop its own course.

Contact Your Sources

When you're contacting sources, your responsibility toward them means you should be respectful and courteous, and also that you shouldn't wait until the last minute to try to set up an interview. However, if you're on deadline, you may not be able to give sources as much time as they would like. That's because you have to balance your responsibility to them with your responsibility toward readers to provide timely information. Still, there are several measures you can take to be considerate of your sources, and this holds true whether you're calling someone, emailing. or stopping by in person:

- Identify yourself by name and say you are a reporter.
- Identify your news organization.
- Briefly explain the topic of your story and the area you'd like to ask about in this conversation: "I'm doing a story on the student council meeting tomorrow night, and I wanted to ask you a few questions about why you're planning to stop funding the student literary magazine."
- If you're setting up an interview for later, say how long you expect the interview to take: "I'd like about 20–30 minutes of your time to find out more about funding cuts."
- Whenever you set up an interview, be prepared for an impromptu interview right then. There's always a chance the source might say, "Well, I have a few minutes now—fire away."

The Interview

IN PERSON

As a journalist, you'll be tempted to save time and trouble by interviewing people by phone, text or email, but we strongly encourage you to conduct your interviews face

FIGURE 9-2 In this broadcast interview with Iran's President Hassan Rouhani, NBC's Ann Curry can't help but be part of the story because she's on camera. When you conduct a live broadcast interview, you need to be prepared so that your question sounds good the first time and you're ready to ask follow-up questions to help the conversation flow smoothly.

to face (Fig. 9-2). You learn more, you have a chance to establish a stronger connection with your source and your source has a chance to interact more with you. And it's usually more fun. Also, if your story includes audio, it will almost always sound clearer and better when you've conducted the interview in person. Whenever possible, allow yourself and your source a healthy amount of time for an interview—20 to 30 minutes is usually good.

For an in-person interview, you need to do the following ahead of time:

- Call, email or stop by to schedule the interview.

- Usually, you need to do this well in advance—say, a week ahead of time. However, if you're working on a breaking news story or dealing with a public official, you might need to schedule an interview only a day or two ahead of time or on the same day.

- Fully identify yourself and tell your source the kind of information you'll want to ask him or her about.

- Give the expected length of the interview and make an appointment.

An interview is a good time to think about stewardship: What will your interview subject think about journalism students, or about journalism itself, after talking with you? Basic professionalism usually means conveying a combination of self-respect and respect for the person with whom you're interacting. You should be pleasant but, when necessary, firm.

The little things count: You should plan to arrive 10 to 15 minutes early. That will allow for road construction or parking problems, and it will communicate to your source that you care. While you're waiting, you can review your questions and notes. Depending on the situation, you probably don't need to wear a suit or skirt and jacket, but you do want to look nice (Fig. 9-3). Attention to what you're wearing can help to

FIGURE 9-3 Part of creating a professional demeanor includes dressing appropriately for the interview. One trick is to mimic the clothing of the person you'll interview. For instance, if you were interviewing an attorney in an office, you'd be more likely to wear a blazer or suit jacket and nice shoes; if you were interviewing a farmer in a field, that outfit might distance you from your source. But there are limits: saggy jeans or low-cut tops are probably not a good choice, ever.

establish immediately for your interview subject a basic sense that you respect the person and take him seriously.

You may know that it's helpful to look a person in the eye and give a firm hand-shake without overdoing it—don't injure your source, of course. Introduce yourself again and remind the source about the subject of your story. To establish rapport, you might comment on the weather or a recent soccer match or a picture on the wall. Sources understand that you're treating them personably before you delve into the work of the interview.

Starting with small talk also gives you time to unobtrusively get out a tablet, and a recorder, if you have one. And you do need to take notes, even if you're recording the interview. Sources notice when you don't, and it makes them skeptical about your accuracy—and they're right. Plus, you'll want notes as back up if your recording is garbled or erased, which happens.

Your first interview questions can be those that are easy to answer. Some reporters like to get the basic factual information out of the way first, while others like to ask more open-ended questions to try to set their interview subjects at ease. During the interview, you should be guiding the conversation. When your source detours too far from the subject, steer the person back by asking another question or using a transition to get back to the focus of the interview. If a source fails to answer a question, politely ask it again: "I want to come back to a subject we were talking about earlier."

If there's anything you don't understand, it's fine to say, "Would you please repeat that?" Or, "Would you please explain what you mean by X?" It's all in how you do this: If you're polite and specific, if it's clear that you're listening, your interview subject will often be happy to repeat or explain. Your source will seldom think you're stupid for asking for explanations. But even if he does, it's worth asking. If you don't understand a word or phrase or explanation, you won't be able to describe it clearly in your story.

At the end of the interview, you can put your tablet aside—but keep it close. Ask your source for ideas about other possible sources, and ways to contact that person if you need to clarify any information. And ask if there's anything you should have asked, but didn't. Maybe your source has an important point to convey, but couldn't find a good place to fit it into the interview. This broad question at least gives that person the chance to fill you in. Then thank your source for his or her time and ask when a good time will be to reach your source in case you have follow-up questions or need clarifications. Confirm that you have the best telephone number.

As soon as you have a moment (in your car, or back at your news organization's office), write down your impressions and notes to yourself about what seemed especially important.

BY PHONE

Sometimes, it's just not practical to schedule an interview with someone in person. Your source may be halfway across the country or your deadline may not allow the time. And a telephone conversation may be less intimidating or easier to fit into a busy schedule for your source.

Imagine being called up out of the blue to comment on an issue—any issue. As an interview subject, you have to think on your feet, yet you have little control over what parts of your answers will be included in a story or in what context. In a telephone interview, you can't make eye contact to see if the reporter is sympathetic or even understands your point.

If you're the reporter, keeping the source's point of view in mind can help you be courteous without giving up your autonomy. You should also keep in mind the following guidelines for a telephone interview:

- Here, too, always identify yourself by name and news organization and say you're a reporter. Never pretend that you're someone you are not—this is not only unethical, but can be illegal in some cases.

- If you're contacting someone at home, apologize and say that you'll take as little of the source's time as possible. Briefly explain the issue and make sure the source understands why you're contacting her or him.

As you interview, you may find that you need to provide your source with some basic information about recent developments on an issue. Let's say you're doing a story about higher tuition. If your source is a professor or a student, that person might not know much about the issue. In order to get an intelligent response, you may need to do some explaining. Also, your story will usually be stronger if you ask specific questions. For instance, what if you ask students or professors something like the following:

Weaker: *How do you feel about the proposed tuition increase?*

You may be implicitly encouraging someone to give you a gut response based on pre-conceived notions: "They're always raising tuition, so I'm not surprised," or, "Those x*&** administrators are always trying to get more money out of us." Obviously, an answer like this doesn't further understanding. But what if you asked questions like the following instead:

- **Better:** Did low tuition rates affect your decision to attend this particular college?

- **Better:** Have you had trouble meeting expenses while you've been paying the current tuition rates?

- **Better:** Do you have student loans?

Note that such specific questions can make your story more complete, more accurate and more interesting. They encourage sources to answer from their experience or expertise, rather than saying what they feel or giving only a vague answer.

On the other hand, if the source is a state legislator or president of the college—that is, someone involved in the process—that person should be prepared for your call. Such a person has been thinking about the issue for a long time, and is a public figure who has some power. Because of that power and the public position, such sources have a responsibility to explain their decisions to the public. For them, it's more likely that an open question such as, "What do you think about the higher tuition rates?" could lead to thoughtful answers. You still need to extend to them the same courtesy and professionalism that you do to all your sources, but public officials or people in positions of authority can be expected to be more comfortable with your questions and with the interview in general. That means you can usually expect to do less handholding in an interview with them than with other sources.

BY EMAIL OR TEXT

Remember that speaking directly to the sources who are closest to the news provides the best information. We call this the **immediacy rule**—that, other factors being equal, you should have as few as possible mediating agencies, people or obstacles between you and the news. That means not only that you should talk with sources who had the most immediate, or closest, contact with the news or event, but also that it's better to talk with your sources than to text or email them, and it's better to talk to them in person than by telephone. It means that you should try as hard as you can to talk with sources, rather than accepting a press release and interview from a public relations person. For all you know, the public relations person made up the quotes attributed to your primary sources.

Sometimes hurried reporters are tempted to agree to an email interview. Some journalists say that electronic communications allow them more access to busy public officials and can provide a helpful "paper" trail to refer to later. And you'll see plenty of news stories that refer to email interviews. But we strongly recommend that whenever possible, you interview people in person. If that's not possible, a telephone interview is acceptable. Email is problematic. It's not private, for instance, and so information that you haven't verified yet might be spread without your knowing it. Also, it's possible that the email account of your intended source is being used by someone else, even if the return address seems to match the source you hope to interview. That's also true for texting. It's easy enough to get an email account with a name similar to someone else's, or to text from someone else's phone.

Interviewing by email makes it harder to ask follow-up questions, takes away from the spontaneity of an interview and makes it more difficult to positively identify your source. However, email can be a great way to follow up once you've established a connection through an in-person interview. You might use a text or email to double-check a number, a fact or a seeming contradiction in two quotes. Or a source may be able to clarify an explanation better in writing. Also, if you have the choice of getting an interview with a key source by email or not at all, email may be the best choice. Add a phrase in your story that makes this clear—something like "X said in an email"—so that your audience can take this into account. And be sure that the person who emails you knows that you're a journalist who's asking questions for publication. Your source might otherwise have an expectation of privacy.

Privacy—Some Information Can't Go into Your Story

Good journalists are as respectful of their sources' privacy as possible, while still trying to provide important information to the public. But there's another kind of privacy: The law says that some kinds of information and some places are protected. Two areas that should raise warning flags for reporters when they're interviewing are **private facts** and **intrusion**.

PRIVATE FACTS

Private facts are embarrassing facts that a person has a reasonable belief should remain private, and that person has tried very hard to keep private. When someone posts a comment on a Facebook wall, that person might forget that it's not private, but that memory lapse is not considered reasonable. But if a journalist somehow gains access to a person's medical or education records, there's a good chance the subject *should* expect privacy. In that case, you need to proceed with extra caution. Revealing such facts is illegal in some states, if they are sufficiently intimate and embarrassing to a reasonable person—as opposed to just personally embarrassing. People have sued over the revelation of a person's sexual orientation, the fact that a person was a stripper and the details of a person's sex life, to name just three examples. In one case, the *Wonkette*, a well-known political gossip blog, published a link to a Congressional aide's graphic blog post detailing her sexual liaisons, including one with a Washington lawyer identified by his initials. When the lawyer sued, the courts found the *Wonkette* blogger not guilty because the details were already published online and therefore could not be considered private (*Steinbuch v. Cutler*, 2007).

In a case such as this, notice that there's no question about whether the information is true. It can be true and still illegal to publish under privacy laws. Even after verifying information, a reporter needs to be sure that the information is public or of sufficient public interest. Of course, if the person is running for president of the United States, the information may be deemed of enough public interest to merit publication or broadcast. If information is newsworthy, or in some cases, only if it has social utility—that is, not just is newsworthy, but is useful somehow to the public—it will not be considered private.

INTRUSION

Intrusion refers to invading a person's private affairs or physically invading his private property without permission. This concept encompasses trespassing, secret surveillance, and misrepresentation of a reporter's identity. Trespassing is illegal, and reporters need a clear understanding of their rights and the limits of those rights to be on others' property. Journalists who are on public property are usually free to video, photograph or report on what they can see and hear on the theory that anyone standing in the same place could also see or hear it, so there's no presumption of privacy. Government buildings that are open to the public are open to all members of the public. That is, a county courthouse can't usually ban some reporters and not others, or some members of the public and not others. But parts of public buildings may be off limits to the general public. Hospitals, schools and jails, while sometimes owned and operated by the government, don't allow general public admittance, and therefore journalists usually need permission to enter parts of these buildings.

Private businesses such as restaurants and theaters have given implied permission to the general public to enter the premises, but they can withdraw that permission at any time. If a journalist attends a theater and the manager asks her to leave, legally the journalist must comply with that request. Reporters also have to be careful that permission they receive to enter a building or room comes from someone who has the power to give it. It's not completely clear when public becomes private; for instance, a doorstep may be considered public in one case while not in another (Fig. 9-4). But when you

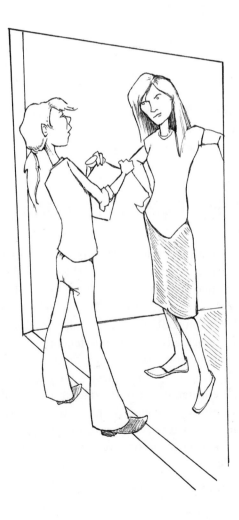

FIGURE 9-4 You need permission to enter any person's residence, including a dorm room.

enter a private dwelling, you're risking intrusion, even if a police officer has given you permission.

Intrusion does not necessarily mean that you've physically crossed a boundary. For instance, photojournalists with a long lens may be guilty of trespassing if that technology allows them to see what a person without it, standing in the same place, could not. A reporter can legally report on or take pictures of what she can see with unaided eyes from public property. If a journalist could see into someone's basement window from a public sidewalk, that journalist could usually report what was seen. But if the journalist needed binoculars or a zoom lens to see into that window, the reporter would be trespassing. Likewise, it may be intrusion if a camera is hidden on a reporter's body for an interview or if the reporter places secret recorders in someone's business or home to record information. Secretly recording telephone conversations is illegal in some states. In some states, as long as one party knows that the conversation is being recorded, it is legal—although not ethical to your sources. (You can check the Student Press Law Center or Reporters Committee for Freedom of the Press online to find out your state's laws.)

It is not illegal to misrepresent your identity, but it is illegal to use such a misrepresentation to gain admittance that would ordinarily be denied to you. For instance, if you as a reporter represented yourself as someone interested in attending several colleges and filled out applications to places where you had no interest in attending, your actions would probably be legal. That's because you have the right to apply to colleges, and your misrepresentation did not give you access to something that would otherwise be off limits. However, if you pretended to be a doctor in order to look at someone's medical records, or a janitor in order to gain access to a building that was off limits to the public, you might be intruding.

THE ELECTRONIC COMMUNICATIONS PRIVACY ACT

The Electronic Communications Privacy Act aims to protect the privacy of at least some electronic communications that were not covered under previous laws. It covers, among other things, streaming videos, voicemail, telephone interceptions, emails and videos of private conversations. The law made it illegal to knowingly intercept and record cellphone calls, but the U.S. Supreme Court has ruled that if an issue is of public concern, actually *airing* the content of such calls is not illegal. That is, while the person who surreptitiously intercepts a cellphone call is acting illegally, if that person gives the recording to a journalist, the journalist may be within the law in broadcasting the material if it is of sufficient public interest. The Act also made it illegal to hack into other people's computer files without their knowledge or permission, to monitor computer keystrokes or to publish electronic communications of a user if you know or might have reason to know that those communications were obtained illegally.

Journalists themselves should never intercept phone calls or computer files. Not only is this immoral, it's also illegal: In 2011, media mogul Rupert Murdoch's news companies made international headlines for illegally hacking into people's telephones in Great Britain. What first scandalized the public was the news that Murdoch's tabloid, *News of the World,* was accused of hacking the mobile phone of Missy Dowler, a 13-year-old who had been kidnapped in a highly publicized case in 2002. At the time of the phone hacking, no one knew that she had been murdered. The hackers apparently deleted some messages, leading family and investigators to hope she might still be alive. Days after the *News of the World* was publicly connected to hacking Dowler's phone, the newspaper, which had been in business since 1843, closed its doors. Furthermore, the illegal activity had implications for Murdoch's holdings in the United States: Soon after the phone interceptions in Great Britain were publicized, the FBI began investigating whether Murdoch's News Corporation had hacked into the telephones of families of victims of 9/11. While privacy laws in Great Britain and the United States are very different, such phone hacking is illegal and ultimately can have long-lasting consequences for those who engage in it.

It's also a good idea to determine whether texts and emails are private before you use them in a news story. For instance, if you didn't make it clear that you were a journalist—or misrepresented yourself in some other way in an email or text exchange—and someone told you embarrassing information, that person might have a reasonable expectation of privacy. But in other cases, a person's expectation of privacy might *not* be reasonable. For instance, in the spring of 2011, Wisconsin Gov. Scott Walker signed a law with severe new union restrictions, and tens of thousands of protesters gathered outside the state Capitol. An Indiana deputy prosecutor sent an email to the governor suggesting that a fake attack on the governor be staged to make the unions look bad. The prosecutor, Carlos F. Lam, later resigned when his email was publicized by the Wisconsin Center for Investigative Journalism. The center had found the email among those released after an open records lawsuit (Golden, 2011). While Lam might have thought the email was private, the journalists were well within their rights in publishing it because it was sent from one public employee to another about government business. It's worth noting that the center double-checked with Lam to be sure that it was actually his email address, that the Internet provider address matched the place where the prosecutor was and that other details matched up.

If Lam had spoken at a public meeting, he would have known that his comments would make the news. So one of the flags for journalists when they're considering privacy law is to ask themselves, Would this source believe his comments or information about him would remain private? And if so, why—should he have a reasonable expectation of privacy or not?

Exercises for Chapter 9

EXERCISE 9-1:

a. You've been assigned to do a story about a new employee on campus. Specifically, you're supposed to find out what drew that person to a job at your school. First, search for new employees, and then do some background research. What can you find out before the interview? Write a description of what you've learned about the person.

b. Based on your research, list a couple of questions or comments that you'd use to establish rapport.

c. List 10 questions you might ask the person you researched. Briefly describe why you would ask each question.

d. Next to each question, briefly describe the type of answer you're anticipating, based on your research.

e. Put the questions in the order you'd ask them and briefly explain why you put them in the order that you did.

EXERCISE 9-2: How would you introduce yourself as you set up an interview? In a few sentences, write up your introduction.

EXERCISE 9-3:

a. You're going to interview an administrator at your school. What would you wear? What wouldn't you wear? What issues would you consider? How did you make your decision? In writing, describe your outfit and your reasoning for it.

b. You're going to interview the owner of a new bar in town. What would you wear? What wouldn't you wear? What issues would you consider? How did you make a decision? In writing, describe your outfit and your reasoning for it.

EXERCISE 9-4: You need to interview someone, but the only way you can contact that person to set up the interview is through email. What would your email say?

EXERCISE 9-5: You are in charge of covering the next student government meeting. You find out that the student body president was just arrested on a DUI—and this is public information. Would you ask the student body president about this? What would you ask? What might you include in a story? List the issues that come up for you.

EXERCISE 9-6: Get the agenda for a local meeting. In writing, describe what issues are on the agenda. Pose a couple of questions you'd want answered if you were covering it.

CHAPTER 10

HOW DO YOU REPORT WHAT SOURCES SAY?

Between your interview and your final news story, sources undergo a transformation from the human beings who talked with you into names associated with sound bites, quotes or paraphrases. To make this process as fair as possible, you need to be truthful and accurate in selecting quotes and conveying context. It's also your job as a reporter to be mindful of sources' underlying humanity, and to think about how you would want to be treated if you were in their shoes.

In most news stories, the majority of what your interview subject says will be para-phrased or won't make it into your story at all. That means that it's very important that you think carefully about which quotes to include.

Guidelines for Quoting

As you write your story, you may notice that something a source said is especially to the point. Maybe the words sparkle. Maybe the source has described a difficult concept especially clearly, or has articulated that source's position on a controversial issue. The quotes you include should convey the spirit of your source's comments overall.

Let's look at a hypothetical example. Imagine that you're interviewing musician Ricardo Baca, who's reasonably well known by your audience. Baca has discovered that his music was included on a student website and a DVD without Baca's permission. The student has since withdrawn the DVD from sale and removed the music from her website. Here's an excerpt from what the musician tells you in response to your questions:

> [You start by asking Baca about his musical background.]
>
> I play the bass guitar, you know, and I play classical and rock and sometimes a little jazz. I guess it's just in my blood. I grew up near Oberlin College. I've spent some time doing other jobs, but I'm a musician first and foremost. There's something about music—how can I say it—it's like what bread, or salt and pepper or sunshine is to other people. I need it to get through daily life. I grew up hearing my parents practice chamber music in the living room, and I was studying music when my friends were playing Little League.
>
> [Now you ask how the musician feels about the fact that his music has been included, without his permission, on a student's DVD she was selling.]
>
> Um, you really want to know what I think? Hmmm, well, I think that's stealing; that's the long and short of it. It was wrong for that student to do that. I'm not going to sue her or anything because I'm sure she didn't think it through, but somebody needs to teach her that musicians have to make a living too.
>
> When I first found out about the DVD, I was mad. I was really mad. But then I tried to remember back to when I was a teenager and some of the stuff I've done, and I'd just like that student to know, and other teenagers, that making money off somebody else's music without their permission is dishonest.

As you decide what to quote in your story, you might be tempted to simply report that Baca said, "I was mad. I was really mad." Baca *did* say these words. But without the context of his other remarks, this quote is misleading about his general response to the incident. Instead, you might include the quote about Baca saying he tried to remember back to when he was a teenager, or his statement that he's sure the student didn't think it through. These statements are closer to getting at his condemnation of the student's action tempered by his willingness to forgive her.

It's this kind of attempt to communicate the nuances of what someone said that can help make your news story quotes more accurate.

PARAPHRASE

When sources provide basic information in ordinary language, direct quotes are unnecessary. That means you probably won't quote the following line: *"I play the bass guitar, you know, and I play classical and rock and sometimes a little jazz,"* he said. There's no reason to use Baca's exact words here. Much of what you include from an interview will be paraphrased—that is, you'll restate what the source said in your own words. In this case, you can simply say the following: *Baca, who plays the bass guitar, focuses on classical and rock music, although he also sometimes plays jazz.*

Even if you use words your source actually said, you don't need to quote those if it's very basic, simple language. For instance, you might write the following paraphrase: *Ricardo Baca grew up near Oberlin College.* Although the end of this sentence uses Baca's exact words, you don't need to use quotation marks around them because this is a very simple, short statement using ordinary language.

When you paraphrase, you still need **attribution**—the "he said" or "she said" that provides the source for a statement or ideas. This is especially important if the material is a statement of opinion, a piece of little-known information or a statement about a controversial or contested issue. If you chose to paraphrase Baca's statement that he was angry, you would attribute the information. You might write the paraphrase this way: *Baca said he was angry when he first found out about the DVD.*

How do you know when to quote and when to paraphrase? Remember that your first thought should be to paraphrase. Look for especially interesting language—for quotes that say something in a unique way, or that give a sense of someone as an individual. For instance, in the preceding hypothetical interview, Baca uses an unusual comparison between music and bread or salt or pepper. While the other information is relevant and may show up in your story—where Baca grew up, what instrument he plays—there's no good reason to present it in the form of actual quotations. Statements of fact are seldom quoted except in the case of some big political or criminal revelation: *"I did it," said Mayor X, who had been charged with stealing parking meters.*

When you're covering a speech, you're often looking for a sentence or two that succinctly states the speaker's main point, something that gets at the heart of what the speaker was saying. This is also true in interviews. However, when you do this, try to avoid quoting clichés—such as when a football coach says, "We'll just go out there and do our best, and may the best man win." Even though such a phrase may sum up the speaker's approach, it uses tired language that doesn't say much. When you encounter clichéd responses, try to ask more specific or deeper questions: "How do you think training in the off season will affect your team's performance?" Or, "Considering the forecast for heavy rain, how much do you think you'll use your running game?"

IN GENERAL, DON'T MARK DIALECT IN QUOTES

For example, a journalist usually doesn't write "gonna" rather than "going to," or "runnin'" rather than "running." Most people who say "gonna" would write "going to." Such quotes are also harder to read.

Journalists also don't usually include the nonlinguistic utterances that often serve as placeholders in spoken language. They don't usually include words like "uh," "er," and "um" in a quotation. Let's say you wanted to include the following from the preceding hypothetical interview: *"Um, you really want to know what I think? Hmmm . . . well,*

I think that's stealing; that's the long and short of it." You could skip the first sentence entirely. And you could start the second sentence at "I think."

QUOTATION MARKS MEAN THAT WHAT APPEARS BETWEEN THEM IS WHAT SOMEONE ACTUALLY SAID

You may hear about journalists making up quotes or fixing someone's grammar. You should not make up quotes. Ever.

But when you're trying to translate how people speak into a written form, you'll come up against some grayer areas. For instance, many professional journalists will "clean up" quotes by correcting a source's grammar or mechanical errors. Journalists often feel that correcting grammar is a service to readers as well as sources because it could help to clarify meaning as well as save a source embarrassment.

However, many other journalists believe that reporters should never change the words between sets of quotation marks. We agree, and we advise you to avoid adding or subtracting any words from what the speaker actually said. If a quote is not clear or a speaker's grammar is unnecessarily embarrassing, then a reporter should paraphrase. This will help you to avoid misleading readers and raising questions about what you're omitting or adding.

For the same reason, quotes should not include ellipses, the three periods that show something has been left out, unless there is a very important reason for omitting material in a quote. These gaps can raise questions about what the reporter has left out, or they can confuse the reader.

Just as you should avoid omitting information from a quote, you should also stay away from inserting your own words into a quotation with parentheses or brackets. This can be tempting when you have a near-perfect quote that uses an unclear pronoun, or that doesn't quite make sense without something the source said a few minutes earlier. But the bracketed information can also confuse readers, who may still believe those words were spoken by the source. Or readers may wonder what, exactly, was replaced by the parenthetical remarks, or whether they would agree with the reporter about what the source intended to say. One way around this predicament is to provide an explanation outside the quotation to clarify any confusing statements.

Weaker: *"I guess [music is] just in my blood," he said.*

Revised: *Baca grew up listening to music.*

"I guess it's just in my blood," he said.

For all the reader knows, what Baca *really* said in the first example was, "I guess gardening is just in my blood." If it's too awkward to provide an explanation outside the quotation marks, then simply paraphrase: *Baca grew up listening to music, which he said is just in his blood.* While you lose some of the zing of Baca's actual words, you can still deliver the general feel of what a source said. And for journalists, clarity and accuracy are more important than zing.

PROVIDE CONTEXT AND EXPLANATIONS BEFORE A QUOTE, RATHER THAN AFTER

Sometimes, you'll need to provide a brief explanation for a quote to make sense. In that case, it's much better to do the explaining *before* the quotation, rather than after:

Weaker: *"It's like what bread, or salt and pepper or sunshine is to other people," Baca said, referring to his music.*

Revised: *Baca said he needed music to get through his daily life.*

"It's like what bread, or salt and pepper or sunshine is to other people," he said.

Furthermore, when your story changes speakers, you should start a new paragraph and establish that someone new is being quoted:

Example: *Baca said he needed music to get through his daily life.*

"It's like what bread, or salt and pepper or sunshine is to other people," he said.

Joseph Peterson, Baca's friend and former professor, said music has always been central to Baca's life.

"I remember how Ricardo would show up in my office just crushed about some band producing a song he thought was inferior," he said.

A REPORTER SHOULD NOT TAKE QUOTES OUT OF CONTEXT

This means you don't just pull certain words and sentences out of an interview and refit them to your purposes. Don't move answers from one question to another, and don't change your question in production. You need to be sure that the parts of an interview you include match what you think your source was trying to get across.

But what do you do when you want to quote two different parts from the same section of an interview? For instance, you might want to quote one sentence, and then skip a sentence before quoting what follows. Let's look at an example. Here's what Baca said:

> It was wrong for that student to do that. I'm not going to sue her or anything because I'm sure she didn't think it through, but somebody needs to teach her that musicians have to make a living too.
> When I first found out about the DVD, I was mad. I was really mad.

Let's say you want to omit the sentence in the middle. Here's how you point out to the reader that information may be missing:

> "It was wrong for that student to do that," Baca said.
> He said using his music without his permission was probably a thoughtless action, and he didn't plan to take legal action against the student, but he wasn't happy about what the student did.
> "When I first found out about the DVD, I was mad," he said. "I was really mad."

In the previous example, there's an attribution, a paragraph break and a transition before the story resumes—all signals to the reader that the statements in the first and second quotes may not have been contiguous.

JUST BECAUSE A SOURCE SAYS SOMETHING DOES NOT MEAN YOU HAVE TO REPORT IT

If material is potentially libelous, you can and should omit it from your story. Remember that you could be accused of libel even if a statement is quoted. You should also avoid obscenities and profanities, unless they are part of direct quotations *and* there is a compelling reason to use them. It's easy to paraphrase and omit these. Also, if a source makes a statement of fact that you know or suspect to be false, you should either check the information with another source or omit this quote.

When a source makes a statement about another person or something in which you know he has no expertise or knowledge, don't include the information. For instance, if a student says an instructor was not rehired because the college didn't like that instructor's politics, check first what leads the student to think that. If he doesn't have some factual basis, then don't include the information. Remember, as a good journalist, you're trying to be truthful. The fact that you're quoting someone else doesn't absolve you of that responsibility.

NEWS STORIES EMPHASIZE THE SPEAKER RATHER THAN THE REPORTER

This means that in your story, you should stress the answer rather than your question.

Weaker: *When asked about what he thought of the student DVD, Baca said it made him angry at first.*

Revised: *Baca said the student DVD made him angry at first.*

Try to avoid saying, "when asked about," or "in answer to a question." These phrases are awkward and they draw attention to your questions, which are not the focus of your story.

NEWS STORIES USE "SAID" OR "SAYS"

News stories report what was said as fairly as possible. Because of this, the words "said" or "says" are the main words you'll use for attribution—not "claimed," "mentioned," "remarked," "stated," "muttered" or "expressed," which introduce nuances of meaning that "said" does not, and which draw attention to themselves. For instance, "claimed" implies that what someone said may not be true, unfairly casting doubt on the words of one source while allowing other sources in your story to simply have "said" their statements.

When you say that someone "mentioned" something, you're saying that the person said it as an aside, that it was not the main point. "Remarked" has a similar emphasis

BOX 10-1

FOR BROADCAST STORIES, ATTRIBUTION COMES FIRST

The quotation marks are invisible in most radio, television and webcast stories. That means that when you cut to a quote or sound bite, you need to be as clear as possible that there's a new speaker, and identify that person. When the sound bite is finished, you need to provide a transition back to the narrator.

on the casual brevity of what someone has said, while "stated" is usually associated with official documents or statements. Each of these words stands out more in a sentence than "said," unduly emphasizing how you think a speaker said something. Using "said" may seem repetitive at first, but the attributions won't stand out to the reader. They serve the specific function of providing the reader with your source of information.

FOLLOW BASIC PUNCTUATION RULES FOR QUOTES

- "Punctuation goes inside quotations if the quote ends in a period or a comma."
- Use a comma in a quote before attribution: "I grew up hearing my parents practice chamber music in the living room, and I was studying music when my friends were playing Little League," Baca said.
- For print and written online stories, attribution should usually come at the end of the first full sentence of a quote: "When I first found out about the DVD, I was mad," Baca said. "I was really mad. But then I tried to remember back to when I was a teenager and some of the stuff I've done, and I'd just like that student to know, and other teenagers, that making money off somebody else's music without their permission is dishonest." Note that within the same paragraph, a quote needs attribution only once. Even though there are three sentences in the preceding example, only one *Baca said* is necessary and correct (Box 10-1).

Quoting Multiple Sources

The previous examples deal mostly with quotes from one source, but news stories typically include multiple sources. As you make decisions about quotes in your story, it's important not only to represent what each source has to say, but also at least to be aware of how you represent sources in relation to each other. Teun van Dijk, a professor of discourse studies, has described how people can legitimize or marginalize voices as they choose what sources to include, and where and how often to place them in a story (1988). Another way that reporters indicate the importance of sources is by determining which sources get to say what they want in their own words. This is similar to the idea of framing, in the sense that you're drawing attention to the people you allow to speak.

When you use direct quotes or recordings, there's basically no other filter between a source's words and the audience's eyes and ears. Being quoted is like acting in a starring role, being paraphrased is like having a nonspeaking role, and being referred to is like being an extra. When you quote someone, that person is more legitimized than if you paraphrase what was said.

And then there are people or groups who are referred to in a story but given nothing to say. Although they're rendered mute, they are present. When you see coverage of a presidential visit, if protesters are there, they'll be included in a story, but they may not be given voice. Instead, the report might simply say something like, *"Protesters lined one side of the street as the presidential entourage drove slowly by."*

The protesters are visible, which is good because their presence is important context for the story, but they don't get to say anything (Fig. 10-1). The story could legitimize the group more by paraphrasing their concerns: *"Protesters lined one side of the*

FIGURE 10-1
Acknowledging that protesters were present at an event is not the same as paraphrasing or quoting what they have to say.

FIGURE 10-2 In visual media, including readable images of protesters' signs is one way to add legitimacy to the group's position. You can make sure that audio includes a clear recording of their point, rather than a background roar. If sources are important enough to include in your story, they usually deserve a chance to speak their message.

street chanting anti-corporate bail-out slogans as the presidential entourage drove slowly by." Further legitimacy would come with one or more quotes (Fig. 10-2), such as in the following example:

> "When's the President going to stop giving billions to banks and start giving billions to taxpayers?" asked protester Suzie Cisneros of Dallas. "The old way of doing business needs to end now, and we need to let the big businesses and banks suffer the consequences for their own risk-taking."

Finally, you signal a source's importance by how fully you identify a person or a group in your story. If you identify someone by name and title, you confer a level of distinction on that person. If "Secretary of State John Kerry" visits Sudan and its president, Omar al-Bashir, is identified as "the Sudanese leader," he is more vaguely identified than Kerry, and therefore less distinguished. If the report says, "Secretary of State John Kerry visited with Sudanese officials," the difference in legitimacy is more marked because it's not clear which officials he met with or whether al-Bashir was even there. We wouldn't expect Kerry to disappear in a sentence such as, "an American leader met with Sudanese President Omar al-Bashir," or "American officials met with Sudanese President Omar al-Bashir." We would expect Kerry to be precisely identified because of his importance. The president of another country should rank with him.

Following are some examples of how careless identification can play out in your local stories.

- **If you give your school administration officials full name and title, but then refer to the faculty or the student body as a group:**

  Students say they want a new recreation building and are petitioning the provost's office for a meeting to discuss the idea in detail.
  "A new building sounds like a great idea," Provost Ethan Jones said. "Unfortunately, we don't have any money, and that will be a challenge."

- **If you refer to your own team's athletes by name and position but not the opponent's:**

  Buffalo Danielle Frost spiked the ball over the net, but the Demons returned it for a score.

- **If you refer to men by full name and title but not women:**

  Mayor Jim Hernandez and his wife made the announcement along with local business owner Harold Reuben.

If your story includes a lot of sources, you might end up with too many names and titles piled up. If you find this happening, rethink your approach to the story and see if other organizing options come to mind, such as summarizing the issue and paraphrasing positions rather than worrying about individual voices getting included. It's not wrong to give more priority to one source than another—one of a news story's jobs is to establish hierarchy of information. However, make sure that your choices are thoughtful.

For example, imagine that students at your school are complaining about a lack of diversity in the faculty. Diversity can refer to gender and heritage or it can refer to other markers such as socioeconomic status, age, sexual orientation, disability, religion, nationality, and political views. Let's say this particular complaint is about a lack of ethnic minorities on the faculty. You could go around campus to get the stakeholders to comment—some student and faculty voices. You could go to the administration to find out the university's official position and response.

Now, to whom will you give voice? This is a difficult decision because it's hard to discern who can speak for each group. The school administration may have a spokesperson whose job it is to represent the school, but whom do you seek out for the student position? The student body president would be a good person to start with, because that person presumably was elected to represent students. However, the president may not know about this specific complaint or diversity issues in general. You could seek out the complainants or ask leaders of campus minority groups for comment, and that would be a pretty typical next step. But can one person speak for all members of a group? Can a person of Chinese descent speak for all Asians, including those of Taiwanese, Japanese, Korean or Cambodian heritage? That's assuming that there's some common, essential quality to being Asian, which is a vast oversimplification of history and human experience. When journalists run to people to ask for a quote to represent a side in a story, they risk lumping people together in just this way. Yet, to avoid this mistake, aren't reporters forced to interview many more individuals, resulting in a mishmash of quotes and confusion?

Let's go back to what the audience needs to know, and what this story is really about. The complaint is a **news hook**: It's the timely event on which your story hangs (Fig. 10-3).

FIGURE 10-3

If you set the players up as vying against one another, then who gets quoted first and who gets more voice in the story is significant. But if, for example, you're doing a story explaining why diversity is an important consideration, you could note the disagreement in a one-paragraph paraphrase in the middle of the story. That way, you're less likely to inadvertently legitimize one side over the others because you're changing the frame from competing opinions to a focus on the issue.

In this second scenario, the story becomes about how your school fits into the larger issue of diversity at colleges and universities. You can lead with the problem, explain why underrepresentation or overrepresentation concerns people, what your school does, if anything, to bring minorities on board and how effective that plan is. The story takes on more of a problem/solution structure. Your mission now is to describe to your audience what is happening at the local institution, including enough context and background to assess the situation and decide whether and how to act. This structure puts the issue, not an actor, in the spotlight.

It will often be challenging to avoid legitimizing some voices over others, but if you can't achieve parity in each story, you can keep your eye on overall patterns across coverage. Do you spotlight the same issues repeatedly, while overlooking equally important ones? Do you go to a certain source frequently because he can be relied on to "give a good quote," bypassing the knowledge offered by less articulate people? If you do, you may create an inaccurate picture for your audience, and you may contribute to the invisibility of some groups. Again, you can help balance news coverage in general by keeping an eye on which sources and groups dominate the media spotlight.

Defamation: When People Say You've Lied

The courts have consistently protected the right to publish factual information. If what you write is true, then you cannot defame someone: Truth is an absolute defense against an accusation of defamation.

However, journalists sometimes make mistakes. If those mistakes cause damage to a person's reputation, the journalist and his news organization could be sued for **libel**. Libel is published, false information that causes damage to a person's reputation. It is usually written, in contrast to **slander**, which is *spoken* defamation. Slander was initially established as a lesser crime because it was assumed the damage was not as far-reaching as that from written defamation. However, with the advent of radio, television and the Internet, the distinction made less sense. Therefore, slander usually refers to spoken defamation with limited impact and distribution, while libel refers to defamation broadcast on television, radio and Internet, or published in print or online.

Defamation law is a two-edged sword for reporters because it protects sources from reporters' mistakes, but it also protects reporters who make mistakes. In the United States, in order to encourage free speech, the burden of proof rests with the plaintiff—the person suing a journalist or news organization for libel. That means you don't have to prove that what you wrote was true; instead, the plaintiff has to prove that you libeled that person. You can publish or broadcast false information, or even information that damages someone's reputation—and you may still be found not guilty of libel. The courts have often ruled in favor of news organizations that mistakenly publish false information. Society's concern is to protect open debate and encourage a free flow of ideas, and the courts have assumed people will make mistakes under such circumstances.

Despite the courts' concern with protecting free speech, you may still publish information that's carefully attributed to a source and that you honestly believe to be true—and you may be found guilty of libel. It's impossible to predict what juries will decide in libel cases, and the courts are sometimes inconsistent because there's a tension between two important rights in libel cases: the right of someone to protect his or her reputation, and the right to freedom of the press (Fig. 10-4).

FIGURE 10-4 Ideally, libel laws protect both rigorous debate and the free flow of ideas, on one hand—and the people whose reputations and livelihoods can be ruined by careless or spiteful lies or rumors, on the other. In the early 1950s, the powerful Hollywood gossip magazine *Confidential* published scandalous stories about celebrities with little regard to the truth. The movie stars Maureen O'Hara (left) and Dorothy Dandridge successfully sued the magazine for libel (O'Hara's brother, James FitzSimons, is the man between the two stars in the photo).

To help you navigate this tricky area, here are the five questions courts usually consider in determining libel suits—the same questions you should ask yourself about any information before publishing.

Could the information be seen as damaging someone's reputation? That is, is the information something more than personal embarrassment—is it information that might make someone lose his job or permanently damage his reputation?

A. Can the plaintiff prove harm? If the information you publish could hurt someone's reputation—for instance, if it suggests a person has committed a crime—that still doesn't mean that person's reputation *has* been harmed, which is what the plaintiff must also prove. The harm suffered by a defamed person could be financial, it could be mental suffering and anguish, or it could be loss of standing in the community.

B. Can the person be identified? Someone's identity might be clear from a job description or physical description, not just from being named.

C. Has the information been published? You don't have to have posted, printed or broadcast a story for the information to have been published. A story is considered published if the information is conveyed to someone other than the subject of the story.

D. Did you fail to take appropriate steps to verify information?

The first four questions about possible libel cases focus on whether someone's reputation was harmed—they focus on the plaintiff. This last question asks not whether damage was done—not whether you made a mistake and actually defamed someone—but whether you followed professional practice as you gathered and reported the information (Box 10-2).

Remember, in some cases, juries will allow an innocent person's reputation to be harmed in order to protect a free press. The constitutional protection of free speech was established to ensure that people could exchange ideas and make political and social changes. This interest in public accountability and freedom to criticize the government has also come to mean that public officials and figures are often held to a higher level of proof in libel cases than private individuals. This is because of a landmark U.S. Supreme Court case, *New York Times Company v. Sullivan* (1964). In this case, the Supreme Court effectively made it much more difficult for public officials to sue for libel than private citizens. The court said that public officials must prove **actual malice**, which has a specific meaning in libel law: It means that you either published a statement knowing that it was false or that you showed a reckless disregard for the truth. (The legal meaning of actual malice does *not* refer to malicious or mean-spirited intent.) The court now extends this burden of proof to public figures. For private citizens, the plaintiff need only establish that a news organization was negligent—that it did not show ordinary care in ensuring accuracy. (However, some states, like Colorado, require even private figures to prove actual malice.)

But what does it mean to show a reckless disregard for the truth? In this case, the defendant's methods are what are important. Courts often refer to a comparison of two Supreme Court libel case decisions written by Justice John Marshall Harlan. In one of the cases, a piece in the *Saturday Evening Post* stated that an athletic director, Wally Butts, had fixed a game in a phone conversation with the opposing coach (*Curtis Publishing Co. v. Butts, 1967*). While Harlan did not accuse the *Saturday Evening Post* of lying or of knowingly publishing false information about Butts, he did find that the publication had shown reckless disregard for the truth. Harlan's summary explained that the *Saturday Evening Post* had failed to follow standard journalistic procedures.

STANDARD PRACTICE

What did a Supreme Court Justice expect a journalist to do as normal practice? In his summary, Harlan noted that the *Saturday Evening Post* had "recognized the need for a thorough investigation of the serious charges"—that is, journalists at the magazine knew the story's information about a coach fixing a game might be defamatory. He pointed out that the story, a magazine feature, was not **hot news**, or news "which required immediate dissemination." That meant the magazine had time to carefully check the accuracy of information before publishing it.

In addition, Harlan noted the journalist's source was on probation in connection with charges for writing bad checks, indicating that the source might not be trustworthy. Harlan said the *Post* knew about the source's probation, and yet failed to try to get independent support for his story. The *Post* knew a witness was supposedly with the source when he overheard the phone call, but the *Post* did not interview the witness. Harlan noted that the *Post* didn't try to screen films of the game to see if the information was true. At the trial, football experts testified that the information in the source's notes would have been obvious or unimportant to any opposing coach. The *Post* writer wasn't a football writer, and yet he didn't try to check out his story with a football expert.

In the other case decided by Justice Harlan, *Associated Press v. Walker* (1967), an Associated Press story stated that Edwin Walker had led riots on the University of Mississippi campus. In contrast to the *Post* case, Harlan said that the Associated Press story was hot news. Since this ruling, courts sometimes take into consideration in libel cases whether a story is time-sensitive, breaking news. Urgency can be a factor in determining the extent of a news organization's responsibility to continue researching and interviewing more sources to confirm information. The court also had the following to say about the reporter's steps in the Associated Press case:

> Harlan noted that the reporter observed the riot firsthand and "gave every indication of being trustworthy and competent." The reporter's dispatches would have seemed reasonable to anyone familiar with the subject's previous statements in public. For instance, Walker had made a statement on the radio earlier urging people to "rise to a stand beside Governor Ross Barnett at Jackson, Mississippi". (*Curtis Publishing Co. v. Butts*, 1967)

BOX 10-2

HOW DO YOU MAKE SURE YOU'RE NOT DEFAMING SOMEONE?

If your story is about someone who is accused of murder, it's easy to see that the potential for permanent harm becomes more serious than, say, misspelling a child's name in a story about a Little League game. If there's potential for harming someone's reputation, journalists must be extra careful about triple-checking their facts.

But accusing someone of murder isn't the only way you can hurt his reputation. If you falsely say that someone is adulterous or crazy or steals candy from Wal-Mart, you may also be defaming your subject. False statements about someone's political beliefs can be defamatory:

In *Gertz v. Welch* (1974), the Supreme Court ruled that it was defamatory to accuse Gertz of being a "Communist-fronter" and "Leninist." On the other hand, the California Court of Appeals has ruled that when a website called two public officials "dumb asses," the insult was not defamatory (*Vogel v. Felice*, 2005). While jokes that make fun of a person are not usually defamatory, ridicule that results in extreme suffering can be. If you suggest that someone doesn't have the necessary skills to perform her job—say, that a professor doesn't really have the Ph.D. that she claims, or that a medical doctor is an alcoholic, there's a good chance you're harming that person's reputation to a significant degree, even if you don't explicitly say that she is not a good professor or doctor. On the other hand, the courts have ruled that a statement about a professional making a single mistake does not necessarily harm that person's reputation, because it's a given that even good doctors, mechanics, lawyers, secretaries and other professionals will make some mistakes.

What do the courts generally consider damaging when it comes to a person's reputation? Court decisions vary, of course, but reporters should know to look out for the following areas:

- Suggestions that a person is sexually promiscuous or involved in uncommon or socially unaccepted sexual practices
- Suggestions that a person has committed a crime
- Suggestions that affect a person's ability to continue in his profession or work
- Suggestions that lead to contempt or ridicule in the community
- Suggestions that a person has a communicable and debilitating disease, such as HIV-AIDS.

Injury: Can the plaintiff prove harm?

Just because the information you publish *could* hurt someone's reputation doesn't mean that it *has* harmed her reputation. The plaintiff has to prove this. If the subject of a story has lost his job, or if his spouse has left him after a defamatory story portrays him having an adulterous affair, these events show injury. The plaintiff also might testify that acquaintances and friends avoided him after a libelous statement, or he was passed over for a promotion.

Identification: Can the person be identified?

If your story names a subject, then it's clear you have identified her. But there are other ways a news story might identify a subject—by title, job description or physical description, including a unique and recognizable way of dressing.

Here's an example of identifying someone without actually giving his name: A young woman on campus said she had been raped by her boyfriend, but he was found not guilty in court. When writing a newspaper column about the incident, the young woman's friend knew enough not to include the name of the boyfriend, but she wrote a draft that did include the rape victim's name, the court date and the allegation that the rape was committed by the victim's boyfriend. The columnist toned down the column on the advice of editors and advisers. But if she had used the original, she might well have conveyed enough information about the boyfriend for many people on campus to identify him.

What if the story is about a group of people, and you identify the group but not the individuals? In most cases, groups of people cannot be libeled. However, if a group is small enough, the members may be able to sue for libel as individuals. For instance, if you say the poetry club is dealing drugs and the poetry club at your college consists of five people, they might sue for libel because the reputations of their individual members have been damaged. And even if the group is large, a prominent member of the group may sue for libel. For instance, when a magazine ran a story in the late 1950s suggesting the University of Oklahoma football team used amphetamines, a well-known fullback successfully sued the magazine (*Fawcett Publications, v. Morris*, 1962). While the team itself could not be libeled, the fullback argued he was individually libeled because he was a prominent member of the team.

Another kind of group *can* be libeled: corporations. That's because corporations are considered persons under the law. Especially if a corporation is accused of poor business practices, it can be libeled in the same way an individual can.

Publication: Has the information been published?
Information has clearly been published if it appears on a news website or in a newspaper, but this term also has a broader meaning in libel than it does elsewhere. For instance, if other people in the newsroom see the information on your computer screen or if you email the story to friends, it might be considered published. You may need to discuss the story with your supervisor, but remember that until you're sure the information is true, talking about it with your roommate or other reporters could be considered publication in a defamation lawsuit.

If you're not working for a formal news organization, the question of *who* publishes information may become important. That is, if you post information online, who is your publisher, and is this person or company potentially responsible for libelous information? According to Section 230 of the 1996 Communications Decency Act, your Internet service provider or social networking site is not the same as a publisher: "No provider or user of an interactive computer service shall be treated as the publisher or speaker of any information provided by another information content provider." This protection has been extended to bloggers, too. In general, you are not legally responsible if someone else posts a libelous comment to your blog, or for libelous comments you've copied from other websites. But of course you are responsible for your own content on such a site.

Standard of fault: Did you fail to take appropriate steps to verify information?
This question asks whether you followed standard practices in determining whether information was accurate. As you see in the main text, a journalist should have a good idea of what the courts may consider standard practices.

Note some of Harlan's assumptions in the preceding two cases:

- If other sources are available, the reporter has a responsibility to check information with more than one source.

- If the reporter is not an expert in the field she's is writing about, she should find an expert.

- If there's a serious possibility of defamation, a news organization is expected to look for ways to check the facts, like screening video footage of the actual football game in this case.

- If a reporter is an eyewitness, that fact is helpful in establishing that the events she reports on actually happened.

- If there's any indication a source might be untrustworthy, it's especially important that a reporter confirm information with independent sources.

It's good to keep these expectations for journalists in mind as they will help you be more accurate, as well as helping to protect you against libel charges.

Let's look at a couple of other examples of standard journalism procedures. If you're doing a story on a fatal car accident and you include a witness's statement, without verification, that the driver was drunk, then you have not taken the requisite steps of a good reporter in determining the truth of important information. The witness might have mistaken the symptoms of shock for drunkenness. Reporting based on assumptions is never a good idea, but it could be particularly damaging in this instance because drinking under the influence is a crime, while being in a state of shock is not. You need to find out from an official source—the police officer on duty, an arrest warrant or a spokesperson for the police department—that the driver has actually been arrested in connection with driving under the influence before you include this information in your story. Then, make sure you attribute the information to that source.

You also need to be very clear in your story what the fact is: You still don't know that the driver actually was drunk. What you know is that he was arrested because the police think he may have been drunk. Note that he still hasn't been charged. Police are not usually the ones who make criminal charges. This is usually the job of a prosecutor, so charges would typically happen later. Even if you say someone was "arrested for" a crime or "arrested on charges of" committing a crime, you still imply that he's actually been charged. While "arrested in connection with" is wordier, it is the most accurate way to explain what has happened.

A similar problem happens when you use "alleged" or "allegedly." If you call someone an "alleged thief," and he has not yet been charged, then you're simply saying someone called him a thief. Publishing this defamatory statement could be considered libel. Even if you're quoting someone calling the person an alleged thief, you may not be protected if that turns out to be false. In contrast, if you report that someone has been arrested in connection with a theft, then even if she is innocent, you have not libeled her because you've reported what actually transpired.

Look again at the previous example of a fatal accident. You know the information could be defamatory—not only does it suggest the driver committed the crime of drunk driving, but it also suggests he killed someone. That should be a red flag, a signal that as you report it, you should be extra careful in making sure all information is both accurate and thoroughly researched. You should be sure you have the correct identity of the driver, and that he wouldn't easily be confused with someone else. You should include other identifying information from the police report, such as the driver's full name, address or at least the name of the town where he lives and his age. Checking the actual police report is important, but even police reports can be wrong. Try to confirm the person's identity with another source. And at the very least, when you provide the name of the driver, attribute the information: James T. Jones, 22, was arrested in connection with driving under the influence of alcohol, Sgt. Dwayne Tomkins of the Carbondale Police Department said.

Keep in mind that although middle initials are one way to distinguish identities, you might also have two people with the same name in the same town. Consider this scenario: If you find on a police report that Janet Smith was arrested in connection with growing marijuana, and the mayor's name is Janet M. Smith, you're not ready to publish a story that the mayor has been arrested for growing marijuana. You need to cross-check addresses and talk with police officials to verify that this is the same Janet M. Smith who is mayor—not someone else—and make that clear in the story.

In all news stories, adhering to good, ethical practices can help to ensure accuracy. With any story that has the potential to damage a person's reputation, you need to be especially aware of the importance of triple-checking all of your facts and being professional.

> Press freedom is essential to our democracy, but the press must not abuse this license. We must be careful with our power. We must avoid, where possible, publicity circuses that make the right of fair trial a right difficult to uphold. We must avoid unwarranted intrusions upon people's privacy. Liberty and, no less, one's reputation in the community are terribly precious things, and they must not be dealt with lightly or endangered by capricious claims of special privilege
>
> *WALTER CRONKITE, AMERICAN BROADCAST JOURNALIST*

DEFENSES AGAINST LIBEL SUITS

Despite taking several measures to help avoid libel suits, you may still be accused of libel, so you should be acquainted with specific defenses.

Truth

Remember that if the information in your story is true, it cannot be libelous. But even if you feel you *know* something to be true and you absolutely trust your source, the information still may not be demonstrably true when you're in court, defending yourself in a libel suit. For instance, what if you posted a story based on the statements of one witness of a crime, but the plaintiff can produce two witnesses in court who will testify the exact opposite? While you may be sure your witness is the only one telling the truth, this may be more difficult for a jury to determine. Or, if you have agreed not to name your source for your story, then it's difficult to back up your information in court.

Fair Comment and Criticism and Rhetorical Hyperbole

As you read more about libel, you may wonder how news organizations get away with saying terrible things about actors, say, or chefs or authors. What about harsh reviews like this excerpt from Anthony Lane in *The New Yorker*?

> I was unprepared, having missed "Les Misérables" onstage, for the remarkable battle that flames between music and lyrics, each vying to be more uninspired than the other. The lyrics put up a good fight, but you have to hand it to the score: a cauldron of harmonic mush, with barely a hint of spice or a note of surprise. . . . I screamed a scream as time went by. (2013, para. 3)

Les Misérables and other musicals—or books, movies, theatrical performances and restaurants, to name a few—are offered up for public consumption and judgment. Courts have taken this into account in providing more protection for criticism of these works.

Furthermore, an expression of opinion has traditionally been protected by the courts. In *Gertz v. Welch*, Justice Lewis Powell explained why the courts distinguish between opinion and fact in libel cases:

> Under the First Amendment there is no such thing as a false idea. However pernicious an idea may seem, we depend for its correction not on the conscience of judges and juries but on the competition of other ideas. But there is no constitutional value in false statements of fact. (1974)

Fair comment, or the right to criticize, also protects **rhetorical hyperbole**, obvious overstatement or exaggeration.

In *Milkovich v. Lorain Journal Co.* (1990), the Supreme Court ruled that even a column clearly labeled as opinion, or a statement that says it is an opinion, may be grounds for a libel suit. If a statement is something that can be proven true or false, the Supreme Court determined that it is a statement of fact, no matter what it's labeled. If you say, "I think the woman has committed a crime," it can probably be determined relatively easily whether she is indeed a criminal. If she is not, then the "I think" does not protect your statement from being libelous.

Privilege

The courts have recognized the **absolute privilege** of certain individuals, speaking in certain situations, to be protected from libel. People in this group include participants in court proceedings, like attorneys or witnesses, or participants in legislative proceedings, like members of Congress or state legislators. This protection is extended to members of the public in official proceedings because it is so important that they be able to speak freely without fear of being slapped with defamation suits. Any citizen criticizing the government has absolute immunity from libel.

Reporters do not qualify for absolute privilege. However, reporters—and anyone else, for that matter—have a **qualified privilege** to report what people with absolute privilege say, as long as that report is full, fair and accurate. If a prosecutor is making the case in

FIGURE 10-5 You can quote what public officials say during public proceedings as long as your report is full, fair and accurate—even if what they say is potentially libelous. The same protection does not always apply if someone is speaking outside an official capacity.

court against a man charged with murder and says he's sleazy and adulterous, and a murderous criminal, the prosecutor can't be charged with libel, even if the accused man is found not guilty. The prosecutor has absolute privilege when speaking in court. A journalist who, under qualified privilege, reports the prosecutor's words also can't be charged with libel, as long as the journalist's stories are **full, fair and accurate**.

So what does it mean for a report to be "full, fair and accurate"? If the prosecutor makes a case on one day and the defense attorney on another, then each day's story will be one-sided. That's okay—as long as you don't skip one side of the case altogether. You obviously don't have to include everything said in court, but your reporting wouldn't be full or fair if you only reported on what the witnesses for the prosecution said. And if you get a quote completely accurate but publish it misleadingly out of context, then your reporting isn't fair.

It's important to remember that your qualified privilege is contingent on your subject's absolute privilege. Absolute privilege is granted during official, public proceedings, but not outside them. If an attorney says something to you in an interview outside the courtroom, that attorney's words are no longer protected by absolute privilege, nor are yours under qualified privilege (Fig. 10-5).

Exercises for Chapter 10

EXERCISE 10-1: Go to your favorite news site and select a news story that contains several quotes. Select a quote to paraphrase, and do so with proper attribution. Include the original quote for comparison, including proper credit to the source.

EXERCISE 10-2: You're following up on a story about why student fees are going up $113 at the start of the next academic year. The student government had to approve these fees before the administration approved them, so you interview the student body president, Rick Boure. He says, "Yeah, it sucks that fees are going up, but I gotta tell you, there's really no gettin' around it. Everything costs more these days, and someone's gotta pay the bills. State funding isn't comin' close to payin' for everything so unfortunately students have to pick up the difference."

    a. What, if anything, would you quote? Write that quote in appropriate news style, including attribution.

    b. What, if anything, would you paraphrase? Write that paraphrase in appropriate news style, including attribution.

    c. Now write the full treatment of the passage as you'd put it in your story, including appropriate context.

EXERCISE 10-3: What are the five elements a plaintiff must prove to bring a successful libel suit? What is the one absolute defense against libel? Why is it a defense? In writing, articulate your answer.

EXERCISE 10-4: Suppose you're doing a story on the company that runs the campus cafeteria. You interview a source who used to work for the company. Your source says, "Oh, they violate safety standards all the time. I wouldn't eat there, after what I've seen." What, if any, issues raise warning flags for you? What would you do with this quote?

EXERCISE 10-5: Suppose you're doing a story on a band playing in town for the weekend. After the first show, you ask some people for their reactions. One person says, "They were horrible. It was like they were all drunk or high or something. They should be fired." What, if any, issues raise warning flags for you? What would you do with this quote?

CHAPTER 11

WORKING A BEAT

Immediately after the Sandy Hook Elementary School massacre, the national news media descended on the town of Newtown, Conn. The community was often bewildered and upset by the invasion of strangers, but they felt very differently about their local news organization, the Newtown *Bee*:

> Newtown's first selectwoman, Pat Llodra, forbade members of the media to enter the firehouse, but it never occurred to her to ask John Voket, the Bee's government reporter, to leave. Almost daily, he visits her office, the repurposed dining hall of a mental asylum, to ask for comments on the town's agenda, and Llodra always takes time to respond. (Aviv, 2013, para. 7)

As a government reporter, Voket covered a **beat**, an area of news coverage that involves a set of regular checks with key, relevant sources (Fig. 11-1). After years of working with the same sources and living in the community, Voket, like many of the *Bee*'s other journalists, cared about his community and his sources, and community members knew that. When a crisis happened, the journalists had built a sense of trust with their usual sources and other residents. That made their reporting better, which meant, in turn, that it served the community better.

" an area of news coverage that involves a set of regular checks with key relevant sources. "

FIGURE 11-1

Some Basic Assumptions about Beats

As a reporter, you also will probably be assigned a beat. For instance, if you were assigned the education beat, you might be expected to cover kindergarten through 12th grade for your community and attend board of education meetings as well as talking with principals, teachers, parents, students and superintendents. By regularly covering the same beat, you will get to know important sources and they will get to know you. As you build trust and rapport, sources are more likely to alert you to issues or talk more honestly with you. Over time, your understanding of the issues on your beat will deepen, and you will gain a sense of the background and history of ongoing problems.

Covering a beat carries certain responsibilities, and if you are assigned a particular beat, your supervisors, sources and audience will expect you to know these. For most beats, the assumptions about your responsibilities are as follows:

- You will serve as watchdog, making sure that those who are responsible to the public are fulfilling their responsibilities.

- You will be expected to report newsworthy events in a timely manner. If you are the education reporter and the district superintendent is fired, you should know about the firing. In practice, this also means knowing about a newsworthy event *first*—before other news organizations and before word is out on the street.

- Timeliness doesn't trump everything else. You'll still be expected to double- or triple-check information, talk with a diversity of sources, treat others with respect and follow good journalistic practice.

- You will be expected to learn the issues and trends for that beat. If a state is planning to cut art classes to focus on science classes, an education reporter should know whether such cuts are controversial locally.

Many journalists start out as **general assignment** reporters: An editor or producer assigns them stories in multiple areas, depending on what's needed most. General assignment reporters don't work an actual beat, but they still often find themselves returning to some of the same sources. That means they also try to make sure that public officials are fulfilling their responsibilities, keep an eye on newsworthy events related to the stories they've covered and let producers and editors know about them immediately.

There is also a set of underlying assumptions about the beat itself:

- The first assumption is that this is an area worthy of coverage. That is, there's an implicit assumption that your beat is one that needs to be prioritized over other areas that don't get covered. Because journalists can never publish all the news, the news they do cover says much about what they think is not important. For instance, your news organization may assign education as a regular beat, but not poverty. Business may be a beat, but not labor, or parenting, or the environment. As you get to know the issues better, you can help a news organization think through the areas it fails to cover, or fill in the gaps on your own beat.

- Another assumption is that your news organization's beat divisions are the most effective way to divide news coverage. Perhaps a small community newspaper chooses to divide its coverage into eight beats: county government, city government, education, health, sports, the environment, police and the courts, and arts and entertainment. These areas would be covered differently if, say, health and the environment were combined, opening up a new beat for covering issues that affect people between the ages of 18 and 25.

- Yet another assumption is that news should be divided up into beats at all. Some media organizations have experimented with using collaborative teams to report on issues. Or consider the possibility of a news site devoted to only one or two issues a day. This might result in reporters working more closely together, interviewing a wider range of sources. On the other hand, reporters might lose the in-depth knowledge of certain issues and rapport with sources that regular beats help to build.

- Often, news organizations assume that you will abide by the convention of authoritativeness, speaking with the highest-ranking officials. This proves that you know your beat and that you know who is important. It also demonstrates your access to people at the top. But as Sigal and Chomsky point out, the convention of authoritativeness also reinforces the status quo and government hierarchy. Informed reporters who think critically can address this problem in part by talking both to high-ranking officials and to sources who are closer to events and issues. As long as you don't ignore high-ranking officials, you can fulfill the expectations created by prevailing news practices and also meet the challenge of reporting more accurately.

The first set of assumptions is basic to your job. But, eventually, you will want to apply the ideas from your newswriting class to make sure that you look more closely at the second set of assumptions about the beat itself in order to report as fairly and thoroughly as possible.

Professional Relationships with Sources

RESEARCH BEFORE YOU TALK TO PEOPLE

To address your first goal as a reporter—that of gathering *some* news—you'll want to familiarize yourself with the background and history relevant to your beat. If you have educated yourself about the issues, you're less likely to be taken advantage of by sources and more likely to make informed choices in selecting sources. And you'll have a better chance of finding alternative sources who were previously voiceless. This background work seldom actually appears in a published news story, but it's critical to the depth and accuracy of your coverage.

Most reporters begin their jobs by reading. What you find in your news organization's previous stories may warrant a mention in your first story, or nothing at all. Remember, however, that the information you learn from old news stories is what has been covered before. You won't necessarily cover the beat in the same way, or talk to the same sources as your predecessor. And to avoid repeating mistakes, you should always double-check such information before using any of it in a story. Reading old news stories is simply a crucial step in learning the names and issues important to your beat—not a substitute for actual reporting.

Next, you'll want to start getting to know your sources. Beginning journalists can fall into one of two traps: They immediately approach sources as adversaries, or they are overly friendly with sources. Neither is the best way to interact with the people from whom you gather information.

TREAT YOUR SOURCES WITH DIGNITY

Ambitious reporters sometimes objectify their sources, treating them as a means to an end. They focus on the information they want without considering whether they treat those sources with basic respect and fairness. This is unethical: It ignores the sources' humanity. Reporters may be facing tight deadlines, or they may simply be focused on the story itself and the quotes they expect from sources. But neither of these excuses is a good reason for treating people with anything less than respect.

People who are interviewed frequently by the news media say that they simply wish to be treated with dignity. For reporters, that means slowing down enough to think about your source's point of view. And it means taking the time, where possible, to acquaint yourself with sources before the big story hits and you need them.

Often, veteran journalists will introduce new reporters to sources. But even if this doesn't happen, it's important to seek out potential sources ahead of time, introduce yourself and allow time for a chat about recent issues. Ideally, such chats should be get-to-know-you sessions with no resulting product or news story. This establishes that your concern about a story won't override your concern about them as fellow human beings. If necessary, though, you can combine introductory interviews with newsgathering for noncontroversial news stories about the city's new community garden project, for instance, or an innovative new school program. Introductory interviews are the best way to begin getting a sense of what's important to the sources on your beat. And those interviews should be conducted in person.

Face-to-face meetings, as opposed to interviews conducted on the telephone, are the best way to consistently build rapport with sources so they'll be honest with you about sensitive subjects and tip you off to stories you don't know about. Your reporting over time will show the difference, too. When you talk with your subjects in person, you benefit from the human contact.

KEEP A PROFESSIONAL DISTANCE

At the other extreme from objectifying your sources is getting too close to them. If you work a beat, you will probably spend a lot of time with the same people. And as *American Journalism Review* managing editor Lori Robertson pointed out, walking the line between friendly and too close is sometimes difficult:

> But the reporter-source relationship is an intimate one to begin with. Reporters want to be warm and friendly. They need trust, respect, rapport. A source may be giving them information that could cost the source his job. It's no surprise that, at times, these interactions turn to affect, whether it's a romance or a friendship. (2002, p. 45)

Getting too friendly with a source can damage a reporter's ability to think objectively and professionally, and thus get accurate information.

One temptation is to keep returning to the same sources without expanding into the rest of your beat—talking with city councilors you know, say, rather than taking the time to meet those you don't know as well, or city workers or residents. If you rely on the same standard sources, their viewpoints may start to sound like the most logical, and it's easy to see these viewpoints as the most important or the norm—or the only views it's necessary to report at all.

To avoid such one-sided reporting, it helps to keep a certain distance from your sources, thinking about all information critically. It's possible to have a friendly *and* professional relationship with regular sources—good beat reporters can learn to get to know sources well while also making it clear to them that the journalist will still report stories that include information the sources don't like. Many sources respect reporters for maintaining that kind of separation.

What does this kind of reporting—checking with some of the same sources, building trust, finding stories on a beat—look like on the ground? Let's take a closer look.

A Scenario: The Education Beat

Say that you're assigned to the education beat, and there's a board of education meeting the first night. You read recent stories about what's been going on and learn that there's a controversial new test for teachers that's up for approval at the meeting. If you get the chance, you'll talk with sources *before* that night's meeting, and find out what they think of the tests. Based on the convention of authoritativeness, you speak with the superintendent, the chair of the board of education and maybe one of the school principals. But you think about Sigal's points and realize that the people most directly affected by the tests would be the teachers. So you call up the teachers union and speak with two representatives. At the meeting, most of the people present object strongly to the test, but the board decides to use it on a probationary basis for a year. You get reactions from some of the teachers, reasons from board members for their decision and a statement from the superintendent. You're ready to roll, and you report a solid story for the next day's broadcast or publication and, later, an update for the website.

After the story runs, you immediately start to worry about what to write about next. Based on a search of past education stories, you know that typical coverage has included subjects such as board meetings, PTA meetings when something especially newsworthy is happening, graduations and budget issues, as well as administrator evaluations and faculty pay. To start getting to know people on your beat, you arrange interviews with the PTA chairman, a science teacher and the school superintendent. You call up one of the representatives of the teachers union and arrange an interview. You sign up for some online publications that cover education nationally and in your state, and you start a Twitter feed on area education.

You wonder about who didn't get covered in your first story (Fig. 11-2). What about the students? If you interview them while they're at school, you'll need permission from someone in authority. Once you have that permission, you talk with several students and you learn that they're pretty mad that teachers are putting up such a fuss about a test for themselves when teachers give students so many tests. And some of the students also think that if teachers had to take tests, they would be more sympathetic with what students have to go through when they prepare for and take tests.

Because this local issue is also connected with proposed testing of teachers across the state, you decide to provide more context for your audience. You look at the state teachers organization publication online, and you see an interesting article about testing teachers. You look at the name at the bottom of the piece, email the writer and do a telephone interview with him to find out how teachers in other communities are responding to the proposed tests. You write an interesting follow-up story in which you address the students' and parents' concerns, and also provide the wider context of reactions of teachers in other communities.

Then it's the next day, and you're looking for other important school issues that need to be covered. You've arranged more interviews—with other teachers, with parents, with students, but in the meantime, you remember that at the board meeting the

FIGURE 11-2

high school principal mentioned a memorial fund for a student who had committed suicide the year before. You wonder how frequent such student suicides are, so you call up the school superintendent, who says the principal has kept statistics for the past 10 years. You learn that two students from the local high school committed suicide this year, and three the year before, and as far as you can tell, this has been the pattern for the past 10 years. You check with state figures, and you learn that the local suicide rate is one of the highest in the state. You interview counselors and some of the students' friends, and you do a story that focuses on coping with depression, as well as a sidebar that reports the suicide rate. Although you receive an angry online comment from a school-board member who says you're focusing on the negative, your editor and you are both pleased with your enterprise in researching this subject, and in providing helpful insights about deeper issues that affect teenagers and the community as a whole.

A couple of weeks later, you're once again trying to think of important stories that haven't been reported. You've written a profile of a math teacher who uses innovative teaching techniques, a story about students who graduate early and another piece on the principal's goals for the next five years. You've covered that year's senior projects.

You've been making regular checks of some online publications and chat groups for state and national educational issues, and you've localized two of these: One concerns the brain drain resulting from low teacher salaries in small towns like your community, and the other concerns a new, more effective approach to teaching.

As you think about which stories to cover, you're also building relationships with sources and taking steps to report the most meaningful stories. At the board of education meetings, you serve as a watchdog, making sure that the public's interests are served. Your stories will help readers learn about the people involved in the system, but you know that you need to keep checking for gaps in your coverage. You realize you're not covering the students who have dropped out. Schools may well be failing these teens in important ways, but people who opt out of the system don't usually make it onto a regular beat checklist. You do some digging around, and you end up with a series of stories based on interviews with teens who have dropped out—a series that not only is helpful to the community, but is also your best work yet.

In your interviews for that series, several people mention as an aside something about the ethnic divide between Mexican-American and Anglo students. You're very much aware of the issue, but without a news hook, you've simply noted the idea in a "Future Story Ideas" file on your computer. You also keep a **tickler file**, a file of issues to keep checking on, such as an upcoming hearing of a teacher charged with drunken driving and the first report on the effectiveness of teacher testing. This is the way many journalists make sure they follow up on important continuing issues.

Two people contact you through Twitter and ask whether you know about rising ethnic tensions at the high school. You do some background research and find out about such tensions elsewhere in your state. You interview the school principal and the head of the history department, who teaches a class on cultural clashes in the United States You learn about a mediator who has been called in to some of the schools in one of the bigger cities, and you call that person to provide wider context.

But when you sit down to write your story, you realize that the people you've been talking to are all people in positions of power. You don't have any student voices. So you interview the student president and two members of the Latinos/Latinas Club. But you realize that just because someone belongs to a particular ethnic group doesn't mean that person speaks for that group. So you go back to the history teacher and ask if the teacher thinks anyone in the class might have interesting points to add. Based on the names the teacher gives you, you talk with two Anglo students, one of whom is responding to tensions by joining the Latino/Latinas Club, the other of whom was in a recent fight with a Mexican-American student. Then you write your story.

As you continue to work your beat, you keep examining trends in your reporting. Perhaps you notice that in story after story, the students and teachers you interview tend to be the same sex you are. Or you keep returning to sources who share your ethnicity. You realize that because of your position, you have been overlooking significant communities within your beat. Because of this realization, you consciously try to gather other perspectives in order to keep your reporting more accurate and interesting.

As a reporter in the preceding hypothetical scenario, you are still, for the most part, operating under the convention of authority and other assumptions critiqued by

FIGURE 11-3 When you try to include diverse sources and subjects in your beat reporting—or any reporting—you should also try to represent them as complex human beings. So while Somalia has been plagued for decades by poverty and famine, Somalians should not always appear in the news as miserable and suffering. And although the Syrian government used chemical weapons against its own people in 2013, Syrian citizens should not always be represented as injured war victims. Pakistani girls like the three shown in the photo here may live in a country torn by warring factions . . . but they also sometimes jump up and down on trampolines for fun.

Sigal, Chomsky and Herman. For instance, you are consulting official, government sources first and most frequently, thereby reinforcing the status quo. You are interviewing the teachers or students who are easiest for you to contact or most willing to talk with you.

Nevertheless, the previous example is meant to serve as a role model for how to marry practical needs and theoretical ideals. Through keeping media critiques in mind, you are also talking with sources who are interviewed less often, and thinking about people outside your group of peers and acquaintances. Of course, you won't immediately solve deep, systemic flaws in media reporting; but through your awareness of those flaws, you will have done fairer and more representative reporting.

Good journalists distinguish themselves by continuing to interrogate their own practices. The steps we've outlined in this section should help you apply your critical thinking skills to working a beat. Whenever you interview sources, remember to keep in mind the elements of good journalism. You need to guard your freedom as a journalist by keeping a professional distance from your sources. You also need to be responsible to those sources, treating them humanely and respectfully. You need to think about your entire community of coverage, and report fully and accurately on as many different kinds of people and problems as possible (Fig. 11-3).

Watchdog Beats

While the press serves as a watchdog in almost any story it covers, certain beats focus more directly on public business and public officials. Beginning reporters are often assigned one of these "watchdog beats"—beats that cover local government, courts or police and crime. These beats share important traits: They tend to have a regular fountain of facts and news, through meetings or police blotters, and much of that information is required by law to be public. This means that a reporter's challenge is not so much finding information in the first place, as it is reaching out to find more interesting, useful information that represents the whole community, rather than just those who have easy access to news or are especially outspoken (Fig. 11-4).

For instance, if you were assigned to cover the city council, you could spend your time covering meetings and doing follow-up stories. Those regular meetings tend to be the meat and potatoes of a lot of government reporting, and it's key that a reporter attend and keep an eye on what happens and what is said. But sometimes, a meeting doesn't warrant a story. There's simply not enough going on. A reporter might do a better job of informing the community through **enterprise reporting**—that is, by finding a story through talking with a variety of people or investigating, rather than through regular meetings, blotters or press releases. This means getting to know the people on your beat and looking out for issues that don't show up on an agenda.

FIGURE 11-4 Gary Coronado took this award-winning photo for a project about Central Americans jumping trains, and risking their lives, to make their way north for jobs in the United States It's a good example of one of the ways that journalists act as watchdogs over unjust conditions.

TIPS FOR REPORTING THE CRIME AND POLICE BEATS

One of the classic watchdog beats is covering crime and police. The steady flow of information here comes from the police blotter and sometimes the scanner, which transmits whatever is coming across police and firefighters' radios. That way, reporters can often make it to the scene of an emergency themselves and find out information firsthand. But even if you're at the scene of a crime or accident, you'll find out more useful information if you've already developed a relationship with your sources.

Getting to Know the Beat

If you're assigned to cover the crime and police beat, you'll almost certainly be dealing with the same sources quite often. That makes it even more important than usual that you get to know your sources and that you learn some basics about the beat early on. How does a beginning reporter go about learning the police beat?

- You'd start, of course, by reading through transcripts or stories from your news organization that deal with crime. Take notes: Are there trends that keep repeating? What are the biggest stories involving police—Thefts? Murders? Hate crimes? Police corruption? Also, look for the names of police sources. These are the people who were most willing to talk with your predecessor, so odds are good that they'll be willing to talk with you.

- Schedule an interview with the police captain and/or public relations officer. Take a list of questions with you. Find out what issues the police are most interested in educating the public about, what their biggest problem areas have been and their goals for the year and any procedures that would be most helpful for you to follow. Be sure to take a business card with your cellphone number and email address.

- Visit all the police stations and sheriff's offices, and introduce yourself to as many people as possible and ask for a tour (Fig. 11-5). Find out where the police blotter is kept, and ask someone to help you familiarize yourself with standard terms.

- Find out crime statistics for your area. A good place to start is with the FBI's Uniform Crime Reports. The statistics in these reports are provided voluntarily by local agencies, so they may or may not play down unsolved crimes. However, you can get a sense of which crimes are a problem in your area and how this compares with similar places.

- You might also check the National Crime Victimization Survey at the Bureau of Justice Statistics to find out more about crime victims in your area.

- Ask for a copy of standard operating procedures, and study it.

- Ask a police officer to tell you about local arrest procedures.

- Remembering Sigal's criticism of the convention of authoritativeness, think about people other than officials you might cultivate as sources. Most communities have a hotline for victims of sexual assault, and they frequently have a shelter for victims

FIGURE 11-5

of domestic abuse. Schedule interviews with program directors, volunteers and people at the shelters. Visit places like soup kitchens, where you're likely to encounter people who've fallen on hard times. Talk with them to find out how they're treated in the community. Keep an eye out for neighborhood groups and victims associations, and talk with their representatives. Talk with probation officers and social workers.

The preceding steps will help you start meeting and cultivating sources, and that's how you'll learn more helpful information about area crime for your audience. Keep digging deeper. When you meet one good source, ask for names of other possible sources. And keep asking people you meet what stories they see in your community.

GETTING BEYOND SNAPSHOTS OF VIOLENCE

Reporters also need to keep in mind the purpose of their reporting. One criticism of crime reporting is that it fails to reflect a community accurately because it doesn't take into account the big picture. Crime stories may imply that crime is increasing when in fact it's on the decline. Or crime stories may give readers a false idea about what crimes are most common in the community, because journalists tend to report on the most unusual or deadliest crimes. Here's how David Krajicek described the problem in an online manual for journalists reporting on crime:

> Lori Dorfman, director of the California-based Berkeley Media Studies Group, advocates a public-health approach to reporting violence. She says news consumers

would be better informed if crime reporting were less anecdotal and episodic and more contextual and scientific.

That means more big-picture context and less focus on details, which she sometimes sees as picayune embellishments—the color of a victim's socks, for example. Dorfman suggests increased attention to epidemiological "risk factors" affiliated with violence, such as alcohol and drug use or socioeconomic status. And she says reporters should dish fewer fears-and-tears stories and devote more time and space to investigations of the consequences of violence, both from the perspective of families and communities and in terms of taxpayer costs to the health-care and criminal justice systems.

The Berkeley Media Studies Group conducted a yearlong analysis of stories about youth violence in three large California newspapers, the *Los Angeles Times*, *San Francisco Chronicle* and *The Sacramento Bee*. The researchers concluded that two-thirds of the 3,174 stories they found were episodic "snapshots" about a violent incident. Just one-third were "thematic, examining the big picture, providing context, and exploring trends."

Dorfman's organization suggests the media apply the same coverage standard to all violence, whether extraordinary or routine, and it urges reporters to expand sourcing beyond the usual-suspect officers and prosecutors to include health professionals, advocates and independent experts. (2003–2010, para. 1–4)

Crime and police reporters need to know the basics of what's going on, which means they need to make regular checks on police blotters and talk frequently with police officers. But they also need to know about the basics that might not show up in those regular checks. That's why it's so important to keep getting out into the community and meeting people who might otherwise remain below the radar.

Campus Crime: A Special Case

Finding out about campus crime can sometimes be tricky, because universities are often covered by more than one police agency. At some schools, the campus police or security deal with minor crimes, and the local police deal with suspected felonies. Campus police or security officers may provide incomplete information if they feel it's in the college's best interests to emphasize its safety.

If you're at a public college or university, you have a right to see campus crime reports. Furthermore, the **Clery Act** requires colleges and universities that receive public funding to make annual reports of crime statistics on campus. You can read more about this at the Student Press Law Center's website. It's a good idea to find out when your university's crime reports are published, and to follow this up with an interview with campus security or police and a story.

A Checklist for Stories about Accidents or Crimes

If you cover crime and police, you'll end up writing many different kinds of stories— stories about the effectiveness of local law enforcement, about victims of crime, about ways to prevent crime, about drug raids, murders and robberies. But as you start out, you may immediately need to know how to write a story about a single accident or crime.

To help you, here's a list of the basic information you will need to find out for a typical story about an accident (a traffic accident, or an accident in which someone is hurt) or a crime:

- Who was involved? You need the names, ages and addresses of victims and, if they exist, suspects. If it's a vehicle accident, you need to try to get the names of drivers and passengers.
- When did it happen? What day and what time?
- Where did it happen? If it's a vehicle accident, what's the intersection or address? If it's a crime, what's the home or business address?
- What was the damage? If people were hurt, how badly? You may need to call the local hospital to find out (in some cases, the hospital can at least tell you if someone was checked in, although privacy laws make it difficult for hospitals to give a patient's condition). In the case of vehicles, how much were the vehicles damaged? If there was a break-in, what was damaged and how much? In the case of a theft, how much was stolen?
- What happened? You need a description of the accident or crime, or as much of it as a police official or victim can tell you. Remember that you need to get this from someone who has witnessed it firsthand, or else an official who has the authority to speak about it.

Enterprise Beats

Reporters are often assigned to cover beats that don't rely on one or two central organizations. That means there's no steady flow of information from a single source. These beats, which depend on a culmination of information from various sources, are called enterprise beats and they include subjects such as business, health, and arts and entertainment. Instead of a stream of input from meetings or police blotters, you're more likely to receive an inbox full of press releases. Let's examine how working one particular enterprise beat, the business beat, might look out in the field.

COVERING BUSINESS

The business beat can mean many things, depending on whether you're in a small community or a big city. But, no matter the community's size, a business journalist tries to report on the health of the business community. And that's more complicated than covering a group of business owners and local chamber of commerce concerns. Business reporting includes reporting on people with real power—power to shape communities, and to do both tremendous good and tremendous harm. Business owners range from landscapers to gym owners to owners of multimillion-dollar banks and construction companies. They often operate behind the scenes to give to soup kitchens and educational institutions, to offer opportunities to people down on their luck or just starting out. They may also seek to influence public affairs through political donations, donations that are now difficult to track because the Supreme Court has ruled that they can remain anonymous. Or they may have relationships with law enforcement or the courts—or with each other—that are a bit too cozy. Keep in mind that your responsibility as a journalist is to cover the whole community.

Reporters need to think about who is affected by business decisions. This includes workers, who might be helped or hindered by businesses or industries new to a community, or who are also affected when businesses don't do well or don't take care of their employees. It includes residents who live near a business or industry, or who might be affected by pollution or developments. It includes consumers, who stand to benefit from diversity and low prices. It includes other businesses, who can benefit from cheaper supplies nearby, or by learning from other businesses' innovations, but who can lose money if the competition is given unfair advantages.

Workers

When you're doing background research for the business beat, you should find out who the biggest local employers are, and what kinds of jobs they provide. It's also a good idea to find out how highly skilled workers need to be to get these jobs and how much they would make. How long have the primary employers been in town, and what sorts of layoffs or shake-ups have they had? Expansions and hires? Does your community have a reputation as a union town, or an anti-union town—and why?

You can look up the local unemployment rate at the Bureau of Labor Statistics website, and compare it with state and national figures. You can also get a sense of the

FIGURE 11-6 In this case, the most credible sources are the people who are making minimum wage. They are directly affected and have firsthand knowledge about the issue.

kind of work available in your region. The government keeps track of jobs because employment affects everyone.

But whether people have work is only one part of the information about jobs. A journalist needs to check on what kind of work that is—how well are local workers paid, and does it match the cost of living in your area (Fig. 11-6)? How well are workers treated? You can look up the government's Occupational Safety and Health Administration's website to check for local violations, for instance. You can also check for on-the-job accident statistics, although these sometimes only tell part of the story if employees are discouraged from reporting them.

Reporting on whether people have jobs and making sure that they're safe and compensated decently is part of a journalist's watchdog function. But it's also crucial to let your community know what employers and employees are doing right. Some employers go out of their way to provide a paid leave of absence for child care, for instance, or to offer good insurance policies or memberships to local gyms. It's easy enough for a journalist to use Twitter to ask community members who's the best employer in town and why, and to follow that up with stories. Sometimes employers and employees are able to overcome disagreements and work out compromises smoothly. These stories provide helpful models for everyone else, and they provide hope, inspiring your audience to act in ways that will make their world better.

Businesses as Neighbors

Industries and businesses usually have a larger impact on a community's environment than residential households. That's to be expected, because they typically serve more people. But it's a journalist's job to make sure that businesses are good neighbors. Are they obeying environmental laws and regulations? This isn't the kind of information a business would usually volunteer unless it's good, so you need to check elsewhere. One place to look is on the EPA website. If you look under the A–Z search, you can scroll down to "ZIP code" under Z. Enter your community ZIP code, and you can find out several different kinds of information about the environmental impacts of local businesses. You can click on "EPA-regulated facilities" to find out what local businesses are regulated in your area, along with what wastes a business is permitted to discharge.

An industry might be too noisy. It might add illegal pollutants into the water, ground or air. And neighbors might also have other objections. In Durango, Colorado, for instance, when an adult boutique moved to a street not far from an elementary school, some residents raised concerns. The city had no regulations preventing stores from selling risqué clothing near schools, but the newspaper published a story airing the concerns. The business owner responded by saying she would tone down window displays so they'd be appropriate for elementary students passing by the store.

Business for Consumers

When a new business comes to town, a business journalist thinks about whether that information is interesting or useful to readers. A new Thai restaurant may introduce more diversity to local cuisine. A new doctor's office or dental practice might provide more medical choices and possibilities. The Home Depot store might bring lower prices—but such large, nationally owned stores might also compete with locally owned hardware stores, eventually contributing to their closures. When a new business moves to town, a good business journalist looks ahead at both the good possibilities and the bad.

Reporters can also provide consumers with helpful information about established businesses. If customers make complaints, you need to be fair both to consumers and businesses, but a good place to start is with the local Better Business Bureau. For restaurants, you can check the results of regular public health inspections. You can also do stories that don't name particular businesses. For instance, you can provide strategies and tips about how to buy a used car or how to find a good medical provider or how to get the best price for a new home.

What Do Other Businesses Need to Know about Each Other?

When the local and national economies were struggling in 2010, the *Durango Herald* did a story about businesses that were continuing to grow and prosper. The story acknowledged the depressed economy and the downward spiral that can happen when one series of layoffs leads to another, but pointed out that the reverse was also true: "For every job gained, further movement is added to the local economy" (Scofield, 2010, para. 7). Several local businesses that were doing well despite the economy were profiled next to the story.

Reporting on one local business's success or experiment can be helpful, if you're as fair to other businesses as possible. If you do a story on a local shoe store's expansion, for instance, you'll be providing that store with free publicity. To share the benefit, you could include information on what's available at other similar stores.

Local business innovations are fun to read about, and new ideas can inspire other businesses. When local businesses band together to form new groups, those efforts may also warrant a story. In Durango, a local resident started a weekly gathering called the Green Business Roundtable. The group has grown steadily, and the mix of weekly speakers often inspires area businesses to take small steps toward greater energy efficiency. The local newspaper covers speakers when they seem especially interesting and newsworthy.

There are real, useful stories you can do that move beyond public relations or delivering a steady report of business openings, closings or quarterly earnings. It's useful to know whether your town is suffering from a recession as much as other towns, for instance—these stories give a sense of how healthy the community is. But you can also provide more depth and inspiration by keeping the big picture in mind when you cover business: How do businesses affect the community as a whole, and what could they do better?

This approach applies to any beat. Beginning reporters may find themselves scrambling for story ideas at first but will soon develop a rhythm for places to look. That's fine as long as you remember your responsibilities to represent the many different facets of your beat, seeking out people who don't get to talk to the news media often, and looking beyond tradition to what your community most needs to know.

Exercises for Chapter 11

EXERCISE 11-1: Choose one of the following: Skim your local newspaper for a week, watch a local evening broadcast one night or listen to a radio program one night. What beats does the news outlet seem to cover? Can you think of a few others it should develop? In writing, discuss your findings and thoughts.

EXERCISE 11-2: Select a state. Then select two news sites from that state. Make a list of the beats they cover. What, if anything, do they have in common in the beats they list? Are there any beats unique to either news site?

EXERCISE 11-3: As a follow-up to Exercise 11-2, select a different state. Once again, select two news sites from that state, and then look at the beats they cover. Considering the beats you've identified in Exercise 11-2, do you see any patterns in the beats they cover? In writing, discuss your findings.

EXERCISE 11-4: Choose a reporter from a major news organization. Do a search and skim through five of that reporter's stories. Then complete the following activities:

a. List the main issue covered in each story.

b. List the jobs or identifications (a local activist, a man who recently lost his job, etc.) of the sources in each story.

c. Identify the reporter's beat.

d. See if you can find a bio or description that describes the reporter's beat. What does it say?

STORYTELLING
IN OTHER
FORMS

Habits of Mind

Journalists know that sources can use questionable logic when presenting their point of view. Learning logical fallacies helps journalists to assess arguments and conclusions for their logical validity, adding another layer of skepticism and accuracy.

What Does it Mean to be Skeptical?

Journalists are skeptical: They double-check information that other people might take at face value. They ask who or what the sources of information are, and they think about the possible motives behind what sources say. They don't accept a news tip or information from a source—or rumors or gossip or what everyone else is saying—until they have a chance to evaluate the evidence (Fig. 12-1).

But good journalists don't let their skepticism get in the way of accepting evidence and reason. Think of the conspiracy websites that claimed the 2011 massacre in Tucson never happened. The website authors assumed that the police, news media, victims and politicians must all be lying in order to provide ammunition for gun-control laws. Or, what about the claims of "birthers," a group of people who believe that President Obama was not born in the United States, and that his birth certificate is a hoax—despite the release of the document and reassurances from government agencies and even the governor of Hawaii. Are these legitimate voices whose views you should report? Or are they employing logical fallacies to promote an agenda?

Journalists typically trust sources with demonstrated records of telling the truth, especially when there's no reason to think they'd lie. And journalists also talk to multiple sources about each issue, which gives them a built-in way to double-check what any one source says. They learn to be on the lookout for hoaxes, lies and mistakes: For instance, phoned-in obituaries are, sadly, a classic place for pranksters "reporting" the death of someone who is very much alive.

Journalists also become adept at listening for the logic—or lack thereof—in what sources say. In this section, you'll learn ways to apply that skepticism by evaluating statements, information and sources, and also by examining the reasoning behind people's statements. Knowing how to spot flawed reasoning is especially important when you delve into the realms of commentary and blogs. Let's start with a look at some of the ways that both journalists and sources might reach erroneous conclusions.

LOGICAL FALLACIES

Logical fallacies are errors in reasoning, and these were famously analyzed and classified by Aristotle (Box 12-1). A source may be accurate in the facts, but still come to

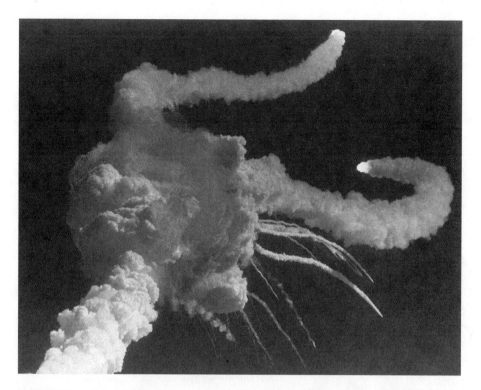

FIGURE 12-1 Good journalists learn to respond automatically to new information with skepticism. For instance, a journalist asks how credible the sources are, what their motivations might be and whether they'd have access to the most accurate information. But journalists also apply that same skepticism to those who continue to doubt facts without good reason and despite plenty of supporting evidence. For instance, websites and groups that claim the Challenger space shuttle explosion in 1986—pictured here— was a hoax deserve to be treated especially skeptically because that claim is inconsistent with the evidence and reasonable thinking.

an erroneous conclusion—or one without enough evidence. Skeptical journalists recognize when sources employ logical fallacies. Let's look at an example.

False Generalizations

According to a legend in India, six blind men once decided to find out what an elephant was like. The first man touched the elephant's trunk and said the elephant was just like a snake; another fell against the elephant's side and decided the elephant was like a wall; another felt along its tusk and said elephants were like arrows or spears, and so on (Fig. 12-2). The men were employing a **false generalization**, jumping to a conclusion based on insufficient evidence. Let's say you visited a college campus for the first time and saw three students wearing Birkenstock sandals. If you concluded that most of the students at the campus were hippies, or even that most wore Birkenstocks, you'd be making a false generalization.

BOX 12-1

A LIST OF FALLACIES IN ARGUMENTS

While Aristotle was the first Western thinker to catalog logical fallacies, other thinkers have been modifying and building on that list for hundreds of years. In addition to those mentioned earlier, the following is a partial list of other fallacies:

Ad Populum: Because most people think a position is correct, it is. *Example*: Eighteen million people can't be wrong.

Appeal to Tradition: The arguer says something is correct because it has always been done that way. *Example*: The news editor has always been promoted to managing editor, so we have to promote this year's news editor, too.

Begging the Question: This is also known as *circular argument*; the arguer's statement assumes that the point in question has already been proven. *Example*: The government can't run anything, so no wonder the Obamacare rollout was such a disaster. (Also, "begs the question" has come to be used imprecisely to mean "raises the question.")

False Analogy: The arguer asserts that two dissimilar things are similar, when in fact they aren't. *Example*: A household has to stick to a budget, so the federal government has to stick to one, too—no deficit spending.

Non Sequitur: The conclusion doesn't logically follow from the original statement; there's a gap in logic. *Example*: Washington legalized marijuana—what a bunch of hippies. (Also, *post hoc* and *slippery slope* are examples of non sequiturs.)

Post Hoc: The arguer says that because something comes after something else, there is a cause-and-effect relationship: The first event caused the second event. *Example*: Every time I watch the game, my team loses.

Red Herring: The arguer attempts to distract the opposition by bringing up an irrelevant topic and pretending that it's relevant. *Example*: He shouldn't be elected president—the garage in his newest house has an elevator for his cars.

Single Cause: The arguer asserts that there is only one cause for a problem when several factors actually contribute to it. *Example*: We should abolish welfare because it keeps people poor.

Slippery Slope: A step in a particular direction will lead inevitably to going to the extreme of that direction. *Example*: If we let the mayor ban supersized soft drinks, the next thing you know, he will try to outlaw everything we eat.

Anecdotal Evidence

Journalists make such false generalizations most often when they rely on only **anecdotal evidence**—that is, individual stories, events or observations that don't justify a broad conclusion. For instance, imagine that you talk with two friends who say they've had trouble getting summer jobs because the economy isn't doing well. If you conclude that

FIGURE 12-2 False generalization.

summer jobs are less available than they once were, you're basing your conclusion on anecdotal evidence—the stories of two people. You certainly wouldn't want to produce a news story about a "trend" based on this kind of anecdotal evidence.

In a story about job satisfaction, you wouldn't lead with, "Most people dislike their bosses," based on interviews with a few disgruntled former employees. Interviews with sources who have been personally affected by issues in the news—unemployment, an increase in violent crimes, a sinking economy—don't typically provide a sense of what's going on in the big picture. However, such interviews can still provide insights, as long as you treat them appropriately. Anecdotes are a powerful part of journalism when they are used to illustrate evidence based on facts. When you learn from the Bureau of Labor Statistics that the jobless rate is up, then the stories of those who have no employment can help an audience imagine the reality behind abstract numbers and understand some of the possible consequences of this trend. But it's crucial that you remember the difference between **anecdotes**—stories that help to show readers some of the individual faces and lives behind facts and statistics—and evidence.

False Dilemmas

As a journalist, you have to examine not just your own reasoning, but that of your sources. Another logical fallacy, one that you'll see in many arguments people make to win others to their side, is called a **false dilemma** (Fig. 12-3).

Here's an example: Imagine that Student A and Student B take a test. When they get their tests back, Student A has scored a 95 percent and Student B a 75 percent. Student B says to Student A: "Did you cheat?" Student A replies: "No, I didn't." Student B then says: "Then the professor must like you better than he likes me."

This false dilemma is an argument in which the speaker implies there's a choice between only two possibilities when there are actually other possibilities: If you didn't do X, then you must have done Y, or, if X isn't true, then Y must be true.

FIGURE 12-3 False dilemma.

In news reporting, erroneous reasoning can lead to more wide-ranging consequences. For instance, what about the age-old saying, "He who is not with me is against me," which implies that someone who doesn't back a particular method or solution, or doesn't support a cause 100 percent, is therefore against the whole cause? Such an argument can discourage moderation and reasoned discussion of multiple options.

The Straw Man

A similar fallacy is the **straw man**, when someone presents a weaker version of the opponent's argument, dismisses it, then claims to have won the argument. After all, it's easier to topple a straw man than the real thing. For instance, in the early days of global climate change discussions, some people who lived in places where the winter was colder than usual said that the colder winter was evidence that global warming wasn't happening. In fact, scientists had predicted that as the earth's climate warmed, some local climates would grow colder temporarily. Furthermore, scientists said that small, localized climate changes were meaningless in the context of long-term, global changes in climate.

Again, as a journalist aware of logical fallacies, you might talk to a scientist to gain a better understanding of the complexity of the issue and avoid communicating flawed reasoning.

Ad Hominem Attacks

Like the straw man argument, an **ad hominem** (Latin for "to the person") attack uses a distraction to try to win a debate. In this case, the arguer attacks the person with

FIGURE 12-4 Ad hominem.

whom the arguer disagrees rather than that person's argument or point (Fig. 12-4). When people who disagreed with former President George W. Bush resorted to insulting his grammar or word pronunciation rather than discussing his policies, they were making ad hominem attacks. When political opponents criticized Hillary Clinton's fashion choices rather than her positions on the issues, they were also using this faulty argument strategy.

Sometimes, it's difficult to separate ad hominem attacks from relevant criticisms of a person's character, especially if that person is running for office. How much did voters need to know about South Carolina Governor Mark Sanford's marital infidelities, for instance, or those of former President Bill Clinton? When there is the possibility that such infidelities involved lawbreaking, a journalist needs to report on them. When the argument is that they reveal an elected official's character, the issue gets murkier.

Ideally, journalists balance considerations like fairness and stewardship with the public's need to know the information. For instance, when John F. Kennedy was president, journalists did not publicize his extramarital affairs: "what reporters covering the White House knew about his promiscuity never saw its way into print. It just wasn't considered relevant" (Shepard, 1999, p. 25). The information was accurate, but news organizations felt that any public interest served by reporting the president's extramarital affairs was not enough to outweigh the potential harm to the president, the First Lady and good taste. Until Senator Larry Craig (R-Idaho) was arrested in connection with soliciting sex in a Minneapolis airport restroom, the mainstream media saw no reason to report on his sex life (Goodnough, 2007). One factor in whether the news media publicizes stories about public officials' private behavior has been whether such secrets contradict that official's stance on related issues:

> In the mainstream media, the recent standard for pursuing open secrets has been murky, but generally guided by the notion that private behavior matters when it is at odds with public declarations. . . . Mr. Craig supported a 2006 amendment to the Idaho Constitution barring gay marriage and civil unions and has voted in Congress against gay rights. (Goodnough, 2007, para. 8)

One way to avoid including ad hominem attacks in your work is to make sure that the information is accurate and fair, and that it serves an ethically justifiable purpose—that it goes to the heart of an issue. If the information serves to distract from the issue, or if it seems disjointed from news of public interest, it's probably just an ad hominem.

This unit focuses on writing leads and stories that are different from the inverted pyramid structure. These stories are often longer, and include many more sources. The unit also introduces you to non-news writing such as blogs and other commentary.

Especially as you look at journalism commentary, practice listening for the logic—or lack thereof—of what both journalists and sources say, and the conclusions they reach. Check the logic of your stories, the overall narrative, and the conclusions your story might lead the audience to draw. Check the logic of blogs you read and the ones you write.

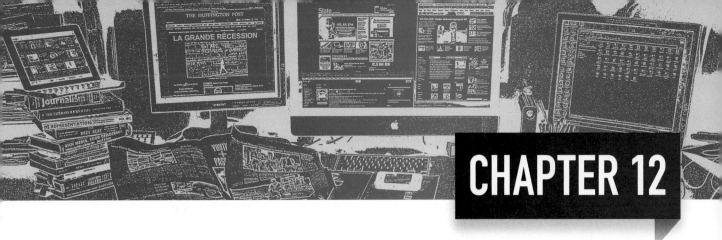

CHAPTER 12

LEADING
WITH SOMETHING
DIFFERENT

Here's the beginning of a CNN.com story from the fall of 2013:

> For some, it's an emotional punch to the gut. For others, the consequences could be truly life-changing.
>
> On the third day of the government shutdown, the impact is only beginning to be felt.
>
> Federal employees and contractors felt the pinch first. But the ripple only started with them. It's now radiating throughout the country. (Payne, 2013, para. 1–3)

The story begins without even identifying its subject—the October government shutdown—a far cry from an inverted pyramid style lead that starts with the most important point and answers *who*, *what*, *when*, *where* and possibly *how* and *why*. But the second paragraph quickly makes that subject clear. That's also true for the following lead from NBCwashington.com:

> No national parks. No Smithsonian. (And no Panda Cam.) No new small business loans, no tax audits, no way to check that the employee you want to hire is a citizen.
>
> The government officially shut down at midnight Oct. 1. Hundreds of thousands of federal workers were furloughed, and some of the D.C.-based services tourists and locals alike rely on will be closed. (DiMargo, 2013, para. 1–2)

Both stories were dealing with the complexities of the 16-day U.S. government shutdown in October 2013. Congress has to vote every year (or more frequently, if it has passed stopgap funding in the past) to fund most of the federal government's operations. This time, a majority of Republicans had refused to vote for funding unless the Affordable Care Act was delayed or defunded.

While legislators negotiated, hundreds of thousands of federal employees were sent home and parts of the government were closed. The U.S. was still recovering from a recession, and people worried that the shutdown might jeopardize that recovery. And analysts were concerned about an additional issue: The federal government was about to reach its debt ceiling around Oct. 17, and some worried that for the first time, Congress might fail to vote to lift that ceiling. Most economists predicted that this would have dire, long-term consequences for the U.S. economy.

That meant the news media needed to cover the shutdown well to provide people with information they might need. Because this issue was so complicated and in the news so frequently, journalists often used forms other than the inverted pyramid to report on it: They varied their leads, changed their tone—and even tried humor to help communicate useful information on a topic that had been saturating the news for weeks.

The variety of leads served readers and viewers well for an issue everyone knew something about—and it's a good example of a time when journalists were less likely to use traditional news leads. Although reporters use inverted pyramid style for most of their stories, hardly any use it for *every* story. And if journalists think a different form will serve their audience best for a particular story, the most common place they vary that form is in the lead.

When to Use Other Kinds of Leads

As a journalist, you'll often write stories that start more slowly, focusing on an individual, a description, background or a telling anecdote. You'll sometimes see labels for these leads: summary leads, multiple-element leads or focus leads. With experience, you'll learn how to create many different kinds of leads, but we'd like you to start by thinking critically about *when* you might start a news story with a lead that doesn't get to what's most important first, and what kind of lead would fit the story content best.

Let's take a look at some examples where journalists have decided that a different kind of lead is suitable, or might even be better than an inverted pyramid lead. The situations we describe following—like making an abstract story concrete or clarifying a complex story—may overlap, so you'll sometimes have to make a judgment call based on the material you've gathered in your reporting.

As you read these other types of leads, you may notice something: Each of the stories still includes the same information that would be included in an inverted pyramid-style lead. For these stories, the paragraph containing that information will simply appear later—and we'll discuss that in a minute.

MAKING AN ABSTRACT STORY CONCRETE

Journalists often find themselves reporting stories about national trends or statistics: the number of people killed in a particular battle or war, the general downward or upward turn of the economy or the jobless rate. These numbers can be hard to absorb, and sometimes their meaning gets lost in the telling. To help their audience grasp difficult and complex stories, reporters often start by telling about one particular individual who has been affected (Fig. 12-5). Here's an example:

> BRATTLEBORO, Vt.—Facing eviction from her Tennessee apartment after several months of unpaid rent, Alexandra Jarrin packed up whatever she could fit into her two-door coupe recently and drove out of town.
>
> Ms. Jarrin, 49, wound up at a motel here, putting down $260 she had managed to scrape together from friends and from selling her living room set, enough for a weeklong stay. It was essentially all the money she had left after her unemployment benefits expired in March. Now she is facing a previously unimaginable situation for a woman who, not that long ago, had a corporate job near New York City and was enrolled in a graduate business school, whose sticker is still emblazoned on her back windshield.
>
> "Barring a miracle, I'm going to be in my car," she said.
>
> Ms. Jarrin is part of a hard-luck group of jobless Americans whose members have taken to calling themselves "99ers," because they have exhausted the maximum 99 weeks of unemployment insurance benefits that they can claim.
>
> For them, the resolution recently of the lengthy Senate impasse over extending jobless benefits was no balm. The measure renewed two federal programs that extended jobless benefits in this recession beyond the traditional 26 weeks to anywhere from 60 to 99 weeks, depending on the state's unemployment rate. But many jobless have now exceeded those limits. They are adjusting to a new, harsh reality with no income. (Luo, 2010, para. 1–5)

Jarrin was not a prominent person, but the reporter focused on her particular experience to help people understand the predicament of 99ers without becoming tangled up in bureaucratic jargon (Fig. 12-6). The last paragraph of this excerpt arrives at the main point of the story: that when the Senate extended unemployment benefits, it didn't help a large group of unemployed people who had been drawing on those benefits for more than 99 weeks. But if the reporter had started with this information, he might have lost readers by overwhelming them immediately with explanations about bureaucratic process. Instead, he presented Jarrin's plight first and then connected it with the problem.

Focusing on individual people who are not in themselves newsworthy can be a powerful way to make your story more interesting. But you have to do so sparingly, and be sure that you don't **bury the lead**—that is, don't wait too long to get to what's important. Even in the previous example, a reader has to work through three paragraphs before arriving at a connection between Jarrin and a national issue. Furthermore, when you overuse any unusual lead structure, it can lose its effectiveness. If most of the stories on your news site start with a focus on an individual, you risk boring your

FIGURE 12-5 Because it was online, the Washingtonpost.com had the space to tell Lu Lingzi's story, the stories of everyone else who died and those of people who were still recovering after the Boston Marathon bombing. But the technique remains the same—focusing on individuals helped make the story human and concrete.

"On a gorgeous spring day, Lu Lingzi and two of her friends at Boston University ventured to the finish line of the Boston Marathon to observe one of the most storied traditions of their adopted city. Lu was from Shenyang, one of the largest cities in northeastern China, and had moved last year to Boston, a city brimming with students and youthful energy. Before heading out that morning, she posted online a photo of a fruit salad she called 'my wonderful breakfast'" (Johnson & Mufson, 2013, para. 1).

readers or forcing them to wade through too many tangential anecdotes to find out the news they need.

Some Tips for Creating Leads That Focus on Individuals

- The best times to focus on individuals are when the overall situation you're reporting might be overwhelming. This is often true if a story involves large amounts of money or large numbers of people—or large numbers in general. For example, you might try this approach if you're localizing a story about a

FIGURE 12-6 A lead focusing on an individual can ground an abstract story. However, be careful not to wait too long before you clarify the connection between that individual and the story's impact on the audience.

government report saying the unemployment rate is up. You could interview people at the local unemployment office, and you could also ask on Twitter or Facebook for people who have recently been laid off.

- As you interview, keep in mind that you might need more personal details than you would for other stories. In the lead about Jarrin, notice that the reporter knows how much the week in the motel is costing her ($260), and that she still has the sticker from graduate school on her windshield. One of these facts probably came from careful interviewing, and the other from the reporter's observations. If you interview someone in her home, look around and jot down descriptive details. If your subject tells you a particularly interesting story, ask follow-up questions to make sure you could retell it. You might or might not end up using the information in your lead, but you won't have the choice if you don't have the information.

NUT GRAPHS

When news stories start with a lead that doesn't immediately get to the main point, they need to include a **nut graph**, a paragraph somewhere early in the story that explains what's newsworthy (Fig. 12-7). This is where journalists answer *so what?* about their news story. Even some inverted pyramid stories will include a nut graph,

FIGURE 12-7 The nut graph answers the question, "so what?" It indicates why your story is timely and important.

three or four paragraphs in, that states implicitly or explicitly: "This is important because . . ."

For stories with nontraditional leads, the nut graph is especially important. It's typically the third, fourth or fifth paragraph, although in a long piece, it may be placed even later. If you wait too long, people don't know *why* they're reading a particular anecdote or description.

After a lead that starts with a little-known individual, *why* is just what the reader is wondering. In the story about 99ers, for instance, the reporter details Alexandra Jarrin's plight for the first three paragraphs. Her hardships are interesting, but they're not newsworthy in and of themselves. Then, there's the following transitional paragraph:

> Ms. Jarrin is part of a hard-luck group of jobless Americans whose members have taken to calling themselves "99ers," because they have exhausted the maximum 99 weeks of unemployment insurance benefits that they can claim. (Luo, 2010, para. 4)

Here, the reporter starts to indicate Jarrin's importance to the audience by emphasizing the connection between her and a national group of people. But at this point in the story, readers still don't know why this group is especially newsworthy. They find this out in the next paragraph, which serves as a nut graph:

> For them, the resolution recently of the lengthy Senate impasse over extending jobless benefits was no balm. The measure renewed two federal programs that extended jobless benefits in this recession beyond the traditional 26 weeks to anywhere from 60 to 99 weeks, depending on the state's unemployment rate. But many jobless have now exceeded those limits. They are adjusting to a new, harsh reality with no income.

In this example, the reporter uses a nut graph to clarify the connection between the people who drew you into the story and a newsworthy trend or event. This paragraph provides the same kind of information that an inverted pyramid-style lead would. It tells readers what's most important or why they should care: Do they know that the Senate's decision is having this kind of impact? The difference is in where the paragraph occurs in the story.

Sometimes, reporters are even more direct. Their nut graphs will actually say, "This is important because . . ." That's often a good way to make sure you're communicating that information to the reader. When you write a story with a nontraditional lead, check that it includes a paragraph that begins with this phrase—or that *could* begin with it.

CLARIFYING A COMPLICATED STORY

It's not just abstract numbers that can become confusing for your audience. Sometimes, you'll find that a particular news story is so complicated that an inverted pyramid lead doesn't do it justice. In this case, you might start with some basic background information to lay a foundation for the main point.

For instance, after sifting through hundreds of financial documents, *McClatchy News* reporters Greg Gordon and Chris Adams began their news story like this:

> In December 2006, Goldman Sachs embarked on a frantic effort to shed billions of dollars in risky mortgage securities and purchase exotic insurance to protect itself against what it had concluded could be the collapse of America's housing market.
>
> Yet for nine months, until Sept. 20, 2007, the Wall Street giant didn't disclose its actions in key filings with the Securities and Exchange Commission, in telephone conferences with analysts or in its press releases.
>
> A McClatchy review of hundreds of pages of subpoenaed company records released by a Senate panel Tuesday, as well as Goldman's SEC filings, has revealed how closely the company guarded its secret exit plan.
>
> Goldman's failure to tell the investors who bought its risky mortgage securities that it had made an array of wagers against housing is at the heart of the furor now enveloping the nation's premier investment house, the only major Wall Street firm to exit the subprime mortgage market with minimal damage. (2010, para. 1–4)

The story begins slowly, focusing on telling events in the order in which they happened to clarify for readers some of the complexity of the financial mess. This makes it easier for people to understand what's going on. But as with any of the slower leads discussed in this chapter, you should weigh the benefit against the potential risk of losing your readers' interest by taking too long to get to the meat of the story.

Some Tips for Bringing Background to the Beginning of a Story

- Notice that in this story, the events and the amount of background information are what could become confusing, as opposed to the large numbers of people or amount of money involved.

- If your story has a complicated history that you need to include, think about how to break it up into bite-sized chunks. You can begin with the most important three or four of these, and then fill in others later in the story. For instance, let's say you're reporting on the controversial firing of a local coach after the issue has been going on a long time, and the story has become very tangled and involved. You might start with the coach's action that sparked the trouble, say in the next paragraph that he was fired and then sum up the angry response in the next paragraph. Details about issues such as the firing or the coach's past problems or popularity could come later in the story.

- Make sure that whatever you start with is sufficiently interesting to pull the reader into the story.

COVERING AN EVENT WITH SEVERAL NEWSWORTHY ISSUES

If several events fall under the same umbrella—a meeting concerning more than one newsworthy topic or an election involving several different important elements—reporters sometimes include several main points in the lead. Here's an example from a CNN story on primary election night:

> President Obama and former President Bill Clinton are on opposite sides of a divisive Democratic Senate primary and a former pro-wrestling executive could take a big step toward winning election to the Senate—those are just two of the storylines as Colorado, Connecticut, Georgia and Minnesota hold primary contests Tuesday. (Steinhauser & Brusk, 2010, para. 1)

CNN and other news media ran individual stories about the important election contests across the country, but this particular story helped readers get an overview of what was going on in several different states. Sometimes, this is the most efficient way for readers to grasp what the major contests and issues are.

PROVIDING A SENSE OF PLACE

Sometimes, it's important to provide your audience with a sense of place. Maybe the setting is especially intense—a protest, a shooting or a large natural disaster. Or perhaps the setting helps provide a sense of the subject or issue. Setting a scene in your lead invites readers to attend to a story they might otherwise pass by. In a news story about banks financing drug cartels in Mexico, for instance, the financial news website Bloomberg.com begins with the following: "Just before sunset on April 10, 2006" (Smith, 2010, para. 1). A journalist wouldn't usually begin with the day or date, especially when that date is four years earlier. But in this case, the reporter is not only setting up a scene, but also the expectation that something big is about to happen. Think about how well this lead works as you read the first few paragraphs:

> Just before sunset on April 10, 2006, a DC-9 jet landed at the international airport in the port city of Ciudad del Carmen, 500 miles east of Mexico City. As soldiers

on the ground approached the plane, the crew tried to shoo them away, saying there was a dangerous oil leak. So the troops grew suspicious and searched the jet.

They found 128 black suitcases, packed with 5.7 tons of cocaine, valued at $100 million. The stash was supposed to have been delivered from Caracas to drug traffickers in Toluca, near Mexico City, Mexican prosecutors later found. Law enforcement officials also discovered something else.

The smugglers had bought the DC-9 with laundered funds they transferred through two of the biggest banks in the U.S.: Wachovia Corp. and Bank of America Corp., Bloomberg Markets magazine reports in its August 2010 issue. (Smith, 2010, para. 1–3)

The rest of the story details the breaking news of Bloomberg's exposé. But look again at that first paragraph. The lead launches immediately into a tense situation on an airport tarmac in Mexico. In the next paragraph, the story continues its description of a crime that sounds as if it might have come from a thriller movie. It's not until paragraph three that the story gets to its main point—that two large U.S. investment banks were financing the crime. This type of lead is not as tightly written as a traditional inverted pyramid lead, and it takes even longer than the previous examples to get to its point, running a greater risk of losing readers. On the other hand, when you succeed with this kind of story beginning, your readers may have a better understanding of the situation before you delve into the details. And readers also may be more willing to read further because the story is not only relevant— it's riveting.

Some Tips for Starting with Description

- Just as you do when you start by focusing on an individual, you need to observe especially carefully and take good notes for this kind of lead. Or, as in this case, you need to interview carefully to get the details. The reporter doesn't seem to have been present at the scene, but he's managed to find out the time of day, the lie the crew told to keep people away from the plane and the fact that there were 128 black suitcases filled with cocaine.

- Jot down all the descriptive details you can think of—if a person was driving, for instance, what kind of car was it? How new or old, and what color? It's very possible that none of this information will make it into your story, but you'll be giving yourself the choice.

You need to be careful about using this kind of technique for breaking news. But it can work. Here's an example:

James Shepherd learned to sail as a boy and was considered an accomplished sailor with a wealth of racing trophies to his credit.

But early Friday morning, his grandfather's sailboat got away from him on Lake Michigan.

Shepherd, 21, drowned after he and three others left the 31-foot Joan's Arc for a late night swim. (Schlikerman, Lee, & Dizikes, 2010, para. 1–3)

In this story about a young man's death, reporters usually would have started with some version of the third paragraph. Instead, these reporters communicated a sense of the poignancy of the accident by juxtaposing Shepherd's skill and experience with the fact that the boat got away from him. The first paragraph doesn't signal what follows, so there's a greater chance of losing readers. It's also important to think about whether family and friends of the victim might consider this lead too casual, and therefore disrespectful of their grief and the young man's memory.

However, we think this lead works. It doesn't waste much time getting to the heart of the story, but along the way, the reporters communicate some sense of Shepherd's individual circumstances. In doing so, the lead communicates a more personal sense of this particular tragedy.

FOLLOWING UP ON BREAKING NEWS

Once a breaking news story has been reported, it's often standard practice to do follow-up stories that report additional information as it becomes available. Journalists use these stories to flesh out the original news stories by filling in gaps, adding atmosphere or details or explanations. Because journalists assume that the audience knows the basic news events already, there's less pressure to get to the main point fast. That means that follow-up stories don't always use inverted pyramid style. In this next example, the news that 10 aid workers had been killed in Afghanistan had already been published and aired. The main point of this particular follow-up story, then, was not their deaths but that the workers had made personal sacrifices to go to Afghanistan. Notice how the story's lead does this:

> Their devotion was perhaps most evident in what they gave up to carry out their mission: Dr. Thomas L. Grams, 51, left a thriving dental practice; Dr. Karen Woo, 36, walked away from a surgeon's salary; Cheryl Beckett, 32, had no time for courtship or marriage. (Dewan & Nordland, 2010, para. 1)

This first paragraph is basically a list—that's a technique you'll also see in other leads. Here, the list adds rhythm through repetition (Grams left a practice; Woo walked away; Beckett had no time). And the details are more powerful than a generalization that simply says they all made personal sacrifices. This emphasis on the victims' humanity might be the difference that draws your readers into the story.

Notice the contrast between the lead and the second paragraph, which states the story's main point but only gives the number of aid workers killed and their nationalities:

> Most of all, the 10 medical workers massacred in northern Afghanistan last week—six Americans, one German, one Briton and two Afghans—sacrificed their own safety, in a calculated gamble that weighed the risk against the distribution of eyeglasses and toothbrushes, pain relief and prenatal care to remote villages they reached on foot. (Dewan & Nordland, 2010, para. 2)

An inverted pyramid lead would have started with some version of this second paragraph, and that would have been accurate and appropriate. When the reporters chose to use a different kind of lead, they made a judgment call—and succeeded in emphasizing the victims' sacrifices, humanizing the people affected and drawing in readers.

Some Tips for Leading with a List

- The kind of list we're discussing here is not like a laundry list, where you name the main events that happened at a meeting. This is a list in which the elements are particularly interesting, or there's a point to be made through the repetition of a phrase.

- Think about the cumulative effect of the items listed. For example, note the repetition of "the square" in this hypothetical lead:

> The rebels had stood in the square for weeks. They had held signs in the square calling for their leader's ouster. They had eaten in the square and slept in the square. Now they were rejoicing in the same square.

The "square" is simply a place in the first sentence, but the word gains symbolic importance through repetition.

ESTABLISHING TONE

Sometimes, journalists want to signal readers that their subject is light—to say, in effect, "Relax. You may have been reading about famine or terrorist attacks or a bad economy, but this story is less serious." Or sometimes, a particular news outlet wants to establish a snappy approach. The following lead from a Planet Money story fits both criteria. Planet Money is a news outlet that emphasizes being interesting and fun, and the story itself, although about an important topic, doesn't involve life-and-death issues:

> When you talk about the patent system among techies in Silicon Valley, there's usually an audible groan. (Blumberg & Sydell, 2011, para. 4)

This lead doesn't get to the main point right away; instead, it indicates the general direction of the story, and in a style that aims to connect with its audience.

Another news outlet, ProPublica, is an online nonprofit that focuses on investigative journalism—pretty heavy stuff. But its website takes an informal approach to the news, with headlines like the following: "The Financial Crisis as Conversion Experience—An Event" (on Feb. 28, 2013), or "Friends in Low Places: Where the Real Lobbying Happens" (on Feb. 20, 2013), or "Do as We Say, Congress Says, Then Does What It Wants" (on Jan. 13, 2013). The tone of the site is conversational and fun, and that tone carries over to many of the site's news leads. For instance, a story about the FAA begins this way:

> Thought Congress had averted a government shutdown by striking a 2011 budget deal back in April? That's only partly true. (Wang, 2011, para. 1)

Notice that this lead omits the noun (as in, *You thought Congress had averted . . .*). Furthermore, the lead starts with a question, and then provides a short answer, setting up a little suspense. We know the rest of the story will provide an explanation.

Some Tips for Communicating a Lighter Tone in your Lead

- In the previous examples, the tone is informal and even jaunty, but it's not sloppy. The writers use sentence fragments, but they do so skillfully to communicate complete thoughts.

- These leads aren't laugh-out-loud funny; they tend to be wry or allusive. The tone still signals to readers that the reporter is serious about communicating important, accurate information.

- If you're trying to match the tone of your news outlet, read or listen carefully through as many stories as possible. You might even take notes. Is there a lot of humor? How sophisticated do the stories expect an audience to be? How informal are leads, and when do they seem to be more traditional?

As you've seen, using leads that provide narrative tension, humor or a personal experience can be an effective method of introducing news stories. These techniques can communicate information better and make your stories more interesting. You should try it—after you make sure you've learned how to write a standard, inverted pyramid-style story. Remember that your primary job as a journalist is to provide your audience the information it needs. If you're dealing with urgent, breaking news or a story where the impact has to be clear right away, you'll need to save these longer, less traditional leads for another time.

Exercises for Chapter 12

EXERCISE 12-1: Find a lead that serves to make an abstract story more concrete. How does it do this, specifically? Is it effective or not? Why? Write a summary of the story, discuss why you selected it and give your assessment of it. Include the lead and a proper citation for the story.

EXERCISE 12-2: Find a lead that serves to clarify a complicated story. How does it do this, specifically? Is it effective or not? Why? Write a summary of the story, discuss why you selected it and give your assessment of it. Include the lead and a proper citation for the story.

EXERCISE 12-3: Find a lead that sets a scene. How does it do this, specifically? Is it effective or not? Why? Write a summary of the story, discuss why you selected it and give your assessment of it. Include the lead and a proper citation for the story.

EXERCISE 12-4: Find a story that has a nut graph. In writing, describe how the paragraph answers the "so what?" question. Include an excerpt from the story that includes the lead, the nut graph and all the material between the two. Provide a proper citation for the story.

EXERCISE 12-5: Find an alternative, slower lead that has a nut graph. In writing, describe how the paragraph answers the "so what?" question. Include an excerpt from the story that includes the lead, the nut graph and all the material between the two. Provide a proper citation for the story.

CHAPTER 13

WHAT ABOUT OTHER KINDS OF NEWS STORIES?

Choosing how to write a news story that doesn't fit the traditional inverted pyramid style isn't as simple as plunking information into the right-sized container. It's a much more organic process. Nontraditional news stories—that is, news stories that don't start with an inverted pyramid style lead and then deliver the rest of their information in the order of descending importance—can follow as many different structures as a reporter's imagination can create. Here's an example from the first story in a Pulitzer Prize-winning series from InsideClimate News, a nonprofit online news organization:

> An acrid stench had already enveloped John LaForge's five-bedroom house when he opened the door just after 6 a.m. on July 26, 2010. By the time the building contractor hurried the few feet to the refuge of his Dodge Ram pickup, his throat was stinging and his head was throbbing.
>
> LaForge was at work excavating a basement when his wife called a couple of hours later. The odor had become even more sickening, Lorraine told him. And a fire truck was parked in front of their house, where Talmadge Creek rippled toward the Kalamazoo River.
>
> LaForge headed home. By the time he arrived, the stink was so intense that he could barely keep his breakfast down.

> Something else was wrong, too.
>
> Water from the usually tame creek had inundated his yard, the way it often did after heavy rains. But this time a black goo coated swaths of his golf course-green grass. It stopped just 10 feet from the metal cap that marked his drinking water well. Walking on the tarry mess was like stepping on chewing gum.
>
> LaForge said he was stooped over the creek, looking for the source of the gunk, when two men in a white truck marked Enbridge pulled up just before 10 a.m. One rushed to LaForge's open front door and disappeared inside with an air-monitoring instrument.
>
> The man emerged less than a minute later, and uttered the words that still haunt LaForge today: It's not safe to be here. You're going to have to leave your house. Now.
>
> John and Lorraine LaForge, their grown daughter and one of the three grandchildren living with them at the time piled into the pickup and their minivan as fast as they could, given Lorraine's health problems. They didn't pause to grab toys for the baby or extra clothes for the two children at preschool. They didn't even lock up the house.
>
> Within a half hour, they had checked into two rooms at a Holiday Inn Express, which the family of six would call home for the next 61 days.
>
> Their lives had been turned upside down by the first major spill of Canadian diluted bitumen in a U.S. river. Diluted bitumen is the same type of oil that could someday be carried by the much-debated Keystone XL pipeline. If that project is approved, the section that runs through Nebraska will cross the Ogallala aquifer, which supplies drinking water for eight states as well as 30 percent of the nation's irrigation water. (McGowan & Song, 2012, para. 2–5)

In this series opener, the journalists told the LaForges' story to ease the reader into what would be a compelling but also highly technical and complex series. They took nine paragraphs to tell the anecdote, with the news hook—a massive oil spill in southwestern Michigan—arriving in paragraph 10. You can see that's quite a bit different from the inverted pyramid structure.

This chapter offers alternative ways to structure a story. It won't give you a list of all the different types of news stories—for one thing, that's just not possible. More importantly, we'd like you to start thinking from the very first about how to fit a story's form to its purpose. So we'll start by providing you with ideas about how to organize piles of information. Then we'll guide you through three different scenarios and the kinds of stories reporters wrote to deal with each. Finally, we'll discuss how you can make sure your story organization is as fair to your sources as possible—without providing a false sense of balance or failing to alert your audience when a particular view on an issue just isn't supported by evidence.

Organizing News Stories into Pods

The information you gather for a story is likely to be grouped in your notes according to each source, but that's seldom how a news story is told. Try this: Think about grouping the information into **pods**, or small clusters of related information. You can think of each pod as its own mini inverted pyramid, in which the most important information goes first, followed by the rest of the information in descending order of importance (Fig. 13-1).

To illustrate this concept, let's start with a short, straightforward story. Here's the information in the police report:

- Driver: James R. Hart, age 37, of Durango, Colorado.

- Number of passengers: 0

- Time of accident: approximately 11:30 p.m. Tuesday

- Accident description: A Dodge truck was heading west on Wildcat Canyon Road, near the intersection with U.S. Highway 550. The truck apparently hit a patch of ice and swerved off the road. The truck rolled down the embankment on the east side of Wildcat Canyon Road, turning over twice. No other vehicles were involved. Hart was unconscious when police were called to the scene.

- Conditions: The accident happened approximately one half-hour after a steady sleet began.

First, you interview police Capt. Christian Rivera, who confirms the information in the report. He says the department was flooded with calls shortly after the ice storm, and five car accidents happened within the next hour or so. He says, "There was black ice everywhere, and we had about five accidents with vehicle damage. Nobody was injured in the other accidents, though."

Next, you call Mercy Medical Center, where the victim was taken. You learn that he has died.

Now you have three groups of information: the facts from the police report, the notes from your interview with Rivera and the information from Mercy Medical Center that the driver is dead. But to write your story, you'll need to reposition these facts into small groups of related information.

Think about what should go into the lead: What news is most important? Think about how you can answer the *who*, *what*, *when* and *where* of the story (and the *how* or *why*, if these answers are available and newsworthy).

Pod one: Because the accident victim is not the mayor or a controversial local figure or celebrity, you wouldn't include his name in the lead. Remember that you want the most important facts first, followed by information in descending order of importance. In your lead, the most important information is that a local man was killed—and that's what starts your sentence. In this case, how he was killed is important enough to make the lead, and this goes next. The "when" is often hard to slip gracefully into a sentence, but it seldom starts the lead; the same is true of the "where," which in this case comes at the end of the sentence.

Review your groups of information again. Can you arrange the remaining facts according to subject? What about a pod about the driver, one about the accident and one that deals with the weather conditions?

Pod two: This pod focuses on what you know about the driver, James R. Hart, of Durango, Colorado, and what happened to him.

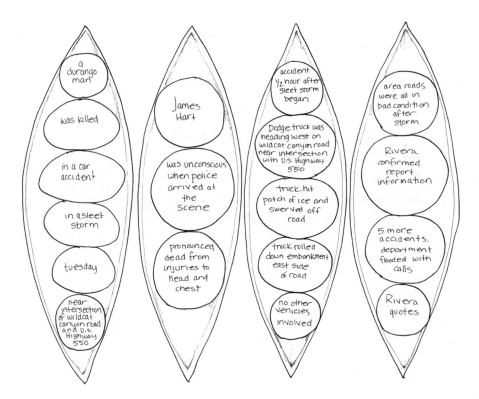

FIGURE 13-1 Grouping your information into pods can help you organize your story logically, which will make it flow more smoothly.

Pod three: This pod includes all the details about the accident.

Pod four: Here, you include some information about the general bad conditions of the road.

Once you're satisfied that these groupings work, think about whether their order reflects their importance and best serves the reader. We've already decided that the first pod should be the lead. Typically, a news story would provide the full identity of a person and what happened to him soon after the lead, so pod two should be next. The description of the accident also helps to answer questions raised in the lead (how, exactly, did the accident happen?), so it would probably come next. That's where we put it; however, you could also place the information about weather and road conditions first because of the potential impact on local readers. Here's what we've got so far:

- A Durango man was killed in a car accident in a sleet storm Tuesday near the intersection of Wildcat Canyon Road and U.S. Highway 550.

- James R. Hart, of Durango, was unconscious when police were called to the scene. He was pronounced dead from injuries to the head and chest at approximately 11:45 p.m.

- A Dodge truck was heading west on Wildcat Canyon Road, near the intersection with U.S. Highway 550. The truck apparently hit a patch of ice and swerved off the road. The truck rolled down the embankment on the east side of Wildcat Canyon Road, turning over twice. No other vehicles were involved.

- Rivera confirms the information in the report. He says the department was flooded with calls shortly after the ice storm, and five car accidents happened within the next hour or so. "There was black ice everywhere, and we had about five accidents with vehicle damage. Nobody was injured in the other accidents, though."

Transitions

Once you've organized the pods, you need to provide connections among sentences, thoughts and paragraphs. In the following, these transitions appear in bold:

- A Durango man was killed in a car accident in a sleet storm Tuesday near the intersection of Wildcat Canyon Road and U.S. Highway 550.

- James R. Hart, of Durango (**we joined the two sentences here**), was unconscious when police arrived, **but** he was pronounced dead from injuries to the head and chest when he arrived at Mercy Medical Center about 15 minutes later, according to a police report.

- **Hart was driving his** Dodge truck west on Wildcat Canyon Road at about 11:30 Tuesday evening when he apparently hit a patch of ice near the intersection with U.S. Highway 550, the report said.

- The truck swerved off the road **and** rolled down the embankment on the east side of Wildcat Canyon Road, turning over twice, the report said. No other vehicles were involved, and Hart had no passengers.

- **Hart's accident happened** about a half-hour after a sleet storm began, said police Capt. Christian Rivera.

- **The ice storm affected other drivers, too**. The police department was flooded with calls shortly after the ice storm, Rivera said.

- "There was black ice everywhere, and we had about five accidents with vehicle damage," Rivera said.

- No one was injured in the other accidents, Rivera said.

As you can see, the transitions don't have to be elaborate. They can be as simple as using a conjunction to join two sentences, or following up one paragraph with a quote about the same subject. But you do have to think about fitting your story together smoothly, supplying transitions for readers to make those connections clear. Let's take a look at the difference such transitions can make. Here's an example from *The Times-Picayune* that we've rewritten to remove the transition:

Weaker: *In the five years since Hurricane Katrina made landfall and devastated communities across the Gulf Coast, the New Orleans area has gained and retained 93,800 jobs, according to a University of New Orleans report.*

Local employment has been brought to 86 percent of the pre-storm mark, according to the report from the Division of Business and Economic Research that was published to coincide with Katrina's fifth anniversary. (Pope, 2010, para. 1–2)

Notice that the reader has to make a logical jump to the second paragraph. Here's the second paragraph as it was originally written, but with the transition in bold:

Better: This achievement *brings the local employment level to 86 percent of the pre-storm mark, according to the report from the Division of Business and Economic Research that was published to coincide with Katrina's fifth anniversary.*

In the second example, "this achievement" provides a connection with the story's lead, letting readers know how the 86 percent of employment relates to the first paragraph of the story. You can see that a word as simple as "this" clarifies for readers that the reporter is referring to a subject that's already been introduced. Words like "that," "these," "those" and "such" do the same thing. They make it clear to readers that what follows refers to a subject you've already addressed. So do phrases such as "one of the X" or "some of the," as you'll see in the following example. First, look at the introductory two paragraphs from an NPR story where we've removed the transition:

Weaker: *California Gov. Arnold Schwarzenegger has set an ambitious plan that requires a third of the state's electricity to come from renewable sources by 2020. But a fight over where to build large clean-energy projects is slowing the green revolution.*

Panoche Valley, ringed by rolling, scrub-covered hills in California's rural San Benito County, was used mostly for cattle grazing, and it has escaped the notice of many Californians. Until now. (Kissack, 2010, para. 1–2)

Here's the second paragraph, with the transitional phrase reinserted and in bold:

Better: One of these battlegrounds *is Panoche Valley, ringed by rolling, scrub-covered hills. Located in California's rural San Benito County, the area was used mostly for cattle grazing, and it has escaped the notice of many Californians. Until now. (Kissack, 2010)*

In this example, "one of these battlegrounds" shows the relationship between the reporter's description of Panoche Valley and Schwarzenegger's plans to convert California to renewable energy. In both this case and the New Orleans employment story, the transitional phrase is only a few words, but those words show audiences the connections between thoughts and paragraphs. Without those connections, readers can get lost or have to reread your story—or, once again, they may give up on it altogether and stop reading.

Pods and transitions should give you some tools to craft a story that's not an inverted pyramid. Now we'll focus on the best narrative framework for telling your story. This, again, depends on what the purpose of the story is. We'll look at three examples here: stories that tell people how things work, stories that discuss a problem and potential solutions and stories that need to weave in historical context.

Stories that Explain *How to* or *Why*

Stories that explain how things work can be especially useful because they help people understand processes that are vital to society, or how things got to be the way they are. Often they're linked to breaking news, but not always. During election season, a news organization might do a story on the electoral college, or on why some states have caucuses and others have primaries. Sometimes, news stories provide the steps for how to do something—how to better insulate your apartment or house, for instance, or how to make home-brewed beer. You can organize stories like these by describing the "how to," step by step. You might open the story with a pod that introduces the subject and explains or implies its relevance. Then, each subsequent pod takes the reader through the next step in the process. Let's look at how one news feature does this: "How much does it cost to make a hit song?"

When pop singer Rihanna's new album in 2011 included several top hits, Planet Money decided to explore the finances behind turning a popular song into a hit. In her story, reporter Zoe Chace described the making of Rihanna's album. This story reads almost like a recipe: You take X, add Y and Z and presto!—you have a process for making hit albums. The theme that ties this particular story together is cost. Here's how Chace describes the first important expense in making a hit song:

> The words hit factory used to mean an actual building where radio-ready pop songs got written. These days, hit factories still exist but they're temporary. They're called writing camps. A record label hires the best and the brightest music writers in the country and drops them into the nicest recording studios in town for about two weeks. (2011, para. 4)

Chace then describes what the writing camp is like, and explains that this is where songwriters meet producers with music tracks, and together they create songs. Chace doesn't get caught up in trying to convey too many details about writing camp. She describes the songwriters humming. She describes a little of what it's like in the studio rooms, briefly introduces the audience to a songwriter, Ray Daniels, with a few interview questions and then returns to the story's theme:

Mr. Daniels: "Let's say we've got 10 rooms working. Every day, the rooms are costing anywhere between $2,000 to $2,500 per day, per room. You've got 10 rooms going, that's $25,000 per day."

Chace: "That's not including the hotel costs, the rental cars and the nice dinners. At the end of the two weeks, Rihanna picks her favorite." (para. 11–12)

For each song, the writing camp costs about $18,000, Chace says. But there's more. After Rihanna chooses the song, the writer and producer each get their fees, $15,000 and $20,000, respectively. Then a vocal producer works with Rihanna to make sure she gets the sound right—that can cost $10,000 to $15,000, Chace reports. Again, she summarizes the cost so far: about $78,000.

The next section of the story deals with marketing a hit, which adds up to about $1 million. Chace provides some of the details: This money will be used to get

Rihanna's song to the top of iTunes, to get her face on billboards, to send the star on a tour and to try to get radio program directors to play her tunes. Then, there's the video. Chace has a sound bite of Daniels saying that there's no guarantee all the costs will even pay off. Finally, Chace provides the following conclusion:

> Indeed, "Man Down" has not sold that well and radio play has been minimal. But Def Jam makes up the shortfall by releasing other singles. And only then, after the label recoups, will Rihanna herself get paid. (para. 41)

Chace has neatly described a step-by-step process, taking her audience behind the scenes of a hit song. And by sticking with her theme of how much money it costs, she's kept the story clear and interesting.

A Problem That Needs A Solution

Journalists sometimes explain complex problems by dividing a story into two main parts. The first part describes a problem, and the second part presents possible solutions. In this case, the description of the problem quickly illustrates the *so what?* In this first part, reporters may also provide some background and history about how the problem came to be.

Let's look at a story that appeared in the *Daily Beast* about the mountain pine beetle, which was killing thousands of trees in Colorado and elsewhere in the West. The lead described the sound of chain saws cutting down dying trees in Beaver Creek Resort in Colorado. Then the story presented the problem more fully:

> After ravaging 22 million acres of pine trees in Canada over the last 12 years, the rice-sized insects have been feasting their way southward. Their favorite meal: the majestic lodgepole pine, which makes up 8 percent of Colorado's 22 million acres of forests. Before landing in Beaver Creek, the pine beetles tore through neighboring Vail, Winter Park, Breckenridge and several areas around Steamboat Springs. So far, say state foresters, the beetles have eaten through 1.5 million acres, about 70 percent of all the state's lodgepole pines. The tree's entire population will be wiped out in the next few years, Colorado state foresters predict, leaving behind a deforested area about the size of Rhode Island. (Moscou, 2008, para. 2)

The extent of the current problem is now clear. Notice that the reporter has also included a little history and context: We know that the beetles have affected 70 percent of the state's lodgepole pines, and we know where key beetle-kill areas are. A forest ecologist is quoted as saying it's the worst outbreak in U.S. history. Their interest piqued, the readers may well want to know about past outbreaks.

Now the story takes a turn and looks at potential solutions—or in this case, why a solution might be elusive:

> Coming up with solutions isn't easy. "It's clear these beetles don't read the book," says Ingrid Aguayo, the top forest entomologist for the Colorado State Forest

Service and a lecturer at Colorado State University. The beetles are breaking all the rules taught in forestry school. The last few relatively warm winters have allowed the beetle population to flourish and enabled them to attack trees at much higher altitudes, like the 10,000-foot forests around Beaver Creek (2008, para. 4).

In this example, the story next provides information about why the beetle outbreak may have occurred—trees were weakened by years of drought, people have put out wildfires and so many of the trees are old. The story ends by returning to the resort to describe its particular methods for dealing with the spread of the beetles.

A Story with a Complicated History

This kind of story is an interesting read because it works the way a lot of fictional stories do. It typically starts somewhere near the beginning of events, provides a nut graph, then builds to the most important information. Journalists often start with an inverted pyramid-style lead, and then switch to a partly chronological retelling of the story. Reporters need skill to do this well because they have to start with a particularly riveting story or they'll lose their audience. Think of it this way: If you're telling your friends about a time you, say, ran a marathon, chances are they'll bear with you as you start from the beginning and tell about the start of the race, then mile five, then mile ten, and so on until the celebration at the end of the race. But if you tell the story the same way in class, people might give you funny looks because they don't know why you're taking so long to get to the point. For news stories, readers need to know why they're spending more time with the subject.

Let's look at an example from the beginning of a story on *All Things Considered*. This story covered a major change in science—an event that wasn't exactly breaking news (the breakthrough took place over weeks and months, not days) but was about a newsworthy change with the potential for a large impact on many people. The story started with this lead-in from NPR host Melissa Block:

> The world of biology is undergoing a revolution. Genetics is no longer all about genes. Just as important are smaller sequences of DNA between genes that tell the genes what to do. NPR's Joe Palca reports on a new study that suggests changes in these non-gene sequences of DNA may hold the key to explaining how all species evolved. (Palca, 2011, para. 17)

This neatly summarizes the importance of the story. But to explain what's new and different, the reporter had to first describe what scientists used to think. So Palca takes listeners back in time and gradually works up to the present:

> To better understand this revolution in biology, we have to go back about a century. At that time, nobody knew exactly what a gene was. The concept was that a gene was responsible for a particular trait.
>
> "There was a gene for blue eyes, a gene for curly hair, etc., etc." Gregory Wray is a geneticist at Duke University.

But the notion of what a gene was became more concrete in 1953 when Watson and Crick showed that genes were made of DNA and that DNA was the chemical that allowed genes to be passed from parent to child.

[Wray]: "We came to understand the gene as a stretch of DNA that codes for a protein and the protein is involved in producing that trait, whatever we're interested in—eye color, hair, so forth."

Proteins make up the enzymes and hormones and membranes that make eyes and hair and all the rest of our bits. Wray says that biologists spent the next several decades exploring the steps involved in turning genetic instructions into protein.

[Wray]: "How do you make a protein? What does that protein do? What's the piece of DNA that codes for that protein?"

Scientists turned out tens of thousands of scientific papers in the latter half of the twentieth century explaining all that.

[Wray]: "And now we're really coming to realize that's only half the picture."

And this is where the revolution is taking place—understanding this other half of the picture. Not about genes, but stretches of DNA that tell genes what to do, regulate them, determine when and where they make proteins.

In the first paragraph, Palca sets up the structure: He tells listeners that he's going to provide some history, and he says why. A reporter might or might not need to say this explicitly as Palca does here, but you'd want to be sure the audience understood why you were delving into the past.

You can easily give the audience information overload in a story like this. Notice that Palca doesn't go back to the beginning of the study of biology. He goes back to the earliest understanding of what a gene was, and then the discovery of DNA and its purposes and then the most recent change in genetics. The story continues, but in the last paragraph of what we've excerpted here, the reporter has looped back to what's so revolutionary in the field of genetics.

These examples should help you learn to structure your own stories. Keep in mind that you base a story's form on the information you have. Your goal is to make the information as fair and as accessible and useful to your audience as possible.

Structure and Fairness

PLACEMENT OF SOURCES

As you structure your news stories, you'll need to think about what's fair, not just what reads well. You'll deal with this issue most often when your story includes different viewpoints on contested issues. If the first voice in a story—that is, the first source, quote or viewpoint—is regarded as the most prominent, the voices lower down will be seen as less important. You could say that in the typical news story, the first voice states the premise of the piece, to which those following will react.

News websites often use the lead or the first couple of paragraphs to give the reader the gist of the story before linking them to the full text. If the reader never makes that jump, then the first sources quoted are the only ones. One way to mitigate the influence of this effect is to vary the first voice across coverage of an event, or across stories on your beat.

In the broadcast media, the first voice is legitimized for the same reasons. That person gets the first word and therefore sets the tone of the piece. The audience is likely to catch that voice before they have a chance to shift their attention elsewhere should the story not interest them. However, the final voice in a broadcast segment is also legitimized because that person has the last word.

Time and repetition are important factors in the broadcast media. Because time is at a premium in a typical newscast, every second confers legitimacy. In the visual media, you can add another dimension: face time. Television and radio newscasts by their very format make any lengthy examination of issues rare. A typical broadcast television half-hour includes only 22 minutes of programming. The result can be the sound-bite phenomenon, where a source has a sentence or two to convey an idea—think political candidates' message points. The more time you give to a source and the more often you give that time, the more you allow the source to expand on that position.

The print equivalent of airtime is the amount of space that sources are given in a story. If one voice gets significantly more space, that person's point can be made more eloquently, or the person can provide more complex positions than those voices with less space. At first, it may seem that the answer to fair reporting is to give each side roughly the same amount of space in your story—to present them in a balanced way.

A QUESTION OF BALANCE

The idea behind balance is laudable. Journalists shouldn't let one voice dominate a story to the exclusion of other voices with something to contribute. But remember that different sources may not have made equally relevant comments, or may not bring equal expertise to an issue. Too often an attempt to provide balance is distilled into getting just two sides of the story. This often leaves it up to the audience to decide who is right. But on what basis can people make a sound decision?

When you see a story with proponents—of stem-cell research, environmental protections or the latest edition of a video game containing violence—you'll typically hear from opponents, too. However, a story rarely falls naturally into two parts, and just because two sides are represented doesn't mean the story is fully told. Also, the tendency to dichotomize a story leads reporters to highlight two extreme sides, ignoring the subtleties between them or the range of views in the middle. Such a story is incomplete.

A story that simply presents two contradictory sides as equals, with equivalent space or time, may lead readers to think that no middle views exist and that therefore no resolution is possible or no action is needed. Think about stories on abortion and what voices are usually heard: Planned Parenthood and National Right to Life, for example. Yet, most people in the United States fall into the great middle of the debate. They don't want to outlaw the procedure, but they accept that there should be some limitations such as parental notification. Also, people representing both ends of the spectrum agree that it's important to decrease the need for abortions; the conflict is that they can't fully agree on how to accomplish their common goal. A shift away from the pro–con structure might change the focus of public discussion and facilitate useful change.

Think about stories covering national politics, where reporters routinely seek comments from Republicans and comments from Democrats. This doesn't include the Tea Party, an influential group within the Republican Party. What about other political parties, such as the Green Party, the Socialist Party USA or the Libertarian Party? What might national discourse look like if other voices were routinely part of the story? When we just have dueling opinions from "both sides," there's little sense of what actions readers can take to effect change.

If the reporter treats sides A and B equally in terms of space or time allotted, then we judge it as balanced. Like the scales of justice, the commitment is a genuine attempt at fairness. But is this what's actually achieved?

Ira Stoll, in a *Columbia Journalism Review* article about coverage of events in the Middle East, observed the following:

> Imagine a "balanced" account of September 11, 2001: "Nearly 3,000 New Yorkers were killed yesterday in what Americans decried as a brutal terrorist attack but what al Qaeda viewed as an important victory in its struggle to reduce American imperialist influence and to advance Islamic beliefs." (as cited in Hassan, 2003, p. 54)

Balancing the American perspective with that of al-Qaida suggests that they are just two opinions from opposing sides. It's easy to see why lending such legitimacy to al-Qaida would have been wrong: The organization was blaming victims for a

FIGURE 13-2 Passengers on the ferry from Staten Island to Manhattan look at their city after it has been attacked.

murderous attack of civilians (Fig. 13-2). Strict allegiance to balance for the sake of balance, without any other justification for including the material, can lead to disconnected and even unprofessional reporting when it distracts journalists from trying to get at the truth.

The balance you'll need to strike as a journalist structuring a news story will often be between fairness and accuracy, thinking about representing different voices in a way that makes it easiest for audiences to see what's accurate. While determining who is most truthful and what your audience needs to know the most isn't easy, journalists make these judgments all the time.

Longer stories like the ones in this chapter take much more time, both for reporting and writing. But adapting these techniques will help you as you produce features and even your short news stories. In the meantime, as you gain more experience and if you're working a beat, you may find that you'll have other information that would be useful to your audience in the form of a blog or opinion piece, which is where we turn now.

Exercises for Chapter 13

EXERCISE 13-1: Review the story in this chapter about the car accident concerning James R. Hart. Using the tips on pods and transitions, write the story.

EXERCISE 13-2: Go to a broadcast news site, such as one of the networks', and select a video of at least a minute long.

 a. How is it structured? In writing, describe the structure you see.

 b. Who are the sources? About how much time are they given, relative to each other? In what order do they appear? In writing, comment on whether the story treats the sources fairly, based on your analysis.

EXERCISE 13-3: Go to a news site that features longer stories, such as *The New York Times*, and select a story of at least 15 paragraphs and at least three sources. How is it structured? In writing, describe the structure you see.

EXERCISE 13-4: Go to a news site that features longer stories and select a story of at least 15 paragraphs and at least three sources. List any transitions you find. Do you see any patterns? If so, describe the patterns you see.

EXERCISE 13-5: Search for a news story that explains how things work. Summarize what the story says about how things work.

CHAPTER 14

IMHO: EXPRESSING YOUR OPINIONS AS A JOURNALIST

What Does Commentary Add?

Blogs and other opinion pieces provide more analysis or interpretation than a straight news story about, say, road construction that is causing delays (Fig. 14-1). This makes sense: The first thing readers or viewers want to know is what's going on, not someone's opinion that the delays are caused by lazy construction workers, or someone else's opinion that the delays are really caused by a multicar accident that the government is trying to cover up. They need the information first so they can change their travel plans or leave home earlier, if they need to. The same is true for other, more serious stories: People often need to absorb the news before they're ready to hear even valid criticism of the parties involved.

Eventually, though, audiences profit from thoughtful analysis, from further relevant information and from informed opinions. For instance, let's say a journalist reports a story about the lack of city aid for homeless people in extreme weather conditions. A blogger might refer to the original story and provide links to organizations where people can volunteer or donate money, as well as to sites where readers might learn more about who the homeless in the city are and who helps them. A news editor might follow up on the news story with a post scolding the city for not doing more, or calling on citizens to press for a change in city laws. In this example, the

FIGURE 14-1 Opinions don't have to be expressed in words. The British artist who goes by the one-word name of Banksy is known internationally for his subversive style and graffiti, which often take the form of biting critiques of governments or the status quo. His oversized paintings often show up overnight on the walls of buildings, as they did during a 2013 stint in New York City. And Banksy's documentary, *Exit through the Gift Shop*, was nominated for an Academy Award in 2010.

blogger provides additional information that can help audiences to act on the news, while the editor provides informed thoughts about how the system or government could be changed to address an issue (Fig. 14-2).

PROVIDING CONTEXT AND ANALYSIS

When issues are particularly complex, a good journalist can provide the background, context and analysis that help to make sense of it all. In an award-winning piece we've referred to in Chapter 1, "The Giant Pool of Money," NPR's Planet Money set out to explain the roots of the economic crisis of 2008 in an hour-long story that mixed original reporting, analysis and opinion. Let's look at just one example from the story.

Alex Blumberg, the Planet Money reporter, describes a particularly irresponsible kind of loan, the "no income, no asset" loan. He says that mortgage brokers offered these loans often, and didn't require proof of income or assets, which he found confusing:

> And it turns out even the people who got them found them confusing. For example, a guy I met named Clarence Nathan. He worked three part-time, not very steady jobs, and made a total of $45,000 a year, roughly. He got himself into trouble and needed money, so he took out a loan against his house. A big one. (Blumberg & Davidson, 2008, para. 23)

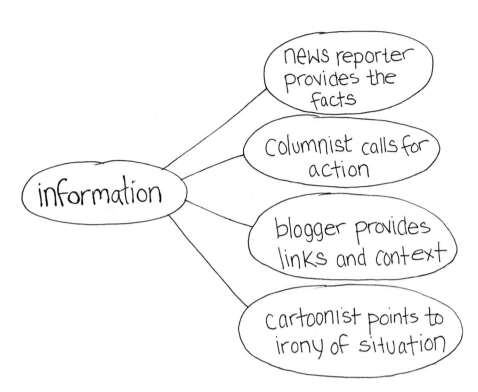

FIGURE 14-2 Each of these people might respond to the work of any of the others, but each makes a contribution to the community's understanding of what's going on.

Blumberg interviews Nathan, who had borrowed approximately $540,000 from a bank that didn't verify his income. On the program, Blumberg asks Nathan if he would have loaned himself the money, and here's what Nathan says:

> I wouldn't have loaned me the money. And nobody that I know would have loaned me the money. I know guys who are criminals who wouldn't loan me that and they'd break your knee-caps. So [LAUGHING] yeah, I don't know why the bank did it. (2008, para. 29)

Then Blumberg provides his analysis:

> By the time I talked to him, Clarence hadn't made a payment in almost a year, and his house was in the process of foreclosure.
>
> And stories like this have been in the news for months. And they often feature an innocent homeowner who was duped by a lying, greedy mortgage banker. Or, if you're more of *The Wall Street Journal* editorial page type, an innocent mortgage banker who was duped by a lying, greedy homeowner. And no doubt, both categories exist, but Clarence's case is more nuanced . . . and much more common.
>
> **Clarence Nathan:** Nobody came and told me a lie, and told me a story, and said, oh, just close your eyes and all your problems will go away. That wasn't the situation. The situation was that I needed the money. And I'm not trying to absolve myself of anything.
>
> I had a situation. And I thought that I could do this, and then get out of it within six to nine months. The six to nine month plan didn't work, so I'm stuck.

But if somebody had told me, you couldn't borrow the money, I probably would have had to do something else more drastic and dramatic, and not be in this situation now. The bank made an imprudent loan. I made an imprudent loan. So the bank and I are partners in this deal.

Alex Blumberg: This imprudent partnership is new. And it's at the heart of the current housing crisis. For most of the history of banking, bankers wouldn't have loaned Clarence their money either. They didn't let people like Clarence near their money, in fact, people with part-time employment and unpaid debts in their past.

And then suddenly in the early 2000s, everything changed. Banking turned on its head and went out looking for partnerships with people like Clarence, loaning him half a million dollars without even checking to see if he had a job. What happened? (para. 30–35)

In these excerpts, we do get firsthand reporting about the housing crisis, but only in the form of an interview with one source who is affected by the issue, not an expert on it. Blumberg is making a larger point, one that the interview with Nathan serves to illustrate: The housing crisis happened through a mixture of bad decisions by both banks and homeowners, but the conditions that allowed that mixture to happen were new. Blumberg provides historical context in the form of explaining that banks had not routinely made such risky loans in the past. And he also summarizes and analyzes some of the facts that he explains in the rest of the story.

Elsewhere in the story, "The Giant Pool of Money" does original reporting—Blumberg and his fellow reporter, Adam Davidson, talk with financial experts and bankers who help to explain more about the financial crisis. But what about commentary that doesn't provide anything besides analysis?

Paul Krugman is a Pulitzer Prize-winning columnist for *The New York Times* and an economist. He also writes shorter pieces in his *Times* blog, where he responds to comments and often comments on those comments (you can see why people sometimes refer to online commentary as an echo chamber). In one of his columns associated with the Pulitzer, Krugman wrote about the economic consequences of the war in the Caucasus, an area on the border between Europe and Asia:

> If you're wondering what I'm talking about, here's what you need to know: our grandfathers lived in a world of largely self-sufficient, inward-looking national economies—but our great-great grandfathers lived, as we do, in a world of large-scale international trade and investment, a world destroyed by nationalism.
>
> Writing in 1919, the great British economist John Maynard Keynes described the world economy as it was on the eve of World War I. "The inhabitant of London could order by telephone, sipping his morning tea in bed, the various products of the whole earth . . . he could at the same moment and by the same means adventure his wealth in the natural resources and new enterprises of any quarter of the world."
>
> And Keynes' Londoner "regarded this state of affairs as normal, certain, and permanent, except in the direction of further improvement. . . . The projects and politics of militarism and imperialism, of racial and cultural rivalries, of monopolies, restrictions, and exclusion . . . appeared to exercise almost no influence at all

on the ordinary course of social and economic life, the internationalization of which was nearly complete in practice."

But then came three decades of war, revolution, political instability, depression and more war. By the end of World War II, the world was fragmented economically as well as politically. And it took a couple of generations to put it back together.

So, can things fall apart again? Yes, they can. (2008, para. 2–6)

Krugman has established himself as an expert on economic affairs: He earned a Ph.D. in economics, taught at Yale, MIT and Stanford and is still an economics and international affairs professor at Princeton University. Furthermore, he has been writing about economic issues for years, and his contributions were recognized with the Pulitzer Prize in 2009. He uses his knowledge in the discipline to provide historical context. And he uses his knowledge in the field to provide analysis from a famous economist from another time, Keynes. Through this context, history and comment, Krugman hopes to shed light on a current subject in the news. (For another example of a writer who provides context and history, see 14-3.)

FIGURE 14-3 Film critic Roger Ebert provided a different kind of context and history to his opinion pieces through his movie reviews. Ebert spent decades establishing his professional persona. His opinion mattered, and he was trusted and respected by audiences because of his experience, expertise and thoughtful work. (Also, notice in the picture how Robert O'Daniell has framed the photo to focus on Ebert's spectacle-clad eyes—emphasizing his expertise—and has hidden Ebert's jaw, which had been damaged by disease and the treatments to save his life.)

BOX 14-1

"THE INVISIBLE PRIMARY"—COMMENTARY WITH CONTEXT

As the Republican primary was heating up late in the summer of 2011, political columnist Jay Cost did a piece for the conservative *The Weekly Standard* on the "invisible primary," an idea introduced by political scientists Marty Cohen, David Karol, Hans Noel and John Zaller. In the invisible primary, party leaders rather than the voting public get to decide who the presidential candidate is:

> The invisible primary is essentially a long-running national conversation among members of each party coalition about who can best unite the party and win the next presidential election. The conversation occurs in newspapers, on Sunday morning television talk shows, among activist friends over beer, in chatter at party events, and, most recently, in the blogosphere. (as cited in Cost, 2011, para. 9)

In a news story, a reporter almost never uses books or articles as sources, because these are secondhand sources and the information is typically already dated. But opinion pieces can helpfully alert the public to the highlights of an important new book, or to the historical lessons of scholars or ideas better known within a discipline than outside it. Cost begins his column by quoting from a source that's not only an article, but ancient, in news terms. It's a 1962 piece by sociologists Peter Bachrach and Morton Baratz that explains that if one group narrows the choices of a second group to issues that don't hurt the first group, the second group doesn't have real choices and therefore has very little power:

> Of course power is exercised when A participates in the making of decisions that affect B. But power is also exercised when A devotes his energies to creating or reinforcing social and political values and institutional practices that limit the scope of the political process to public consideration of only those issues which are comparatively innocuous to A. To the extent that A succeeds in doing this, B is prevented, for all practical purposes, from bringing to the fore any issues that might in their resolution be seriously detrimental to A's set of preferences. (as cited in Cost, 2011, para. 3)

MAKING CONNECTIONS FOR READERS

Opinion pieces often do the footwork for readers and let them know what's out there. For instance, the Pew Research Center's Amy Mitchell offers a daily briefing of news about the news that consists of just a short summary of headlines and a list of links. The subject here—the information Mitchell is providing—is what's most important about events and trends in the news media industry. This means her "news gathering" is actually made up of reading, watching and listening to what others are saying, and then, through her knowledge and experience, highlighting particularly important information for her audience.

Megan McArdle, who writes about economic issues for BloombergView, provides more analysis and discussion for her readers than the Pew Research Center briefing. But, like many other bloggers and columnists, one of the crucial services McArdle provides her readers is links to the original reports and stories whose subjects she discusses.

Through his own background knowledge and reading, Cost provides his readers with relevant ideas that cast a new light on current events. Then, Cost points out some of the implications of these established ideas for recent presidential candidates:

> In the last 40 years, the invisible primary has become extremely important, for two reasons. First, the cost of campaigning has increased exponentially (consider: television advertisements, campaign consultants, and get out the vote organizations). Meanwhile, the utility of public funds has decreased in the last 15 or so years; public financing imposes hard spending limits that knee-capped Bob Dole in the summer of 1996, and all serious contenders have declined public funds for the primary ever since. Thus, it is hard to imagine anybody winning the nomination having raised less than $75 million on their own.
>
> Second, frontloading has altered the nature of the nomination battle. In 1976, Jimmy Carter could start small—with virtually no establishment support—but pile win upon win for weeks on end, so that by the time people caught on to the strength of his candidacy, nobody could stop him. That's not the case anymore. On February 5, 2008, there were a whopping 21 Republican primaries or caucuses—just one month after Iowa. To be competitive, a candidate must either have strong name recognition (like McCain and Clinton) or competent statewide organizations already in place (like Obama) by the end of the pre-primary year. That's no little feat, and to do that they need the support of local politicians and plenty of cash. In other words: they need to win or place in the invisible primary. (para. 11–12)

After describing some of the changes in electoral politics caused by the invisible primary, Cost then applied those ideas to the current Republican contest. He said that those candidates who were not sanctioned by party leaders had either dropped out or would never be first-tier candidates: Newt Gingrich, Tim Pawlenty, Mitch Daniels, Ron Paul. He said that both Mitt Romney and Rick Perry were contenders to win the invisible primary, but that he thought that "the jury is still out" about Michele Bachman, a front runner at the time.

Media critic Jim Romenesko writes about journalism in a blog called "JimRomenesko.com—a blog about media and other things I'm interested in." Like Mitchell and McArdle, Romenesko plays the role of alerting readers to news in their subject area—and that news is reported by others. He also provides commentary on some of those stories, and will sometimes call sources to follow up on issues. For instance, after a North Carolina editor made a controversial request for the names of concealed-weapons permit holders—and that editor resigned—Romenesko called the former editor. Romenesko included some of the editor's comments in his blog, plus the full story of his resignation that was slated for the next day's newspaper.

In his "Morning Report," Romenesko includes headlines and links to full stories about subjects such as a journalist who received an important award, a controversy surrounding a noted journalist, hirings and firings and news organizations going out of business or starting up new businesses.

You can see that the interpretations, context, analysis and thoughtful comments of the journalists we've discussed can help people understand the news. Such commentary can provide a framework that helps to make up for the fragmented way we often receive daily news. But sometimes, commentary doesn't contribute to people's understanding of the issues.

> What is unique, and uniquely concerning, about digital media is the speed with which properly packaged (dis)information can spread and how hard it is for fact and reason to catch up.
>
> *MICHAEL HIRSCHORN, CONTRIBUTING EDITOR TO THE ATLANTIC*

When Are Opinions Not Helpful?

Any kind of publication—on air, in newspapers or magazines, online or podcasts—serves to further ideas. When something is repeated, it gains credence. People talk about the amplifier effect of the media because of this, an effect that can be harmful when it brings added attention to rumors or false information (Fig. 14-4). When one blog after another picks up on a thread or idea or event, repeating and discussing it—in what people call the **blogosphere**—sophisticated readers look for a grounding in fact.

When television programming provides one commentator arguing with another, their voices gradually rising, a viewer might well ask: How is this helpful? And that's just what a journalist should ask—in what ways does a piece of analysis or opinion help the audience? If the answer is not many, or not any, then the journalist shouldn't write it or publish, air or post it.

WHEN ARGUMENTS AREN'T GROUNDED IN EVIDENCE

Most of us get information from a variety of sources: our friends and family, or our extended universe via the social media, blogs and other Internet sources. These sources may be largely opinion, or they may have evidence to back up their claims. And all of the sources people consult will undoubtedly have some influence on their perceptions of the issues at hand. But good blogs or other pieces of journalism are based on evidence, either gathered by the journalist or by other credible sources such as news organizations, scientists or other scholars. When you offer analysis, you start with facts. When you provide an opinion, you ground it in your expertise or information you have researched or that can be verified. Think of the difference between these two statements:

- Chocolate is good.
- Dark chocolate is beneficial to your health.

The first statement is one of opinion: My opinion is that I think chocolate is good. But, in and of itself, it is only an opinion. Suppose my friend disagrees with me

FIGURE 14-4 The Internet has made it easy for a rumor or opinion to get repeated so often that it almost seems like fact. As a journalist, you shouldn't join in.

("Chocolate is bad"). We can argue a little about who is right or wrong, but beyond that, all we have is a conversation about our respective opinions. My friend could argue that I don't really believe that chocolate is good, but we would just go back and forth, never reaching a conclusion because there is no evidence presented yet. In journalism, this kind of statement doesn't contribute much to public knowledge.

In the second statement I give a reason why I think dark chocolate is good: It's beneficial to people's health. That second part of the sentence is a truth claim—I am providing an assertion to support my opinion about chocolate. And that is a statement that could be researched, and therefore supported or not based on the evidence someone finds. If a reader finds that I am correct that chocolate is healthful, then a reasonable person should be persuaded that, at least for that reason, chocolate is good. A reasonable person would draw the opposite conclusion if the evidence refuted my claim.

How does this relate to journalism? Although the audience may consult a variety of sources for opinions on a matter, it is the journalist's responsibility to provide only opinions based on the best evidence for any claim so that the audience can make a reasoned decision. For instance, when Congress was deciding whether to allow a controversial new pipeline from Canada through several states, an opinion writer might have said the following, without providing any support:

Weak: *"The Keystone XL pipeline is an idiotic scheme. The government shouldn't build it."*

Such an opinion doesn't provide readers with any help in deciding whether their governmental representatives are serving them well, whether the pipeline is threatening the environment or whether the jobs and the access to an energy source are crucial. Contrast the preceding weak version with the following opinion:

Better: *"The Keystone XL pipeline is a bad project because it poses a strong risk to the environment. For instance, the U.S. Department of State's report says that several threatened or endangered species could be harmed by the project."*

This opinion serves the public better because it provides support in the form of a specific reason, backed up by a government report.

It is true that the number and variety of publishing platforms are exploding in the Internet age. But very few of these entities are engaged in original reporting. In short, we face a situation in which sources of *opinion* are proliferating, but sources of *facts* on which those opinions are based are shrinking. The former phenomenon is almost certainly, on balance, a societal good; the latter is surely a problem.

PROPUBLICA, "ABOUT US"

WHEN TOO MUCH IS BASED ON SECONDHAND INFORMATION

As you can see in the examples of analysis and opinion, these are mostly built on the scaffolding of other reporting. While journalists often do include firsthand reporting in their opinion pieces, a lot of their work is to provide interpretation and analysis about stories that have already been reported. That's fine—except when the structure of information gets too top-heavy.

For instance, the Pew Research Center's Project for Excellence in Journalism did a weeklong study in 2010 of all the news outlets in one city, Baltimore, Md. In its story, "How News Happens: A Study of the News Ecosystem of One American City," the center reported some telling findings:

Fully eight out of ten stories studied simply repeated or repackaged previously published information.

And of the stories that did contain new information nearly all, 95%, came from traditional media—most of them newspapers. These stories then tended to set the narrative agenda for most other media outlets. (2010, para. 6–7)

This is what we mean by "top-heavy": If there are fewer original news stories and more commentators, then too much of what's available to readers is people's opinions, as opposed to real, helpful information.

WHEN OPINIONS ARE BASED ON SLOPPY JOURNALISM

Some opinion pieces are written by people with a solid background in the area they discuss—like Paul Krugman and Megan McArdle, for example, when they deal with economics. But many are not, and on the Internet, it's easy to publish blogs that haven't been vetted or checked for accuracy by anyone else, or that simply repeat inaccurate information. Here's the way that the Pew Research Center's Project for Excellence in Journalism distinguished between traditional journalism and blogs:

> There are now several models of journalism, and the trajectory increasingly is toward those that are faster, looser, and cheaper. The traditional press model—the journalism of verification—is one in which journalists are concerned first with trying to substantiate facts. It has ceded ground for years on talk shows and cable to a new journalism of assertion, where information is offered with little time and little attempt to independently verify its veracity. Consider the allegations by the "Swift Boat Veterans for Truth," and the weeks of reporting required to find that their claims were unsubstantiated. The blogosphere, while adding the richness of citizen voices, expands this culture of assertion exponentially, and brings to it an affirmative philosophy: publish anything, especially points of view, and the reporting and verification will occur afterward in the response of fellow bloggers. The result is sometimes true and sometimes false. Blogs helped unmask errors at CBS, but also spread the unfounded conspiracy theory that the GOP stole the presidential election in Ohio. All this makes it easier for those who would manipulate public opinion—government, interest groups and corporations—to deliver unchecked messages, through independent outlets or their own faux-news Web sites, video and text news releases and paid commentators. Next, computerized editing has the potential to take this further, blending all these elements into a mix. (2005, para. 2)

Obviously, good journalists have to be concerned with reporting and verification *before* publishing. You can't settle for "sometimes true and sometimes false"—not even in opinion pieces.

Writing in the First Person

Blogs and other opinion pieces tend to emphasize the voice of the writer or speaker more than stories about breaking news. Establishing a strong voice or tone can be helpful in reminding readers of those views. This tendency—using "I" or "me" for news—is an intriguing shift in journalism and can make certain kinds of stories more interesting. While it doesn't work for breaking news—it's still considered inappropriate for most news stories—it's very effective and useful in the right forum.

PERSONA

Over time, a commentator develops a strong voice and **persona**, or the character that the writer projects (Fig. 14-5). This is true of people who write columns as well as those who do audio for broadcast or podcast.

Think, for example, of Alex Blumberg's voice in the excerpt earlier in the chapter. His tone is casual—he says he "met a guy," rather than introducing his source, Clarence Nathan, more formally. Blumberg is even more informal in other parts of the story: When he misses part of Davidson's full title as NPR's international business and economics correspondent, he says, "Oh, sorry. It actually sounds more impressive." And when he introduces the giant pool of money for which the story is named, he addresses a section of his audience directly:

> And by the way, before you finance enthusiasts start writing any letters, we do know that $70 trillion technically refers to that subset of global savings called fixed income securities. Everyone else can just ignore what I just said. (Blumberg & Davidson, 2008, para. 49)

FIGURE 14-5 The persona you project will change, depending on your audience, the material and your purpose.

Blumberg presents himself as a layman, someone who found the banks' willingness to provide easy loans "confusing." When Davidson, the business reporter, is explaining the amount of money that the world is saving at the moment, he provides an analogy to show just how much it is—all the money that all the people in the world spend in a year, plus everything Bill Gates bought, plus all the rice sold in China, plus more. Blumberg's response? "Wow." He's often drily funny. For instance, after Nathan says that even criminals he knows wouldn't have loaned him the $540,000, Blumberg says the following: "As it turns out, Clarence's friends, acquaintances and shadowy criminal contacts would have been right not to lend him the money" (2008, para. 30).

Blumberg and Davidson's voices and style were no accident. Here they discuss their program's tone in an interview with Karen Everhart of current.org:

> **Davidson:** The single clearest influence for us would be *Radio Lab* with Robert Krulwich and Jad Abumrad and their way of co-hosting. It was sort of an accident that we ended up co-hosting, but we found that it's really useful to explain complicated things. There's something about two people reacting to each other and slowing the pace down, if needed, that's very effective and helpful.
>
> **Blumberg:** And one person in the group can play the role of the audience— "That seems crazy! That's weird! Wait!" So you can stop and slow down. Sort of like a Greek chorus to represent what the listener is feeling or thinking. (Everhart, 2009, para. 62–63)

Blumberg and Davidson thought about the tone and voices of their program. When Blumberg responds to information with a "wow," or a question, he's often role-playing. The informality, though it seems to come naturally from both reporters, doesn't indicate sloppiness. For instance, even as Blumberg jokes about whether he has Davidson's exact title right, he's making sure that the correct information is communicated to listeners.

A writer's voice doesn't have to be as pronounced as Blumberg's or Davidson's. Much of what establishes a tone can be the references or sources a writer includes. Think of the Krugman column excerpt earlier in the chapter. His language is relatively simple and hardly formal. But by including an extensive quote from John Maynard Keynes, Krugman sets himself up as a scholar and, by association, expects readers to respond with serious attention. In the same vein, a humorous columnist expects that his audience will at least be receptive to comedy and will define his own persona according to the style of humor he employs.

Journalists use the first person when they believe there's a good reason to be part of the story. If it is an opinion piece, for example, the author's take on an issue is the point. But what about those rare occasions when you use first person for a news story? For a story based on an interview with a famous subject, a writer will sometimes describe the setting and her own reactions to the subject. If done skillfully, this helps readers imagine themselves in the writer's place, sitting across from a musician or writer or artist. Details about the writer's interview experience can make a story more vivid for an audience. But too often, writers include unnecessary clutter about the food they ordered or their trivial responses to a subject. Then, the story becomes less informative.

Sometimes, a writer's own experiences can illuminate and enrich the story. Following is an excerpt from Denise Grady's column, "Second Opinion," where this is done especially well:

> Last month, Dr. Otis Brawley, the American Cancer Society's chief medical officer, told *The New York Times* that the medical profession had exaggerated the benefits of cancer screening, and that if a woman refused mammography, "I would not think badly of her, but I would like her to get it."
>
> Then, the cancer society issued a statement saying women over 40 should keep having mammograms every year, because seven studies have shown that the test decreases the risk of death from breast cancer.
>
> But the statement also said mammography can "miss cancers that need treatment, and in some cases finds disease that does not need treatment." In other words, the test may lead to some women being treated, and being exposed to serious side effects, for cancers that would not have killed them. Some researchers estimate that as many as one-third of cancers picked up by screening would not be fatal even if left untreated. But right now, nobody knows which ones.
>
> So what are women supposed to do?
>
> Mammograms are no fun, to put it mildly. Like many women, I have been putting up with them in hopes that, if I get cancer, they might find it early enough to save my life and maybe help me avoid extensive surgery and chemotherapy. Have I been kidding myself?
>
> Hoping to make sense of it all, I consulted several experts. All said mammograms were still important—after all, breast cancer kills 40,000 women a year in this country—but they differed about who really needed them and how often. All agreed that research was badly needed to figure out how to tell dangerous tumors from the so-called indolent ones. (2009, para. 2–7)

The column went on to cite the experts, including their advice and helpful information, explanations and statistics. Then, Grady ended her column with the following paragraph:

> By the time I finished the interviews I decided that, because I'm between 50 and 60, I'll keep having mammograms. But I've requested the report from my last one to find out about my tissue density, and if it's low, I might stretch the interval to 18 months or even 2 years. And I'll hope that in the meantime research does find a way to tell which tumors will kill you, and which will just sit there and mind their own business until you die of something else. (2009, para. 31)

This is an example of a helpful, first-person voice. The first four paragraphs describe the problem: Women were receiving conflicting information about the benefits of mammograms. Then, Grady enters with her own experience: She wonders whether her mammograms were pointless. She returns to the experts for the bulk of the column. Finally, at the end of the piece, Grady shares her own, now-more-informed decision: She'll continue having mammograms because of her age, but she might have them less often. Her experience doesn't dominate the piece but makes it more accessible.

FEATURES OF A NEWS BLOG

You'll see a lot of opinionated pieces that are categorized as news or news related. Many are not acceptable journalism, and many others fail in some important respect to serve their audiences. If you're writing an opinionated piece, keep in mind the following points:

A News Blog Sticks to Basic Journalistic Principles

That is, journalists rely on facts and don't repeat rumors, they carefully cite sources and they move beyond "he said, she said" reporting to provide information that readers can use. The fact that a journalist is writing a blog or column is no excuse for resorting to sloppy or unethical writing practices. And bloggers and columnists still have to be careful to avoid libel.

A News Blog Presents Informed Opinions

Your opinion as a writer matters only if there's a reason you might have more access to information than most of your audience. Political columnists are often former reporters whose years of experience reporting on Washington or state politics mean they know a lot about the political process and about the history of particular political figures and issues. Therefore, these columnists' opinions carry more weight.

But even columnists who have a wealth of background experience continue to do original reporting. For instance, Nicholas Kristof spends much of his time traveling to other countries to see firsthand conditions that have led to the wars or political situations on which he reports. An article in the *American Journalism Review* differentiates between informed opinion writers, who base their writing on "shoe leather reporting," and writers who start out with their opinions already formed. The article quotes Tom Rosenstiel, the journalism critic:

> He distinguishes traditional opinion reporting from what he calls the journalism of affirmation, where writers "expect to arrive at preconceived notions." Pundits such as Rush Limbaugh and Rachel Maddow "see themselves as agents of a movement," and many bloggers feel the same way, Rosenstiel says. (Carmichael, 2010, para. 18)

That is, good opinion writers report first and form their opinions afterward, as opposed to the other way around.

A News Blog Can Provide In-Depth Information About Niche Subjects

Like McArdle and Romenesko, many bloggers provide more depth about narrow subjects that don't get as much coverage in the mainstream news media. For instance, Techcrunch, which was started by Michael Arrington, covers Internet companies and products. Jenna Wortham's Bits blog at *The New York Times* provides a similar focus. At Grist.org, the blogs about climate change and organic food emphasize environmental news.

Blogs and other opinion pieces can provide important connections, analysis and contextualizing of other information in the news (Box 14-2).

BOX 14-2

WRITING A NEWS BLOG

Blogs on news sites run by professional news media have a decidedly different tone than more casual celebrity gossip blogs, and they are more fact based than provocative political sites. Their purposes are different, and so are the bloggers' personas. News blogs may very well be more relaxed than articles and editorials by the same writers, but they still have a professional distance and structure. A well-crafted news blog usually includes the following elements: a **purpose**, **evidence** and a **takeaway**.

Start with a news story that you've written and write a blog post about it. Try following these steps:

1. Determine the focus of your blog. Determine first what news you found in reporting and writing the story.
   a. Ask yourself what interesting items you found that you left out of the news story. Would any of these items have an impact on your reader? On the people in your story?
   b. Ask yourself whether you can offer personal insight about the topic based on facts you uncovered in your reporting. Are there any actions you'd like a reader to take?
2. Once you have a focus, you can start writing your blog. In the first paragraph, state your **purpose**. This is where you state what the post is about and why you're discussing this topic, now: Is there a news hook, or compelling news value? For instance, an approaching deadline for signing up for insurance under the Affordable Health Care Act might serve as the news hook for a blog about the Act itself, its implementation or health care in the United States.

3. In your next few paragraphs, present your **evidence**, the pertinent, useful facts that flesh out the purpose of the post.
   a. This can include information that you gathered for a related news story.
   b. Or it can be based on information from other people's reporting. If you use facts gathered by others, you need to be sure they come from credible sources. These can include reputable news organizations, government organizations or well-respected research organizations.
   c. If the information from other reports is central to your blog, you'll want to link to those reports so your readers can read the full report or the rest of the news stories.
   d. You may want to include a block quote from another report as part of your evidence. Be sure to identify your source.
4. End with the **takeaway**, or what you want the reader to remember or do. This can be a call for some sort of action—"That's why it's so important that you vote, even in this off-year election." But the takeaway can also provide a caution, an insight that will simply make readers wiser, or an argument in favor of a particular point of view— "The Environmental Center is one of the most important clubs on campus."
5. Review what you've written. Is everything factually accurate? Is every assertion supported here or in the links you provide? Is your post free of logical fallacies? Is your persona professional? Would the impact be clear to the reader?

Exercises for Chapter 14

EXERCISE 14-1: Select two or three logical fallacies. Search online to find a column or blog post containing one or more of them.

EXERCISE 14-2: Go to a celebrity blog such as perezhilton.com. Analyze a day's posts: What is the blog's purpose? What news values do you see? Who are the sources? What types of evidence do you see? Is there a takeaway? In writing, discuss your findings.

EXERCISE 14-3: Go to a blog written by someone you know. Analyze several posts: What is the blog's purpose? What firsthand information is there? Secondhand information? What information is useful to you, if any, and why? In writing, first discuss what you find. Then describe what a professional journalist would be expected to do differently, if anything.

EXERCISE 14-4: Go to a professional journalist's blog (search "journalist blogs" for ideas). What news values do you see? Who are the sources? What types of evidence do you see?

EXERCISE 14-5: Find two blogs that comment on the same issue. Summarize the issue. (You might need to check some news stories to understand it fully.) Then, compare and contrast the posts. You might examine purpose, sourcing, evidence, tone and fallacious reasoning.

CHAPTER 15

CONCLUSION
How Storytelling Connects to Larger Forces

The shape a story takes is affected by larger, amorphous forces—forces such as culture, society and the audience itself. Good journalists continue to reexamine the people and systems at play in an event and in a story, and they keep in mind that their ultimate goal is to provide their audience with relevant and accurate information.

Thinking about the Audience

One of the hardest things for a beginning reporter to learn is how to get a sense of the audience. Sometimes, just one angry comment can haunt you, even when you think you've done a good job. Sometimes several complimentary comments can give you a false idea of how important a story is. And sometimes it can seem as if you're just sending your careful work into a void.

What we can tell you is that not everyone will interpret your work the way you intend it. People will bring their lenses, their biases, to your work and perceive it in ways that are consistent with their previously held opinions, attitudes and beliefs (Box 15-1).

So, even if you've done your best to create a piece that is fair, in context and useful, you may very well find there are people who say your piece is biased—and other people who say the very same piece is perfect. The meaning they create isn't something you can control.

311

BOX 15-1

AUDIENCE REACTIONS: A CASE STUDY

People find this photo shocking (Fig. 15-1). We include it because the photo raises important questions we'd like you to consider: Should it have been published? Does it serve a purpose, and can you articulate the precise reasons for your answers?

It helps to know something about the photo's backstory: The young boy in the body bag is dead, drowned at Hart Park Lake in Bakersfield, California. Most of the people standing around him are family members, including his brother, who stands in anguish on the right side of the frame. The man kneeling over the child is his father.

This drowning was not an isolated incident. Drownings were a problem in the area, and two other people had drowned very recently (Lewis, 1995, p. 242). The photographer has said that he shot eight frames of this scene (p. 240). The editor has said that he ran this particular picture to show readers the reality of drowning so that it might prompt people to be more careful while swimming (Christians et al., 1991, p. 153).

When we use this picture in class, students react in several ways. Some students find the picture a necessarily intense image of community danger. They argue that only graphic photos or stories will make a point strongly enough to get people to respond. Proponents of this argument typically identify their attitude as one of "tough love": Don't sugarcoat reality, they say. A second and related attitude these students express is that the press shouldn't be in the business

FIGURE 15-1

of withholding information. A third attitude they frequently identify is that the public won't pay as much attention to a written text as to a graphic photo. These students emphasize their belief in the freedom of the press and its responsibility to provide information to the public.

A BIT OF HISTORY

Early in communications research, scholars conceived of the sender—the journalist, in this case—as all-powerful and the reader as passive. The hypodermic-needle theory is one example of the **powerful-sender** model that held sway from about the beginning of the 20th century through the 1930s (McQuail, 1987, p. 252; see Fig. 15-2).

The idea was that if a sender sent a message—like a story—it would be interpreted by the audience in the way it was intended. People would glean the same general meaning from that message, and even act on it according to the sender's intentions in

Another set of students views this photo as entirely too graphic. Their opinion is that this photo should not run because it needlessly sensationalizes an event that is painful for the survivors. Their attitude is that the news media, in general, are too sensational and intrusive, and they say that this photo exemplifies that. They believe in the freedom of the press and agree that a journalist's responsibility is to inform—just like the first group—but they also believe that journalists need to consider the feelings of the subjects of a story or photo when making their decisions.

When they work through these conflicting beliefs, they come up with alternatives. Some students argue that a descriptive story would accomplish the same goals as the photo, so they decide to run a piece without the photo. This way, they can be consistent with both sets of beliefs, although one may trump the other this time—they decide to withhold the picture to protect the survivors. On the other hand, they don't deny that a story must be told, so they are honoring their belief in the responsibilities of the press in that way.

Another solution students come up with is to crop the picture so the dead boy will be edited out, but the raw emotion on the others' faces remains. In this way, students try to minimize the harm in terms of the graphic nature of the photo while maintaining the truth supplied by the picture. Perhaps you can feel the slight shift in emphasis between this group and the group that would cut the picture altogether. This group uses the photo but tries to take out what they assume would be most painful to the family. It's a subtle shift away from emphasizing humaneness, and toward emphasizing press autonomy and responsibility.

When this last group of students actually tries to crop the photo, they find they can't without cutting off people's heads or limbs. Because the cropping alternative is unworkable, they go back to square one and the question of whether to run the photo. In some cases, they choose to publish one of the other photos that the journalist took— which is essentially a decision not to publish the photo. Their opinion has shifted from agreeing to print some version or portion of this photo to not wanting it printed at all, and this shift, just like the other positions, is based on what these students believe is most important.

You can see here the variety of responses people can have to the exact same text—and how strong those feelings can be. If a small group in one classroom can hold such different views, imagine the variety of positions the larger audience of news consumers might bring to it. In fact, the public responded negatively to the publication. The editor wrote later that he shouldn't have run the picture, although the photographer stood by his belief that it was right to publish it (Lewis, 1995, p. 242).

This case illustrates that people really do care about what journalists publish. In this example, the journalists had an ethical justification for their decision to take and publish the photo: They thought they were serving their readers by graphically illustrating a community danger. But they couldn't know, really, if people would agree.

generally the same way. Years of research have shown this view of audiences to be too linear and simplistic.

Over the course of the 20th century, scholars came to realize that the relationship between sender and receiver is not just one-way—the interaction is more complex. The **powerful-reader theories** emerging at that time said that people use the media in conscious and deliberate ways, rather than being controlled by powerful senders. Scholars started to understand that people select which media messages they'll pay attention to, how they'll perceive them and what they'll do with the

FIGURE 15-2 The relationship among journalists and audience members is far more complex than this early one-way model suggests.

information, for specific purposes that are consistent with the way they view the world.

Technology now lets people choose from a seemingly endless supply of information. They can easily follow others on social media and select niche news sites that match their preexisting beliefs and interests. If they don't like particular points of view, they seldom have to see them. They can pick and choose, in effect tailoring the kind of information they see.

And people use the media to satisfy their needs and desires. For example, one of the reasons people might turn on the television is to catch the weather on a morning talk show. Later in the day, the TV might just serve as background noise. Similarly, people might check their favorite blogs so that they can talk with friends about the day's posts, a social interaction they'd be excluded from if they didn't read the blogs.

Also, readers can be senders themselves in their online communities. Through websites like Tumblr or Pinterest, they can select and pass on the information that *they* find important. And, user-generated material like the videos on Vimeo and YouTube bypasses the legacy media altogether and therefore has expanded the level of audience power.

Still, while people's choices may seem endless, those choices are actually finite. People can only select from within the range of what's available to them in the first place. Some information is simply unavailable, and some stories don't exist because no one has told them, for example. As media scholar Stuart Hall argues, while encoders, such as journalists, can't determine how readers will respond to the message, they still set some of the boundaries within which readers make meaning (2001, p. 173). The concept of agenda setting—that journalists can't determine what the audience will think, but they can influence what it thinks about—is consistent with this view. So your purpose as a journalist remains the same: to provide relevant, accurate information that audience members can use, whether and how they choose.

The audience isn't the only force you'll negotiate. Economic decisions and cultural values can also play into whether and how you tell a news story, for example. You may find stories that you feel are important never get told because your news organization doesn't have the money to spend on an investigative series, for instance, or your producer decides that community norms deem some visuals too graphic for the evening news. It's this kind of larger, systemic, concern to which we turn now.

Forces Behind the Scenes

Recall from Chapter 2 the story of Lori "Star" Sutherland, who was shot to death one morning in the boutique where she worked. Sutherland's friends and other community members were upset with the local newspaper for including information about her drug and alcohol use, and also for including her accused murderer's opinion that she was a neglectful mother. Critics said the newspaper was unnecessarily sullying the victim's memory and causing the family further pain. The newspaper argued that including the information served as a "cautionary tale" against drug use and dangerous behavior.

Notice what happened here: A conversation took place among community members and journalists. That conversation was about whether sensitive information should be made public in a news story. But why were the facts that someone used meth and was legally drunk at 11 a.m. sensitive? Is that information inherently different than if Sutherland had consumed aspirin and caffeine?

Let's look at some cultural and societal assumptions embedded in the story and the resulting dialogue:

- Coming to work drunk is bad.
- Meth use is bad—for the user, the family and the community.
- Being a neglectful mother is bad.
- Publishing unsubstantiated allegations by a murderer about his victim is bad.
- Publishing information or opinions that might harm a child is bad.
- Publishing information or opinions that might harm a victim's family is bad.
- Tainting the reputation of a dead person is bad.
- Cautionary tales are good.

Some of these are truth claims and some are value claims—the point here is that they are an invisible foundation on which the story, and the conversation about it, relies. Because these values are operating below the surface, they are all the more powerful for being assumed. To the extent that the story leaves assumptions like these unquestioned, it legitimizes them.

We return to the Sutherland story to show how cultural assumptions can influence a journalist's understanding of what is relevant to a story, and how they can seep into a story or an editorial, even unintentionally. External factors such as culture, society, political and economic structures and history influence storytelling because the events and people you cover cannot help but be influenced by them—nor can you, nor can your audience. The goal is to be fully aware of what you're saying, with all of its implications, and judicious about which values you reinforce.

CULTURE AND SOCIETY

One way to view the relationship between **culture** and **society** is to think about society as the manifestation of the culture that creates it. In this model, culture is a shared internal understanding about the world. Society is the external creation of that collective vision with all its norms and taboos, and the concrete laws and institutions. If the culture sees meth use as damaging to the individual, the family and the greater good, the community would institute a law forbidding it. A community that values children would create laws to protect them, for instance.

You don't necessarily learn all of this from formal instruction: Can you name the precise moment you learned it was not okay to be a cannibal? Society's rules often seem to be the things we just know. You may not agree with them or follow them—and when people push back, it can get interesting—but you naturally assimilate your culture's values and norms.

Both society and culture are living, changing entities, each influencing the other. For instance, as cultural attitudes toward marijuana have changed, so have some states' laws. And reduced penalties or legalization in those states might lead in turn to a further shift in people's attitudes toward marijuana.

WHAT DOES THIS MEAN FOR A WORKING JOURNALIST?

People who are socialized within a system can talk and behave in ways that might at first seem natural or normal but, on closer inspection, reveal a value system. As a reporter, you can question particular values.

Suppose you are doing a story on the opening of a new soup kitchen, and a person you interview says, "People shouldn't ask for a handout." Such a statement is not a factual statement. It's an opinion that reflects values and assumptions such as the following: *It's important to be a productive member of society, have a good work ethic and be self-sufficient.* The source's statement is also grounded in the assumption that if you have to ask for charity, you are somehow in that position through choice—that you didn't work hard enough, or you didn't save your money wisely or you didn't study when you were in school. Including the quote in your story might reinforce that belief.

> In the best traditions of American journalism in the public service, we seek to stimulate positive change. We uncover unsavory practices in order to stimulate reform. We do this in an entirely nonpartisan and non-ideological manner, adhering to the strictest standards of journalistic impartiality. We won't lobby. We won't ally with politicians or advocacy groups. We look hard at the critical functions of business and of government, the two biggest centers of power, in areas ranging from product safety to securities fraud, from flaws in our system of criminal justice to practices that undermine fair elections. But we also focus on such institutions as unions, universities, hospitals, foundations and on the media when they constitute the strong exploiting or oppressing the weak, or when they are abusing the public trust.
>
> *PROPUBLICA, "ABOUT US"*

News stories report on people's judgments and values, but they should not do so unquestioningly. By understanding that the negative comment about "handouts" is not a statement of fact, you can thoughtfully determine whether or how to use it in your story. The point is that you recognize the statement not as a truth claim but as a value claim, and that you judge it on that basis.

Culture and society are two forces you'll negotiate, but there are others, such as political, economic and historical forces. The **political system** doesn't just refer to Republican–Democrat politics; that's too narrow a definition. Sure, we need to consider the political system of the country—how can we fully understand elections without doing so? But thinking about politics doesn't need to end there. Media scholar Graeme Turner offers a broader definition. He writes that politics

> refers to the distribution and operation of power. It is not confined to electoral or party politics, nor to the consideration only of the operation of power by the state. The ways in which power operates, the range of sites upon which power is constituted, the mechanisms through which power is distributed throughout the society, are many and various. (1996, p. 216)

When we're thinking about the politics of an event, for instance, we look at how power is operating—who has it, who doesn't and who wants it. In a campus meeting about which student groups get funded, the meeting facilitator could structure the meeting so that, say, an administrator gets to speak first, for as long as he wants, followed by student comments as time allows. That gives a lot of power to the administrator. He could choose to use the whole meeting, effectively silencing the student voice. Or, the facilitator could decide just the opposite, letting students speak first until all comments are heard, only then letting the administrator have a turn. This would give more power to the students.

We can think of **economic forces** in a similar way—as the distribution of resources, which often refers to money, but not exclusively so. For instance, national forests or oil reserves or a highly skilled workforce would also be thought of as resources. The economic element takes into account that the United States is a capitalist economy where free market approaches are valued.

Where monetary resources are directed indicates the relative importance, and also power, of the recipient. Economic choices are linked when resources are limited. When one recipient takes, others must give. What the federal government spends on the military or farm subsidies is money not spent on other agencies vying for funding, such as veterans' hospitals, alternative energy and education, to name a few that have been in the news.

When you're reporting, attention to the economic aspects of a story may help you determine how to tell it. When you hear a developer argue to city officials that a new Wal-Mart in town will bring jobs, for example, you understand that a bargain is being struck. The developer has an interest in building the store, but that developer knows that she or he has to offer something to the community in return, especially if the locals don't want the store to come to town. The developer also knows that it's a wise political strategy to offer city officials the promise of more jobs in their district: It's hard for the officials to say their community doesn't need any more jobs.

As a reporter, if you see this implicit deal being struck, you can start reporting the story by researching the company's prior track record, and even the results of other stores moving into other towns, to see if the citizens actually got more jobs, whether they were high-quality jobs and whether the town got what the developer promised. That would be a much more useful story than one that simply quotes the developer's opinion or a resident's objection, legitimizing them without providing context to help the audience understand.

Viewing human experience through a historical lens opens up the possibilities for thinking about what might be and learning from what has been, releasing us from the present. You can see the **historical moment** in some of the examples we've already used in this chapter. For instance, the meth use in the Sutherland story would not have come up before meth was invented or had become a widespread problem, so the story is directly influenced by the time in history that the event occurred.

Having a sense of the historical moment can pop you out of the naturalness of the present. This awareness helps you to articulate in your work how today is grounded in the past, how the future depends on what happens today and how different historical forces merge or conflict at our point in time. A reporter with a sense of history knows that what appears to be inevitable or natural may be neither. A sense of history can remind you that claims that a trend or event never happened before may not be true. So when someone complains about the influence of immigration in the United States, it's helpful for the reporter to know that this country's history is made up of a series of waves of immigration. That knowledge can add perspective and accuracy to stories about the issue.

FIGURE 15-3 Unseen influences such as cultural expectations, political pressures and economic decisions affect both journalists and their stories. The more journalists can learn about those influences and navigate through them, the better they can do their jobs.

The forces we've described here are interwoven, and they morph and shift and move together. As a journalist, you'll need to do your best to understand them—their power and their players—and to recognize them when you encounter them as you report.

Looking at how they operate is akin to looking at what's underneath or behind a story—and doing so will help you discern what's at stake, where people might be coming from, what opinions might be masquerading as fact (Fig. 15-3).

When the people in question are powerful, and when their decisions affect citizens, it's especially important to expose buried assumptions and avoid being a vessel into which your sources can simply place their messages for transmission to others intact. For even if these messages are not negative or detrimental, simply by including them, you're affirming their legitimacy. Therefore, you need to decide whether you're going to follow that script or take your reporting in a different, perhaps more ethically justifiable, direction that will be more useful for the audience.

Final Thoughts

As *Democracy Now!* journalist Amy Goodman says, journalists need to make sure they represent the powerless and that they make it possible for people to inspire each other:

> Media should not be a tool only of the powerful. The media can be a platform for the most important debates of our day: war and peace, freedom and tyranny. The debate must be wide-ranging—not just a narrow discussion between Democrats and Republicans embedded in the establishment. We need to break open the box, tear down the boundaries that currently define acceptable discussion. We need a democratic media.
>
> A democratic media gives us hope. It chronicles the movements and organizations that are making history today. When people hear their neighbors given a voice, see their struggles in what they watch and read, spirits are lifted. People feel like they can make a difference.
>
> Social change does not spring forth from the minds of generals or presidents—in fact, change is often blocked by the powerful. Change starts with ordinary people working in their communities. And that's where media should start as well. (Goodman & Goodman, 2004, pp. 310–311)

The challenge for journalists is to tune in to their audiences and really listen to what people are saying, while still trying to challenge those audiences. When newly elected Federal Communications Commission chairman Newton Minow addressed the National Association of Broadcasters in a famous speech in 1961, he emphasized the difference between acting in the public interest and simply providing an audience with immediate gratification:

> You must provide a wider range of choices, more diversity, more alternatives. It is not enough to cater to the nation's whims; you must also serve the nation's needs. And I would add this: that if some of you persist in a relentless search for the

highest rating and the lowest common denominator, you may very well lose your audience. Because, to paraphrase a great American who was recently my law partner, the people are wise, wiser than some of the broadcasters—and politicians—think. (Minow, 1961, para. 31)

Good journalists understand their duty to provide a range of facts and ideas from which the audience can sample and learn. If you think about what happens when that range is limited, you see the problem: Underinformed people can't make wise choices. When those choices can take the form of votes or petitions or mass protests, the decisions people make affect everyone. So, good journalists try to extend that range as far as possible. There's no guarantee that people will take advantage of the information journalists provide, nor that they will use it wisely. But you should still strive to provide the information and fulfill your duty to the public.

Award-winning journalist David Boardman offers a compelling account of how his love of writing evolved into a passion, a fire in the belly, to bring justice. He says

For me, it didn't start out with that public service drive.

I was more motivated by love for writing, and then over time I found I had a real passion for politics. Journalism seemed like a place to bring those two things together.

The greatest piece of the passion is moving the rock of society. Really making a difference. I've tended to think of making the difference on more of a macro level, not just in a person's life as they read the paper. Righting wrongs and fixing things. I feel we have an obligation, this sacred trust. If we pursue this, in a best-case scenario, will it have any impact? If not, maybe we need to turn to something else that will have an impact because there are so many things that need addressing. (as cited in Bock, 2002, p. 93)

We challenge you to use the ideas and skills presented in this book to give people the information they need to make their lives better. We challenge you to try to move the rock.

Glossary

A

Absolute privilege is the privilege recognized by the courts of certain individuals, speaking in certain situations, to be protected from libel. People in this group include participants in court proceedings, like attorneys or witnesses, or participants in legislative proceedings, like members of Congress or state legislators.

Actual malice has a specific meaning in libel law: It means that you either published a statement knowing that it was false or that you showed a reckless disregard for the truth. The legal meaning of actual malice does not refer to malicious or mean-spirited intent.

Ad hominem is a logical fallacy. As a distraction, the arguer attacks the person with whom he disagrees, rather than that person's argument or point.

Ad populum is a logical fallacy. It says that because most people think a position is correct, it is.

Aggregator sites are websites that compile information from other news organizations, although sites such as the Huffington Post and Yahoo! News also provide news from their own reporters.

Agenda setting means influencing what people discuss and think about by deciding what gets presented.

Alliteration is the use of several words close together that begin with the same letter or sound.

Anecdotal evidence is a logical fallacy. The arguer tries to use individual stories, events or observations to justify a broad conclusion.

Anecdotes are short stories that help to show readers some of the individual faces and lives behind facts and statistics, adding human interest to an otherwise data-heavy story, for example.

Appeal to tradition is a logical fallacy. The arguer says something is correct because it's always been done that way.

Appearance of conflict of interest is a situation where no *actual* conflict of interest may exist, but it might appear that there is a conflict of interest to an outside observer.

ARPANET was a precursor to the Internet. Initially the connection of a few computers at different locations, it laid the foundation that made the Internet workable across nations, allowing computers and smaller networks to connect with each other.

Associated Press Stylebook is a reference, available online or as a book, that includes industry-standard usage, spelling and punctuation. It's a journalist's way of ensuring clarity, consistency and accuracy across stories and coverage.

Attribution is the "he said" or "she said" that provides the source for a statement or idea. This is especially important if the material is a statement of opinion, a piece of little-known information or a statement about a controversial or contested issue.

Autonomy is part of the principle of freedom, and it refers to the idea that journalists should maintain a professional distance from sources, subjects of stories or others who might want to exert influence on them.

B

Beat is a reporter's specialized area of news coverage that involves regular checks with key, relevant sources. Some examples include the education beat, the police and courts beat and the city government beat.

Begging the question is a logical fallacy. The arguer uses a circular argument, assuming that the point in question has already been proven.

Blogosphere refers to the phenomenon of one blog after another picking up on a thread or idea or event, repeating and discussing it.

B-roll in video reporting is secondary footage other than interviews. It is used to intercut with footage of interviews, especially to illustrate a point or provide transitions.

Burying the lead means waiting too long to get to what's important in a story. This is to be avoided.

C

Cautionary tales are warnings to audience members that are sometimes embedded in a news story. For instance, when a story of a fatal car accident includes the fact that the victim wasn't wearing a seat belt, the story serves as a cautionary tale about the danger of not wearing a seat belt.

Checks and balances refers to the idea that the press, in performing its watchdog function, serves to keep powerful people and institutions accountable.

Citizen journalists are ordinary people who are typically untrained and unpaid volunteer news gatherers. They are often on the scene before trained news reporters have time to make it there. They can report issues that the mainstream news media don't cover.

The Clery Act is a law requiring colleges and universities that receive public funding to make annual reports of crime statistics on campus.

Conflict is a news value typically defined as some sort of battle between competing forces or ideas.

Conflict of interest refers to situations where a reporter is too close to a source or story, risking a loss of autonomy and therefore credibility. Even if no actual conflict exists, even the *appearance* of a conflict is bad. This is why standard practice is that reporters don't interview friends or family for their stories, for example, nor accept gifts or freebies.

Contextual truth is part of the principle of truth telling, along with factual accuracy. Contextual truth refers to the deeper truths behind a story that help the audience make greater sense of it. Facts that are technically accurate may still mislead the audience because they're incomplete or don't connect the dots.

The convention of authoritative sources is Leon Sigal's idea that reporters have come to think that the higher an official's position within an organization, the better a source that person makes, which isn't necessarily the case.

Crowdsourcing is soliciting information from citizen journalists. For example, as a reporter gathering news, you might ask your readers for tips or help for a continuing story, you might ask for insider sources for an investigative piece or you might ask for people who have experienced the effects of an issue or trend firsthand.

Curiosity is a characteristic of good journalists, involving asking questions and seeking answers in the quest to help people understand the world around them, and the events that occur in it.

D

A **deck** is a secondary, longer headline that provides additional explanation.

Defamation is a legal term referring to someone damaging another person's reputation. Libel is published, false information that is usually *written*, in contrast to slander, which is *spoken* defamation.

Demographics refers to a way to categorize people, such as by age, sex, level of education and socioeconomic status.

E

The **Electronic Communications Privacy Act** aims to protect the privacy of at least some electronic communications that were not covered under previous laws. It covers, among other things, streaming videos, voicemail, telephone interceptions, emails and videos of private conversations. The law made it illegal to knowingly intercept and record cellphone calls.

Enterprise reporting is finding a story by seeking out a variety of people or investigating, rather than through regular meetings, blotters or press releases.

Establishing shots in video reporting are those that give an overview of each location.

External goods is moral philosopher Alisdair MacIntyre's term for benefits and rewards that people reap from outside, or external to, a practice. Fame, fortune and prizes are examples of external goods.

F

Factual accuracy is part of the principle of truth telling, along with contextual truth. It means that all facts must be confirmed with a credible source to ensure their accuracy. Facts in quotes must be substantively true—that the person uttered the words does not automatically make them accurate.

Fair comment is the legal right to criticize. Within limits, the law allows people to make comments of opinion, even if they're very critical, especially about entertainment or services that are offered to the general public. This is a defense in a defamation lawsuit.

Fair Use Doctrine allows people to use limited amounts of copyrighted work for certain purposes without permission or paying fees, with some restrictions. This doctrine was developed because courts decided that, without it, copyright laws might stem the flow of ideas and free speech.

False analogy is a logical fallacy. The arguer says two dissimilar things are similar in order to support an argument.

False debates refer to perceptions journalists might convey when, striving for balance, they create a story that makes it seem as if there's more conflict among experts than there actually is by giving "both sides" equal voice.

False dilemma is a logical fallacy. The arguer implies there's a choice between only two possibilities when there are actually other possibilities.

False generalization is a logical fallacy. The arguer jumps to a conclusion based on insufficient evidence.

The **First Amendment** is part of the Bill of Rights in the U.S. Constitution. The amendment addresses government—as opposed to private—interference with freedom of speech, religion and the press. It reads as follows: "Congress shall make no law respecting an establishment of religion, or prohibiting the free exercise thereof; or abridging the freedom of speech, or of the press; or the right of the people peaceably to assemble, and to petition the Government for a redress of grievances."

Follow-up stories, sometimes called *folos*, are stories that provide updates, further details or added context to the original story.

Folos, also called *follow-up stories*, are stories that provide updates, further details or added context to the original story.

Framing refers to the idea that news constructs a partial reality for the audience, but the reality it constructs isn't complete because so much is left outside of the frame. Gaye Tuchman originated this idea to discuss the frame of television news, but it has been applied to print, radio and online news as well.

Freedom is an ethical principle that refers to the idea that journalists enjoy a great deal of freedom because of the First Amendment, and that journalists are responsible for maintaining their independence.

G

Gatekeepers are the people and organizations who decide what information passes through the news media on to the audience, which sources are given a voice and what topics garner attention. Traditionally this has meant reporters, producers and editors, but now it might also apply to citizen journalists and crowdsourcing.

General assignment reporters are those who aren't working a beat. An editor or producer assigns them stories in multiple areas, depending on what's needed most.

Geographical proximity is part of the news value called proximity, along with psychological proximity. It means that a story is newsworthy because it's happening in your area or close to your area.

H

Habits of mind represent a core set of ideals that guide each journalistic decision, such as evaluating information, choosing sources and telling a story well.

Horse-race coverage refers to journalists covering elections and politicians by focusing on who is ahead in the polls rather than the candidates' positions on issues. It's criticized as providing superficial information that doesn't help voters, rather than substantive information that does.

Hot news is important, breaking news that an organization needs to publish or air right away. This is a defense in a defamation lawsuit because it emphasizes the public's right to know.

Humaneness is the ethical principle that directs journalists to minimize harm to sources and story subjects.

Human interest is an emotional interest in a story that often informs the other timeliness, impact, proximity, conflict, prominence, and novelty. People are often drawn to stories of ordinary human beings who experience tragedies, or who encounter adventures or miraculously good fortunes, for example.

The **Hutchins Commission** is the informal name given to the Commission on Freedom of the Press, which sought to examine the state of the U.S. press and make recommendations about how it should serve democracy better. Although subject to some criticism on its release in 1947, the report is considered a milestone in journalism history partly because it underscores the importance of the press in a democracy and its obligation to serve the public.

I

The **immediacy rule** says that, other factors being equal, a journalist should have as few as possible mediating agencies, people or obstacles between the journalist and the news.

Impact is a news value that refers to the real or probable effect an event will have on a story's stakeholders.

Inattentional blindness refers to the phenomenon found in the results of multiple studies: People don't see everything, even what's right before their eyes, especially if they are too focused on a specific task.

Inferences are generalizations drawn from known facts. They are one category of information that Hayakawa describes, and they are different from judgments and reports. An inference can be faulty if it is drawn from incomplete information, or if it is based on incorrect assumptions.

Initiative is a characteristic of good journalists, in which they take it upon themselves to network with sources, track down a story, investigate and make connections.

Internal goods is moral philosopher Alisdair MacIntyre's term for the moral force driving a person to seek excellence for its own sake. In contrast to external goods, internal goods originate inside a practice. The more that the people involved strive for these internal goods, the better they and the practice as a whole become.

Intrusion, a part of privacy law, refers to invading a person's private affairs or physically invading his private property without permission. This concept encompasses trespassing, secret surveillance and misrepresentation of a reporter's identity.

Inverted pyramid is a news story structure that starts with the most important information and delivers the rest in descending order of importance.

J

Judgments are one category of information that Hayakawa describes, and they are different from inferences and reports because they express a person's opinion regarding the topic he is discussing.

Justice is an ethical principle referring to the idea that a journalist's job is to provide information that helps people right wrongs and make the world more egalitarian.

L

Lead, which is sometimes spelled *lede*, is the first paragraph of a news story. In a straightforward inverted pyramid story, it's the gist of the story, usually including at least the *who, what, when* and *where* and less frequently the *why* and *how*. It's usually made up of one sentence (now and then, two). It's not too long, not too detailed, but not overly simplified either.

Leading questions are those posed in an interview that push a source to a particular response rather than letting the source respond more organically.

Lede, which is sometimes spelled *lead*, is the first paragraph of a news story. In a straightforward inverted pyramid story, it's the gist of the story, usually including at least the *who, what, when* and *where* and less frequently the *why* and *how*. It's usually made up of one sentence (now and then, two). It's not too long, not too detailed, but not overly simplified either.

Lenses is a metaphor that is one way to think about your position. When you put on a pair of sunglasses, the color of the lenses alters your vision. Along the same lines, your position colors the way you see the world and the stories you tell.

Libel, part of defamation law, is published, false information that causes damage to a person's reputation. It is usually written, in contrast to slander, which is *spoken* defamation.

The **Libertarian Theory of the press** sees the press as a monitor of the government, keeping an eye on those in power and seeking the truth. Under this philosophy, the press contributes to self-governance by helping to inform the people.

Literary journalism emphasizes a different kind of storytelling that uses several of the following literary traditions: detailed descriptions of the setting and people in a story, metaphors, suspense, dialogue, first-person voice and an emphasis on the writer's persona.

Localize, or localizing a story is reporting the local effects or implications of a national issue for people in your area.

N

Natural sound (Nat Sound or NatSOT) is video with ambient sound that's good enough to use without narration.

News hook is the timely event on which your story hangs.

News values are characteristics that indicate the newsworthiness of a story. These commonly include timeliness, impact, proximity, conflict, prominence, novelty, and human interest.

Non sequitur is a logical fallacy. The conclusion doesn't logically follow from the original statement.

Novelty is a news value typically defined as a unique or unusual story: It's

not news if a dog bites a person, the saying goes, because that happens with some regularity, but if a person bites a dog, that's news because it's unusual.

Nut graph is a paragraph other than the lead somewhere early in a story that provides the main point of the story and explains what's newsworthy. This is where journalists answer *"so what?"* about their news story.

O

Objectivity refers to the ideal that journalists should be unbiased.

P

A **package** is a story made up of several different elements. For broadcast, those elements might be a stand-up, a sound bite and a voice-over. For print, they might be a story, a graphic and photos.

Paraphrasing means taking information out of quotation marks and then rewording it so that the writing is more concise or more effective. Paraphrases need to be attributed to the source of the original information, and the facts and context must be consistent with the original.

Passive voice is a verb construction that uses a form of the verb "to be" and the past participle of the main verb. In the passive construction *She was given a present,* the verb "to be" is *was,* and the past participle of the verb "to give" is *given.* This moves the actor to a less prominent part of the sentence—or out of a sentence completely. Passive constructions also de-emphasize the individuals responsible for actions, and in some cases allow reporters to omit them entirely.

Persistence is a characteristic of good journalists in which they exhibit determination in reporting the story even in the face of opposition and roadblocks.

Persona is the character that the writer projects.

Personalization means using anecdotes and stories based on individual personalities to lighten complex stories that

people might otherwise not engage with. The risk of personalization is that the experiences of the individuals affected by the issues are told at the expense of explanations of the issues themselves.

Plagiarism is using other people's work without giving them proper credit.

Pod is a metaphor that can help you think about structuring a news story, especially longer stories. Pods are clusters of related information.

Position is another word for your worldview. Recognizing your position can help you recognize your biases and blind spots and therefore mitigate their influence on your work.

Post hoc is a logical fallacy. The arguer says that because something comes after something else, there is a cause-and-effect relationship.

Powerful-reader theories are communications theories that say audiences use the media in conscious and deliberate ways, rather than being controlled by powerful senders.

Powerful-sender theories, such as the hypodermic-needle theory, are communications theories that say the sender is very powerful and the reader is passive. The powerful-sender model, which held sway from about the beginning of the 20th century through the 1930s, is now understood to be too limited and simplistic an explanation of the communications process.

Private facts, an element of privacy law, are embarrassing facts that a person has a reasonable belief should remain private, and has tried very hard to keep private. Revealing such facts is illegal in some states, if they are sufficiently intimate and embarrassing to a reasonable person—as opposed to just personally embarrassing.

Prominence is a news value referring to the idea that prominent people are newsworthy. Because prominent people are often in positions to make decisions that concern the rest of us, what they do is frequently newsworthy, but not always.

Proximity is a news value referring to the idea that the closer an event is to the audience, the more newsworthy it is. See *geographical proximity* and *psychological proximity*.

Psychological proximity is part of the news value called proximity, along with geographical proximity. It means that a story is newsworthy because an audience feels emotionally close to its subjects because they share beliefs, cultural backgrounds or some other value or experience.

Public domain means belonging to the general public. An item in the public domain is available for everyone's use without the risk of copyright infringement.

Q

Qualified privilege is the legal privilege to report what people with absolute privilege express, as long as that report is full, fair and accurate.

R

Red herring is a logical fallacy. The arguer attempts to distract the opposition by bringing up an irrelevant topic and pretending that it's relevant.

Reports are verifiable statements. These are one of the categories of information that Hayakawa describes, and they are different from inferences and judgments.

Rhetorical hyperbole is an obvious overstatement or exaggeration. It's a defense in a defamation lawsuit.

S

Sensational news is information that includes graphic details about sex, violence or crime that satisfy an audience's curiosity—a curiosity that's usually viewed as unhealthy and superficial. Critics accuse journalists of sensationalizing the news by emphasizing such details in their coverage.

Shield laws have been enacted by many states to protect reporters who want to keep secret the identity of sources who give them important information at some risk to themselves. However, these shield laws vary radically from state to state and ultimately may not offer much protection for reporters or sources.

Single cause is a logical fallacy. The arguer asserts that there is only one cause for a problem when several factors actually contribute to it.

Slander is spoken, false information that causes damage to a person's reputation, as opposed to libel, which is usually *written* defamation.

Slippery slope is a logical fallacy. The arguer asserts that a step in a particular direction will lead inevitably to going to the extreme of that direction.

A **sound bite (sound on tape or SOT)** in audio and visual media is a snippet from your interview with a source, and the equivalent of a quote in print media.

Sound on tape (SOT) is another term for a sound bite.

Stakeholders are the people who might be affected by an issue or event and therefore a news story. They typically include a story's subject, sources and the news audience.

A **stand-up** is a particular kind of video or television news story or part of a story. It is characterized by the reporter's presence on camera, speaking to the viewer.

Stewardship is an ethical principle referring to the idea that journalists should be caretakers of the profession.

Straw man is a logical fallacy. The arguer presents a weaker version of an opponent's argument, dismisses it and then claims to have won the argument.

T

Throwaway line is often the first sentence in any news story with audio. It often provides a general sense of the topic, then returns to a more specific sentence that repeats this information. The throwaway line gives audience members time to turn their attention to the story.

Tickler file is a file of issues to keep checking on, such as an upcoming hearing, and dates on which to check them. It can help you make sure that you follow up on important continuing stories.

Timeliness is a news value that's essential to the very definition of news—what distinguishes it from history or science or any other kind of information: A story should be new, present a new development or link to a current event.

Transparency refers to the idea that journalists should be clear about why—and sometimes how—they do what they do. An editorial might explain to the audience why editors decided to include graphic photos with a story, for example.

Truth telling is an ethical principle that has two elements: factual accuracy and contextual truth. It refers to the idea that journalists seek out and report useful, relevant, true information.

V

A **voice-over (VO)** is a reporter or anchor's narration over visuals.

W

Watchdog is a metaphor referring to the idea that journalists stay keenly focused on matters of public interest and keep an eye on the powerful, particularly those who are in a decision-making role—government institutions and officials and corporations and their officers—as well as other prominent people who have power or influence over the lives of individuals.

References

Abad-Santos, A. (2013, April 22). Reddit's "Find Boston bombers" founder says "It was a disaster" but "incredible." Retrieved from http://www.theatlanticwire.com/national/2013/04/reddit-find-boston-bombers-founder-interview/64455/

Abbate, J. (1999). *Inventing the Internet* (2nd ed.). Cambridge, MA: MIT Press.

Abel, D., & Noonan, R. (2010, November 11). Hazing penalty defended: Message had to be sent, officials say. *The Boston Globe.* Retrieved from articles.Boston.com.

About Planet Money. (2013). *Planet Money.* Retrieved from www.npr.org/blogs/money/

Abramson, L., & Cornish, A. (2012, October 29). Waves pound Maryland coast as hurricane nears. National Public Radio. Retrieved from www.npr.org/2012/10/29/163896137/waves-pound-maryland-coast-as-hurricane-nears

Alderman, J. H. (2006, June 16). Police: Man in crash had wife's head in car. *Durango Herald*, p. 11A.

Al Jazeera. (2014, April 15). Armed men kidnap schoolgirls in Nigeria. Retrieved from http://www.aljazeera.com/news/africa/2014/04/armed-men-kidnap-schoolgirls-nigeria-2014415134310107956.html

Associated Press. (2010). AP history. Retrieved from www.ap.org

Associated Press. (2013). *Associated Press Stylebook and Briefing on Media Law 2013* (46th ed.). New York: Basic Books.

Associated Press v. Walker. 388 U.S. 130 (1967).

Auletta, K. (2005, December). Whom do journalists work for? In *The Red Smith Lecture in Journalism* (pp. 9–16). Kansas City: Universal Press Syndicate.

Aviv, R. (2013, March 4). Local story. *The New Yorker.* Retrieved from http://www.newyorker.com/reporting/2013/03/04/130304fa_fact_aviv

Barabak, M. (2008, November 5). It's Obama: decisive victory makes history. *Los Angeles Times.* Retrieved from http://articles.latimes.com/keyword/electoral-college/recent/2

Barger, W., & Barney, R. (2004, September 1). Media-citizen reciprocity as a moral mandate. *Journal of Mass Media Ethics,* 19(3), 191–206. Retrieved from http://dx.doi.org/10.1207/s15327728jmme1903&4_4

Barron, J. (2012, October 30). Storm picks up speed and disrupts millions of lives. *The New York Times.* Retrieved from LexisNexis Academic database.

Beaubien, J. (2013, December 5). Nelson Mandela, inspiration to world, dies at 95. National Public Radio. Retrieved from http://www.npr.org/2013/12/05/136590582/nelson-mandela-inspiration-to-world-dies-at-95

Benjamin, S. (2005, May 24). Coroner reports shooting victim used alcohol, meth. *Durango Herald*, p. 3A.

Benjamin, S. (2011a, June 6). Fatal crash spurs signal changes. *Durango Herald.* Retrieved from http://durangoherald.com/article/20110611/NEWS01/706119962/Fatal-crash-spurs-signal-changes

Benjamin, S. (2011b, June 10). Couple die in collision. *Durango Herald.* Retrieved from http://durangoherald.com/article/20110610/NEWS01/706109999/Couple-die-in-collision

Bennett, W. L. (1996). *News: The Politics of Illusion* (3rd ed.). White Plains, NY: Longman.

Bennett, W. L. (2005). *News: The Politics of Illusion* (6th ed.). New York: Pearson Longman.

Bloomberg News. (2013, December 11). Retrieved from www.bloomberg.com/news/

Blum, R. (2010, August 4). Alex Rodriguez hits home run No. 600. Associated Press. Retrieved from Yahoo!news.com

Blumberg, A., & Davidson, A. (2008, May 9). The giant pool of money. *Planet Money.* Retrieved from www.thisamericanlife.org

Blumberg, A., & Sydell, L. (2011, July 22). When patents attack. *Planet Money.* Retrieved from www.thisamericanlife.org

Bock, P. (2002). One journalist's sense of mission and purpose. In Clark, R. P., & Campbell, C. C., *Values and Craft of American Journalism: Essays from The Poynter Institute* (pp. 92–102). Gainesville: University Press of Florida.

Boorstin, D. (1992). *Image: A guide to pseudo-events in America.* New York: Vintage Books.

Branch, J. (2012, December 20). Snow Fall. *The New York Times.* Retrieved from http://www.nytimes.com/projects/2012/snow-fall/

Branzburg v. Hayes. 408 U.S. 664 (1972).

Carey, J. W. (1989). *Communication as Culture: Essays on Media and Society.* Boston: Unwin Hyman.

Carmichael, K. (December/January 2010). Capital investment. *American Journalism Review.* Retrieved on August 24, 2011, from www.ajr.org

Carr, D. (2013, October 20). Tech wealth and ideas are heading into news. *The New York Times.* Retrieved from www.nytimes.com/2013/10/21/business/media/tech-wealth-and-ideas-are-heading-into-news.html?_r=0

Chabris, C., & Simons, D. (2010). *The Invisible Gorilla: And Other Ways Our Intuitions Deceive Us.* New York: Crown Publishing Group.

Chace, Z. (2011, June 30). How much does it cost to make a hit song? *Planet Money.* Retrieved from npr.org

Chomsky, N., & Herman, E. (2002). *Manufacturing Consent: The Political Economy of the Mass Media* (updated ed.). New York: Pantheon Books.

Christians, C., Rotzoll, K., & Fackler, M. (1991). *Media Ethics: Cases and Moral Reasoning* (3rd ed.). New York: Longman.

CNN Newsroom. (2010, January 13). Damage assessment begins after Haiti earthquake; Red Cross says 3 million people affected by earthquake in Haiti; Obama to make remarks on devastation in Haiti. *CNN News.* Retrieved from http://transcripts.cnn.com/TRAN-SCRIPTS/1001/13/cnr.01.html

Cohen v. Cowles Media Co. 501 U.S. 663 (1991).

Cost, J. (2011, August 17). Welcome to the invisible primary. *The Weekly Standard.* Retrieved from sroblog.com

Cronkite, W. (1996). *A Reporter's Life.* New York: Ballantine Books.

Cunningham, B. (2003, July-August). Toward a new ideal: Rethinking objectivity in a world of spin. *Columbia Journalism Review, 24–32.*

Curtis Publishing Co. v. Butts. 388 U.S. 130 (1967).

Dee, J. (2010, January 21). Right-wing Flame War! *The New York Times.* Retrieved from http://www.nytimes.com/2010/01/24/magazine/24Footballs-t.html

Demby, G. (2013, April 15). When our kids own America. Retrieved from http://m.npr.org/news/front/177058100

Denver Post. (2013). Aurora theater shootings. #Theatershooting. Pulitzer Organization. Retrieved from http://www.pulitzer.org/files/2013/breaking-news-reporting/aurorabreakingnews02.pdf

Dewan, S., & Nordland, R. (2010, August 9). Slain aid workers were bound by their sacrifice. Associated Press. Retrieved from nytimes.com

Didion, J. Salvador. In N. Sims (Ed.), *The Literary Journalists* (pp. 72–86). New York: Ballantine.

DiMargo, C. (2013, October 12). What you can and can't do during the government shutdown. Retrieved from http://www.nbcwashington.com/news/local/What-You-Can-and-Cant-Do-During-a-Government-Shutdown-225824691.html

Duggan, M., & Brenner, J. (2013, February 14). The demographics of social media users—2012. Retrieved from pewinternet.org/Reports/2013/Social-media-users/Social-Networking-Site-Users/Demoportrait.aspx

Espo, D. (2008, November 4). Barack Obama elected president. Associated Press. Retrieved from abclocal.go

Everhart, K. (2009, May 15). Planet Money grew "organically" from "A Giant Pool of Money." Retrieved from www.current.org

Faas, H., & Fulton, M. (n.d.). The survivor: Phan Thi Kim Phuc and the photographer Nick Ut. *Digital Journalist.* Retrieved from http://digitaljournalist.org/issue0008/ng_intro.htm

Farhi, P. (2006, June/July). Rocketboom! *American Journalism Review,* 38–43.

Farrell, S., Makhoul, R., Botti, D., McDonald B., Adnan, D., DelViscio, . . . Taha, L. (2011, March 20). A new Arab generation finds its voice. Retrieved from http://www.nytimes.com/interactive/2011/03/20/world/middleeast/middle-east-voices.html?scp=3&sq=multimedia%20arab&st=cse#0

Fawcett Publications v. Morris. 377 P. 2nd 42 Oklahoma (1962).

Fenwick, A. (2009, August 13). Q & A: *The New York Times*'s Damon Winter. *Columbia Journalism Review.* Retrieved from http://www.cjr.org/campaign_desk/q_a_the_new_york_timess_damon_1.php?page=all

Fort Lewis College Institutional Research. (2013). *Fort Lewis College Fact Sheet.* Durango, CO.

Freelon, D. (2011, February 5). Sorting through claims about the Internet and revolutions, Part 1. Dfreelon.org. Retrieved from dfreelon.org

Gabrielson, R. (2013, November 26). Beating at development center goes unpunished after years of delays. Center for Investigative Reporting. Retrieved from cironline.org

Gertz v. Welch. 418 U.S. 323 (1974).

Gellman, B., & Poitras, L. (2013, June 6). U. S., British mining data from nine U.S. Internet companies in broad secret program. *Washingtonpost.com.* Retrieved from http://www.washingtonpost.com/investigations/us-intelligence-mining-data-from-nine-us-internet-companies-in-broad-secret-program/2013/06/06/3a0c0da8-cebf-11e2-8845-d970ccb04497_story.html

Golden, K. (2011, March 24). Indiana prosecutor resigns over Walker email. Retrieved from www.wisconsinwatch.org

Goodman, A., & Goodman, D. (2004). *The Exception to the Rulers: Exposing Oily Politicians, War Profiteers, and the Media that Love Them.* New York: Hyperion.

Goodnough, Abby. (2007, September 2). Oh, *everyone* knows that (except you). *The New York Times,* Section 4, p. 1.

Gordon, G., & Adams, C. (2010, April 30). Goldman didn't tell SEC about mortgage moves for months. McClatchy DC <*McClatchyDC*>. Retrieved from mcclatchydc.com

Gottlieb, J., & Vives, R. (2010, June 15). Is a city manager worth $800,000?

Los Angeles Times. Retrieved from http://articles.latimes.com

Grady, D. (2009, November 2). Quandary with mammograms: Get a screening, or just skip it? *The New York Times*. Retrieved from www.nytimes.com

Grisham, L. (2012, September 1). Pulling the curtain back on NPR's election coverage. National Public Radio. Retrieved from http://www.npr.org/blogs/ombudsman/2012/08/31/160406441/pulling-the-curtain-back-on-npr-s-election-coverage

Hall, S. (1997). *Representation: Cultural Representation and Signifying Practices*. London: Sage.

Hall, S. (2001). Encoding/decoding. In M. Durham & D. Kellner (Eds.), *Media and Cultural Studies: Keywords* (pp. 166–176). Malden, MA: Blackwell.

Hassan, A. (2003, May/June). The Other War: A debate. *Columbia Journalism Review*, 54–57.

Hastings, M. (2010, June 22). The runaway general: The Rolling Stone profile of Stanley McChrystal that changed history. *Rolling Stone*. Retrieved from http://www.rollingstone.com/politics/news/the-runaway-general-20100622

Hayakawa, S. I. (2006). Reports, inferences, judgments. In G. S. Adam & R. P. Clark (Eds.), *Journalism: The Democratic Craft* (pp. 256–262). New York: Oxford University Press.

Hedges, C., & Al-Arian, L. (2007, July 30). The other war: Iraq vets bear witness. *The Nation*. Retrieved from http://www.thenation.com/doc/20070730/hedges

Henn, S. (2012, August 17). At this camp, kids learn to question authority (and hack it). *All Tech Considered*. Retrieved from http://www.npr.org/blogs/alltechconsidered/2012/08/17/159015235/at-defcon-kids-camp-young-hackers-learn-to-pop-locks-and-drop-it

Hertzberg, H. (2005, May 9). The Matt and Judy show. *The New Yorker*. Retrieved from http://www.newyorker.com/archive/2005/05/09/050509ta_talk_hertzberg

Hill, A. (2013, December 20). Pennsylvania court: Towns can restrict fracking. *Marketplace*. Podcast retrieved from http://www.marketplace.org/topics/sustainability/pennsylvania-court-towns-can-restrict-fracking

Hirschorn, M. (2010, October 4). Truth lies here: How can Americans talk to one another—let alone engage in political debate—when the Web allows every side to invent its own facts? *The Atlantic*. Retrieved from http://www.theatlantic.com/magazine/archive/2010/11/truth-lies-here/308246/

Hughes, C. (2013, January 27). Welcome to our redesign: A letter from *The New Republic*'s publisher and editor-in-chief. *The New Republic*. Retrieved from http://www.newrepublic.com/article/112191/new-republic-redesign-chris-hughes-welcomes-readers

"Hurricane Sandy Photographs." (n.d.). *Snopes.com*. Retrieved from www.snopes.com/photos/natural/sandy.asp

"Hurtful facts." (2007, May 6). *Durango Herald*. Retrieved from http://www.durangoherald.com/aspbin/printable_article_generation.asp?article_path=/opinion/opin070506_2.htm

Johnson, J., & Mufson, S. (2013, April 23). Lu Lingzi, 23. Retrieved from http://www.washingtonpost.com/wp-srv/special/national/boston-marathon-bombing-victims/

Kant, G. (2006). *How to Write Television News*. Boston: McGraw Hill.

Kirchner, L. (2011, February 14). "Information wars" on Al Jazeera English: An all-star panel discusses social media and political revolution. *Columbia Journalism Review*. Retrieved from www.cjr.org

Kissack, A. (2010, August 17). "Big solar" struggles to find home in California. National Public Radio. Retrieved from npr.org

Kovach, K., & Rosenstiel, T. (2007). *The Elements of Journalism: What Newspeople Should Know and the Public Should Expect* (Rev. ed.). New York: Three Rivers Press.

Krajicek, D. (2003–2010). The Crime Beat. Retrieved from http://justicejournalism.org/justnews/crimeguide/chapter01/chapter01_pg06.html#thepublichealthperspective

Krakauer, J. (1997). *Into Thin Air: A Personal Account of the Mount Everest Disaster*. New York: Doubleday.

Krugman, P. (2008, August 15). The great illusion. *The New York Times*. Retrieved from www.nytimes.com

Lambeth, E. B. (1992). *Committed Journalism: An Ethic for the Profession* (2nd ed.). Bloomington: Indiana University Press.

Lane, A. (2013, January 7). Love hurts: "Les Misérables," "Django Unchained," and "Amour." *The New Yorker*. Retrieved from http://www.newyorker.com/arts/critics/cinema/2013/01/07/130107crci_cinema_lane

Lewis, G. (1995). *Photojournalism: Content and Technique*. Madison, WI: Brown and Benchmark.

Linkon, S. (2013, March 1). In B. Cunningham, Class warriors: Creators of the late Center for Working Class Studies at Youngstown State University discuss class in America. *Columbia Journalism Review*. Retrieved from www.cjr.org/currents/class_warriors.php

Liptak, A., & Newman, M. (2005, July 6). New York Times reporter jailed for keeping source secret. *The New York Times*. Retrieved from http://www.nytimes.com/2005/07/06/politics/06cnd-leak.html

Little, M. (2011, May 20). The human algorithm [Web log post]. Retrieved from http://blog.storyful.com/2011/05/20/the-human-algorithm-2/#.UfwB3TnR2Jo

Lopez, R., Holtz, A., & Arrow, E. (2010, April 9). Bet against the American dream. *Planet Money*. Retrieved from http://www.npr.org/blogs/money/2010/04/americandream.html

Los Angeles Times v. Free Republic. 54 U.S. P.Q. 2d 1453 CCH, California (2000).

Lo Wang, H. (2013, November 4). Hit with rough patch, Howard University faces flagging morale. *All Things Considered*. Retrieved from http://www.npr.org/2013/11/04/243073789/hit-wth-rough-patch-howard-university-faces-flagging-morale

Luo, M. (2010, August 2). 99 weeks later, jobless have only desperation. *The New York Times*. Retrieved from nytimes.com

Maass, P. (1997). *Love Thy Neighbor: A Story of War*. New York: Vintage Books.

MacIntyre, A. (1985). The nature of the virtues. In N. Bowie (Ed.), *Making Ethical Decisions* (pp. 248–264). New York: McGraw-Hill.

Madden, Mary. (2012, February 24). Privacy management on social media sites. Retrieved from http://www.pewinternet.org/Reports/2012/Privacy-management-on-social-media.aspx

Marquardt, A. (2013, October 31). Syria meets first critical deadline of chemical weapons deal. *ABC News*. Retrieved from http://abcnews.go.com/WNT/video/syria-meets-critical-deadline-chemical-weapons-deal-20748283

McBride, K., & Rosenstiel, T. (2014). The complicated pursuit of truth. In K. McBride & T. Rosenstiel (Eds.), *The New Ethics of Journalism: Principles for the 21st Century* (pp. 7–8). Los Angeles: CQ Press.

McBride, K., & Rosenstiel, T. (2014). The future of journalism ethics. In K. McBride & T. Rosenstiel (Eds.), *The New Ethics of Journalism: Principles for the 21st Century* (pp. 217–219). Los Angeles: CQ Press.

McChesney, R. (1993). Communication research at the crossroads. *Journal of Communication, 43*(4), 98–105.

McDonough, K. (2013, December 12). Pope Francis slams super salaries for the rich while the poor survive on "crumbs." *Salon.com*. Retrieved from http://www.salon.com/2013/12/12/pope_francis_slams_super_salaries_for_the_rich_while_the_poor_survive_on_crumbs/

McGowan, E., & Song, L. (2012, June 26). The Dilbet disaster: inside the biggest oil spill you've never heard of, part 1. Retrieved from http://insideclimatenews.org/news/20120626/dilbit-diluted-bitumen-enbridge-kalamazoo-river-marshall-michigan-oil-spill-6b-pipeline-epa

McQuail, D. (1987). *Mass Communication Theory: An Introduction* (2nd ed.). London: Sage.

Milkovich v. Lorain Journal Co. 497 U.S. 1 (1990).

Mindich, D. (1993). Edwin M. Stanton, the inverted pyramid, and information control [Monograph]. *Journalism Monographs*, 140.

Minow, N. (1961, May 9). Television and the public interest. *American Rhetoric: Top 100 Speeches*. Retrieved from http://www.americanrhetoric.com/speeches/newtonminow.htm

Moscou, J. (2008, July 21). Beetlemania: How a tiny bug is ravaging Colorado's forests. *Newsweek*. Retrieved from *www.thedailybeast.com*

Moynihan, M. (2012, July 30). Jonah Lehrer's deceptions: The celebrated journalist fabricated Bob Dylan quotes in his new book, *Imagine: How Creativity Works*. *Tablet* magazine. Retrieved from http://www.tabletmag.com/jewish-news-and-politics/107779/jonah-lehrers-deceptions

Munro, T. (2006, November 26). Peace sign creates stir: Pagosa homeowners asked to remove symbol or risk fine. *Durango Herald*. Retrieved from http://archive.durangoherald.com/asp-bin/printable_article_generation.asp?article_path=/news/06/news061126_2.htm

Nashrulla, T. (2013, December 11). 13 news organizations sent a letter to Syrian rebels asking them to stop kidnapping journalists. *BuzzFeed*. Retrieved from http://www.buzzfeed.com/tasneemnashrulla/13-news-organizations-sent-a-letter-to-syrian-rebels-asking

Nazario, S. (2006). *Enrique's Journey: The Story of a Boy's Dangerous Odyssey to Reunite with his Mother*. New York: Random House.

New York Times v. Sullivan. 376 U.S. 254 (1964).

Palca, J. (2011, August 19). Don't throw it out: "Junk DNA" essential in evolution. *All Things Considered*. National Public Radio. Retrieved from www.npr.org

Payne, E. (2013, October 3). The government shutdown: Americans on the edge. *CNN.com*. Retrieved from http://www.cnn.com/2013/10/03/politics/government-shutdown-impact/

Peterson, T. (1963). The social responsibility theory. In F. Siebert, T. Peterson, & W. Schramm (Eds.), *Four Theories of the Press: The Authoritarian, Libertarian, Social Responsibility and Soviet Communist Concepts of What the Press Should Be and Do* (pp. 73–103). Urbana and Chicago: University of Illinois Press.

Pew Research Center's Project for Excellence in Journalism. (2005). Five major trends. *The State of the News Media 2005*. Retrieved from stateofthemedia.org/2005/

Pew Research Center's Project for Excellence in Journalism. (2006). Blogs. *The State of the News Media 2006*. Retrieved from stateofthemedia.org/2006/a-day-in-the-life-of-the-media-intro/blogs/

Pew Research Center's Project for Excellence in Journalism. (2010, January 11). How news happens: A study of the news ecosystem of one American city. Retrieved from http://www.journalism.org/analysis_report/methodology_4

Pew Research Center's Project for Excellence in Journalism. (2011, March 14). Key findings. *The State of the News Media 2011: An Annual Report on American Journalism: Overview*. Retrieved from stateofthemedia.org

Pew Research Center's Project for Excellence in Journalism. (2006–2013). Journalism resources. Retrieved from http://www.journalism.org/resources/about_ccj

Platt, S. (2013, June 14). Newtown residents mark 6-month anniversary of Sandy Hook shootings. Getty Images. Retrieved from http://www.gettyimages.com/Search/Search.aspx?contractUrl=2&language=en-US&family=editorial&assetType=image&p=170545728

Pope, J. (2010, August 16). N.O. adds 93,800 jobs since Katrina. *The Times-Picayune*. Retrieved from www.nola.com

ProPublica. (2013). About us. Retrieved from www.propublica.org/about/

Radosevich, F. (2011, July 25). Man accused in Norway attacks "acted with intent of terror"—judge. *Christian Science Monitor*. Retrieved from http://www.csmonitor.com

Resmer, C. (2006, March 15). Explore New England steals text from Seven Days [Web log post]. Retrieved from http://7d.blogs.com/802online/2006/03/explore_new_eng.html

Ricchiardi, S. (2007, June/July). Hometown horror. *American Journalism Review*. Retrieved from http://www.ajr.org/article_printable.asp?id=4350

Roberts, G., & Klibanoff, H. (2006). *The Race Beat: The Press, the Civil Rights Struggle, and the Awakening of a Nation*. New York: Vintage Books.

Robertson, L. (2002, May). Romancing the source. *American Journalism Review*, 43–49.

Rodebaugh, D. (2005, August 31). Local woman encounters a mountain lion—close up. *Durango Herald*. Retrieved from http://archive.durangoherald.com/asp-bin/printable_article_generation.asp?article_path=news/05/news050821_3.htm

Rosen, J. (August/September 2003). Important if true. *American Journalism Review*, 47–51.

Sampson, H. (2010, August 17). Judge: Student's Facebook rants about teacher are protected speech. *Miami Herald*. Retrieved from MiamiHerald.com

Schudson, M. (1978). *Discovering the News: A Social History of American Newspapers*. New York: Basic Books, Inc.

Schlikerman, B., Lee, W., & Dizikes, C. (2010, August 6). Sailor dies, man missing, 2 rescued in sailing accident. Chicago BreakingNewsCenter. Retrieved from *ChicagoBreakingNewsCenter.com*

Scofield, H. (2010, November 16). Sweet success stories: Evidence shows a recipe for business growth exists in S.W. Colo. *Durango Herald*. Retrieved from www.durangoherald.com

Shepard, A. C. (1999, March). Gatekeepers without gates. *American Journalism Review*, 22–29.

Siebert, F. (1963). The libertarian theory of the press. In F. Siebert, T. Peterson, & W. Schramm (Eds.), *Four Theories of the Press: The Authoritarian, Libertarian, Social Responsibility and Soviet Communist Concepts of What the Press Should Be and Do* (pp. 39–71). Urbana and Chicago: University of Illinois Press.

Sigal, L. (1986). Who? Sources make the news. In R. K. Manoff & M. Schudson (Eds.), *Reading the News* (pp. 9–37). New York: Pantheon.

Silverman, C., & Jenkins, M. (2011). *B. S. Detection for Digital Journalists*. Retrieved from http://ona11.journalists.org/sessions/b-s-detection-for-digital-journalists/

Simon, M., Jean-Francois, E., Darlington, S., Feyerick, D., Smith, M., Meilhan, P., . . . Griggs, B. (2010, January 13). 7.0 quake hits Haiti: "serious loss of life expected." *CNN.com*. Retrieved from http://www.cnn.com/2010/WORLD/americas/01/12/haiti.earthquake/index.html?ref=allsearch

Slackman, M. (2006, January 3). After Cairo police attack, Sudanese have little but rage. *The New York Times*, p. A3.

Smith, D. (1992). *Rocky Mountain Boom Town: A History of Durango, Colorado*. Boulder: University Press of Colorado.

Smith, M. (2010, June 28). Banks financing Mexico gangs admitted in Wells Fargo deal. *Bloomberg*. Retrieved from Bloomberg.com

Smith, M. (2012, October 30). Sandy wreaks havoc across Northeast; at least 11 dead. *CNN.com*. Retrieved from www.cnn.com/2012/10/29/us/tropical-weather-sandy/

Spata, O. (2013, July 4). Support for Snowden. AP Images. Retrieved from http://www.apimages.com/metadata/Index/Support-for-Snowden/3c3b4dfaacc34d9f988292436e2f1376/1/0

Spencer, J. (2007, October/November). Found in (My)Space: Social networking sites like MySpace and Facebook are valuable sources of information for journalists. *American Journalism Review*. Retrieved from www.ajr.org

"Steinbuch v. Cutler." (2007, September 10). *Digital Media Law Project*. Retrieved from http://www.dmlp.org/threats/steinbuch-v-cutler

Steinhauser, P., & Brusk, S. (2010, August 10). High-level backing, wrestling candidate highlight Tuesday primaries. CNN. Retrieved from cnn.com

Stephens, M. (2007). *A History of News*. New York: Oxford University Press.

Student Press Law Center. (2011). *SPLC Guide to Fair Use*. Retrieved from http://www.splc.org/knowyourrights/legal research.asp?id=114

Thompson, H. S. (1979). The Kentucky Derby is decadent and depraved. In *The Great Shark Hunt: Strange Tales from a Strange Time* (pp. 24–38). New York: Rolling Stone Press/Summit Books.

Trahant, M. N. (1995). *Pictures of Our Nobler Selves: A History of Native American Contributions to News Media*. Nashville: The Freedom Forum First Amendment Center.

Tuchman, G. (1978). *Making News: A Study in the Construction of Reality*. New York: The Free Press.

Turner, A. (2012, October 30). Sandy aftermath affects millions in New York and along New Jersey's coast. *PBS NewsHour*. Retrieved from http://www.pbs.org/newshour/bb/weather-july-dec12-sandy_10-30/

Turner, G. (1996). *British Cultural Studies* (2nd ed.). London: Routledge.

van Dijk, T. (1988). *News as Discourse*. Hillsdale, NJ: Lawrence Erlbaum Associates.

Vevea, B. (2012, September 10). Teacher strike in Chicago becomes political. *Morning Edition*. Retrieved from http://www.npr.org/2012/09/10/160899022/teacher-strike-in-chicago-creates-political-issues

Vogel v. Felice. WL 675837. Cal. Court of Appeals (March 25, 2005).

Volunteers of America. (2013a). About us. Retrieved from http://www.voa.org/About-Us

Volunteers of America. (2013b). Our ministry of service. Retrieved from http://www.voa.org/About-Us/Our-Ministry-of-Service

"Walmart intersection to get safety overhaul." (2011, June 13). *Durango Herald*. Retrieved from http://durangoherald.com/article/20110614/NEWS01/706149931/Walmart-intersection-to-get-safety-overhaul

Wang, M. (2011, August 3). FAQ: Why Congress flew home while airport inspectors work without pay. ProPublica. Retrieved from www.propublica.org

Ward, B. (2008). *Communicating on Climate Change: An Essential Resource for Journalists, Scientists, and Educators*. Narragansett, RI: Metcalf Institute for Marine & Environmental Reporting, University of Rhode Island Graduate School of Oceanography.

Williams-Harris, D. (2010, August 16). 16-year-old dead, man wounded in Albany Park shooting. ChicagoBreaking NewsCenter. Retrieved from *Chicago BreakingNewsCenter.com*

Woods, K. (2002). The Woods theorem: A new formula for diversity in American news organizations. In R. P. Clark & C. C. Campbell (Eds.), *Values and Craft of American Journalism: Essays from The Poynter Institute* (pp. 105–115). Gainesville: University Press of Florida.

Yes Men. (2010, January). Sovereign: Let us finally put poverty behind us. Retrieved from http://www.weforum.org/en/events/AnnualMeeting2010/elizabeth.shtml

Credits

Line art illustrations for this book created by Miki Harder

Photos

Page 2—Tom Bartels

Page 11—Bettman/Corbis/AP Images

Page 15—Ole Spata/Picture Alliance/DPA/AP Images

Page 18—Joel Saget/AFP/Getty Images

Page 31—AP Photo/Nick Ut

Page 48—Spencer Platt/Getty Images

Page 52—*The New York Times*/Damon Winter

Page 58—Aaron Ontiveroz/*The Denver Post*

Page 68—AP Photo/*The San Francisco Examiner*/Lacy Atkins

Page 84—Julian Wasser/Time Life Pictures/Getty Images

Page 84—Chris Felver/Getty Images

Page 85—Sonia Nazario

Page 85—John Storey/Time & Life Pictures/Getty Images

Page 114—Jiji Press/AFP/Getty Images

Page 119—Scott Olson

Page 120—AP Photo/Emilio Morenatti

Page 132—U.S. Army

Page 136—*The Denver Post*

Page 148—Charles Menjivar/*The Wall Street Journal*

Page 160—Dorothea Lange/Library of Congress, Prints & Photographs Division, FSA/OWI Collection, [LC-USF34-9058-C]

Page 160—Russell Lee/Library of Congress, Prints & Photographs Division, FSA/OWI Collection, [LC-USF34-072327-D]

Page 174—AP Photo/Oded Balilty

Page 178—Patrick Hertzog/AFP

Page 192—Chip Somodevilla/Getty Images

Page 209—David Lom/NBCNEWS.com

Page 227—David Shankbone

Page 231—AP Photo/Harold Filan

Page 249—AP Photo/Muhammed Muheisen

Page 250—© Gary Coronado/Palm Beach *Post*/zReportage.com/ZUMA

Page 261—AP Photo/Steve Helber

Page 270—AP Photo/Meixu Lu

Page 290—Tom Stoddart Archive

Page 294—Adrian Pingstone

Page 297—AP Photo/The *News-Gazette*/Robert K. O'Daniell

Page 312—John Harte/*Bakersfield Californian*

Index